No. 1428
$17.95

Professional Programming Techniques— Starting with the BASICs

By Richard Galbraith

FIRST EDITION

FIRST PRINTING

Printed in the United States of America

Library of Congress Cataloging in Publication Data

Galbraith, Richard.
Professional programming techniques.

Includes index.
1. Basic (Computer program language)
2. Electronic digital computers—Programming.
I. Title.
QA76.73.B3G34 1982 001.64'24 82-5829
ISBN 0-8306-2428-7 AACR2
ISBN 0-8306-0128-7 (pbk.)

Contents

Introduction

Computer programmers are like musical composers. They create works (programs or songs) for other people to perform. Good composers consider the abilities of the players and the tones of the particular instruments when they develop their music. Good programmers consider the preferences of the people who will be using their programs and the specific features of their particular computer systems.

Composers need to be able to play a musical instrument to develop an ear for music, and they usually play their tunes first to make sure the notes they have written match the sound in their mind. They do not need to be virtuosos; somebody else will do most of the performing. Similarly, programmers need to be able to use a computer system. They should be familiar with the capabilities of the computer and they should try out their programs to see that they work correctly. Typing ability definitely helps, since with most computers you use a keyboard to get information; but programmers do not need to be speed typists nor expert computer operators (somebody else can have those specialties).

A knowledge of electronics and higher mathematics is definitely not necessary for programming. Programmers do not build their own computers any more often than composers build their own pianos.

The essential skills for successful computer programming are fluency in a special language (like BASIC) and a logical approach to problem solving. Both of these skills can be developed by a combination of study and practice.

BASIC is a computer programming language. It is a special set of words and symbols used to describe precisely what the computer is to do. In this respect, it is similar to the set of staves, notes, and other symbols that a composer uses to describe precisely how the music will sound. Before you learn the language, you will find that reading something written in BASIC will be frustrating. You can guess at the meaning of some of the words, but you won't understand the complete work. With some study, you can learn to translate anything written in BASIC into familiar English. You can become truly fluent in BASIC if you regularly practice reading BASIC written by others and writing in BASIC yourself. With experience, you will find that you begin to think in BASIC and can understand a program without having to translate it.

The skill of logical problem solving is often more difficult to develop than fluency in a language. This is the skill that has given programmers the image of being magicians or geniuses. Most programmers are neither. Their minds cannot see all the ramifications of complex problems any better than other people. The secret to their success is a disciplined approach that divides complex problems into a series of simpler problems. The BASIC language does not allow for sentences as complex as normal English. It is used to direct the computer to rapidly perform a series of simple tasks. This limited capability forces programmers to learn to break problems down into simple units. When you first try this approach, it will seem unnatural and clumsy. Do not get discouraged. When you first tried to walk instead of crawl, that was clumsy too. With enough practice, you developed into a "natural" walker. You can also develop into a "natural" problem solver, if you practice enough.

USING THIS BOOK

Do not sit down in a comfortable chair and read this book from cover to cover. *Do* use this book to guide your practice for gaining fluency in BASIC and logical problem solving with computers.

In Chapters 1 and 2 you will find background information on computers, including explanations of commonly used technical terms. Starting with Chapter 3, you should become an active participant. Try all examples on a computer system. These examples were designed so they will work on most popular personal computers and academic time-sharing systems. At the end of each chapter, experiment with variations on the ideas presented in that chapter. Appendix A provides some suggestions for your experimentation. Reading can put ideas into your head. Practice will keep them there.

SHARING EXPERIENCE

Computer programming can be addictive. There is often a temptation to ignore the rest of the world while you are engrossed in work with a computer. The pride that comes from figuring something out for yourself can lead you to waste months trying to reinvent the wheel.

You will learn faster and become a better programmer if you share the experiences of others and share your own work with friends. Reading programs that other people have written will expose you to a variety of techniques and will develop your sense of quality (you can learn as much from errors as from successes). Modifying and improving those programs is an excellent way of sharpening your programming skills. Similarly, someone else may be able to offer ideas that will improve a program you have written. Problem solving is often helped when more than one person's perspective is used.

Good programs, like good books, are seldom the exclusive product of a single author. The title page of this book recognizes one man as its creator, but the material did not flow smoothly into the finished product. The rough drafts were improved by sharing them (or parts of them) with several other people. The final product incorporates improvements resulting from trial and discussions with Lynn Bunting and four children: Maureen Douglas, Jennifer Galbraith, Chris Keller, and Art Povelones.

Chapter 1
The Nature of Computers

Computers are absolutely amazing machines. They perform calculations at truly unimaginable speeds: an unaided human cannot recognize the passage of one-thousandth of a second, yet some of today's computers can add two numbers in one ten-millionth of a second. This astounding speed allows computers to solve gigantic problems (such as checking all the arithmetic on 93 million income-tax returns) that would be too tedious for people to do. Speedy calculations also enable computers to determine the precise maneuvers needed to safely land a space ship. If a man tried to do the calculations himself, he would be hundreds of miles off course before he decided what he should have done.

There is no doubt that computers are changing our lives. Most of our government and business leaders were born before the first computer was invented, yet it is hard to find a government or business organization in the United States that does not use computers or information generated by computers. The average citizen pays most of his bills by writing checks in response to computer-printed bills. His checks are then processed by computers that switch money from his account to the company which sent the bill. These computers also compute the daily interest we earn on our savings (nobody went to the effort to compute daily interest before computers). Our tax rates and insurance premiums are all calculated by computers. Computers provide us with more detailed information on how our businesses and government are doing than we could possibly otherwise know. It has been calculated (with the help of a computer) that it would take five trillion clerical workers (that's 5,000,000,000,000 people) to duplicate all the work currently being done by computers. To do everything that computers now do—without using a computer—would take one thousand extra human workers for each person currently alive in the world. The earth cannot hold that many people.

The large computers used by big businesses and government agencies can cost millions of dollars and fill large rooms. During the past ten years, however, computers have been shrinking. Now computers are built which are small enough to fit inside household appliances and cheap enough to be bought by individuals for their personal use. Special-purpose computers are being built into cars, microwave ovens, and television sets. In offices, computers are replacing typewriters because computers can let secretaries correct errors and change reports without retyping. This book, for instance, was written with the use of a computer.

Computers often seem to work by magic. We commonly refer to them as electronic "brains." Yet computers are not magical and they are not intelligent. Computers are man-made machines that sometimes break down; they produce results determined by the way they are designed and put together. No computer has ever "thought" out a new way of doing anything. Every computer carries out the plans of the people who designed it and the people who wrote its programs. The actions of computers are completely determined by the mechanical laws of electronics and by the instructions people have thought to give computers.

WHAT COMPUTERS REALLY DO

Computers store pieces of information. They move stored information from one place in the computer to another and to devices (like typewriters and tape recorders) connected to the computer. They compare pieces of information and change pieces of information according to mathematical rules. Whenever a piece of information (a number, a word, or some special symbol enters a computer system, it is converted to a coded pattern that can be represented by a series of electrical impulses. To a computer, information has no meaning except as a recognizable pattern of on/off switches.

In order for a computer to solve any problem, some person first must figure out a way to solve that problem using only the limited skills of a computer. The person must be able to describe the steps of storing, moving, comparing, and changing coded patterns which will produce the desired answer. The machinery of the computer can then repeatedly follow the person's instructions step-by-step. The description of the steps the computer follows is the computer's program. The machinery of the computer determines how fast it works and how often it breaks down. The computer program determines how useful the results are. A computer cannot work for people until a person has thought for the computer.

To do a good job of writing programs for a computer, you need to know something about how computers work. Fortunately, you don't have to understand the electronics, fancy mathematics, or special techniques used to design and build computers. It would take years of hard study to learn all of that. You simply need to understand logically what the computer does when you give it instructions.

Every computer system can be split into three functionally different pieces: (1) Memory where the patterns are stored; (2) Central Processing Unit where all the comparing and changing of patterns occurs; and (3) Peripherals, which include a wide variety of special devices that may be connected to the computer.

Computer Memory

The memory is the easiest part of the computer to understand. We can visualize computer memory as a large apartment house divided into small rooms. Each room has its own *address*. Initially, the address of a room is simply a number used to pick out a particular room from all the others. Since there are thousands or millions of identical rooms in the memory of standard computers, it is easy to see why having a numbering system is necessary if you want to store things in the right room and be able to find them again quickly.

When an apartment is occupied by a particular family, we often find it more convenient to refer to it as the "Smith's apartment" instead of "apartment number 2063." A well-managed apartment complex has a directory of current occupants, so that if you know the name of the resident, you can easily locate the right apartment number. Most computer programming systems also include directories so you can use names of "occupants" as substitutes for number addresses (Fig. 1-1). If you want the computer to store the most points scored in a game, you can have it assign a name (MOST-POINTS, for example) or an abbreviation (MP) to a memory apartment. Then you never have to know the actual apartment number. Any time you want to find MOST-POINTS the computer will be able to locate it using the directory. The names or abbreviations used as addresses are called *variables* or *variable names*.

Each numbered memory apartment contains a *value*, which is a specific coded pattern. It is usually easier to think of values as the numbers or letters the patterns represent than to worry about the specific design of the pattern (though sometimes the patterns can be used directly for special effects). For most programming, we consider a value to be either *numeric* (a number) or *alphanumeric* (a series of letters possibly including numbers and spaces). Alphanumeric values are also called *strings*.

Unlike real apartments, each memory apartment is quite small and can only hold one value at a time. The content of a memory address is not an empty room. It is more like there were a bicycle combination lock filling each apartment. If you want to change the number showing on the combination to "350," you spin the dials on the combination until they show "350." If you later decided to store a different number in the same place, you would spin the dials again. The "350" would disappear and a new number would appear. When a computer stores a value in an address, it does not open the

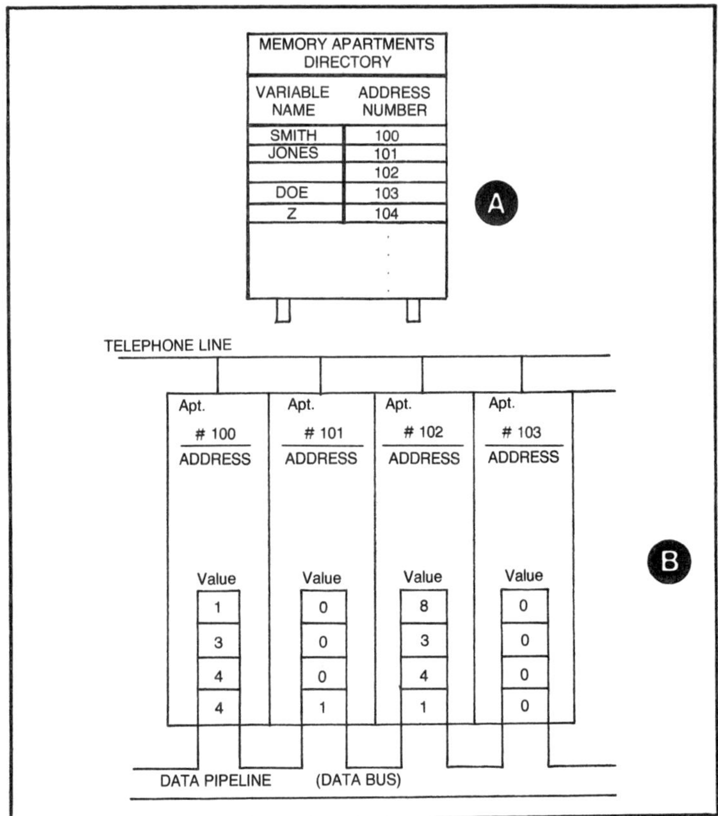

Fig. 1-1. Memory apartments.

door and cram the value inside. Instead it copies the value on the "dials" in the apartment, replacing any value already there. Similarly, when a value (like 350) is moved from apartment no. 5 to apartment no. 44, the dials in apartment no. 44 are changed to copy the value in apartment no. 5. In this example, both apartments no. 5 and no. 44 will hold the value of 350 when the move is complete, and whatever value used to be in apartment no. 44 will be lost.

The main thing to remember about computer memory is that it consists of addresses and values. Addresses (and the variable names used as directory addresses) locate a specific compartment in memory. Each compartment contains one value at a time. Many different compartments may have the same value, but each compartment must have a different address. The address of a compartment stays the same (though the directory of variable names can be different for different programs). The value stored at that address, on the other hand, can be changed many times as part of a computer program.

Central Processing Unit

All of the computing in a computer is done in the central processing unit. It consists of a small number of compartments, called *registers*, which are used to hold values temporarily. The registers are connected by special electronic circuits which can add, multiply, compare, and copy the value in the registers.

One register is used to store the current step on which the computer is working. This is usually called the *instruction register*. Each different instruction (add, multiply, etc.) has its own code, which makes it look like any other value. This means that instructions can also be stored in the memory, just like numbers. When the central processing unit is finished with one instruction, it can get the next instruction from memory and work through a long series of steps without stopping.

Before it can get an instruction from memory, the central processing unit has to know where the instruction is stored. A second register, often called the *program counter*, is used to store the address in memory for the next instruction. As soon as the central processing unit moves an instruction from memory, into the instruction register, it increases the value of the program counter so it will hold the value of the next instruction.

The automatic increasing of the program counter between each step means that the computer will normally do each step in the order in which it is written (and stored in the memory). However, some of the computer's instructions allow the programmer to change the value in the program counter to repeat some steps or to change the order of the steps.

Together, the instruction register and the program counter act as the supervisors for all the work done in the central processing unit.

One or more of the other registers are used for arithmetic. Before the computer can add any values stored in its memory, those values must be copied onto arithmetic or "answer" registers (often called *general purpose registers*). Once the values are in the central processor, the computer can do its arithmetic operations in its work areas and make the answer available to be copied back into memory.

In order to copy answers from the memory into registers and to copy answers back into memory, the central processor must keep track of the addresses of the memory apartments assigned to those specific purposes. It does this by using one of its registers as an *address register*. Remember the addresses are numbers, so they can be handled just like any other values.

Many times it is useful to send and receive messages from devices other than the computer's own memory. To do this the central processor has a series of circuits that can be used to plug wires from peripherals (machines like printers and tape recorders) into the computer. These connections are called *ports*, like the ports that let ships bring freight into a country. A special register can be used to hold messages (coded electrical signals) that come in from the ports or that the computer plans to send out to a machine attached to one of the ports. Microcomputers only send or receive messages through one port at a time. The central processor has a switch that can connect the message register with any one of the machines attached to its ports. However, if a machine sends a message to the computer while the central processor isn't switched to pick it up, then that message will never be noticed by the computer. Every once in a while, you may type something on your keyboard or teletypewriter and discover that the computer ignores you. This can happen either because the central processor was busy sending or receiving a message through a different port, or some other values were copied into the message register before the central processor looked for your keyboard message.

The central processor works much faster than most of the peripherals attached to it. In many practical applications, the central processor spends most of its time doing nothing while it waits for messages from the peripherals.

Peripherals

Peripherals include those machines that are attached around the periphery or edges of the central processor. They are necessary for most computer uses. Because you cannot see what is inside the central processing unit or the memory, you need input devices like typewriter keyboards and joysticks to get your information and commands into the computer. You also need output devices like printers, video displays (televisions or other cathode ray tubes), and loudspeakers to get information out of a computer in a form you can understand. You also need storage devices such as tape recorders and magnetic disk drives to store information and programs permanently and to store the excess information which cannot fit into the computer's memory.

Some input devices use switches to generate coded signals for the computer. Each time one of the letters on a teletypewriter or computer keyboard is depressed, it turns on a specific switch. When each switch is turned on, it lets an electrical current—whose pattern matches the computer code for that letter or symbol—pass on to the computer's port. As soon as the signal has gone through the switch, the switch is turned off. The "shift" key is a kind of master switch, which changes the current pattern connected to each of the other keys. That way, most of the keys can be used for two different signals, like an uppercase letter and its lowercase equivalent.

The joysticks and paddles used with many computer games work in basically the same manner as a keyboard. There are a number of different switch connections (usually eight: front, back, left, right, and four diagonal positions). When the stick is pushed in any direction, it contacts one of the switches, turning the switch on to send a coded signal to the central processor.

Other types of input devices (less commonly found attached to microcomputers) turn sound or light waves into electrical patterns. Microphones with special coding attachments are being used in various experiments to get computers to respond to human voices. Small wands use patterns of light and dark to interpret bar codes (the funny pattern of stripes on many food packages) into computer codes. Other optical scanners with rows of photo-electrical cells are used to "read" the marks on standardized answer sheets into computers. Still other devices translate printing, including the numbers printed on the bottom of checks, into computer codes.

Putting information into computers is not nearly as interesting as getting information back out of a computer. A variety of output devices are available. These translate electrical signals from the computer into something that people can see or hear. Using an amplifier and loudspeaker, it is easy to convert electrical signals into noise and music. Figuring out a way to generate more complicated sounds, like sentences spoken by a person, is difficult, but it is being done.

Printing information from a computer is the reverse of entering information from a keyboard. When the printer receives a coded letter from the computer, it turns on the appropriate switch and the matching key strikes an inked ribbon to make a mark on the paper. This is exactly what happens in an electric typewriter. Many of the printers used with microcomputers only have a single key with seven or nine dots. On these, called ***dot-matrix printers***, the electrical pattern determines which of the dots stick out far enough to mark the paper. Each letter is made by 5 or 7 consecutive hits with different patterns of the vertical dots.

Video displays are the most common output devices on microcomputers. Video displays use a cathode ray tube (or CRT) like a television set. The picture we see on the screen is made up of many rows of tiny dots of light. Electrical signals from a computer can control the way lines and other shapes are "drawn" on the screen. Letters and numbers are created using the dot patterns like those of the dot-matrix printers.

Storage devices are used for both input and output. They record messages received from the central processor into magnetic patterns. These magnetic patterns will stay in place for years on specially coated plastic surfaces (like the magnetic tape used for tape recordings) unless they are changed by a strong magnetic force. Thus, any magnetic material (tapes and diskettes) needs to be protected from magnetic forces like those in radio speakers and large electric motors. As long as the magnetic patterns have not been disturbed, the stored messages can be read back into the computer later. Magnetic storage devices are both to save programs (so they don't have to be typed into the computer each time they are run), and to store organized sets of information (data files) that you may want the computer to change or print several times.

Most microcomputer systems are set up to use either cassette tapes or *floppy disks* (so named because they resemble phonograph disks except they are more flexible) as peripheral storage devices. The cassette tapes can use a normal audio cassette recorder with high-quality tapes. The floppy disks require more elaborate and more expensive machinery, the price you pay for their ability to record and send back information much more rapidly.

INTERFACES

The different parts of a computer system are coordinated by special circuits called *interfaces*. The interface circuits include timing signals, and *handshake* signals that keep messages from getting lost between the central processor and a peripheral. Before sending a message, the central processor can check these signals to make sure the peripheral is ready to receive it. Similarly, most peripherals will wait for a handshake signal from the central processor before sending in a message.

The interface between the central processor and memory is handled by an *address bus* and a *data bus*. These circuits are called busses because they shuttle information around the computer much like city busses shuttle people around a town. The address bus works like a telephone network. It calls the various memory apartments to tell them when to copy their values onto the data bus or to copy the answer from the data bus into their own contents. The data bus acts more like a pipeline that carries values back and forth between memory and the central processor.

To illustrate how all of this works, we can trace the actions of a model computer (Fig. 1-2) through a few commands that add a number from memory to a number typed in at a keyboard.

The central processor starts by calling address no. 1 to copy the first instruction into the data bus. That instruction is then copied into the instruction register ("command") and the program counter (address to find the next command) is increased to be ready to call address no. 2. The central processor determines that this first command tells it to get a number from the keyboard. This is a fairly complicated command that takes several steps to complete. First the computer puts a "?" in the message register. Then it switches on the port to the video display. When it sends the message over the wires, a "?" appears on the video screen so the person watching knows that the computer wants something to be typed. The central processor now switches to the port for the keyboard and waits for the handshaking signal that means something has been typed. Now the central processor can copy the value from the keyboard into its message register.

Having finished with the first command, the central processor calls up the next command (from address no. 2 in the instruction register) and increases the program counter again. The second command may tell the central processor to add a number from address no. 50 to the value of the message. To obey this command, the central processor first calls up address no. 50 on the address bus and has it send its value on the data bus into the "answer" register. Now the central processor can add the values in the message (the number which came from the keyboard) and the answer (the number copied from address no. 50). The result of the addition is left in the answer register.

Another command is needed before the person watching the video screen can see the answer. Since the program counter now has the value of 3, the next command is copied into the instruction register from address no.

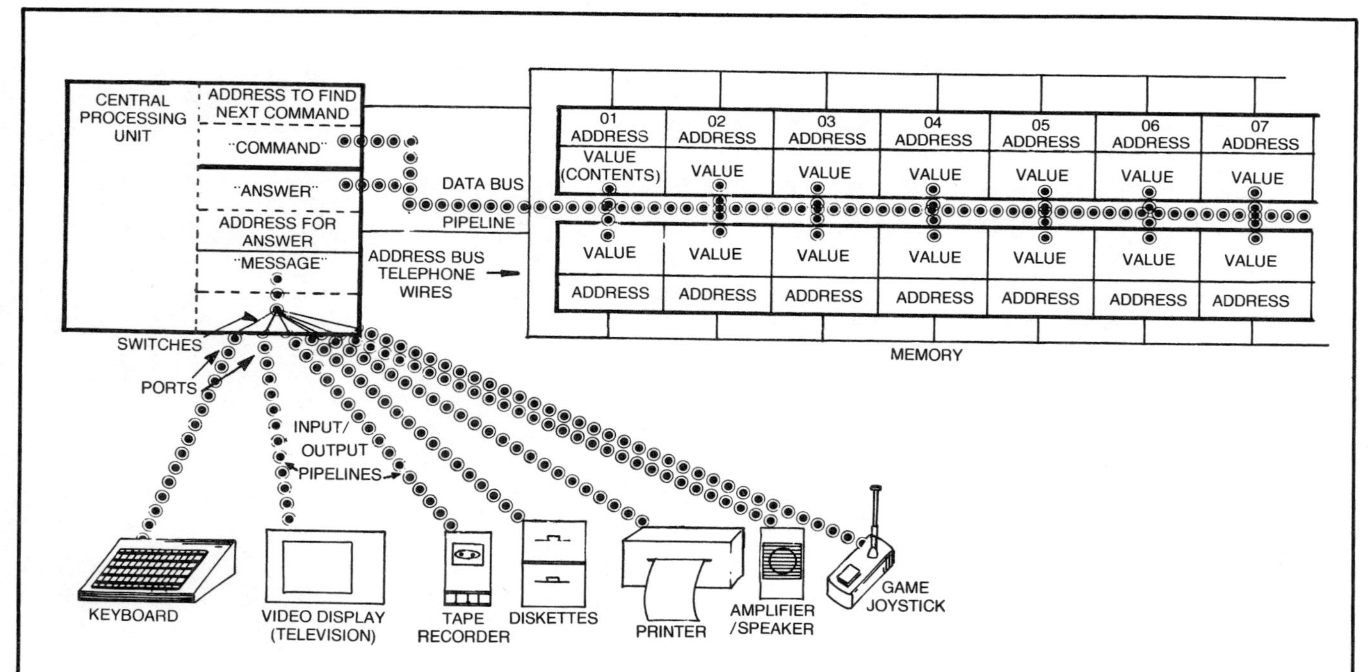

Fig. 1-2. Model of a computer.

3. This command may tell the central processor to copy the answer into the message, switch on the port to the video display, and send the message so it appears on the screen.

All the switching and copying that goes on inside the computer makes even a simple problem seem tedious and complicated. The important things to remember are: (1) A computer does not do fancy operations; it breaks every command down into a series of small, simple steps. (2) A computer does each little step so fast that you usually don't have to worry about how many steps it takes. In the example just used, the answer would seem to appear on the screen at the same time you finished typing the number on the keyboard.

Computer programmers don't have to pay much attention to all the details of what goes on inside the computer, but it does help if they have a general idea of how the computer works. This background will make it easier for you to understand why the commands you give the computer in BASIC (and in other computer languages) must be written in specific ways.

Chapter 2
Computer Languages

Computers work by obeying specific instructions. To set a computer to do what you want it to, you must be able to give it instructions it can understand. No computer can understand English completely, partly because English is such a complicated language and partly because people speaking in English often don't say precisely what they want. When a parent tells a child to "Please, cut it out," the child figures out the meaning from the parent's expression and either gets out a pair of scissors or sits down quietly. Computers cannot guess. They require exact instructions.

People have invented special languages, called *programming languages*, instructions for computers. These programming languages have many similarities to regular languages. They all have verbs, or *operations* (like ADD, PRINT, READ). They all have nouns (addresses and values) and they all have pronouns (*variables* that stand for addresses holding values). And, they all have rules of grammer. Not every combination of English words is an understandable sentence; the words must be arranged according to certain rules to make sense. The grammer of programming languages is usually referred to as *syntax*.

Not all computers speak the same language. Some languages can only be understood by particular machines. Other languages have been designed to solve only certain kinds of problems (like drawing graphs or printing reports). Some languages, like BASIC, are designed to be general-purpose problem-solving tools that people can use to give instructions to many different computers. Like common languages, programming languages have dialects; a program written in BASIC for one computer may not work on a different kind of computer if it uses slang expressions (technically called *language extensions*). This difficulty is similar to the problems an American has when listening to a Cockney Englishman.

MACHINE LANGUAGES

When computers were first invented, there were not a wide variety of programming languages to choose from. The programmers translated all of their instructions into the special codes that the central processor used. This way the computer could do exactly what the programmer told it to do without wasting any time trying to translate the instructions.

The syntax of machine languages is simple. Every sentence starts with a verb or *opcode* (for operation code). Most opcodes have to be followed by one or two nouns (addresses or values). A few opcodes (like the one telling the machine to stop) are complete sentences by themselves. There is no punctuation.

The trouble with machine languages is that they are very difficult for people to understand. Programmers can easily make small mistakes in writing machine-language instructions. Because the computer follows the mistaken codes exactly, it often gives ridiculous answers. Then the poor programmer has to read through the codes hunting for the mistake. The computer works best with binary codes (a series of 1s and 0s that work for on/off switches). So the machine-language code looks something like:

```
0011111000111111110011010011001100000000
01100110100101011000000001110110101001011
00000001011111111000000001100110100110011
0000000001110110
```

If this sample code looks like garbage to you, then you are a human and not a Z-80 microcomputer. Programmers quickly tire of reading rows of 1s and 0s. Some bright programmers started writing special sets of instructions to get the computer to translate its special codes into something easier for people to read. One early step was to get the computer to print a single digit to replace each combination of four 1s and 0s. There are sixteen possible combinations that form the ***hexadecimal*** code ("hex" for six, plus "deci" for ten):

0000 = 0 in hexadecimal
0001 = 1
0010 = 2
0011 = 3
0100 = 4
0101 = 5
0110 = 6
0111 = 7
1000 = 8
1001 = 9
1010 = A (we ran out of number digits)
1011 = B
1100 = C
1101 = D
1110 = E
1111 = F

By using these group codes, and by having the computer only print one statement on each line, the long series of 1s and 0s becomes much easier to read (though it still doesn't make any sense unless you know the special meaning of each code).

```
3E3F
CD3300
CD2B00
ED4B017F
80
CD3300
76
```

Even with these improvements, machine language is so difficult for people to read that it would take weeks or months to write a single program. Just as bad, nobody could sit down and read through a machine-language program and tell what it did (at least, not without tediously decoding each statement).

ASSEMBLER LANGUAGES

The next step in computer-language development was the creation of programs to translate words and abbreviations that make sense to people into codes that the central processor could use. These programs are called *assemblers* because they take the words from the programmer and assemble them into a program. The programmer writing in an assembler language still has to break each problem down into the tiny steps that the computer can follow, but at least he can use words that make more sense to us. In an assembler language, our sample rows of 1s and 0s might be written as:

```
BEGIN LOAD   A,"?"
      CALL   SCREEN
      CALL   KEYBRD
      LOAD   B,(NUMBER)
      ADD    A,B
      CALL   SCREEN
      HALT
```

This set of instructions appears to make sense. We can guess its meaning. First load the "answer" register with the message "?". Next call the video screen (to have it display the message). Third, call the keyboard (and get an answer). Next, copy some number into a register or variable called "B". Then add the number in "B" to the answer (in "A") and send the result to be displayed on the video screen by calling *screen* again. Finally, have the computer stop.

With assembler languages, there are two versions of each program. First, there is a *source* program, which the programmer writes and feeds into the assembler. The assembler produces an *object* program which uses the machine-language codes. Assembler languages let the programmer control each step the central processor takes, and lets him write instructions that make use of a computer's speed. So assembler language is still used for some problems that have to be solved very fast. However, to write good assembler programs, a programmer has to learn to think like a computer and he has to write out every tiny step involved in solving a problem.

HIGH-LEVEL LANGUAGES

Most computer instructions are now written in high-level languages, instead of machine or assembler languages. They are called "high-level" languages because they emulate natural language—and because they consist of extremely powerful instructions to the computer. Tests show that high-level languages require 10 percent *less* programming time than other languages. In these high-level languages people can write statements that describe the way people think about problems, without having to break them down into tiny computer steps. A special language program inside the computer then translates each statement in the high-level language into a whole series of machine language steps. Therefore, high-level language programs usually require fewer steps and are easier to read than assembler programs. Our little sample program uses seven steps in assembler or machine language. The same program can be written with three statements in the high-level BASIC language:

```
10  INPUT  A
20  PRINT  A + N
30  END
```

For more complicated programs, an assembler might require twenty or more times as many instructions as a high-level language. The smaller number of instructions generally make it quicker to solve a problem using the high-level language and easier to read and change the program once it has been written.

High-level languages let you concentrate on how to solve the problem and let the computerized translator do the tedious work of converting the solution into the tiny steps the central processor can understand. High-level languages do not let you solve any problems on the computer that could not be solved by a program written in machine language. Also, the high-level languages still require that the programmer be able to write the instructions precisely. Every statement written in a high-level language must be mechanically converted into machine language (by an already-written program).

Programs written in high-level languages are converted into machine language by two different kinds of programs: *compilers* and *interpreters*. Compilers start with a source program and convert it into an object program (like assemblers, but more complicated). The object program is saved in machine language and can be run on the computer many times. Interpreters convert programs one statement at a time and make the computer follow each instruction as soon as it is translated. Each time the program is run, the interpreter translates it all over again.

If you wanted to translate a speech from English into Japanese, a compiler would be the person who would make you first write out the whole speech in English. Then the compiler would write out a different copy showing you how to pronounce the equivalent sentences in Japanese. You could then read the speech to as many different Japanese audiences as you wanted without having to have the compiler be with you. However, if somebody in the audience asked you what you meant by a particular word, or if you suddenly got an idea for improving the speech, you would be in trouble. You would have to change the English version of the speech, get ahold of the compiler and wait hours for him to give you a new Japanese version.

On the other hand, if you hired an interpreter to stand beside you while you gave speeches, the interpreter would translate each sentence as soon as it was spoken (even if it did not make any sense). If you changed your mind about what you wanted to say, there would be no problem. Of course, you would have to pay the interpreter every time you gave the speech.

As a general rule, if the same program (or speech) is going to be used many times, then it is faster and cheaper to use a compiler. But if a program is only going to be used a few times, or if it may be changed often, then it is easier and cheaper to use an interpreter.

This book concentrates on a single high-level language: BASIC, an acronym for Beginner's All-Purpose Symbolic Instruction Code (actually, the people who invented BASIC first decided that it was a catchy sounding name for a language and then they figured out the words it's supposed to stand for). Most computers use interpreters to translate BASIC statements. There are also some versions of BASIC which use compilers.

The BASIC language has a small vocabulary of words and follows simple syntax or rules of grammar. Learning the words (commands, variables, and values) and the rules of syntax is easy. If you later decide to learn COBOL (an acronym for COmmon Business Oriented Language) or FORTRAN (which stands for FORmula TRANslator), or any other computer language, you will have to learn a different set of vocabulary words and syntax rules.

No matter what language you use, getting the computer to do what you want it to requires that you learn to write your instructions in a very precise and logical form. The computer will try to do exactly what you say. It will not worry about what you really mean. A good set of instructions in any language will include provisions for all different possibilities. The hardest part of learning to write good programs is learning how to plan the solution of problems for stupid machines. People are smart enough to change their own behavior when something unusual happens. If you handed somebody a seven dollar bill, he would notice that something was strange and would probably refuse to give you change. A computer would not notice that anything was wrong UNLESS the person who had written its programs had thought about the possibility of counterfeit money ahead of time and included instructions for sounding an alarm.

The real value of computers is the result of the speed with which computers can follow precise instructions and the intelligence with which people can plan logical solutions to problems. The same skills that make a person a good problem solver with BASIC can be used with any other computer language.

LAYERS OF LANGUAGES

Each computer language (except machine language) is a written program. Modern computers use several different programs at the same time. While your program is running inside the computer, the computer is also running a program called BASIC (which interprets the instructions in your program) and a program called an *operating system* (which interprets instructions for the peripherals and controls which other programs the central processor works on). Thirty or more different programs may share a large computer at the same time.

We can generally divide all programs written for computers into three groups: (1) operating systems, (2) language translators, and (3) application programs.

Operating systems are programs (or groups of programs) written to control how the computer works. They include the instructions the computer follows when it is first turned on (referred to as the *booting* program), instructions for copying other programs into memory (*loads*) and copying changed programs back onto a storage peripheral (*saves* to disks or cassette), and instructions for communicating with peripheral devices (input/output or I/O routines). Fancier operating systems include security instructions to control who can use different programs and information in the computer, accounting instructions used to determine how much each person who uses the computer has to pay, and scheduling instructions that determine when the central processor works on different programs. The different parts of an operating system are designed to handle the mechanical details of coordinating computer use. Most programmers don't think about operating systems very much. They learn the commands to get the operating system to run the programs they want by reading the instructions that come with the computer. Programmers don't really care why these commands work as long as they *do* work. In fact, the main reason for having operating systems is to reduce the number of things programmers have to know about the computer before they can make it work.

Language translators are tools for programmers. They transform the instructions people write into programs that the central processor can run. The way people can write programs to solve problems is limited by what the translators will accept. Good translators make writing programs easier by providing warning messages and explanations when the programmer has made a mistake, by having commands and syntax rules that are flexible and easy to remember, and by allowing programmers to describe the instructions to the computer in a form that is easy to read and understand. Nobody will ever invent the best language translator. People will always disagree on what commands make the most sense and are the easiest to use. Some languages will make more sense to accountants; other languages will be easier for scientists or artists to understand. BASIC is not the best possible language for anyone, but it is pretty good for a lot of different kinds of problems and it is easy for most people to learn.

Application programs are the reason for having computers. These are the sets of instructions written to make the computer solve a specific problem (or play a particular game). Operating systems and language translators only make it easier for people to use computers; they don't make the computer do anything useful by themselves. It takes a good applications program to get anything valuable out of a computer. Just as there is no best language translator, there will never be a best applications program. An application program is good if it lets someone solve a problem quickly, easily, and accurately. An application program is bad if it produces wrong answers or takes more work than it would take to solve the problem without a computer. Beyond these very simple rules for evaluating programs, the quality of a program is determined by how well it satisfies the people who use it. The main limit on what an applications program can do is the imagination of the people who write it.

Chapter 3

BASIC Commands

When you want to give people instructions, you use English sentences to describe each step you want followed. The main unit of the English language is a word, but a bunch of words won't make any sense unless those words are arranged into sentences. The rules of grammar describe the ways different types of words (nouns, verbs, adjectives, conjunctions, etc.) can be arranged to make legitimate sentences. The rules of English grammar are very complicated. However, we do know that every sentence must have a subject and a predicate. (A few sentences appear to violate this rule because we don't always write the subject. For example, the subject of the sentence "Be quiet!" is "you" even though you are only implied.)

When you want to give a computer instructions in BASIC, you use *statements* to describe each step. Each statement is made up of symbols (reserved words, operators, values, and variables) arranged according to the syntax rules (grammar) of BASIC. The rules for BASIC statements are much simpler than the rules for English sentences. Every BASIC statement starts with a command word (verb) that specifies what kind of action the computer is supposed to take. BASIC verbs are short words chosen from English, like PRINT, LET, END, LIST. In most statements the verb is followed by one or more targets of the command. The targets tell what is to be PRINTed, LISTed, copied, or compared.

When the computer interprets your instructions in BASIC (and in most other computer languages) it recognizes four different types of symbols: reserved words, constants, variables, and delimiters.

Reserved words are the main vocabulary of the computer language. Each reserved word has an entry in the permanent dictionary of the language that tells the computer how to translate it into machine actions. Reserved words must be spelled exactly right, and can be used only in places where their dictionary definitions make sense. Computers are very picky about how their reserved words are used. If you typed an instruction to PRIMT something, a person would probably figure out that you wanted it PRINTed, but your BASIC program would simply give you a message stating that it did not understand you. The reserved words for BASIC include all of the BASIC command words (LET, PRINT, END, etc.), the arithmetic symbols (= for equals, + for add, – for subtract, * for multiply, and / for divided by) along with some other words you will learn to use later (AND, OR, TO, THEN, etc.).

Constants are specific values that the computer can print, store in its memory, use for arithmetic, or compare. BASIC constants are either numbers or *strings*. All numbers start with either a digit (0, 1, 2, 3, 4, 5, 6, 7, 8, or 9) or a sign (+ or –). The rest of the number is made up of digits and possibly a decimal point. Generally BASIC numbers look like what we normally think of as numbers, things like 3 or 300.45 or –8. However, there are a lot of things we recognize as numbers that the BASIC computer would not accept. Some example, 1,000,000 isn't accepted in BASIC because BASIC won't allow commas in the middle of its numbers. It thinks that 1,000,000 is three different numbers, a one and two different zeros. Because $5.00 doesn't start with a digit or a sign, BASIC won't recognize that it is a number either.

A *string* or literal is a constant with a non-number value. When a computer prints your name or any written instructions it is using a string. BASIC recognizes anything typed inside of quotation marks (") as a string. If a BASIC statement included the phrase "PRINT ME", it would treat the whole phrase as a single value. If the phrase were typed PRINT "ME", then BASIC would interpret it as a command to print the string value ME.

Think of constants as the nouns of the BASIC language. The pronouns are called *variables*. A variable is a name that BASIC gives to an address in memory. A particular variable can hold lots of different values at different times, but it can hold only a single value at a time. This works just like the English pronoun "it." The word "it" may stand for many different things in the same story, but each time "it" is used you can replace it with some particular noun without changing the meaning of the story. In BASIC, variable names must start with an uppercase letter. It is common to use a single letter (A or I or X) to name a variable. A few computers allow you to use any word (except reserved words) as the name of a variable, but most computers only pay attention to variable names that are one or two letters long. (Some versions of BASIC require that a variable name be either a single letter or a letter followed by a digit, such as A4, B0, or X1.)

When BASIC sees a variable name, it assumes the variable is supposed to hold a number value. If you want a variable to hold a special kind of value (like a string or literal), you have to let BASIC know so that it can set aside the right amount of memory to hold your special value. Using a dollar sign at the end of a variable name will identify that variable as a *string variable*. For example, a variable named N$ would hold a string value such as "Name," while a variable named N would hold a number such as 50.

Delimiters are the punctuation marks of computer languages. BASIC uses commas (,), semicolons (;), quotation marks ("), parentheses ((and)) as delimiters. Commas are used to separate variables or constants. PRINT A,B tells the computer to print the value of the two different variables A and B, while PRINT AB tells the computer to print the value of the single variable AB. In English, we use commas for lots of different purposes (mainly for pauses and to make big numbers like 1,000,000 easier to read), and we use the context to help us understand what they mean. BASIC computers are not as flexible as we are. Whenever the computer sees a comma (unless it is inside quotation marks), it decides that it has reached the end of a value. To the BASIC-programmed computer, 1,000,000 means a value of 1, followed by a value of 000, followed by another value of 000. If you want to give the computer a value of one million, you must type 1000000 (no commas). This rule is a little inconvenient (and there are some fancy ways to get around it when you really have to have commas in your numbers), but that's part of the way the BASIC language was designed. Semicolons are also used to separate variables, but they can be used only with a few commands. The difference between PRINT A,B and PRINT A;B is that A;B will print the two values right next to each other, while A,B will leave more space between them.

The quotation marks delimit the beginning and end of a string value. Parentheses are used to group values together in expressions (which will be explained a little later). Many versions of BASIC also allow the use of either colons (:) or backward slashes (/) to separate statements when more than one statement is typed on the same line. Thus the colon works a lot like the period at the end of a sentence in English, except that it is never used at the end of the last statement on a line. PRINT A:PRINT A would be an acceptable way of telling the computer to print the value of A twice. PRINT A:PRINT A: would not be acceptable because the computer would look for another statement right after the last colon. It might seem simpler to use the period (.) just like English, but remember the computer already thinks the little dot on the typewriter is a decimal point.

Warning: some computers won't let you type more than one statement on a line. Also having several statements on a line usually makes it harder for people to read the commands. So, it is a good idea to get in the habit of writing only one BASIC command on each line.

Blank spaces are not delimiters to BASIC. The computer does not care whether you write "IF A = 5 OR B = 10 THEN C = 15" or "IFA=5?RB=10THENC=15". Nevertheless, it is a good idea to use spaces when you type BASIC statements so you can read your own writing. The easier your statements are to read, the easier it will be to tell what the computer is going to do and to fix mistakes.

GETTING STARTED

Reading about computers and programming is interesting, but it is not the best way to become a good programmer. Computer programming is a skill, like playing the piano. Like playing the piano, it requires practice as well as knowledge (besides, using a computer is usually more exciting and fun than just reading about one). The rest of this chapter will be easier to understand if you work on a microcomputer or computer terminal while reading it.

First, before the computer can follow any BASIC commands you give, it must be turned on and have a BASIC language translator in its memory. Some microcomputers have BASIC permanently in their memory and will be ready for use as soon as you turn them on. If you are using a terminal hooked up to a large computer, you will first have to "sign on" to the system by typing some kind of identification code and password (the exact procedure is slightly different for each computer). With most microcomputers using disks, turning the computer on will load the operating system, but will not load any language translator into the memory. With either the disk-based micros or the computer-terminal systems, you will probably have to ask for BASIC before it will be available to you. To ask for BASIC, you simply type the word BASIC and then press the RETURN key. (On some computers, the RETURN key is labeled either ENTER or CR for carriage return.)

When the BASIC language translator is ready for you to type in a command, it will tell you by displaying a message on the screen (or printing it on your teletypewriter terminal), saying: READY. The line that you are going to type will be marked by some symbol (>, *, or –, depending on your computer) which is called a ***prompt*** because it is a reminder to type something promptly.

The computer will generally ignore anything you type until you press the ***return*** or ***enter*** key. That key signals the computer that your message is finished and the computer should do something. The exception to this rule is provided by the control keys. Somewhere on your keyboard is a key labeled ***break*** or ***interrupt***. Hitting that key will interrupt whatever the computer is doing and get it ready to do your next command. If you type HELLO OUT THERE and hit return, the computer will give you some kind of an error message because it does not know what HELLO OUT THERE means. But, if you type HELLO OUT THERE and hit the break key, the computer will tell you that it is ready again (totally ignoring your message). Note: some keyboards have a special CONTROL key that is used with other keys to send special messages to the computer. If your keyboard has one of these keys, don't play with it (you might disconnect yourself from the computer completely).

Unless you are an expert typist, you will also want to become familiar with the ***backspace*** key (often labeled with an arrow pointing left "←"). This key lets you correct typing errors. For example, if you type HELLO OUT THEIR, you can hit the backspace a couple of times, and the screen will say HELLO OUT THE   . Now you can type the final RE, and your mistake is corrected.

THE PRINT COMMAND

The PRINT command is used to display values on the screen. It tells the computer to print something for people to read.

Enter PRINT "HELLO OUT THERE" on your computer. Type the uppercase letters and the quotation marks exactly as they appear. Don't forget to hit the return or enter key when you are ready for the computer to obey your command. The computer will print on the screen the message, HELLO OUT THERE. The computer parrots the exact string of letters and symbols typed in between the quotation marks. It does not print the quotation marks because they are considered to be delimiters showing where the string begins and ends. The quotation marks are not counted as part of the message.

When you print a number value, you don't need the quotation marks. The computer automatically treats all numbers as values. Enter PRINT 15 and the computer will print the number 15. If you throw in some meaningless zeros, the computer will ignore them and print the number in its simplest decimal form. Enter PRINT 00015.000 and you still get 15. Enter PRINT 0.05 and you get .05 (that one zero is a meaningful placeholder). If you have been trying these examples on a computer, you may have noticed that the results don't print out in a neat column. Instead they look like this:

```
HELLO OUT THERE
15
15
.05
```

The string (HELLO OUT THERE) started at the left hand edge of the screen, but there is a blank space in front of each of the numbers. Whenever BASIC prints a number value, it saves the first space for a sign (– if the number is less than zero, blank if it is a positive number). It also leaves a blank space after the last digit (to keep numbers from getting too crammed together on the screen). BASIC makes no attempt to line up the decimal points in a series of numbers the way we do when writing dollars and cents.

There are several ways to print more than one value on a line. The simplest is to use a single PRINT command with commas between the values. Enter PRINT "TOM","DICK","HARRY" and the computer will print TOM DICK and HARRY on the same line with a bunch of space between each name. The computer divides each line into several columns. Each time it finds a comma in a PRINT command, it moves over to the start of the next column and gets ready to print the next value. If you put two commas right after one value, it will leave a column blank and spread out the message even more. Enter PRINT "TOM",,"DICK","HARRY" to see the difference a comma makes. If you don't like to have so much space between words, use semicolons (another delimiter) instead of commas. Enter PRINT "TOM";"DICK";"HARRY" and the computer replies, TOMDICKHARRY. It would be a little easier to read if you put a few spaces back in. If you want it to print: TOM DICK HARRY, you will have to put some spaces inside the quotation marks, where they will be part of the message.

Enter PRINT "TOM ";"DICK ";"HARRY" or PRINT "TOM";" ";"DICK";" "; "HARRY".PRINT"TOM";"DICK";"HARRY" won't do any good because BASIC ignores blank spaces unless they are part of a string value.

Now print one million. You can do it easily as a strong value. Enter PRINT "ONE MILLION" or PRINT "1,000,000". Now try it as a number value. If you enter: PRINT 1,000,000 the computer replied:

1 0 0

because it treats the commas as delimiters. The computer thought you told it to print three different numbers, one a value of 1 and two with values of zero.

If you ordered your computer to PRINT 1000000 it may have printed back your value of one million the same way you typed it. However, if your computer uses low precision numbers, it may have printed the results in scientific notation: 1E+06. When BASIC runs into really large numbers, it shortens them by printing a number between –10 and 10 followed by an exponent. In this example, the exponent of +06 means that the 1 should be followed by 6 zeros. One trillion (1,000,000,000,000) would be printed as 1E+12. Tiny fractions appear with negative exponents. One one-millionth (0.000001) could be printed as 1E–06. You can do a lot of computer programming without using huge numbers or tiny fractions, but it is nice to know that the computer isn't broken when it suddenly prints the letter E in the middle of a number.

The PRINT verb does not have to be followed by a value. You can enter a lone PRINT and the computer will print a blank line. You can also order the computer to print the value of a variable. Enter PRINT X. This command requires the computer to (1) find the address for the variable called X in its directory; (2) copy the value from that address in memory into the central processor; and then (3) send a copy of the value from the central processor to the screen. The result is that a number appears on the screen. The number is probably zero, since no values have been put into memory, but it could be some strange number left over from something else the computer has been doing.

PRINT is one of the most heavily used verbs in the BASIC language. It is the main command that lets you see what the computer has done. Some versions of BASIC have fancy variations of the PRINT verb that cause messages to appear anywhere you want them to on the screen or which let you print commas in big numbers and line up decimal places in columns of numbers. These special features don't work the same way on all computers. So, it is a good idea to start off using the plain standard version of the PRINT command. Sticking to the standards allows you to run your programs on many different kinds of computers.

GIVING VARIABLES A VALUE

While the PRINT command controls what is printed on the screen, the LET command controls what is stored in memory. Enter LET X = 5 and your computer does not seem to do anything. However, the computer has assigned the value of 5 to the variable X in its memory. Now if you enter PRINT X the computer will print 5 on the screen. A complete LET statement looks like:

LET variable-name = something

This does not work like an equation in algebra. Only a single variable name can be on the left of the equal sign. The computer will not understand a command like LET X + 5 = 10. If you told the computer to LET 5 = X, it would think you wanted to copy whatever value was stored in the address for X into the address for a variable named 5. Since all variable names in BASIC must start with a letter, the computer would give you an error message.

When BASIC translates a LET command, it first figures out the value of the "something" that comes after the equal sign, then it copies that value into the memory address of the variable. The "something" can be a number, a variable, or an arithmetic expression. Enter LET Y = 10 and the variable Y is given a value of 10. (If you don't believe this without seeing for yourself, then enter PRINT Y.) Enter LET Y = X and the value stored in Y will be changed to a copy of the value that already was in X. This statement does not change the value of X. Enter PRINT X,Y to see that the two variables now have the same value.

LET statements are used to make the computer do arithmetic. Enter LET A = 5 + 6 and the computer will figure out that 5 + 6 is 11; then it stores the answer in A. Now enter LET B = A + 4. The computer has to copy the value of A into its arithmetic area (in the central processor) before it can determine that the answer to the arithmetic problem is 15 (4 plus the 11 that was stored in A). After the arithmetic is complete, the answer is copied back into the memory address for B. BASIC will allow you to use the same variable on both sides of the equal sign. You can tell BASIC to LET B = A + B. In this case, it will copy the values sitting in A (which is still 11) and B (which we made 15) into the central processor, add them together, and copy the answer (26) back into the memory address B. The old value of 15 is erased when the new value is stored in B. If you repeat the same command, LET B = A + B, the answer will be different (11 + 26 = 37) the second time.

Many different English commands can be translated into LET statements. "Add 5 to the total" can be written as LET T = T + 5 (assuming we use the variable name T to hold the total). "Take 2 away from John's score" might be written in BASIC as LET J = J − 2. When counting sheep, the words "There's another one!" could produce the BASIC command: LET S = S + 1.

LET is a special verb in many versions of BASIC because it does not have to be written. When the computer sees a statement which starts with a variable name, it assumes that it is a LET statement. (When you see an English command that starts with a verb—"Pay attention" or "Be quiet"—the subject is assumed to be the pronoun "you." The option of omitting the word LET at the beginning of a BASIC statement works the same way.) If your computer allows this shortcut, you can save some typing by entering: A = B + 5 when you mean LET A = B + 5.

One little reminder: String values require a different size of memory address than number values. You can't LET a number variable = a string value. LET N = "ZERO" will produce an error message because there is not enough room in the number variable N to hold the whole word "ZERO." If you want to store a string value, you have to use a string variable. LET N$ = "ZERO" is a good command because the dollar sign indicates that N$ is a string variable (which does not have the same address as N). You also cannot LET a string variable equal a number value. BASIC always gets ready to do some arithmetic when it sees a number. When it sees the name of a string variable, it expects a word. BASIC does not know how to do any arithmetic with words. (Neither do I. What is the answer to Bob + Mary? I've seen that arithmetic problem carved in a tree, but never could figure out its value.)

ARITHMETIC EXPRESSIONS

An arithmetic expression is a series of number values and variables with arithmetic symbols (or operators) between them. The computer can calculate the numeric value of any expression by performing the arithmetic. Most expressions are simple combinations like A + 1, 5 – 3, or X – Y. Whenever BASIC sees a variable as part of an expression, it copies the value of the variable from memory to do the arithmetic. BASIC does not do algebraic translations; it would not change X + X into 2X.

BASIC uses five symbols for arithmetic operations:

+ for addition	Example: 3 + 2 has the value 5
– for subtraction	Example: 3 – 2 has the value 1
* for multiplication	Example: 3* has the value 6
/ for division	Example: 3 / 2 has the value 1.5
↑ for exponentiation	Example: 3 ↑ 2 has the value 9

The symbols for addition and subtraction are the same ones used in elementary arithmetic. The "×" used in arithmetic for multiplication won't work in BASIC because it is the same as the letter "X" which BASIC interprets to be the name of a variable. The asterisk or (*) symbol was chosen for multiplication because it is the closest thing on the keyboard to the large centered dot used for multiplication in standard algebra (example, 3 • 2). The old arithmetic symbol for division (÷) isn't on the keyboard either. We are used to seeing the slash (/) used in typing fractions (like 1/2), and fractions are really division problems (1 divided by 2 is one-half). So the slash makes a good symbol for division. Exponentiation is also known as raising a number to a power, thus the use of the up arrow (↑) symbol. Exponentiation can be thought of as repeated multiplication: 3 ↑ 2 is two threes multiplied together (3*3=9);3 4 is four threes multiplied together (3*3*3*3 = 81), and so on. Some BASIC language translators actually interpret exponentiation as repeated multiplication, so before you depend on your computer to calculate the value of expressions like 3↑0.5or

3↑−4, you need to make sure that your computer does not restrict exponentiation to whole numbers.

There are two ways to get the computer to show you the value of an expression. You can enter a LET command like LET V = 3 * 4 * 5 * 6 * 7 * 8 * 9 , followed by a print command such as PRINT V. The first command calculates the product of all those numbers and stores the resulting value of 181440 in the memory address for V. The PRINT command then copies that value onto the screen. The other way is to simply enter PRINT 3 * 4 * 5 * 6 * 7 * 8 * 9. This will put the value 181440 on the screen almost instantly. It also requires one command instead of two. However, the print command does not store any answers in memory, so if you wanted to use the answer again (say, add 16 to the result), you would have to have the computer do the whole calculation over.

Determining the value of an expression can get complicated if more than one arithmetic operator is involved. The value of something like: 5 * 4 + 6 / 2 − 3 ↑ 2 is not obvious. You have to figure it out by doing one operation at a time and combining the results. If you just started at the left and worked to the right, you would get an answer of 100 (5 times 4 is 20, plus 6 is 26, divided by 2 is 13, minus 3 is 10; 10 to the second power is 10 * 10, or 100). BASIC doesn't work that way; it follows the same rules as algebra and gives some operators precedence (or priority) over others. Exponentiation has the top priority and is done first. Multiplication and division have the same priority, after exponentiation and before addition or subtraction. Addition and subtraction share the bottom of the totem pole. When the computer has to choose between two operations with the same precedence, then it does the one on the left first. Here's how the sample expression is evaluated:

5 * 4 + 6 / 2 − 3 2	Exponentiation (↑) has top priority.
5 * 4 + 6 / 2 − 9	Multiplication (*) and division (/) are equal. Which is first?
20 + 6 / 2 − 9	Division has highest priority
20 + 3 − 9	There are no priorities. Start on the left.
23 − 9	The true value at last.
14	

If you don't use algebra very often, it will take some practice to remember how the computer evaluates expressions. It could be upsetting if you were expecting something to be worth $100 and the computer came back with a final value of $14. It could be downright harmful if you had assumed the computer would do its arithmetic in order from left to right and had used the computer answer without checking it. You may want to take some time to figure out the values for a number of expressions and then test your answers with the computer. Try the following samples:

PRINT 3 + 4 * 5
PRINT 5 * 4 + 3 (Is it the same as # 1?)
PRINT 2 * 20 /5
PRINT 2 * 3 + 4 / 2
PRINT 3 + 4 / 2 * 2 (Is it the same as # 4?)
PRINT 16 – 1 * 3 ↑ 3.

Sometimes the computer's rules get in the way of doing things the way we want them done. People like computers because computers do what people tell them to (that is also one of the reasons some people don't like computers). So, we ought to be able to tell the computer to add 3 and 4, then multiply the result by 5. We could use two different commands LET R = 3 + 4, then PRINT R * 5. There is an easier way: Use parentheses as delimiters to group the operators. BASIC, like elementary algebra, will do arithmetic that is inside a pair of parentheses before it does anything outside of the parentheses. Thus, a pair of parentheses can get around the normal rules of precedence. (3 + 4) * 5 is 7 * 5 or 35. Without the parentheses, the multiplication would be done first, for a final answer of 23.

Using parentheses to group things can make it easier for us to understand expressions, too. If our original expression had been written as: (5 * 4) + (6 / 2) – (3 ↑ 2), the computer would have given the same answer, and people would be less apt to come up with different answers (like 100). Using too many parentheses can make expressions look more confusing: (((5 * 4) + (6 / 2)) – (3 ↑ 2)) and will slow down the computer a little. Nevertheless, it is better to use a pair of parentheses that may not be necessary than to take a chance on having an expression translated wrong because the numbers weren't grouped right.

The most common error is writing BASIC statements with parentheses is to use an odd number of them. Parentheses must always be used in pairs. If there are more symbols telling the computer that this is the start of a group (the left parenthesis), than symbols marking the end of a group (the right parenthesis), then the computer will think it has a group that never stops. On the other hand, an extra ")" tells the computer that it is at the end of a group that never started. Either way, the translator gets confused and sends you an error message.

Speaking of error messages, what is 5 / 0? It is mathematically and physically impossible to divide anything into zero equal parts with no remainder. Very few people try to divide by zero when they see what they are doing. Nearly every computer programmer sooner or later tells his computer to divide by zero because he forgets to check the value of a divisor. When you have written an instruction to print the ratio of wrong answers to right answers as: PRINT W/R., it is easy to forget that somebody might not have any right answers (R=0). When the computer finds a value of zero for a divisor, it won't use magic to come up with an answer. It will simply send out an error message reminding the programmer not to ask for the impossible.

By now, you have enough knowledge of BASIC to get your expensive computer to solve any arithmetic problem, using PRINT and LET statements, that you could solve on a seven-dollar pocket calculator. This may not sound particularly exciting, but PRINT and LET statements, with a variety of expression, form the core of nearly every BASIC program. Before going on to the next chapter, take some time to play calculator with your computer. See how many different answers you can get by putting different combinations of parentheses in the expression: 5 * 4 + 6 / 2 – 3 ↑ 2. Try different calculations using variables with negative numbers or decimal fractions for values. When you are comfortable with computer expressions and the PRINT and LET commands, you will be ready to cross the threshold into the world of computer programming.

Chapter 4

What's a Computer Program?

The great speed of computer calculations is wasted when it gets instructions one step at a time. The computer spends more than 99.99 percent of its time doing nothing but waiting for someone to push the buttons that give it the next command. The only way to make good use of the speed of a computer is to give it a whole series of commands at once. Then the computer can follow all instructions at its own speed without waiting for a slow person.

A computer program is simply a series of commands that a computer can obey as often as you desire. The commands are stored inside the computer. Once you order the computer to start the program, the computer is able to retrieve the commands from its memory one at a time, follow the instructions for that command, then continue on with the next command.

Each step in the program must have an address so the computer will know where to find it in memory. In BASIC program steps are addressed by a *line number* at the start of each instruction. The line number is followed by a command word (like LET or PRINT) and the rest of a command. A short BASIC program looks something like:

```
10 LET R = 5
20 PRINT "THE RADIUS OF A CIRCLE IS";R
30 LET A = 3.14159 * R ↑ 2
40 PRINT "THE AREA OF THAT CIRCLE IS";A
99 END
```

Notice that the steps are not numbered 1, 2, 3, etc. BASIC does not require that line numbers be sequential. Line numbers must be whole numbers. (Some computers allow a line numbered 0, but others won't accept anything less than 1 as a line number.) There is also an upper limit to the size of line numbers. Most computers won't accept a line number higher than 65535. The limit of some sixty-five thousand line numbers is usually not much of a problem since you would probably run out of patience and computer memory long before you wrote sixty-five thousand lines of instructions for a single program.

The line numbers are kept in a directory (like variable names) to locate the memory addresses where the instructions are stored. The directory is sorted so the instructions are listed from the lowest line number to the highest. The directory doesn't care what the lowest number is that you use, or how many numbers you skip. The directory only includes the line numbers that have been entered as part of the program. Most programmers get into the habit of leaving room between line numbers to add more instructions later. This is why the lines in the first sample program are numbered 10, 20, 30, 40, and 99 instead of 1, 2, 3, 4, 5.

The last line of the program (99 END) simply informs the computer that it is finished with the program. When the computer sees the END command, it prints the READY message on the screen and waits for additional instructions. Now, type the sample program on your computer. (Don't forget to press the enter or return key at the end of each line.) The computer does not follow any of the program commands when you type them. Instead, it stores each line in its memory for future use.

To make the computer follow all the instructions stored in the program, enter the command RUN. The computer should respond by doing all commands in the program and then printing:

```
THE RADIUS OF A CIRCLE IS 5
THE AREA OF THAT CIRCLE IS 78.539
```

You can have the computer RUN the same program as often as you like. It will always come back with exactly the same information. This pretty quickly gets boring. If you want to know about a different circle, you will need a different program. To find the area of a circle with a radius of 10, you could write a program that looks just like this first one, except line number 10 would say LET R = 10 instead of LET R = 5. Fortunately, you don't have to enter the whole program all over again. All you have to do is type a new line 10:

```
10 LET R = 10
```

The computer will store your new instruction and put its address in the directory instead of the address of the original line 10. Now when you give the RUN command, the computer prints:

```
THE RADIUS OF A CIRCLE IS 10
THE AREA OF THAT CIRCLE IS 31.4159
```

It is just as easy to add instructions to a program. You just have to enter statements with line numbers that aren't already used in your program. The sample program can be expanded to print the diameter and the circumference of the circle:

```
22 LET D = 2 * R
25 PRINT "THE DIAMETER OF THAT CIRCLE IS";D
50 LET C = 3.14159 * D
60 PRINT "THE CIRCUMFERENCE OF THAT CIRCLE IS";C
 5 PRINT
 7 PRINT
```

The last two lines will make the computer print blank lines so that the results of the program won't be jammed up against all of the other stuff you have been typing. Notice that it doesn't matter what order in which you type the new line numbers. The computer will rearrange the directory so the instructions are obeyed in the order of their line numbers. When you enter: RUN, the computer will respond:

```
THE RADIUS OF A CIRCLE IS 10
THE DIAMETER OF THAT CIRCLE IS 20
THE AREA OF THAT CIRCLE IS 31.4159
THE CIRCUMFERENCE OF THAT CIRCLE IS 62.8318
```

You can now get lots of information about any size of circle by entering replacement line 10s that LET R = the radius of the circle you want and then giving the RUN command.

You can make the computer print a list of the instructions in the program with another command: LIST. The LIST command uses the computer's directory, so the instructions are listed in the order of their line numbers. Enter: LIST and the sample program will appear:

```
 5 PRINT
 7 PRINT
10 LET R = 10
20 PRINT "THE RADIUS OF A CIRCLE IS";R
22 LET D = 2 * R
25 PRINT "THE DIAMETER OF THAT CIRCLE IS";D
30 LET A = 3.14159 * R↑2
40 PRINT "THE AREA OF THAT CIRCLE IS";A
50 LET C = 3.14159 * D
60 PRINT "THE CIRCUMFERENCE OF THAT CIRCLE IS";C
99 END
```

As your programs get longer, you may not want to list all the instructions at once. You can list a single line by putting its line number after the command verb LIST. Enter LIST 22 and the computer will print 22 LET D = 2 * R. To list a group of lines, type the lowest and highest line numbers you want to see with a hyphen (-) between them as part of the list command. Enter: LIST 50-70, and the computer will print lines 50 and 60 of the program. (It would also print line number 70, except this program doesn't have any line numbered 70.)

If your computer has both a video screen and a printer, your BASIC translator probably has a special version of the LIST command that prints the program listing on your printer instead of showing it on the screen. The most common BASIC dialects use the verb LLIST (named after line-printer LIST) to produce printed listings. If the LLIST command works with your computer, then you can also have your programs print information on your line printer by using the LPRINT verb (for line-printer PRINT) instead of the regular PRINT verb.

REVISING PROGRAMS

Most programmers spend more time revising programs than they spend writing them in the first place. Programs get revised so they can solve a similar but different problem (like finding the area for different circle sizes), or because the rules for solving the problem have changed (like altering a payroll program when the tax laws change), or because additional information is wanted (like finding the circumference as well as the area of a circle), or because the programmer has figured out a way to make the program better, or because somebody discovered that the program was producing wrong answers. Revising a program is not an indication that the program was not a very good program to begin with. Of the six reasons just listed for changing a program, only one implies that the programmer made a mistake when he wrote it originally.

One characteristic of a good computer program is that it is easy to change. That is why we commonly number program lines by 10s instead of consecutively. It is also the reason for using familiar variable names. The computer would be just as happy if you used V1, V2, V3, and V4 as the variables for Radius, Diameter, Area, and Circumference. However, when you read a line like: 30 LET A = 3.14159 * R ↑ 2, you are much more likely to recognize it as the "Pi R-squared" formula for the area of a circle than if it had been typed 30 LETV3=3.14159*V1↑2. It is always a good idea to think of a program as a draft copy that you will probably revise later. Then you will write the program in a style that will make revising it later as easy as possible.

You have already revised the circle program in two ways. You added new lines to a program by simply typing them in with line numbers that would insert them in the order you wanted (adding the diameter and circumference calculations). You also changed an existing line (giving the size of the radius) by typing in a replacement line with the same line number. The third type of revision you may need to make is to delete lines from an existing program. Deleting a line has the same effect as changing it to a do-nothing line. So, the way to delete a line in BASIC is to enter a replacement line with just a line number (and no command). To stop your circle program from printing the diameter, just enter 25. Now, if you list the program again, the old line 25 will not appear. It has been eliminated from the directory.

When revising a program, be careful that you do not create problems elsewhere. For example, it seems reasonable to delete line 22 (LET D = 2 * R) at the same time you delete line 25 (printing the diameter). If you did, your program would print zero for the circumference because line 50 used the result of line 22. Line 22 is important not just to old line 25, but to a calculation occurring several steps later in the program.

SAVING PROGRAMS

You have probably noticed that it took you much longer to write a program to print the area, diameter, and circumference of a circle than it would have taken you to figure out the answers. As you become more familiar with programming, it will take you less time to write a program than it does now, but it will still generally take longer to write a computer program that solves a problem than it takes to figure out the answer for one case. Computer programs only save time when they are used often; then the tremendous speed of calculations makes up for the effort required to write a good program.

Once your circle program is in the computer's memory, you can find the area, diameter, and circumference of any circle very quickly. You can change the size of the radius in line 10 and run the program much faster than you could do the arithmetic for the three formulas. The only program is that as soon as you turn off your computer or use it for another program your circle program gets erased from memory.

You don't want to have to type your computer programs at the keyboard each time you want to run a program. All that typing takes too long and gives you too many chances to make mistakes. Instead, you want to save your programs on some peripheral device so you can easily copy them back into memory any time you want to use them.

If your computer has disks (or if you are using a time-sharing system with large disks), the command to copy your program from memory to a disk is: SAVE "program-name". The program-name you put between the quotes will be stored in the directory for the disk, so the computer can find that specific program whenever you ask for it by name. There are some limits on what names you can give your programs. Most systems limit names to short abbreviations, no more than six to eight letters long.

Several problems can arise when saving a program to disk. First, the disk must have sufficient unallocated room (space not used to store other programs or information) to hold a full copy of the program. In using microcomputers, it is a good idea to keep at least one extra disk ready, so that if the computer tells you it is out of disk space, you can switch to the new disk and still save your program. Second, you must have permission to write on the disk. On a time-sharing system, this is a subject to be discussed with the system manager. On microcomputer systems, permission to write is controlled by a rectangular slot on the side of the disk. When this slot is covered (usually with a gummed sticker), the disk is write-protected, and the computer won't write anything on it. Disks are usually write-protected only when they are nearly full and/or contain some valuable programs or information that shouldn't be erased. The usual response to an error message stating that a disk is write-protected is to switch to a spare disk before saving your program. The third problem requires the greatest care.

If there is already something on the computer's disk with the same program-name as the one you are saving, the computer will copy your program in the same part of the disk as whatever had that program-name, erasing the old information in the process. This is good when you are making changes in a program and don't want the old version any more, but it can be expensive if you accidentally wipe out a different program, or your company's current payroll information.

Once a program has been SAVEd onto a disk, it can be copied back into memory to be run again by entering LOAD "program-name". Of course, if no program called "program-name" is on a disk currently hooked up to the computer, you will set an error message. Some systems allow you to take a short-cut in running programs stored on disk. Instead of entering LOAD "name", waiting for the program to be copied, then enter RUN, you may be able to simply enter RUN "name".

Another disk command allows you to erase a program that has already been copied to a disk. Entering: KILL "program-name" will erase the program with that name and make the space on the disk available for another program. You cannot KILL a program from a disk unless you have permission to write on that disk. All four disk program commands consist of a verb (SAVE, LOAD, RUN, or KILL) followed by a short program name enclosed in quotes.

USING TAPE CASSETTES

Many microcomputer systems use tape cassettes instead of (or in addition to) disks. These systems use special cassette versions of the SAVE and LOAD commands—CSAVE (for cassette SAVE) and CLOAD (for cassette LOAD). The CSAVE verb generally requires a "program-name", but the CLOAD verb can be used alone.

Before saving a program to a cassette, it is necessary to have the cassette recorder properly set up, with the cassette in place and the PLAY & RECORD buttons depressed. The cassette must be advanced past the leader or the first part of the program won't be recorded. Once you enter CSAVE "program-name", the computer immediately sends a signal to start the recorder motor and then sends the program as a coded message over the microphone wire. The computer has no way of knowing whether or not there is actually a tape in the recorder or whether the recorder is set to record the message it is sending. Also, if anything else was recorded on the tape before, the new message gets recorded right over whatever was there before.

After recording a program onto a tape, it is a good idea to check to see if it was really recorded properly. Many systems include a special BASIC command—CLOAD?—just for this purpose. Rewind the cassette, depress the PLAY button, then enter CLOAD? (the question mark is part of the verb) on the keyboard. The computer will listen to the program recorded on the tape and compare it to the program in the computer's memory. If there is any difference, it prints an error message which serves as a warning that you need to CSAVE the program again.

CLOAD simply has the computer send a signal to turn on the recorder's motor and then listen to the program recorded on the tape and copy it into memory. To the human ear, most recorded computer programs sound like high-pitched screeching that will never replace disco or rock-and-roll. The computer translates each second of noise into 500 to 1500 (depending on the specific computer system) keyboard characters. This is roughly equivalent to typing ten thousand words per minute. As fast as this sounds, it is considerably slower than loading and saving with disks. It may take several minutes to load a reasonably long program from tape. If the computer runs into trouble while CLOADing, it will display an error message, and you will have to start the tape over at the beginning (probably adjusting the volume control on the recorder to keep the same error from happening again).

TELLING THE COMPUTER WHERE TO GO

Now that you have saved your first circle program, you are ready to try two more little programs. Make the computer print your name. You might try this by entering a two line program:

```
10 LET N$ = "GEORGE WASHINGTON"
20 PRINT N$
```

If you enter the RUN command, the computer will print GEORGE WASHINGTON followed by a bunch of unwanted information about a circle. The computer had no way of knowing that you wanted to write a new program, so it just revised the program that was already in its memory. To cure this problem, there is a BASIC command that erases whatever program is currently sitting in memory and gets the computer ready to receive a new program. This command is simply the verb NEW. (Don't try to convince an English teacher that NEW is a verb, because English teachers don't speak the same language as BASIC computers.) If you try to LIST the program in memory after entering NEW, you will see that there is nothing to list.

Before you print out your name again, let's introduce a new kind of command, the GOTO statement. The computer normally starts with the lowest line number and follows each instruction in order. The GOTO statement lets you change the order in which the instructions are followed. A GOTO statement consists of the verb GOTO (yes, it is one word; the proper English GO TO won't work in BASIC) followed by a line number. When the computer starts to follow an instruction, it has already stored the line number of the next instruction it will get from memory in a special location (register) inside the computer. When it sees a GOTO command, the computer simply replaces the line number of the next instruction with the number in the GOTO command.

Now for an improved name printing program:

```
10 LET N$ = "GEORGE WASHINGTON"
20 PRINT N$;
30 PRINT " IS A FINK !"
40 PRINT "NOBODY";
50 PRINT " CAN BE TRUSTED !"
99 END
```

Run this program, and the computer will give you a pessimistic view of the world. The message can be made much more favorable by adding the line

```
25 GOTO 50
```

Running the revised program tells you that GEORGE WASHINGTON can be trusted, because lines 30 and 40 were skipped when the computer went from line 25 to line 50. You can also use GOTO statements to have the computer go back and repeat something. For example, adding the line 60 GOTO 20 will make the computer go back and print GEORGE WASHINGTON CAN BE TRUSTED ! again. Since each time it finishes printing the message, it will run into the GOTO 20 statement, the computer will keep repeating the message forever. When you get tired of the message, you can stop the computer by pressing the break key (labeled interrupt on some systems). Of course, you can also stop the message by turning the computer off or pulling the plug, but either of those actions will erase your program from memory. The break key leaves your program intact so you can save it, revise it, or run it again. You can also make the program continue where it left off by entering CONT (short for continue).

Now you can change the program into a real optimist by entering the following GOTO statements:

```
55 GOTO 40
45 GOTO 30
35 GOTO 99
```

After you run the program, LIST it. The original program was easy to read even if the message wasn't nice. All those GOTOs may have improved the message, but they also make the program look much more complicated than it has to be.

```
10 LET N$ = "GEORGE WASHINGTON"
20 PRINT N$;
25 GOTO 50
30 PRINT " IS A FINK !"
35 GOTO 99
40 PRINT "NOBODY";
45 GOTO 30
50 PRINT " CAN BE TRUSTED !"
55 GOTO 40
99 END
```

This example illustrates the two biggest problems with the GOTO statement. First, GOTO statements always make it more difficult to read and understand the program. Good programmers make their programs as clear and simple as possible. There are times when the GOTO statement is valuable in a program, but excessive GOTOs are a sign that the programmer did not plan his program properly before writing it. Second; careless use of GOTO statements can make the computer chase its tail forever. It may be useful to repeat a message occasionally, but who wants to see the same sentence about GEORGE WASHINGTON (or anything else) repeated forever?

There is another error you can create with a GOTO statement. Telling the computer to GOTO a line number that doesn't exist in your program (such as GOTO 12 in the above example) will produce an error message.

There are some other BASIC commands that can be used to control the order in which the program instructions are followed. The practical uses of the GOTO statement show up in combination with these more complex commands (discussed in Chapter 6). Before learning any more BASIC commands, you should spend some time (and all of Chapter 5) exploring the steps for designing programs to solve a specific problem or to do a specific job.

By now, you should be fairly comfortable working with your computer. You know how to enter and change programs in the computer's memory. You know the four BASIC verbs that appear in most programs:

LET (which stores the value of an expression in a variable)
PRINT (which sends a message to the video screen)
GOTO (which changes the next instruction to be followed)
END (which stops the program)

You also have used five different commands to control what BASIC does with a program:

LOAD or CLOAD (to bring a program into memory from disk or tape)
SAVE or CSAVE (to copy a program from memory onto a disk or tape)
LIST (to display all of the program lines on the screen)
RUN (to start the computer running a program with its first line)
CONT (to continue running a program after it has been interrupted by the break key)

You have written a useful program to find facts about a circle. You can just as easily write simple programs to solve almost any computational problem using other formulas. For example; convert temperature from Fahrenheit to Centigrade [formula: C=9/5*(F−32)], or find the volume of a sphere (formula: V = 4/3* Pi * F↑3, where R is the radius, V is the volume, and the number Pi is approximated by 3.14159 or 22/7), or convert meters to English lengths (1 inch = .0254 meters; 1 foot = 12 inches; 1 yard = 3 feet; and 1 mile = 5280 feet).

Chapter 5

Designing Programs

If you wanted to build a house, what would your first step be? Before you laid the foundation, before you started digging trenches for the pipes, before you even bought any building materials, you would develop a plan on paper. The plan would let you visualize exactly how the house would look, how big each room would be, and how all of the rooms would fit together. While you were planning your house, you could try out several different designs to see which you like best. When the first draft of your plan was finished, you could easily change it with a pencil and eraser. It is obviously much easier to change the arrangement of a house while it is on the drawing board than after the walls have been built.

Now, suppose you want to build a good computer program. What will your first step be? Before you start typing on the computer, before you write your first BASIC statement, you should develop a plan for the program. As a general rule, the more time you spend designing a complicated program before you start typing it into the computer, the sooner you will get the finished program to work the way you want.

The effort of putting a plan on paper helps you think about all of the things that can make your program be useful and all of the things that can cause problems. It is easy to add ideas to a program while it is still a plan on a piece of paper. It is also much easier to change your plan to solve a problem you overlooked than it is to correct a program that isn't giving the right answers.

A good plan will serve as a map to guide your efforts once you are ready to start writing the actual program statements. For a complicated program, your plan will let you work on one piece at a time, knowing that the pieces will all fit together at the end. Later, when it is time to do some maintenance work to improve your program, the original plan will help you quickly find the right program lines to revise.

For trivial programs, like the sample circle program, all this talk about writing a plan first sounds like using a steam shovel to prepare for planting a rose bush. However, most useful computer programs don't have just five or ten statements. A typical business program or computer game will include hundreds or even thousands of statements. You need some kind of a map to find your way through them.

The plan for a program doesn't have to be elaborate. Many professional programmers routinely work from sketches and lists written on a couple scraps of paper. The essential elements of their plans are:

1. Knowing the purpose of the program
2. Knowing what information the program will produce
3. Listing the information that will have to be provided before the program can produce the desired results
4. Outlining the steps the computer will have to follow to get those results

The last three steps are commonly referred to as the *output* (what the program puts out), the *input* (what is put into the program), and the *process*.

DEFINING THE SCOPE OF A PROGRAM

The first step in designing a computer program should always be to define its purpose. Why do you want this program? The answer to that simple question should be clear in your mind before you start doing any work. There are lots of good reasons for writing a computer program: to save your company money, to save yourself some time, to keep track of the results of the Olympics fast enough to support live television broadcasts, to make sure a rocket lands on a certain part of Mars, to provide students with multiplication drills without tying up a teacher's time, to create a fun game, and to improve your programming skills by getting the computer to do something strange. All of these are legitimate purposes for a computer program.

The purpose of a program may seem obvious. Yet an amazingly large number of programs get thrown away each year because they don't serve any purpose. A computer program is good if it accomplishes a purpose. A computer program is bad (even if it produces a lot of information very quickly) if it does not do what it is supposed to. If you don't know exactly what the goal is, you will not be able to successfully reach it. If you try to write a program that will do everything, it will do nothing very well.

The second step in defining a program is to describe the output. Exactly what do you want the program to produce? For the sample circle program, the output is a series of sentences displaying the diameter, area, and circumference of a circle in normal decimal form. In general, outputs include anything you want the program to display on the screen, print on paper, or record on any peripheral device. In many cases, you will be concerned not only with the information the computer produces, but also with its appearance. When the appearance of the output is important, the design work for the program will include creating mock-ups of each output. Mock-ups are usually written on special forms (*spacing charts*) that help you see exactly how many printed characters (letters and numbers) will fit on each line. Careful design of the outputs can be tedious and time-consuming. It pays off by making your final program look professional and pleasant to use.

The next design task is to determine exactly what information will have to be fed into the program for it to produce the desired output. In the circle program, the only input is the radius of the circle. As soon as you decide what radius to use, the program can calculate the output using standard formulas. It is important to make sure that the information you define to be an input is something that the intended users of your program will know. Many people might be interested in using a horoscope program that required their date of birth as the only input. Very few people could use a program that required them to enter the position of Jupiter at the time of their birth. Often it will be desirable to make your program more complicated in order to simplify the required inputs. Sometimes it will even be necessary to revise your planned output so that it can be produced from the available input information.

Once the input and output have been described, you should be able to list all the data items (variables) needed for your program. This list should include both the abbreviations you will use as the various names in your program, as well as simple English explanations of what they mean. Such a data dictionary will help you translate your ideas into BASIC statements once you start to write your program. Later, it will help you (or anyone else) read your completed program and decide how to make revisions in it.

Purpose, outputs, inputs, data dictionary. It sounds like you have to write a book just to design a simple program. In practice, the design of most commercial programs is completed using four to ten sheets of paper. For a simple program, the important design information can be written on a single piece of paper (Fig. 5-1). This design documentation provides a good description of what the program will be used for, what you need to know to be able to use it, and what it will produce.

If you are writing a program for someone else to use, then you should pause when your design is written and sit down to review the design with the intended user. The purpose of the review meeting (or informal chat) is not to impress the other person with how clever you are or with how hard you worked in writing a good-looking design. The main purpose is to make sure that you do not waste your time writing a program that won't be used. Is the output really what the user needs or likes? Can the user easily supply the information needed for input? If the answer to either of these questions is no, then the program should be redesigned. This is also a good opportunity to get ideas for making your program better. All it takes to fit a new idea into your program at this stage is a couple of minutes with a pencil. Once the program is written, it might take hours to make the same change.

MAPPING THE PROCESS

Once you have defined exactly what you want your program to do, you still have to figure out how to get the computer to produce the desired results. You need some type of a map that shows how the computer can get from the input to the output. This map will describe the process of obtaining the proper results by showing all the major steps you will include in the program.

Programmers use several different methods to map out their programs. Some of the techniques you might learn and use later are: *HIPO* (not a fat animal, but an abbreviation for hierarchical input-process-output) charts, *pseudo-code, Orr* diagrams, and *decision* tables. Different methods are best for mapping different kinds of problems. As a starting point, it is good to learn a single, general-purpose form of map for computer programs: the *flowchart*. Flowcharts let you describe a problem by drawing a series of boxes (showing what steps the computer takes) connected by arrows (showing the order of the steps). Flowcharting is fairly easy to learn and can be used with any computer language. (It can also be used to describe how to solve a problem without a computer).

A flowchart for the circle program is shown in Fig. 5-2. The program starts with the little oval at the top. The arrow shows that the program will first "get the radius." That task could be accomplished by entering a LET R = "some-number" statement, but the same task could be accomplished with some other BASIC statements. While making a flowchart, you do not have to know exactly what BASIC statements you will use. You only have to know that each task you write in a box is something that your computer can do.

The rest of the flowchart describes the tasks of calculating and printing the diameter, area, and circumference in order. The end of the program is

PROGRAM NAME: DIMENSIONS OF A CIRCLE	**SHORT NAME:** CIRCLE **DATE WRITTEN:** SEPT., 1981
PURPOSE: DO THE ARITHMETIC TO FIND THE AREA AND OTHER DIMENSIONS OF A CIRCLE	
OUTPUT: SENTENCES DISPLAYED ON THE SCREEN GIVING THE DIAMETER, THE AREA, AND THE CIRCUMFERENCE OF THE CIRCLE	
INPUT: THE RADIUS OF THE CIRCLE	

VARIABLES:

ABBREV.	**MEANING**
R	RADIUS
D	DIAMETER—DOUBLE THE RADIUS
A	AREA—FROM FORMULA $A = \pi R^2$
C	CIRCUMFERENCE—FROM FORMULA $C = \pi D$
	NOTE: USE 3.14159 AS VALUE OF π

Fig. 5-1. Program design summary.

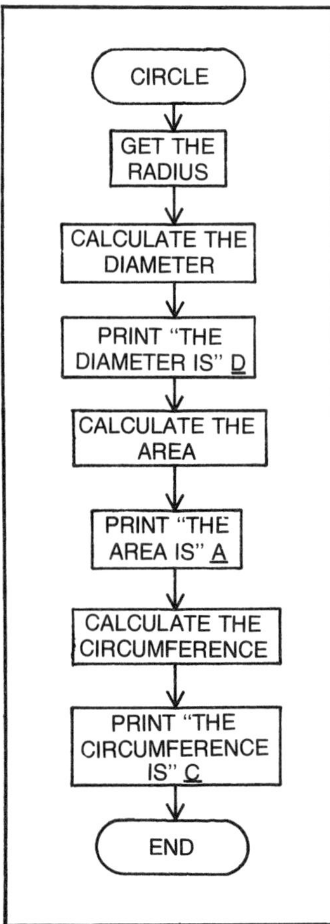

Fig. 5-2. Flowchart for Circle program.

illustrated by the arrow pointing to the bottom oval. The earlier sample program for circle calculations follows this map exactly. However, this is not the only way to produce the results you want. You could just as easily draw an alternate flowchart that did all of the calculations first, then printed all of the results. If you wrote your program using the alternate flowchart, your program would look different and would work differently, but it could still produce the same results and fulfill its purpose.

The circle program is an unusually simple program. Its flowchart is also an unusually simple flowchart. Even when you are working on a much more complicated program, your flowcharts should stay fairly simple. If you make your map too complicated, you may still get lost when you try to follow it to your destination.

All flowcharts can be drawn using just three differently shaped symbols, plus the arrows connecting them (Fig. 5-3). Those symbols are:

Flattened oval to represent a terminal (starting or stopping) point
Rectangle to represent a task to be performed
Diamond to represent a decision or choice point

There should be exactly two terminal symbols on each flowchart. The starting terminal is normally drawn at the top left part of the paper. The stopping terminal is normally drawn at the bottom or right of the paper. It is possible to draw flowcharts that have several different starting or entry points and several different stopping or exit points. However, extra terminals make a flowchart confusing and will make it difficult to ensure the program will work correctly. Nearly all professional programmers agree that each computer process should have a single entry and a single exit. Your maps may show a number of different routes, but everyone following the flowchart should start at the same place and eventually trace their way to the same final destination.

A rectangular box is used to enclose each step in the process. Inside the box, you write a brief description of what is done during that step. In a

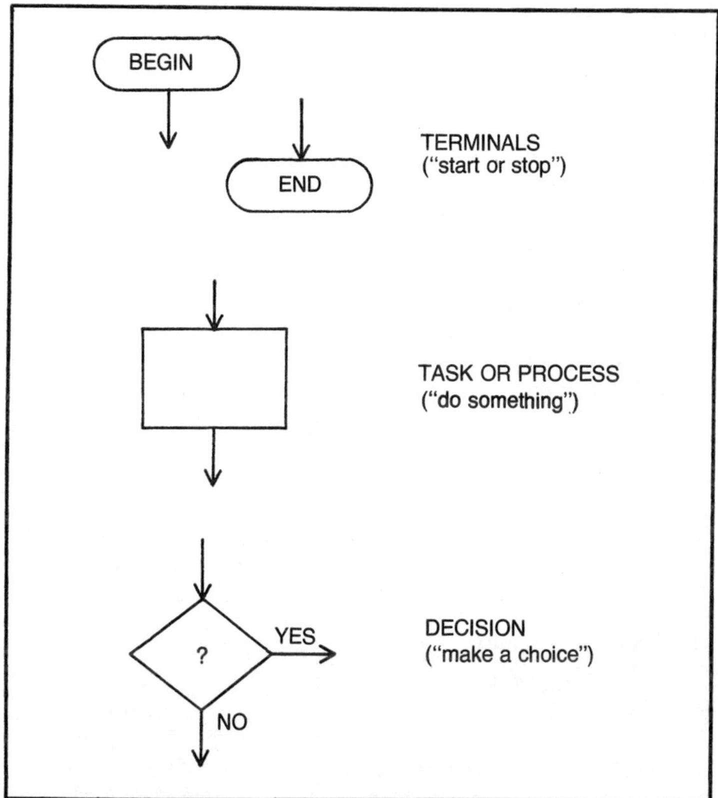

Fig. 5-3. Flowchart symbols.

highly detailed flowchart, there may be one box for each statement. More commonly, a single box will represent a step like "print all the results," which will require several statements in a program. There is no need to worry about how many statements it will take to write each step. The purpose of the flowchart is to describe the important steps in the process and to show how they fit together. The task of translating the flowchart into an actual program does not begin until after the design is completed and makes sense.

Diamond-shaped boxes contain questions. Two different arrows leave each diamond to show that different steps are chosen depending on the answer to the question. The question in a decision diamond is usually worded so that it can be answered either yes or no. Alternatively, the diamond can contain a statement that can be either true or false. It is important to label the two paths out of a diamond in such a way that whenever you trace your way through the flowchart you can answer the question and know which path to take.

The popular game of "heads I win, tails you lose" is illustrated by the flowchart in Fig. 5-4. The first step after the beginning of the same is to flip a coin. Next you have to check to see if it came up heads. If the answer is yes, you follow the yes arrow and claim "I WIN!," then you continue on to the end terminal because the game is over. If the answer is no, then you follow the no arrow to ask if the coin came up tails. This time the yes arrow leads to the conclusion that "YOU LOSE !" and the no arrow says that "YOU WIN !" All paths eventually lead to the same end terminal.

You might not think the second diamond is necessary. You could assume that if the coin is not a heads, then it automatically is a tails. There is a remote chance that the coil will end up balanced on its edge. It may take over a million tosses before this happens, but it is possible. A good flowchart will cover all possibilities.

When you write a program, it will only consider the possibilities you included in your design. If you did not account for a unusual event in your flowchart, then your program will produce the wrong result when that unusual event actually happens. If your program is used very often, all the unusual events will eventually occur, so your design should be prepared ahead of time to handle them. Good programmers believe in Murphy's law: "If anything can go wrong, it will." They try to think up all the strange things that could happen and design their programs so none of those possibilities will make their programs produce the wrong results.

DRAWING A FLOWCHART

You can draw a flowchart to describe the procedure for solving any problem. Flowcharting is simply the process of building an outline. You do not have to know what all the steps will be to get started. You just have to work out the process one step at a time. Your first draft of a flowchart for any problem will probably look sloppy and have to be revised when you remember a step you left out. Remember, the whole purpose of drawing

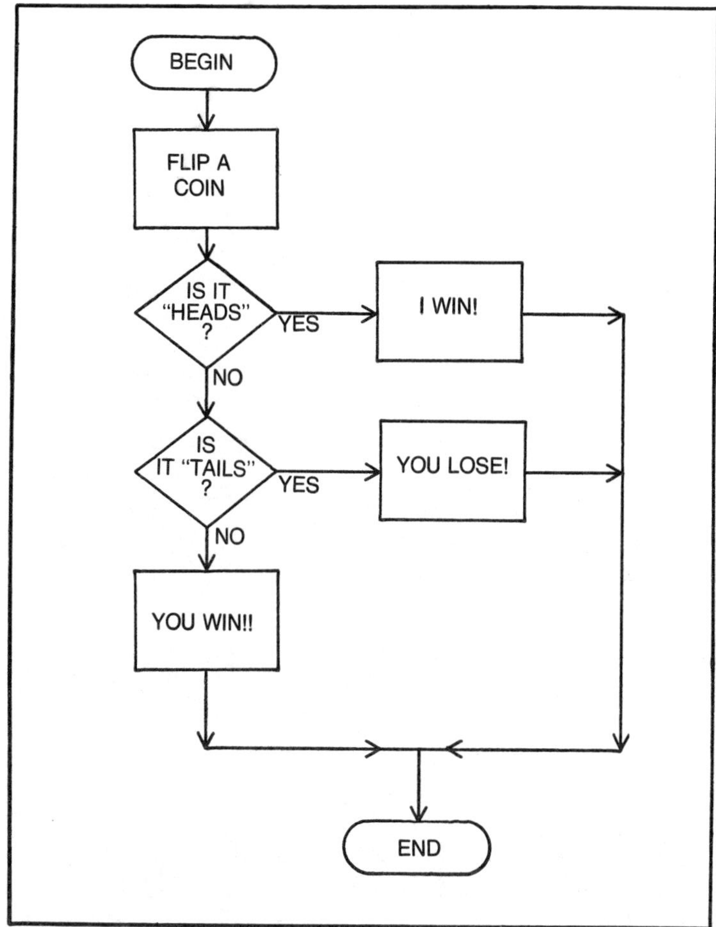

Fig. 5-4. Flowchart with decisions.

flowcharts is to work out good designs for getting the proper results. If you knew exactly what the flowchart should look like before you started, you would not gain anything by taking the time to draw it.

Drawing a flowchart requires that you think about a problem one step at a time. The rough flowchart in Fig. 5-5 is the result of planning to handle a mugger. You know you are being mugged when the mugger demands that you give him your money. That step will occupy the first rectangle after the starting symbol. The first concern of the victim is probably to save his life, so if the mugger is pointing a gun at him, he will choose not to argue. This step gets represented by drawing a diamond with the question: "Does he have a gun?" The yes arrow leads to a box for the step of giving the mugger your money. You now need to decide on the steps to take after he has your

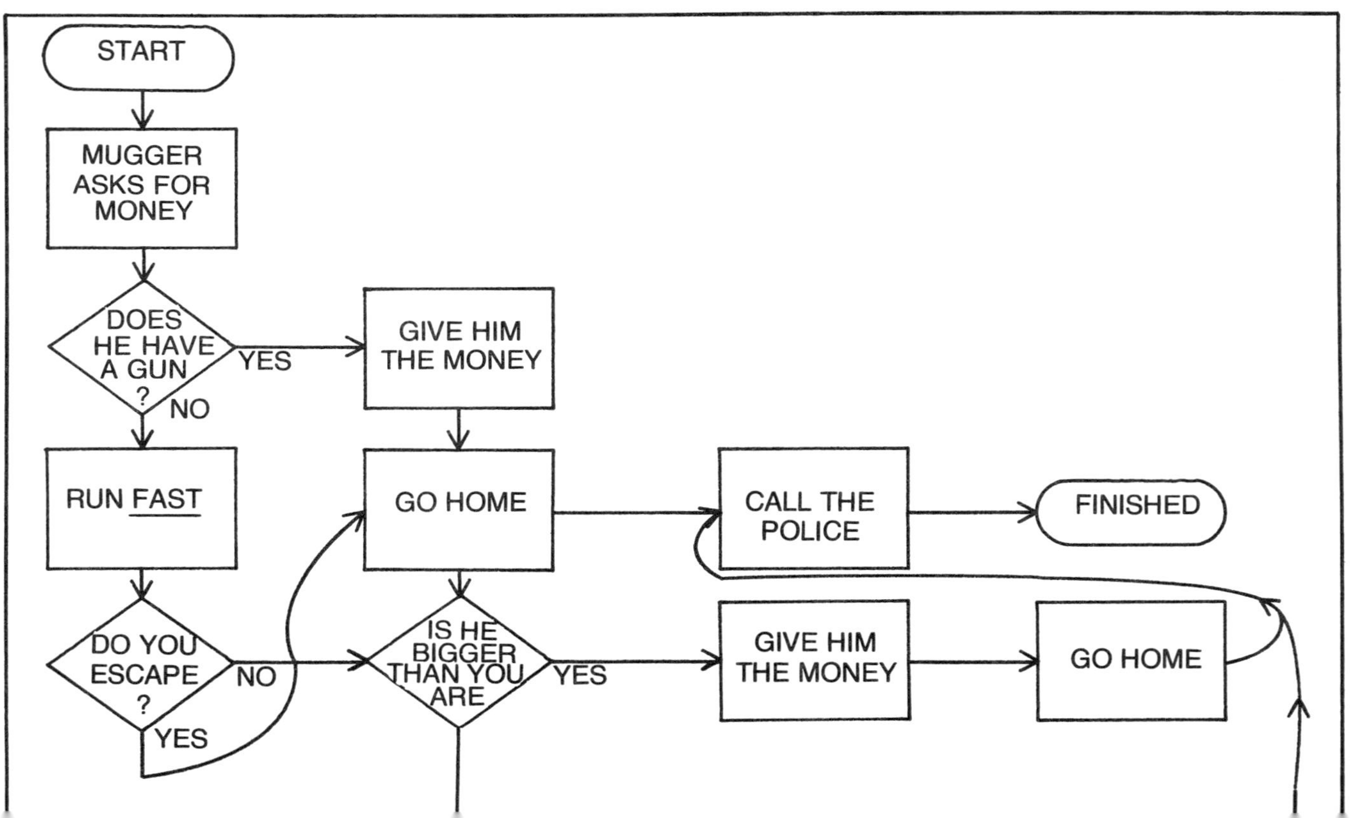
START
MUGGER ASKS FOR MONEY
DOES HE HAVE A GUN ?
YES
NO
GIVE HIM THE MONEY
RUN FAST
GO HOME
CALL THE POLICE
FINISHED
DO YOU ESCAPE ?
NO
YES
IS HE BIGGER THAN YOU ARE
YES
GIVE HIM THE MONEY
GO HOME

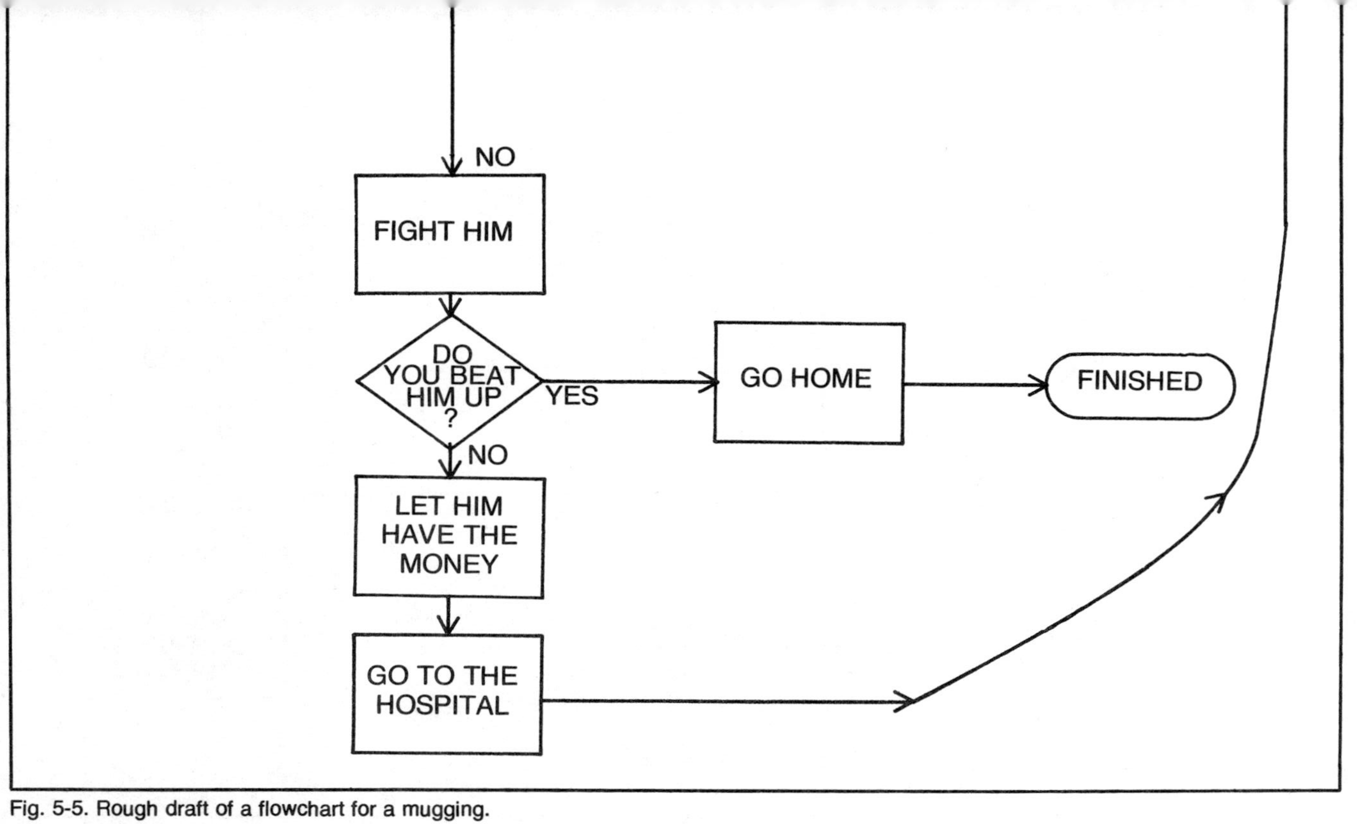

Fig. 5-5. Rough draft of a flowchart for a mugging.

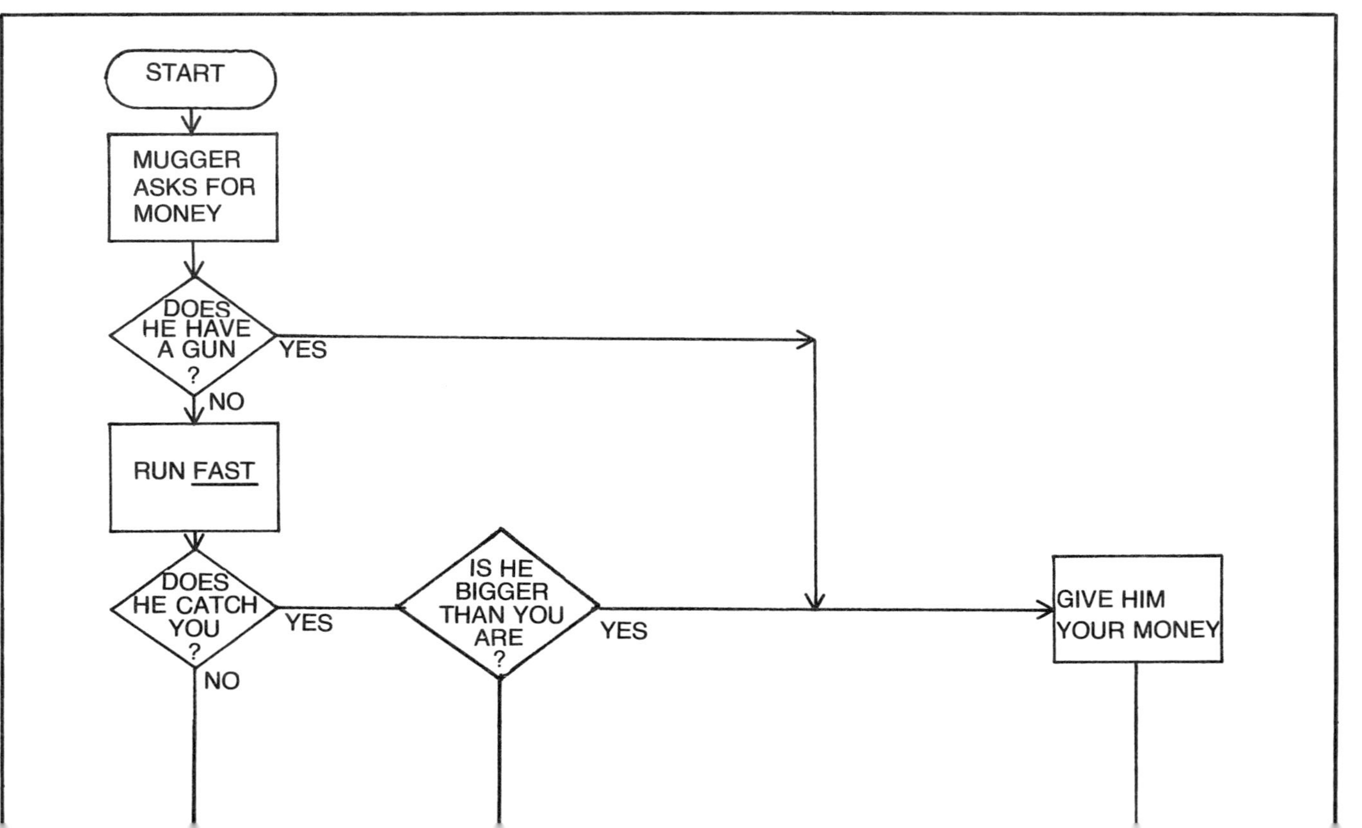

START
MUGGER ASKS FOR MONEY
DOES HE HAVE A GUN ?
YES
NO
RUN FAST
DOES HE CATCH YOU ?
YES
NO
IS HE BIGGER THAN YOU ARE ?
YES
GIVE HIM YOUR MONEY

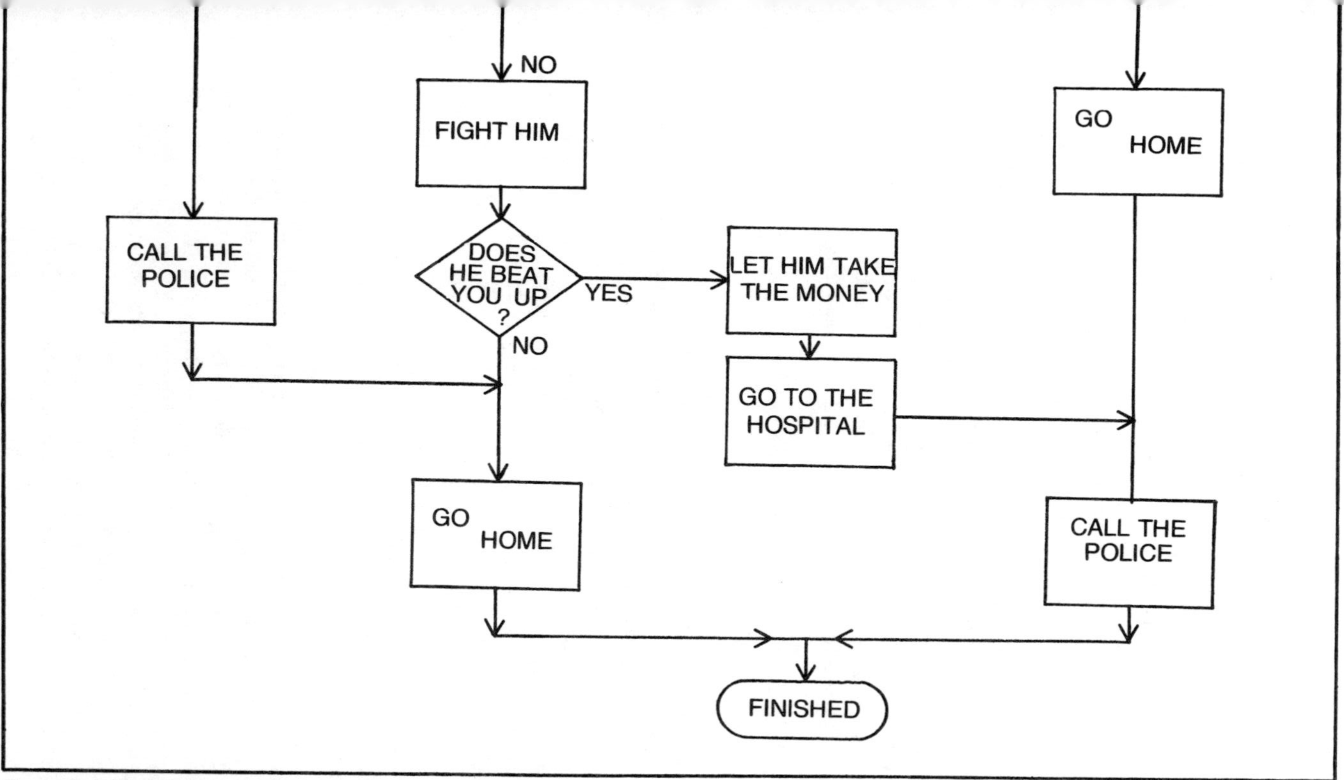

Fig. 5-6. Refined flowchart for a mugging.

money. In the same flowchart, the next steps were chosen to be "go home" and "call the police." Once the police have been called, the mugging situation is finished (as far as the victim is concerned, even though the police still may do something about it). So an arrow is drawn to a terminal symbol for the end.

Only after working out all of the steps to be taken if the mugger has a gun do you have to worry about the alternative. In our example, the victim chooses to run away from his attacker. He will either get away or get caught (another diamond to show both possibilities). If the answer to the "escape" question is yes, it would be reasonable to go home and call the police. Those two steps could be drawn in boxes after the escape diamond, but there are already boxes on the flowchart showing those steps, so you can draw the "yes" arrow to connect with the existing boxes.

The sample flowchart continues with the decisions of fighting (or not fighting) and the possibilities of winning or losing the fight with the mugger. The flowchart is finished when the person drawing it is satisfied that it includes all the steps to be taken for each important choice. If you start at the starting point and follow the arrows, any route eventually gets to a terminal marked "finished."

You may or may not agree with the instructions given by the flowchart. Your own instructions might be to stand up for your rights and fight off the mugger no matter what, or you might prefer to give the mugger some money and forget about the whole thing, or you might want to add alternatives for getting help if there are other people near by. A different set of instructions would lead to a different flowchart.

The quality of the flowchart is a separate issue. You should review the flowchart to determine if it really describes the sequence of choices and actions you intended. If you try to trace the flowchart and the steps do not match the description of the process, or if any of the steps do not make sense, then it is a bad flowchart.

The rough draft given in Fig. 5-5 is not a good flowchart. First drafts seldom turn out perfectly. Some of the arrows wiggle around awkwardly. In one place, two arrows cross each other. That makes the chart look more complicated than necessary. The chart also has two different ending points; that should be fixed.

To produce a good flowchart, you should carefully look at your rough draft and see if you left out any important steps or included unnecessary steps. If so, you need to cross out the unnecessary boxes and draw in your additions. Then you will be ready to draw a neat version, rearranging the boxes so the flowchart is as simple as possible. Figure 5-6 shows the improved mugger flowchart. The final result is clearly easier to read than the first draft. The easier the instructions are to understand, the more likely it is they will be translated and followed accurately.

A good flowchart is a simple description of the steps and decisions involved in a process. It has the following characteristics:

1. It is easy to read.
2. It includes all necessary steps in their proper order.
3. It has only one starting terminal (at the top).
4. It has one and only one ending terminal.
5. It has no dead ends or circular paths that would allow you to follow the flowchart without ever reaching the ending terminal.
6. None of the arrows cross each other.
7. It fits on a single piece of paper.

Fitting on a single piece of paper may seem a strange characteristic. However, once a flowchart is spread over more than one piece of paper, you lose sight of how the steps fit together. A flowchart is not easy to understand if you have to flip through several pages to follow it.

Some problems are so complicated that you could not possibly fit all of the little steps on a one-page flowchart. If there are that many steps, a single flowchart would probably be confusing anyway. The better choice is to break the problem down into a series of simpler parts, then to draw a separate flowchart for each part.

THE TOP-DOWN APPROACH

Many problems are too large to be solved all at once. When you are faced with an overwhelmingly large problem, it is best to first map out a general strategy that describes the large problem as a series of smaller problems. Then you can work out the details of each smaller problem as a separate and easier task. Designing a program by first describing an overall (top-level) solution, and then describing more detailed solutions to the simpler (lower-level) parts of the problem is called top-down programming.

Try to draw a flowchart showing how to play a winning game of Tic Tac Toe. The first step would be a description of how to draw the game board. Then you would have to decide who got the first move. For each turn, you would have to describe how to decide the proper place for your own move. You would also have to describe how to tell when the game is over and who is the winner. You could number each square from 1 to 9 and describe all the decisions based on whether specific combinations of squares already held X's, O's, or were empty. Such a flowchart would quickly grow into a complicated web with dozens of diamonds and rectangles. If you are extraordinarily thorough and precise, you could probably even convert your web of flowcharting symbols into a decent computer program. However, you could easily make an error someplace in the tangled flowchart which no one would notice until after your completed program started making silly or illegal moves.

Using a top-down approach, you would first draw a one-page flowchart giving an overview of the game. One version of the top-level flowchart for Tic Tac Toe is shown in Fig. 5-7. The boxes do not contain anything that can be directly translated into BASIC statements. Before you could write a Tic Tac Toe program from this flowchart, you would have to create instructions

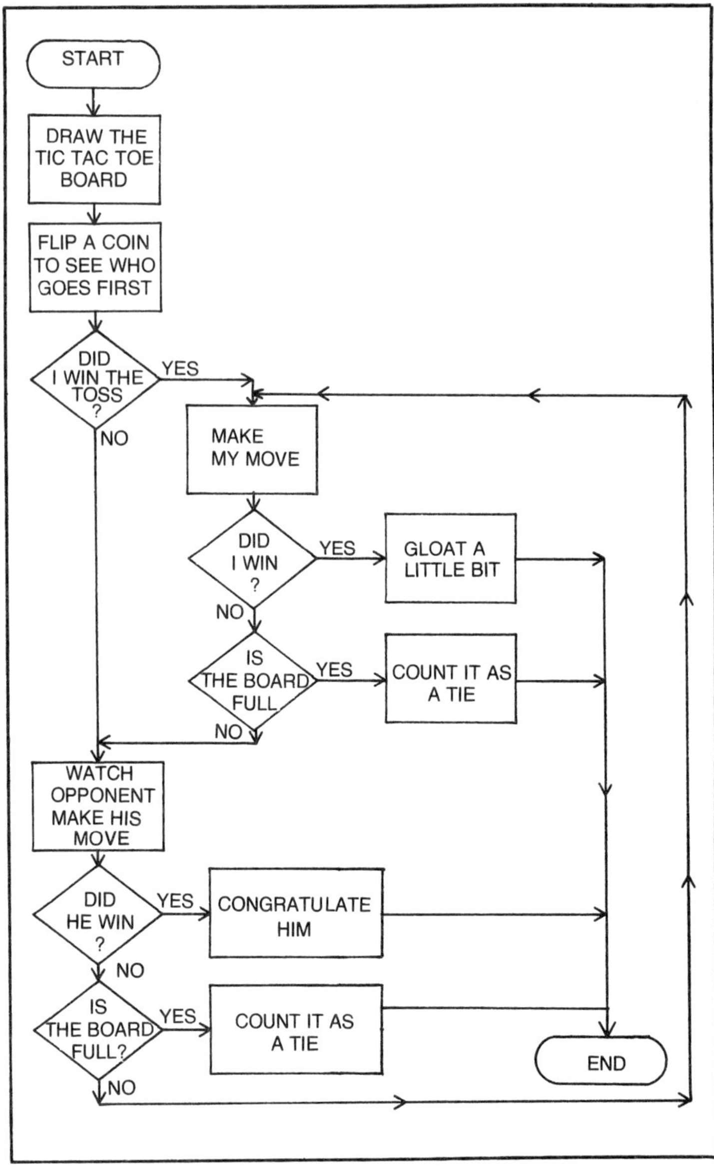

Fig. 5-7. Top-level flowchart for Tic Tac Toe.

for the separate steps of drawing the board, determining who goes first, making a move, checking the opponent's move, and checking to see if someone won. Each of these smaller problems can be described with its own (second-level) flowchart.

The top-level flowchart is fairly easy to read. It has a single starting terminal and a single ending terminal. Every chance for the game to end with a tie or a victory for either side is checked before another move is allowed. The flowchart does contain a *loop*, which is a circular path repeating the same steps. That loop could create a problem if it allowed you to go around in circles forever without ever reaching the end terminal. This

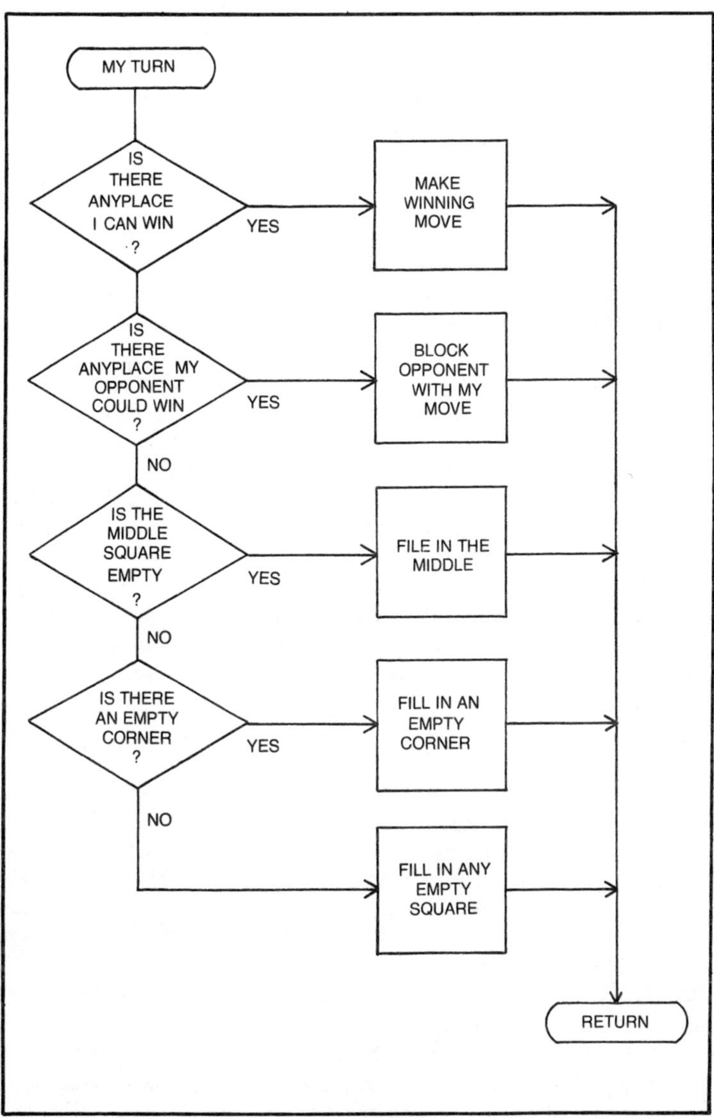

Fig. 5-8. Second-level Tic Tac Toe flowchart.

particular loop avoids that problem. Before you could go around the circle five times, all nine squares would be full and one of the decision diamonds would send you to the end of the flowchart. The reason for the loop is to save you the effort of repeating the instructions for making a move for each turn. It allows you to tell the two players to keep alternating turns until the game is over.

The single box marked "make my move" on the top-level flowchart is expanded into its own full-page flowchart in Fig. 5-8. In this case, the starting terminal has been labeled with the name of the box on the higher-level flowchart. The ending terminal has been labeled RETURN to indicate that when you reach the end of this flowchart, you return to the top-level flowchart to continue the instructions.

This flowchart describes a decent strategy for picking moves in Tic Tac Toe, but you may be able to devise a better strategy. One major advantage of using a top-down approach is that you can revise and improve one level at a time without having to redesign the entire plan. Changing the way you select moves will not change the overall description of the game, nor any of the other sections on drawing the board, checking the opponent's moves, etc.

Before writing a program in BASIC, you would probably need to draw a third level of flowcharts describing each of the choices for making a move. One flowchart would tell how to determine "Is there anywhere I can win?", and another, "Is there anyplace the opponent could win?" Before you are finished flowcharting, you will have drawn at least as many flowcharting symbols as you would have used in drawing a single giant chart showing all of the individual steps.

The top-down approach does not save paper. Instead it helps organize your planning. All the individual boxes in a series of top-down flowcharts are organized into meaningful groups. This makes the flowcharts (and eventually your programs) easier to understand and revise.

You may wish to complete the second level of the Tic Tac Toe flowchart. The chart for checking the opponent's move should include boxes asking for his move and making sure the square he chooses is vacant. Some of the other boxes on the top-level flowchart are simpler and may not require separate flowcharts.

There is no hard-and-fast rule to determine how detailed your flowchart maps should be. Some programmers continue drawing successively more detailed flowcharts until each box contains a single computer instruction. Others prefer to work from more general plans, translating each box on their flowcharts into a whole series of program statements. You should aim to develop flowcharts that help you produce programs with the greatest accuracy and the least total effort.

Before going on to the next chapter, try drawing flowcharts for a few noncomputer situations. Start with something simple like sharpening a pencil, then proceed to something more complicated like a baseball batter's turn at the plate or the steps that end in marriage to a specific partner on a certain day. Have somebody else trace your flowcharts to find important steps or decisions that you forgot to include. Do not be surprised if your flowcharts grow considerably larger after they are tested. It is amazing how complicated some everyday situations appear when you have to describe them with instructions specific enough to work mechanically.

Chapter 6

Building Blocks for Programming

You compose a computer program by combining individual statements to make a logical set of instructions. The arrangement of the statements into structured groups is as important to the resulting program as is the content of the specific statements. You could write a simple program using the following four statements:

```
LET A = 5
LET A = 2 * A
LET A = A - 3
PRINT "THE ANSWER IS";A
```

Depending on the order you chose (by writing line numbers), the program would print an answer of 0, 2, 4, 5, 7, or 10. Done in the order shown, the answer is 7. Putting the PRINT statement first will give an answer of 0, ignoring the calculations done afterwards in the LET statements. Try writing the statements in a different order on your computer to obtain each of the four other answers.

Control structures determine the order in which the computer executes (or obeys) the commands in a program. There are three primary control structures:

1. *sequence* (one command after another)
2. *alternation* (choosing between alternate commands)
3. *loops* (repeating commands a limited number of times).

These control structures (and their variations) are the principal building blocks of computer programming. Each of these building blocks appears as a specific pattern in flowcharts.

The sequence is the simplest and most common control structure. A sequence is a series of steps taken one after another in a specific order. On a flowchart, a sequence appears as two boxes connected by an arrow indicating which one follows the other (Fig. 6-1). Sequences are sometimes referred to as "drop-through" logic because when the computer has completed the statements in the first box on the flowchart, it drops through the bottom of the box to continue with the next statement.

In BASIC, the line numbers determine the sequence of the statements. Unless you write a special control statement (like a GOTO command), the computer will assume that all of the statements in your program form a sequence starting with the statement with the lowest line number and continuing in order to the statement with the largest line number. The Circle program in Chapter 4 is strictly a sequence of LET and PRINT statements.

ALTERNATION OR CHOICE

Alternation is the control structure of decision-making. It allows the computer program to do a specific step only if certain conditions are met.

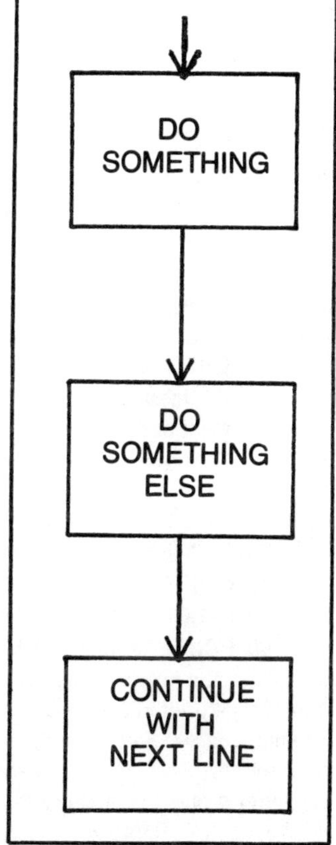

Fig. 6-1. Sequence control structure.

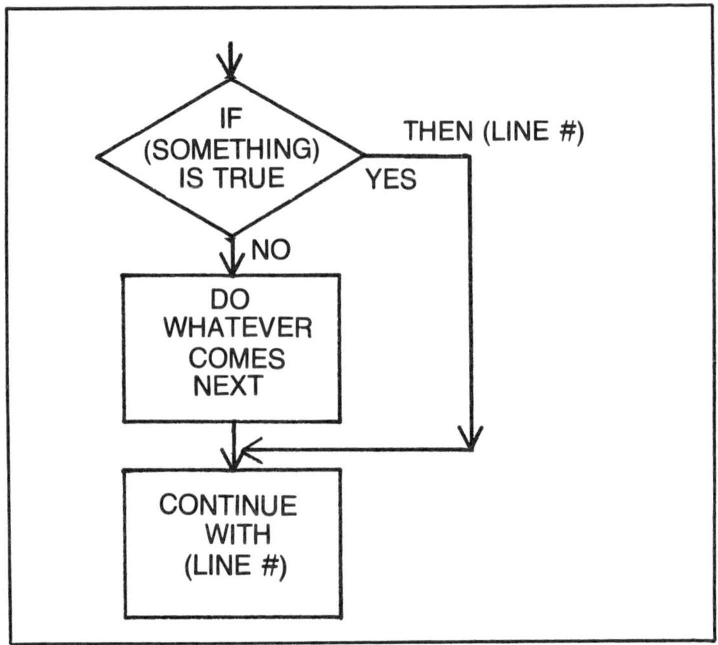

Fig. 6-2. Alernation control structure.

The English instruction, "Turn on the lights only if there is not enough sunlight for reading," is an example of alternation. Figure 6-2 illustrates the way alternation appears on flowcharts. The structure starts with a decision diamond. In this example, the diamond would ask, "Is there enough sunlight?" If the answer is no, the program is directed to do something, like turn on the room lights. If the answer is yes, the following step is skipped.

BASIC has a special command to translate alternation flowcharts. The IF . . . THEN statement is used to conditional skip some steps in a program. This statement has two parts. The IF part contains a condition that can be either true or false. It corresponds to the contents of a decision diamond. The second, or THEN, part of the statement contains a line number the program will skip to when the condition in the IF clause is true. The following BASIC statements show the IF . . . THEN command in action:

```
200 IF R > 1 THEN 230
210 PRINT "THIS CIRCLE HAS A SMALL RADIUS."
230 PRINT "THE DIAMETER IS"; 2 * R
```

When the program reaches this point, it will already have a value for the radius stored in the variable named R. If that value is greater than one, line number 200 will cause the computer to GOTO line number 230 and print the diameter. Only if the radius is less than or equal to one will the computer drop-through line 200 to print the message "THIS CIRCLE HAS A SMALL RADIUS."

In one respect, the IF . . . THEN statement in BASIC works backwards from the way you usually use the word *if* in English. A normal sentence would say; "If such-and-such, then do something." This implies that if such-and-such is not true, then you can forget about the rest of the instruction. In BASIC, the "do something" instructions are separate statement(s) following the IF statement. The computer skips these instructions whenever "such-and-such" is true and follows them only when "such-and-such" is not true. It takes some practice with BASIC to get accustomed to writing IF conditions so the computer will skip or follow the "do something" steps when you want it to.

In many program designs, you will want to choose between doing either one step or another. The primary form of the alternation structure only allows you to choose between doing a step and not doing it. Figure 6-3 shows how the alternation structure can be expanded to provide an either/or choice on a flowchart. This expanded structure can be translated into BASIC by a combination of IF . . . THEN and GOTO statements.

Look at part of a program that writes form letters to women. If the woman is single, she should be addressed as "Miss;" otherwise she should be addressed as "Mrs." This program has a variable named M$ that indicates the woman's marital status and another variable named N$ with

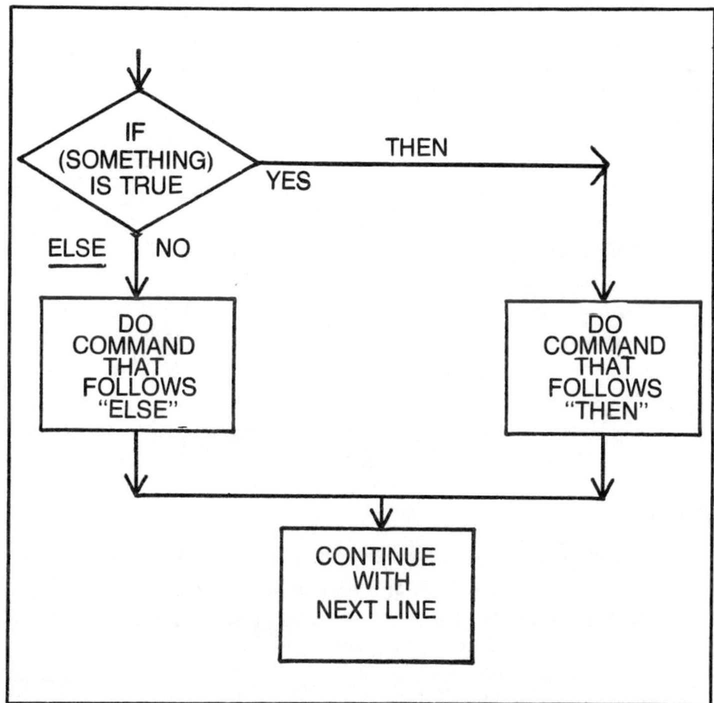

Fig. 6-3. Either/or alternation.

her last name as its value. The alternation structure that chooses to print either "Miss" or "Mrs." is translated into the following BASIC statements:

```
700 IF M$ = "SINGLE" THEN 750
710 PRINT "DEAR MRS. ";
720 GOTO 760
750 PRINT "DEAR MISS ";
760 PRINT N$
```

When the condition of the IF statement is true, the THEN clause causes the computer to skip the message intended for women who are not single. Instead the computer goes to line number 750 to print the single's introduction before printing her last name. When the condition of the IF statement is not true, the computer continues with the next statement, which instructs it to print "DEAR MRS. " The GOTO statement in line 720 is needed to prevent the computer from printing both introductions in sequence. Both paths (for true and for false) eventually lead to the same statement (line 760, which prints the last name). Thus the structural unit of five statements has a single entry point and a single exit point. This allows the structure to be treated as a single box on a flowchart that can easily be combined with other units in a larger program. The five lines in this example could be accurately summarized by the English command; "Print the introductory line (or salutation)."

Some versions of BASIC include an extended form of the IF . . . THEN statement that provides for a choice between two commands. This extended statement is written as IF condition THEN command-1 ELSE command-2. The computer will do command-1 when the condition is true and will do command-2 when the condition is false. If your computer includes this option, then you can replace the five BASIC statements for printing salutations to women with the following pair:

```
700 IF M$="SINGLE" THEN PRINT "DEAR MISS "; ELSE
      PRINT "DEAR MRS. ";
760 PRINT N$
```

It is often convenient to use the "IF condition THEN command" form of the BASIC alternation statement (with or without the ELSE part) to save typing. It also makes programs easier to read than the traditional "IF condition THEN line-number" form. However, the BASIC on many computers only allows the traditional form.

CONDITIONS

The contents of decision diamonds on flowcharts can be any questions with yes/no answers or any statements that have true/false possibilities. When the flowchart is translated into BASIC, the content of each decision diamond has to be translated into the condition of an IF . . . THEN statement. BASIC conditions are comparisons between two expressions (combinations of variables and values).

Three symbols are used to compare expressions in a condition:

= Equals, which means the condition is true when both expressions have the same value.

< Less than, which means the condition is true when the value of the first expression is less than the value of the second.

> Greater than, which means the condition is true when the value of the first expression is greater than the value of the second expression.

The symbols for less than and greater than are designed to look like arrows with the pointed side aimed at the expression with the smaller value and the bigger side of the symbol opened toward the expression with the larger value. The comparison symbols can be used in pairs to create three more comparisons:

< = Less than or equal to. This is the opposite of greater than and can be read as "is not greater than."

> = Greater than or equal to, which is the same as "is not less than."

< > Not equal to (literally, it stands for "is less than or greater than," but nobody would say that in English).

Let the variable X have the value 5. In that case each of the following conditions is true:

```
X + 5 = 10
3 < X
2 * (X - 2) > X
-10 < = -8
-10 > = -2 * X
X < > 0
```

Most conditions use simple comparisons. The simpler the comparisons, the easier it is to read the program. Occasionally, your program design may require more complex comparisons. For those cases, you can build compound comparisons using the conjunctions AND or OR. When two simple conditions are connected by the word AND the compound condition is true only if both simple conditions are true; otherwise it is false. For example, "5 = 5 AND 6 = 6" is true, but "5 = 5 AND 5 = 6", "5 = 4 AND 6 = 6", and "5 = 6 AND 6 = 4" are all false. A compound condition written with the word OR is true if any one of its simple comparisons are true; it is false only if every one of the simple comparisons are false. Thus, "5 = 5 OR 6 = 6" is true. "5 = 5 OR 5 = 6" and "5 = 4 OR 6 = 6" are also true, but "5 = 6 OR 6 = 4" is false.

Most versions of BASIC will let you write compound conditions that have as many comparisons strung together as you can think of. You could write IF A = 5 AND B + 2 > C AND D = 0 AND E < 10 AND F - 2 = A THEN 600. The computer would not mind. However, most humans would be confused by such a complicated statement. It is best to keep your programs simple. Avoid using both AND and OR in the same statement. A statement like IF A = 5 AND B = 3 OR N = 0 THEN 500 invites misinterpretation. Some computers (and some people) would make the

AND comparison first. That way the condition would be considered to be true any time N = 0, no matter what the value of A was. Other computers would make the OR comparison leaving any ANDs for last. This way the final comparison would be false any time the value of A was not 5 (even if the value of N was 0). Writing AND and OR in the same statement introduces ambiguity into a program; the program might not do what you think it does.

The *case structure* is an extension of the alternation structure. Instead of choosing between two paths, the case structure provides for doing something different for each value of a variable. Examples of the case structure include asking a person to choose from a set of actions and have the computer respond appropriately to his choice, using different scales to score a test depending on the student's grade level, and translating number values into printed messages.

Case structures can be written with a combination of IF . . . THEN and GOTO statements. A flowchart for the case structure is shown in Fig. 6-4. The following part of a BASIC program includes a variable M whose value is the number of a month. The case structure prints the English name for the appropriate month.

```
1200 IF M =  1 THEN 1300
1205 IF M =  2 THEN 1310
1210 IF M =  3 THEN 1320
1215 IF M =  4 THEN 1330
1220 IF M =  5 THEN 1340
1225 IF M =  6 THEN 1350
1230 IF M =  7 THEN 1360
1235 IF M =  8 THEN 1370
1240 IF M =  9 THEN 1380
1245 IF M = 10 THEN 1390
1250 IF M = 11 THEN 1400
1255 IF M = 12 THEN 1410
1260 PRINT "INVALID MONTH,";
1265 GOTO 1450
1300 PRINT "JANUARY,";
1305 GOTO 1450
1310 PRINT "FEBRUARY,";
1315 GOTO 1450
1320 PRINT "MARCH,";
1325 GOTO 1450
1330 PRINT "APRIL,";
1335 GOTO 1450
1340 PRINT "MAY,";
1345 GOTO 1450
1350 PRINT "JUNE,";
1355 GOTO 1450
1360 PRINT "JULY,";
1365 GOTO 1450
```

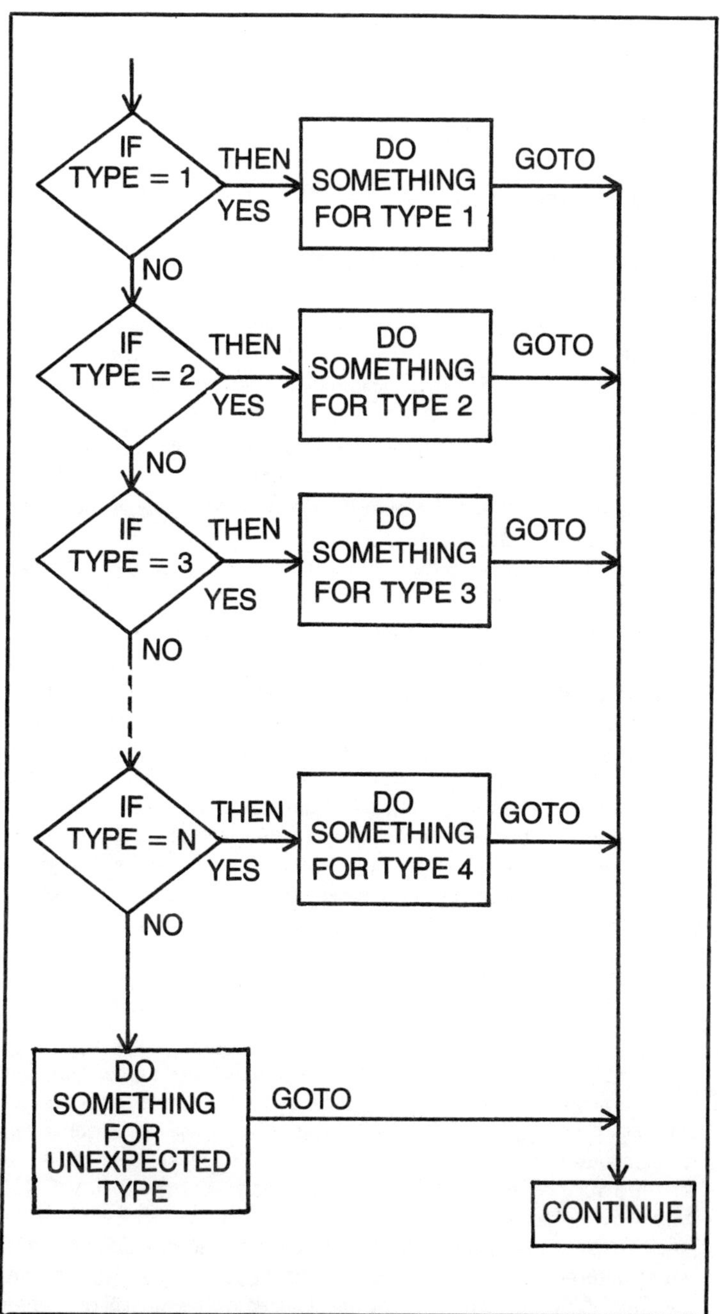

Fig. 6-4. Case structure flowchart.

```
1370 PRINT "AUGUST,";
1375 GOTO 1450
1380 PRINT "SEPTEMBER,";
1385 GOTO 1450
1390 PRINT "OCTOBER,";
1395 GOTO 1450
1400 PRINT "NOVEMBER,";
1405 GOTO 1450
1410 PRINT "DECEMBER,";
1450 PRINT Y                    (Y = the year)
```

Even a fairly simple use of the case structure requires a large number of BASIC statements. In many cases, a whole procedure is written for each case in place of the single PRINT statements in the example. The important features of the case structure include:

1. directing the program to a specific procedure for each expected value of the variable used in the series of IF statements
2. providing for an action to be taken in case the variable has an unexpected value (line 1260 in the sample)
3. ending the action for each case with an instruction that sends the program to a common exit point (line 1450) for the structure

The long series of IF . . . THEN statements, plus the large number of GOTOs, makes writing case structures in BASIC rather tedious. Some versions of BASIC include a command—the ON variable GOTO . . . statement—to simplify writing case structures. This one command replaces a whole series of IF . . . THEN statements. The exact format requires that the word ON be followed by the name of a variable with whole number values. The word GOTO is followed by a list of line numbers (separated by commas). When the value of the variable is one, the computer goes to the first line number on the list. When the value is two, the computer goes to the second line number on the list, etc. Using this format, the twelve IF . . . THEN statements numbered 1200 through 1255 in the example can be replaced by a single statement like:

```
1200 ON M GOTO 1300, 1310, 1320, 1330, 1340, 1350, 1360, 1370,
       1380, 1390, 1400, 1410
```

The remaining statements (1260 through 1450) would remain the same. You still need to plan some action for the computer to take if the value of the variable does not match any of the expected values on the GOTO list, and you still need to have a GOTO at the end of each separate action to send the computer to the common exit point. Figure 6-5 illustrates one way the case structure can be abbreviated on a flowchart using the ON . . . GOTO statement.

The ON . . . GOTO statement is useful only when the different cases you are interested in have consecutive whole number values starting with one. The GOTO list starts with the line number for the value of one. There is no place in the list for a line number corresponding with a value of zero or a negative number. If your cases involve fractions or string variables, the ON . . . GOTO statement will not work. When these limitations on the use of ON . . . GOTO cause problems, you can always write your case structure using a series of IF . . . THEN statements.

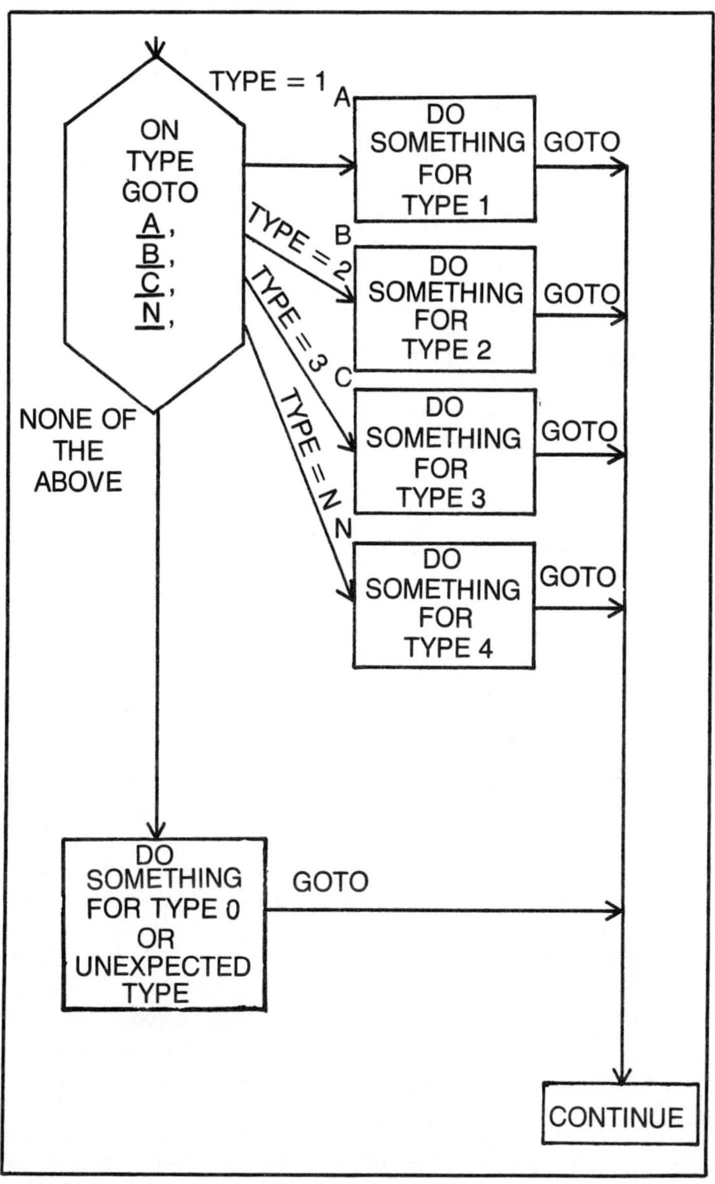

Fig. 6-5. Case structure with "ON . . . GOTO" statement.

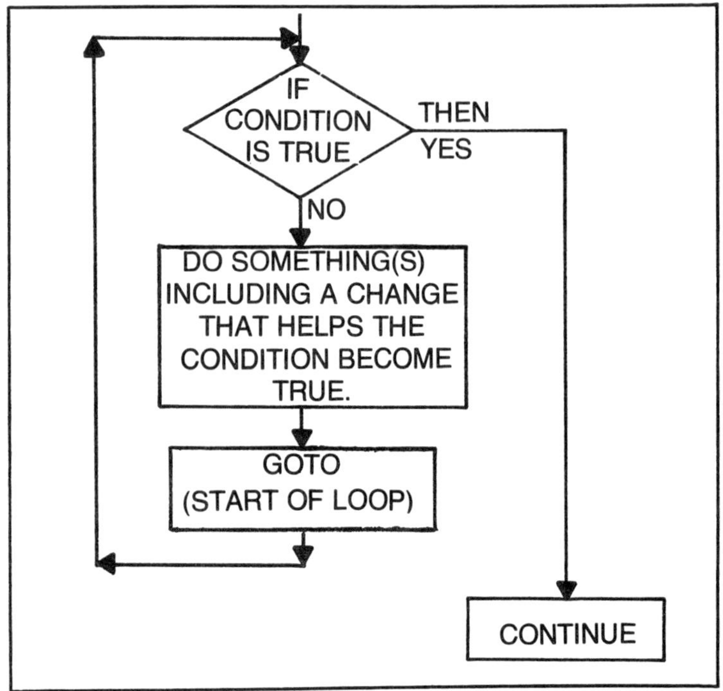

Fig. 6-6. Test-before loop.

LOOPS

The loop structure is one of the most powerful tools a programmer has. Writing a loop allows you to get the computer to repeat the same steps a large number of times without having to write the instructions more than once. The loop structure has three essential parts.

1. A test determines whether the program will continue in the loop or go to the first statement following the loop. The test is often an IF . . . THEN statement.
2. The body of a loop is the set of instructions that are to be repeated. At least one of these instructions should change the value of a variable in the IF clause; otherwise the computer will never get out of the loop.
3. A control statement at the end (bottom) of the loop sends the computer back to the beginning (top) of the loop, so the instructions can be repeated.

The test can be either the first or last statement in a loop. Figure 6-6 is the flowchart of a loop that starts with a test. This design is called a *test-before* loop because the test takes place before the instructions are followed the first time.

One use of a test-before loop occurs in developing scale drawings. Suppose you wanted to print a design on a regular sheet of paper so the longest side of the design is not more than eight inches long. If the length is already less than eight inches, you could make a life-size drawing. Otherwise you could cut all the dimensions in half and make a scale drawing with one inch equaling two inches in real life. If the design was still too big for your paper, you could keep cutting the dimensions in half (and doubling the scale) until the design became small enough to fit. The following BASIC statements include a loop for scaling a drawing. The variable L is used for the length of the line; S is the scale factor.

```
200 LET L = 60
210 LET S = 1
250 IF L < = 8 THEN 300
260 LET L = L / 2
270 LET S = S * 2
280 GOTO 250
300 PRINT "THE SCALE IS 1 INCH =";S;"INCHES"
```

Lines 250 through 280 form the loop. Line 250 tests to see whether the computer should follow the body of the loop or exit the loop. Lines 260 and 270 are the body of the loop. Line 260 makes the value of L get closer to zero each time it is executed, so that sooner or later it will make the value of L less than 8. If the value of L did not get smaller each time you went through the loop, then the computer would keep repeating itself forever. Line 280 sends the computer back to the top of the loop, where it tests to see whether the loop should be repeated again. Lines 200, 210, and 300 are not part of the loop. Lines 200 and 210 determine the starting values for variables used in the loop. Such statements are often referred to as *initializing* a loop. Initializing statements are often needed for loops that involve figuring totals or multiplying a value. Line 300 simply prints the results of the loop. It is included to show the exit point for the structure.

If you run this loop on your computer, it will print a scaling factor of 8. You may want to add a PRINT statement in the body of the loop (like 265 PRINT "LENGTH IS NOW";L) so you can count the number of times the loop is repeated. Then change line 200 to see the results for different starting lengths.

When you write a loop with the test at the end, called a test-after loop, you do not need a GOTO statement. The THEN clause of the test will send the computer back to the top of the loop. Besides saving a statement, writing a *test-after* loop (Fig. 6-7) changes the loop structure in two ways. First, the body of the loop is always executed at least once. In the sample program, the body is skipped completely when L starts with a value less than eight. If the test had been written at the bottom of the loop, the length would have been divided by two even if it were small to begin with. The other difference is that the condition in the IF . . . THEN statement of a test-after loop is written so that the loop is repeated when the condition is true. In a test-before loop, the body of the loop is repeated when the condition is false.

To illustrate the test-after loop, assume you are given one dollar on the day you are born. As a successful investor, you double your money every year. How old will you be when you make your first million? In the following little program, A stands for your age and M is the variable for the amount of money you have. You start the program at birth (A = 0) with one dollar (M = 1). You enter a loop that doubles your money each time you add a year to your age. When your money totals at least one million dollars, you retire. (Note: If you test for your money equaling a million, you will get stuck in the loop forever because your total will double from less than one million to more than a million without ever equaling exactly one million.)

```
400 LET A = 0
410 LET M = 1
450 LET A = A + 1
460 LET M = 2 * M
470 IF M < 1000000 THEN 450
500 PRINT "YOU ARE A MILLIONAIRE AT AGE"; A
510 END
```

Loops are often used to do something a specified number of times. A simple example is a teacher requiring you to write, "I will not make paper airplanes" fifty times. To follow her instructions, you need to count each time you finish writing the sentence, then quit when your total equals fifty.

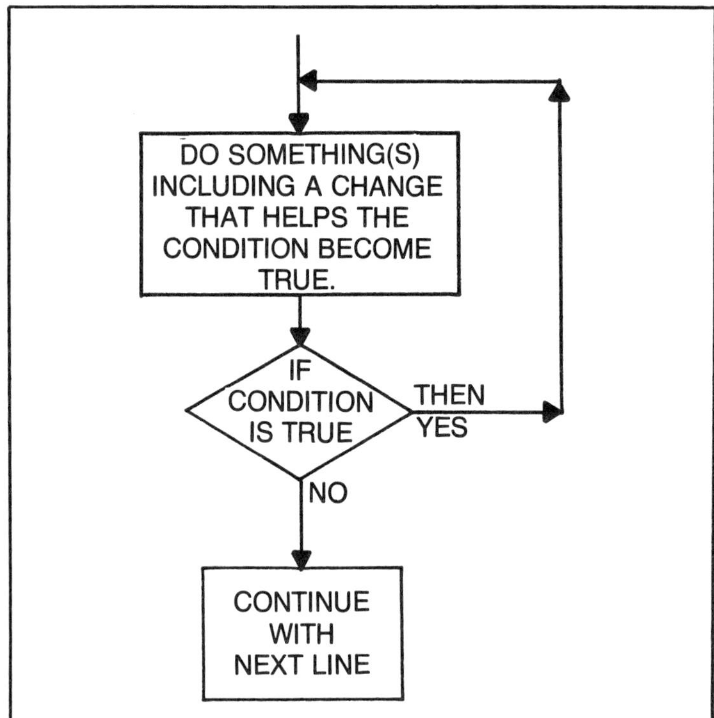

Fig. 6-7. Test-after loop.

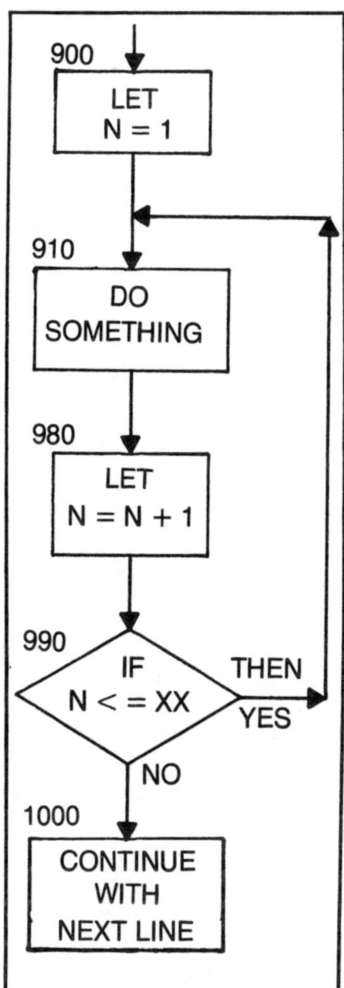

Fig. 6-8. Loop with counter variable.

In BASIC, you need to pick a variable that has no other meaning in your program and use it as a counter for your loop. Figure 6-8 is a flowchart for a loop with a *counter variable* (N in this case). The counter must be initialized before the loop is entered. Usually you start counting with one, but you could start with zero, ten, or any other number. At the end of the body of the loop, you add one to the counter (LET N = N + 1). Then you test to see if the value of the counter is greater than the number of times you want to repeat the loop. If the counter is not greater than your limit, you repeat the body for the Nth time.

The following program will handle the teacher's writing assignment very quickly:

```
 900  LET N = 1
 910  PRINT "I WILL NOT MAKE PAPER AIRPLANES."
 980  LET N = N + 1
 990  IF N < = 50 THEN 910
1000  END
```

This program may fill your screen faster than you can count the lines. You may want to reduce the limit in line 990 to a smaller number (say 10), so you can count the number of times the loop is repeated.

BASIC has a pair of commands designed to make it easier to write loops with counters. They are FOR and NEXT. The FOR command specifies both the initial value of the counter and its upper limit. The exact syntax is FOR variable = initial-value TO limit. The NEXT command combines the actual counting (adding 1 to the value of the variable) with the test (repeating the loop until the limit is passed). The FOR statement is written at the start of the loop. In the program above, replace line 900 with: 900 FOR N = 1 TO 50. The NEXT command is written after the body of the loop. In the sample, replace both line 980 and 990 with: 980 NEXT N.

FOR statements and NEXT statements must always be written in pairs. Also, no statement in the body of the loop should change the value of the counter. If a statement between line 900 and 980 subtracted one from the value of N, then your count would be fouled up and the computer would repeat the loop forever (or until you pressed the break key). Finally, there should not be any GOTOs or IF . . . THEN statements in the body of the loop that might send the computer outside the loop. Such a command would weaken the structure of your program by creating a second exit point. Also, leaving the loop would mean that the computer would not have paired the FOR command with the matching NEXT statement which could cause your program to do something strange the next time it ran into a NEXT command (Fig. 6-9).

Simple FOR . . . NEXT loops can be used to print a number of blank lines on your screen (200 FOR C = 1 TO 6 : 205 PRINT : 210 NEXT C : prints 6 blank lines) to make your printed messages stand out better, or to pause a few seconds before writing more messages on the screen (3000 FORZ=1 TO 1000: 3010 NEXTZ: this loop has no body; it just makes the computer count to a thousand before doing anything else). The initial value and limit in a FOR . . . NEXT loop do not have to be numbers; they can be variables or more complicated expressions. For example, the following loop prints a happy birthday message (with N$ for the person's name) once for each year in the person's age (Y).

```
 10 LET N$ = "TOM"
 20 LET Y = 40
100 FOR J = 1 TO Y
110 PRINT"HAPPY BIRTHDAY, ";N$;"  FOR THE";J;"TH TIME."
120 NEXT J
999 END
```

STRUCTURED PROGRAMMING

Among professional programmers, structured programming has become a popular term to describe a series of techniques for writing good programs in any programming language. Experience has convinced them that structured programs can be written and tested faster than programs that are not well structured. Structured programs are also easier to maintain and modify.

The identifying feature of a structured program is that it is designed and written using structural units: sequences, alternations, loops, and their extensions (like case structures). Each of these structural units has a single entry point and a single exit point. This characteristic allows a large number of structural units to be combined into a complex program without confusion. The programming problem can be broken down into small pieces that can be easily understood.

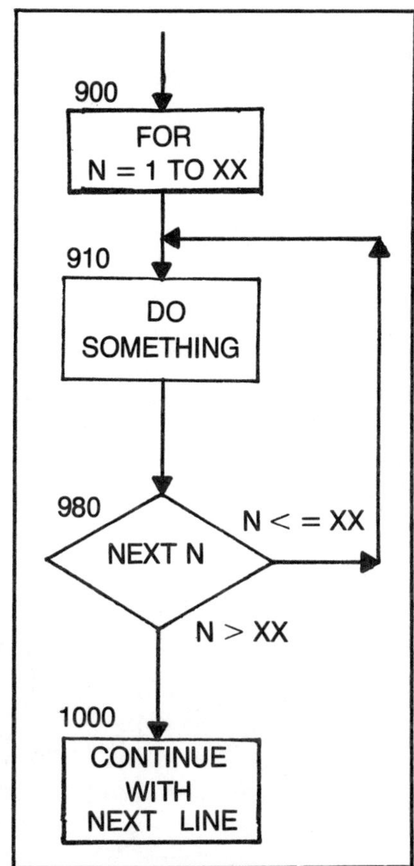

Fig. 6-9. FOR . . . NEXT loop.

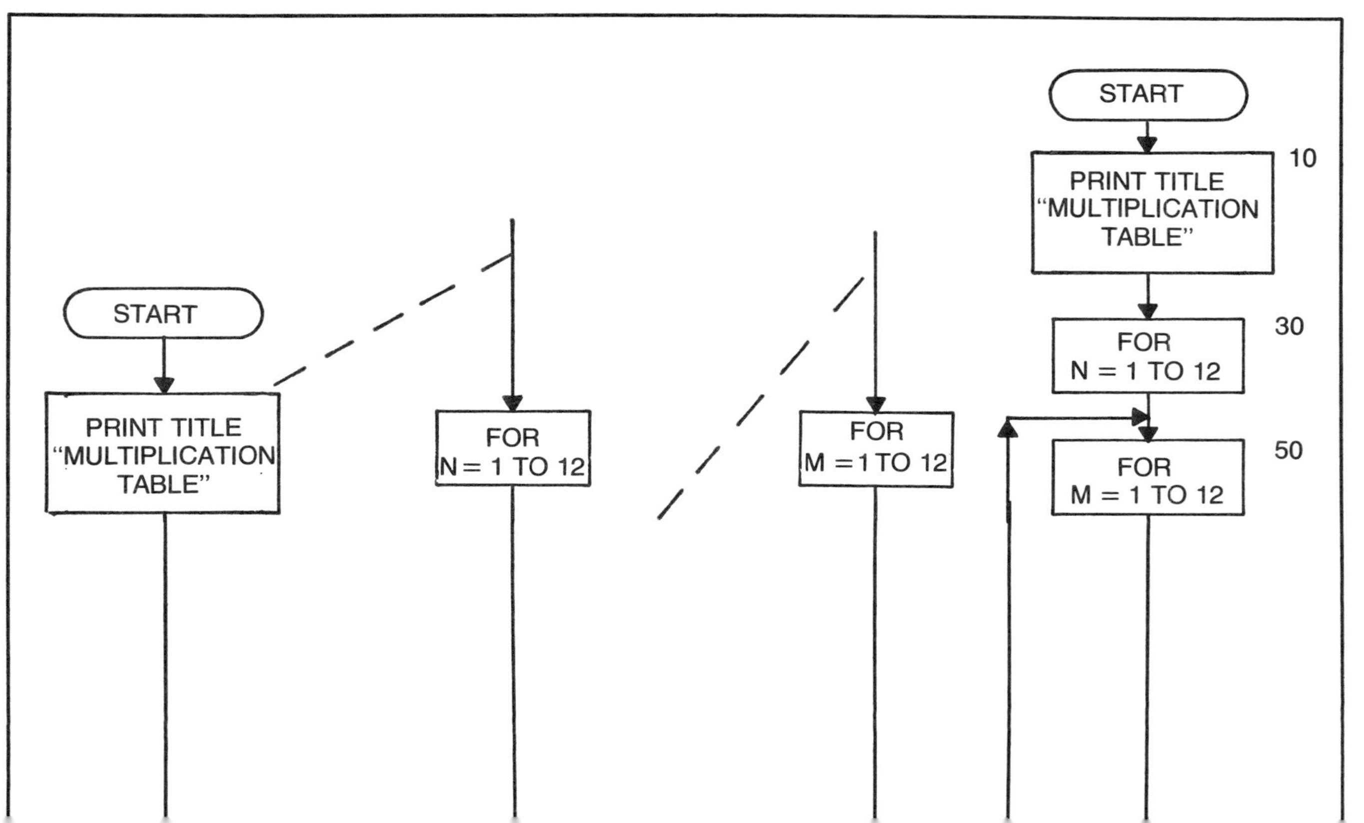

START
PRINT TITLE "MULTIPLICATION TABLE"
FOR N = 1 TO 12
FOR M = 1 TO 12
START
10
PRINT TITLE "MULTIPLICATION TABLE"
30
FOR N = 1 TO 12
50
FOR M = 1 TO 12

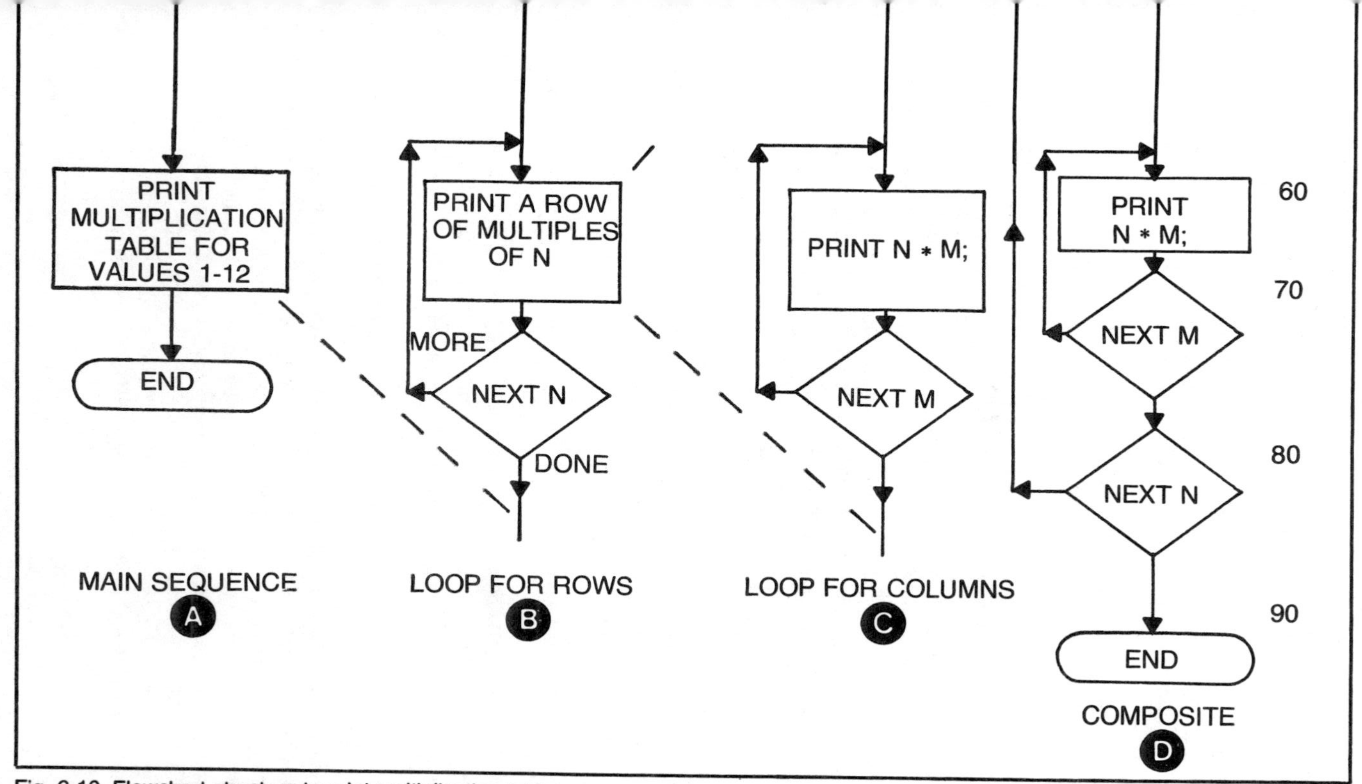

Fig. 6-10. Flowchart structure to print multiplication tables.

Any computer programming problem can be described at the top level as a simple structure (usually a sequence or a loop) with a small number of steps. Each of the steps requires either a single computer instruction or another simple structure with smaller steps. Thus the final program is built with a series of simple structures nested inside each other.

The process of structured programming can be illustrated with a simple problem, printing a multiplication table. At the top level, the program requires a simple sequence of

1. Printing a title to label the table
2. Printing the multiplication table itself
3. Ending (Fig. 6-10A.)

Steps 1 and 3 each require a single BASIC statement. Step 2 involves printing twelve rows of numbers, one for each multiplier. Figure 6-10B expands step 2 of the main sequence into the flowchart of a loop structure. The job of printing each row of products can also be expanded into a loop to print each of twelve products for a multiplier, as shown in Fig. 6-10C. All of the expanded steps can be drawn as a single composite flowchart (Fig. 6-10D). This final flowchart has two loops nested inside the main sequence. After assigning line numbers to each box on a structured flowchart, writing the actual program is a simple translation into BASIC statements:

```
10 PRINT "MULTIPLICATION TABLE"
20 PRINT
30 FOR N = 1 TO 12
50 FOR M = 1 TO 12
60 PRINT N * M;
70 NEXT M
75 PRINT
80 NEXT N
90 END
```

Line 20 prints a blank line to make the title stand out. The semicolon in line 60 is needed to keep the computer from printing each product on a separate line. Line 75 prints blanks at the end of each row to keep the computer from jamming products from different rows on the same print line. The other lines are taken directly from the flowchart.

Structured programming often seems like a lot of extra work to beginners. But as you progress to using the computer to solve more and more complicated problems, you will discover that the discipline of structuring your programs will pay off. The primary structures (and the flowchart designs) of sequence, alternation, and loops are fundamental ideas that can help you solve an immense variety of problems. Using these ideas in a top-down approach to program design will allow you to view an overwhelmingly confusing problem as a series of smaller problems, each of which can be solved (or further simplified) with minimal effort.

Chapter 7
Reusable Programs

The programs presented so far have been limited to solving a problem for a specific set of input values. The area-of-a-circle program would only compute results for a circle with the particular radius spelled out in the LET R = statement. If you wanted to find the area of a different sized circle, you would have to change the program. If all programs had to be changed each time one of the input values was changed, then only programmers could use computers.

Learning to design programs so that people who do not know programming can use them to solve problems was a major milestone in computer history. Programming instructions were developed that allowed the input data to be separate from the actual program. Programs could be written once and saved. Then whenever anyone wanted to use the program, he could put the input values he wanted on a card. The same program could read the values from many cards to find the answers to specific problems.

When BASIC was invented, the use of separate cards for data was a common practice. So the authors of BASIC allowed programmers to continue their habits by including a verb (DATA) to identify a statement as a data card containing input values and another verb (READ) that moved values from the DATA statements into the memory areas assigned to variables.

A specific statement, like "10 LET R = 5", can be replaced by a general input statement, like "10 READ R". The READ command tells the computer to copy a value from a DATA card and store it in the variable R. If there is no DATA card, the computer will print an error message complaining that it cannot READ something that does not exist. The DATA statement must have a line number, but it does not make any difference (to the computer) what line number you use. The DATA statement could be line number 1 so that it comes before any of the program commands, or it could be numbered so that it comes in between any two commands in the program. The computer will treat the DATA statements as input cards which are not part of the program. Traditionally, DATA statements are written after the end of the program.

The following revision of the Circle program uses a READ statement in a simple sequence procedure:

```
 10 LET PI = 3.14159
 40 READ R
 50 LET A = PI * R ↑ 2
 60 PRINT "A CIRCLE WITH A RADIUS OF";R;
      "HAS AN AREA OF";A
 90 END
100 DATA 5
```

Line 10 is not really necessary. The value of pi could have been included in line 50. However, this way it is easier to change the program to use different approximations of pi—such as 22/7. Also, it is easier and faster for the computer to do calculations using variables instead of numbers written in the decimal system. It is also possible that your computer will not allow a two-letter name for a variable, like PI. If that is a problem, use the single letter P for pi in your program.

This simple example does not show any advantage to using a READ R statement instead of a LET R = statement. You still have to change one line each time you run the program for a different sized circle. The savings in effort start appearing when a program uses more than one input value. If you wanted to calculate the volume of rectangular boxes, you would need three input variables: L for length, W for width, and H for height. All three could receive their values from a single DATA statement. A DATA statement can include any number of values as long as they are separated by commas. Thus a program to compute the volume of a box might look like:

```
100 READ L
110 READ W
120 READ H
130 PRINT "THE VOLUME IS"; L * W * H
140 END
150 DATA 8,5,2
```

The computer keeps track of how many data values have been read. Each time it encounters a READ command, it copies the next value on a DATA card. If your program tries to READ more values than you have included on your DATA cards, the computer will print an error message. On the other hand, if you put more values on DATA cards than the program READs, the rest of the values will simply be ignored. In this example, the first READ would store the first value (8) on the DATA card in variable L. The next READ would store the next value (5) in variable W. And the final READ would move the next value (2) to variable H.

Each time you want to run this program to compute the volume of a different box, you only have to change the single DATA statement. If the input values had been included in LET statements, you would have to retype three lines for each box. Another advantage of the READ statement over LET statements is that several variables can be assigned values with a single READ statement. The verb READ can be followed by a whole series of variable names (separated by commas). The following program produces exactly the same results as the last example:

```
10 DATA 8,5,2
50 READ L, W, H
60 PRINT "THE VOLUME IS" ; L * W * H
90 END
```

READ LOOPS

Computers are often used to solve more than one problem at a time. If you wanted to know the areas of four different circles, it would be easier and quicker to put all of the radii on a data card and have the computer repeat a loop to calculate each matching area than it would be to repeatedly type a data card with a single radius and then run the program. Of course, sometimes you might want to find the areas of two, or one, or ten circles at a time. So, it would be best to write your circle program in a way that could handle any number of different radii in one run.

You could start off your program design with a step that determines how many areas will be calculated. That step could be translated into a BASIC READ statement. Then you could write a loop structure to READ each radius from a DATA statement and calculate the area. This design is illustrated by the flowchart in Fig. 7-1, which translates into the following BASIC statements:

```
 10 LET PI = 3.14159
 20 READ N
 30 FOR C = 1 TO N
 40 READ R
 50 LET A = PI * R ↑ 2
 60 PRINT "A CIRCLE WITH RADIUS OF" ; R
      "HAS AN AREA OF";A
 70 NEXT C
 90 END
100 DATA 4
110 DATA 1,2,100,3.5
```

The DATA statements are not really part of the program. With this set of input data, N would be assigned the value of 4. Then each of the next four values on the DATA statements would be read as the value of a radius (R) and the calculated area would be printed. The value of N controls the number of times the FOR...NEXT loop is repeated. If the first data value had been 2 instead of 4, the program would have stopped after printing the

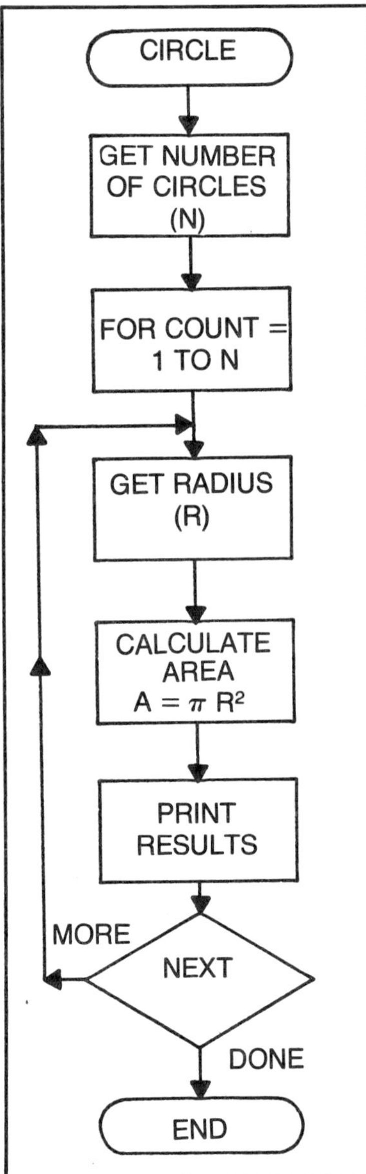

Fig. 7-1. READ loop.

results for two circles (and the remaining values of 100 and 3.5 would have been totally ignored).

The illustration has two DATA statements to emphasize the two different types of input values—one for the number of circles and the other type for the radius. These values could have been typed on a single card; or each value could have been typed on its own separate DATA statement. The computer treats all values on all DATA statements as a single list of input values to be read in order.

This same program could be used with different DATA cards to print the areas of any number of circles. Try the program with line 100 as DATA 1,10,20. It should tell you that a circle with a radius of 10 has an area of 31.4159, then quit. (The first value of the DATA statement tells it to perform the READ loop only once.) Replace line 100 with: DATA 12, 50, .5, 16, 18, 12, 2, 3, 4, 5, 6, 7, 8 and the program will print the areas of twelve different circles before stopping.

This form of READ loop requires that you count the number of different data values you are going to use and that you feed the number into the computer first. This is somewhat inconvenient. People are more apt to think of the list of problems they want to solve and then say "that's all". Counting the problems is a nuisance, and since people do not always count as accurately as computers, provides an extra chance for a mistake to be made.

If you could design your program so that the person using it could tell the computer "that's all," your program would be simpler. Figure 7-2 is the flowchart for a program that uses a "that's all" answer to exit from the READ loop. This design requires that the last value on the DATA statements be a special code that signals the computer to quit. Such a special code is commonly called an *END-OF-FILE* (EOF) or *END-OF-DATA* flag.

There are some restrictions on what value you can use as an end-of-data flag. BASIC will print an error message if it tries to read a string value into a numeric variable. Otherwise, you could just use the word "END" or "FINISHED" as the last entry on your DATA statement. When the program is reading number values, the end-of-data flag must be a number. You would not want the program to stop accidentally because somebody used the end-of-data value as regular data. You can avoid this problem by picking a number that could not possibly be meaningful as input to the problem. The radius of a circle must be a positive number; nobody can draw a circle with a radius of −9. Therefore using a negative number as your end-of-data signal would not stop you from using the program to find the area of any real circle. It is also helpful if the end-of-data flag stands out by looking obviously different than all the real data values. The following program uses −999 to signal the end of the data for that reason.

```
10  LET PI = 3.14159
40  READ R
45  IF R = -999 THEN 90
50  LET A = PI * R ↑ 2
60  PRINT "A CIRCLE WITH RADIUS OF";R;
      "HAS AN AREA OF";A
70  GOTO 40
90  END
```

```
100 DATA 1, 2, 100, 0.5
110 DATA -999
```

This program is one statement shorter than the last version of the circle program. More importantly, it does not require the user to tell the computer how many problems he wishes to solve. The user just lists all of the radii he wants on DATA statements and leaves the end-of-data flag of −999 on the last statement. (By using a separate statement for the end-of-data signal, you reduce the likelihood that the person running the program will forget to type it in when he enters his own data values.)

Many commercial computer applications involve saving up groups of input data (like purchases or payments), then running them through the computer in batches. Nearly all batch programs use READ loops. With other types of jobs, the requirement that all of the data be typed on DATA

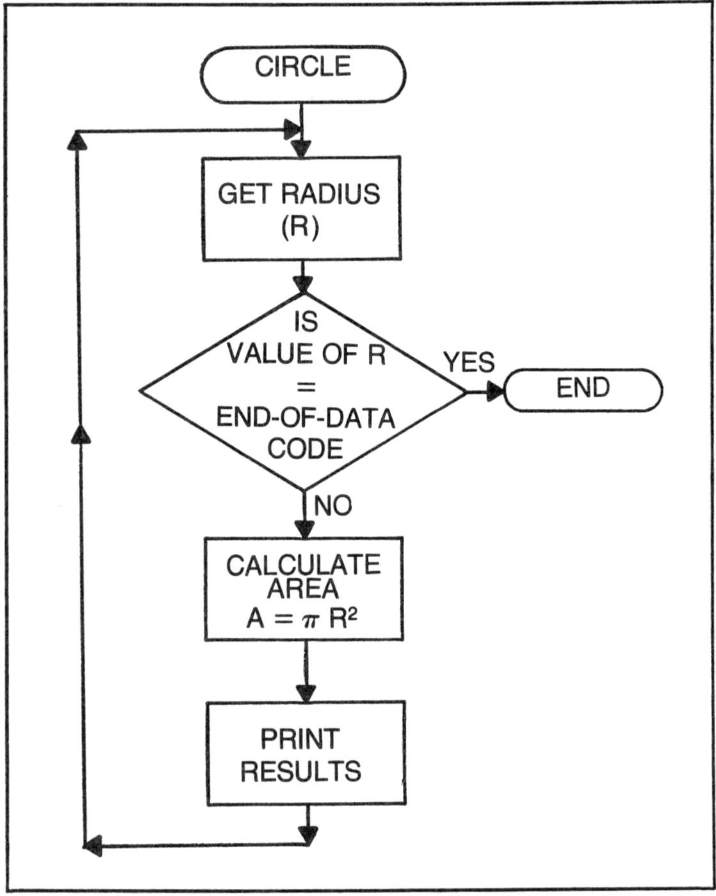

Fig. 7-2. READ loop with end-of-data flag.

statements before the program is run causes serious difficulties. These jobs call for a different type of statement for entering input into the computer.

INPUT STATEMENT

The INPUT verb in BASIC allows input values to be typed into the computer while the program is running. The computer interprets the INPUT command as a request to copy one or more values from the keyboard into the memory area(s) reserved for variables.

To the programmer, an INPUT statement looks like a READ statement and functions like a READ statement. The format of an INPUT statement is the verb INPUT followed by the names of one or more variables. (If several variable names are used, they must be separated by commas.) As a result of the INPUT statement, each variable named in that statement will have been given a new data value. With READ statements, the new values came from DATA statements. With INPUT statements, the computer has to get the values from the person at the keyboard.

The computer tells the keyboard operator that the program is waiting for a value by printing a question mark (?). The computer continues to wait until the operator types in a value and presses the enter or return key. If the INPUT statement includes two or more variable names, the person should type in a value for each variable (separated by commas), before pressing the return key. The following are sample input statements:

```
100 INPUT R
150 INPUT B
200 INPUT N$
250 INPUT A,B
300 INPUT A,B,C
350 INPUT N$,A,B$
```

Each statement would cause the computer to print a single question mark and wait for an answer. Line 100 expects the person running the program to answer with a single number value (like 6 or 345.99); so does line 150. The typed response to line 200 should be a string value. Line 250 requires that two numbers be typed with a comma in between. Line 300 needs three numbers as answers. Line 350 requires that a string (word) value be typed, followed by a comma, then a number, then another comma, and finally a second string. Yet when you look at the screen, each of these statements sends you the same request: a single question mark.

Without any additional explanations, INPUT statements could easily confuse the keyboard operator into making mistakes. This problem can be alleviated by preceding each INPUT statement with a PRINT statement that tells the person what to enter. If you end the PRINT statement with a semicolon (;), the question mark from the INPUT statement will be printed at the end of the PRINT message, making it look like a normal question. The same INPUT statements listed above will appear to make more sense if you match them with PRINT statements similar to the following:

```
100 PRINT "WHAT IS THE RADIUS";
105 INPUT R
150 PRINT "GUESS A NUMBER";
155 INPUT B
200 PRINT "WHAT IS YOUR NAME";
205 INPUT N$
250 PRINT "HEIGHT (IN INCHES) AND WEIGHT (IN POUNDS)";
255 INPUT A,B
300 PRINT "HOW LONG ARE THE 3 SIDES OF YOUR TRI-
      ANGLE";
305 INPUT A,B,C
350 PRINT "WHAT IS YOUR NAME";
355 INPUT N$
360 PRINT "HOW OLD ARE YOU";
365 INPUT A
370 PRINT "WHAT MONTH WERE YOU BORN IN";
375 INPUT B$
```

Printing clear messages for each INPUT statement will make your programs much easier to use. The messages should be specific enough to minimize the chances of somebody making mistakes. If your program assumes certain units of measure (like inches or feet, pounds or kilograms), the printed message should identify those units. If your input statement requires more than one answer, then the message should state how many values are needed (see lines 250 and 300).

Sometimes you will not be able to think of an appropriate message for a group of variables on an INPUT statement (like the INPUT N$,A,B$ example). In that case, you should split the complex INPUT statement into a series of simple statements (like 350-375). The extra typing required only has to be done once when you write the program. The improvement in ease of use will be noticeable each of the many times the program is run.

Despite your best programming efforts, people will occasionally make mistakes when typing in values. BASIC will notice some mistakes, like typing a word answer instead of a number, and then display a warning message. If a person does not enter as many values as the INPUT statement expects, the computer will signal for more input by printing either "??" or "MORE?". You can easily find out what your computer does by running the one-line program "10 INPUT A,B" and entering a single number. If the operator enters more values than the computer expects, the computer will print a warning (like "EXTRA IGNORED") and continue. For example, if you answered a request for a price of a car as 10,000 (for ten thousand dollars), the computer would see the comma as separating two values so it would print the warning message and continue the program using 10 dollars as the price of your car.

Many of the mistakes people make when typing are obviously wrong when you look at them, but would not appear wrong to the computer. If you were asking adults for the year of their birth and you got answers of 1981,

1776, and 2001, you would know they were either mistakes or jokes and you would throw them out. If you were writing bills for a water company and one of the forms had a meter reading lower than the previous month (a negative amount of water used) or as having used one billion gallons of water in a small trailer, you would know that the form was in error. The computer's INPUT statement would not worry about any of these situations. As far as it is concerned, one number is as good as any other number.

If you allow your program to accept obviously bad numbers as input, then it will occasionally produce absurd results. There is an old saying about computers: "garbage in, garbage out". Actually, that saying is true only if the programmer has not thought about possible errors before writing his program. For good programs, the appropriate saying is: "garbage in, warning messages printed out instead of unreasonable results".

You can include IF...THEN statements after each INPUT(or READ) statement to test that the value is reasonable. If an unreasonable answer was entered into the computer, your program could print a message explaining what was wrong. Using INPUT statements, the program could then loop back until a good value was entered (Fig. 7-3).

If you were asking adults for their year of birth, you know that any date after 1970 would be a mistake (the person would either still be a child or would not have been born yet). You could also assume that any date prior to 1800 was a mistake (that person would have to be alive for more than 180 years). The part of your program that asked for the birthdate could stop many mistakes by testing the answer against this range of dates (line 220 in the following). Compare this example of BASIC programming to the flowchart of an input loop in Fig. 7-3.

```
200 PRINT"IN WHAT YEAR WERE YOU BORN";
210 INPUT Y
220 IF Y > 1800 AND Y < 1970 THEN 300
230 PRINT"PLEASE CORRECT YOUR ANSWER."
240 PRINT"YEAR OF BIRTH SHOULD BE BETWEEN 1800 AND
      1970";
250 GOTO 210
```

You can keep the test for bad input simple, or you can include more elaborate editing. You might want to print different messages for dates that are too small or too late. Editing can also provide for automatic correction of data in some cases. If someone entered a number between zero and one hundred as their birth year, you might assume that those were the last two digits of the current century. Your program could then convert the input into a complete year by adding 1900 to the input value. However, any time you have the computer alter input data, you should also print a message to show what change you made. That way, the person using the program will have enough information to trace down the problem if he thinks the results of the program are wrong. The following BASIC statements expand the editing done in lines 220—240 above:

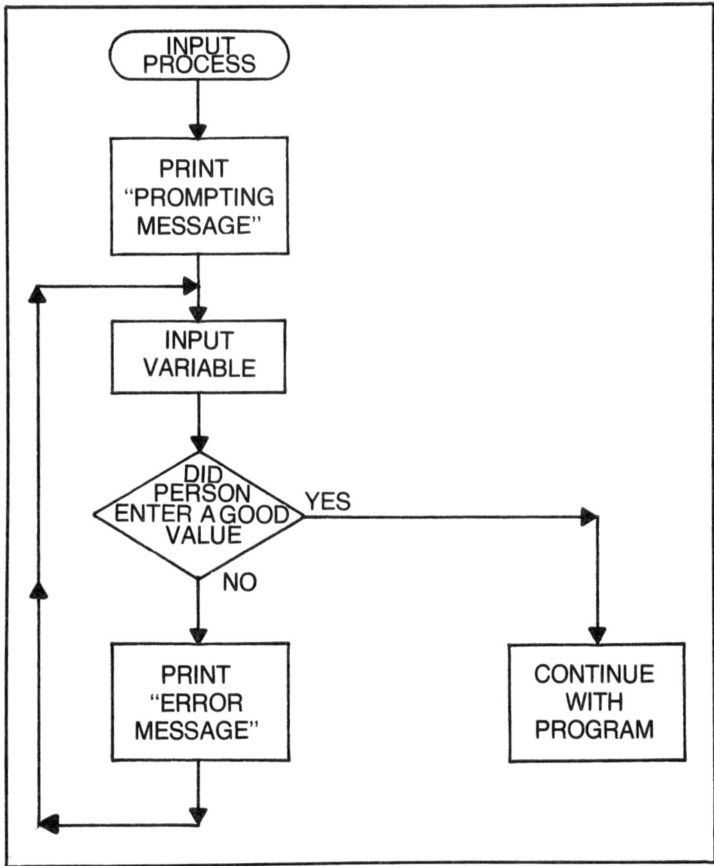

Fig. 7-3. Normal input process.

```
220 IF Y >=0 THEN 230
222 PRINT "DATES MUST BE POSITIVE NUMBERS."
224 GOTO 200
230 IF Y > 99 THEN 240
232 LET Y = Y + 1900
234 PRINT "I HAVE ASSUMED YOU MEAN";Y
240 IF Y > 1800 THEN 250
242 PRINT "IF YOU WERE REALLY BORN IN";Y;
      "YOU WOULD BE IN THE BOOK OF WORLD RECORDS."
244 GOTO 200
250 IF Y < 1970 THEN 300
260 IF Y > 1990 THEN 270
262 PRINT"THIS PROGRAM IS FOR ADULTS. YOU SEEM
      TO BE TOO YOUNG."
```

```
264 GOTO 200
270 PRINT"YOU'RE AHEAD OF THE TIMES. COME BACK
      AFTER YOUR BIRTH !"
272 GOTO 200
```

Humorous messages are appropriate in some programs, particularly games and demonstrations for people who are not used to computers. They would not be appropriate in most business programs, where editing messages should be simple and business-like. The design of a computer program should include thinking about the type of people who are going to use the program, so that the level of editing and messages will be appropriate.

INPUT statements can replace READ statements within the type of read loop shown in Fig. 7-2. Two items require special attention when combining an input routine with a read loop. First, the prompting message for the input should include a comment identifying the end-of-data value. The keyboard operator needs to know what to do when he wants to stop entering more values. Second, the test for end-of-data should come before the tests for bad data. Otherwise, when someone enters the value for end-of-data, the computer will print a message telling them they made a mistake. Applying these ideas to the circle program produces a flowchart consisting of an alternation structure nested inside the main loop (Fig. 7-4).

The final program for circles in this book incorporates these ideas:

```
10 LET PI = 3.14159
30 PRINT "RADIUS (ENTER -999 TO QUIT)";
40 INPUT R
45 IF R = -999 THEN 90
46 IF R > 0 THEN 50
47 PRINT"THE RADIUS OF ANY CIRCLE IS MORE THAN 0."
48 GOTO 30
50 LET A = PI * R ↑ 2
60 PRINT "A CIRCLE WITH RADIUS OF"; R;
   "HAS AN AREA OF"; A
70 GOTO 30
90 END
```

Some versions of BASIC allow you to save typing by combining the prompting message from a PRINT statement with the INPUT statement. Instead of the two lines: 30 PRINT "RADIUS (ENTER −999 TO QUIT)"; and 40 INPUT R, you could type: 30 INPUT "RADIUS (ENTER −999 TO QUIT)"; R. If your computer allows this shortcut, then the verb INPUT is followed by a string value inside quotation marks, a semicolon, then the name of the variable (or variables) to be input. The prompting message must be a simple string to use this format.

Some prompting messages (such as PRINT "WHAT IS YOUR GUESS, ";N$—where N$ is a variable holding a person's name) cannot be used as part of an INPUT statement. If the printed message included a variable name, the INPUT statement would tell the computer to set a new value for that variable instead of displaying the old value. Nevertheless, since you almost never want to use an INPUT statement without a prompting message, putting the message in the INPUT statement can save you a lot of time in typing programs.

MENUS

A prompting message is not always much help to the person using a program. A question like "What do you want me to do?" assumes the person knows what different things he can choose. Then the person must type in his answer in the exact wording the program expects. Unless he uses the same program often, he is unlikely to get the computer to do what he wants, because he will not be familiar with the range of choices or their grammar.

When a program includes a variety of choices, printing a menu which lists those choices makes the program much easier to use. If each item on

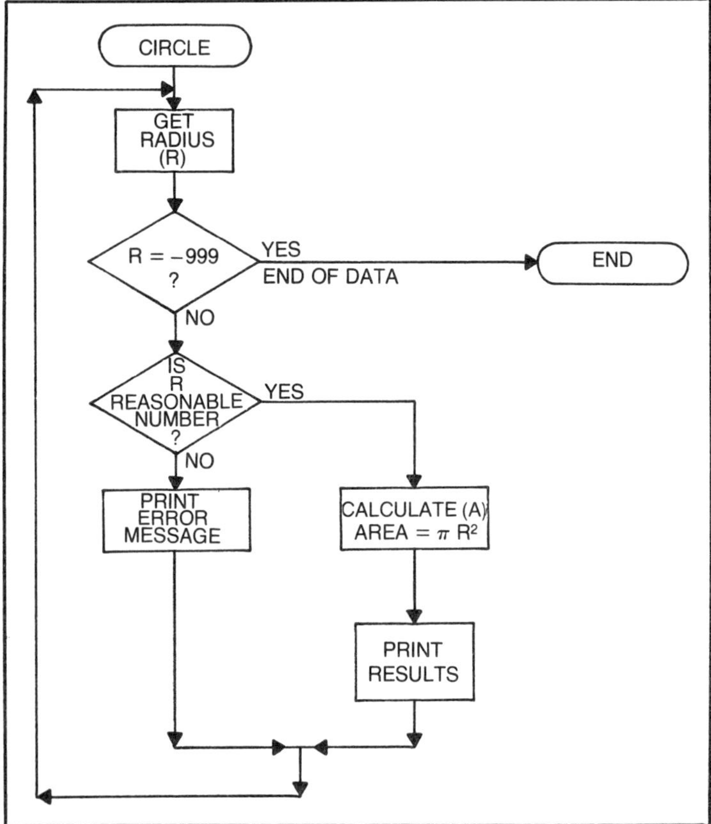

Fig. 7-4. READ loop with input validation.

the menu is identified by a number, then the person reading the menu will only have to enter a single digit for the computer to carry out his wishes.

The beginning of the next program illustrates the use of a menu. This program could be used to combine the earlier circle program with the programs to print a multiplication table or a birthday message into a single program. This combined program uses a case structure (with the ON ...GOTO command) to select the action the computer is to take, then it loops back to the menu to allow the person to try the other options.

```
100 FOR I = 1 TO 6
110 PRINT
120 NEXT I
130 PRINT"THIS PROGRAM CAN DO THE FOLLOWING:"
140 PRINT"  1 — COMPUTE THE AREA OF A CIRCLE"
150 PRINT"  2 — PRINT A MULTIPLICATION TABLE"
160 PRINT"  3 — PRINT A BIRTHDAY GREETING"
170 PRINT"  4 — QUIT"
180 PRINT"WHICH DO YOU WANT IT TO DO";
190 INPUT W
200 ON W GOTO 1000, 2000, 3000, 4000
210 PRINT "CHOOSE A NUMBER FROM 1 TO 4 !!"
220 GOTO 180
1000 PRINT "WHAT IS THE RADIUS";
```

(The rest of the CIRCLE program goes here.)

```
1500 GOTO 100
2000  (statements to print multiplication table)
2500 GOTO 100
3000  (statements for birthday message)
3500 GOTO 100
4000 END
```

Lines 100-120 are a loop that prints blank lines to help the menu stand out on the screen. Lines 130-170 print the actual menu. Lines 180-220 provide the input processing (with validation and error loop). Lines 1500, 2500, and 3500 return the program to the menu after it has completed the requested job.

When you try this program on your computer, you may encounter a minor problem. Before you can read the entire multiplication table, the command sending the program back to the menu may have rolled some of the answers off your video screen. You can cure this by making the computer pause before reaching line 2500. Either of the following pairs of statements will make the computer pause:

```
2400 FOR I = 1 TO 5000
2410 NEXT I
```

or

```
2450 PRINT"PRESS ENTER TO CONTINUE";
2455 INPUT A$
```

The first pair (2400-2410) will make the computer pause for the length of time it takes the computer to count to 5000. You can make the pause longer or shorter by changing the limit in the FOR statement. The second pair (2450-2455) causes the computer to wait as long as the person wants. The variable in the INPUT statement is not used by the computer. You are simply taking advantage of the fact that INPUT makes the computer wait for a message to be sent from the keyboard before it will continue with the next instruction.

Menus come in handy in many programs, especially programs designed for people who do not use computers often. Menus are more convenient to use on computers with video screens than on computer terminals that print everything on paper. A long wait for the computer to print the menu between each action could make a program boring. Also, using menus to list the choices for questions like "What day of the week is it today?" or "Which month were you born in?" is more likely to insult your user than to help him.

Knowing how to write menus does not mean you should use a menu every chance you get. It does mean that you have one more tool to help you design your programs in the manner that will be best for the people who will use them.

DEFAULT VALUES

The INPUT command normally reads a value from the keyboard and stores it in the memory location for the specified variable. Even if no value is entered on the keyboard, the variable will have a value. The value of the variable will be whatever was previously stored in that part of the computer's memory, unless it has been changed by a LET, READ, or INPUT command.

On many computer systems, all variables start with a default value each time you enter a RUN command. Number variables are given an initial value of zero. String variables may either start as spaces or as special null values. These default values save programmers the effort of writing a series of LET statements at the beginning of their programs to make any variables used for totalling start off at zero.

If you respond to an INPUT request by just pressing the return or enter key without typing any value, most BASIC computer systems will leave the value of the variable the same as it was before the INPUT statement. This allows you to create your own default values for variables.

In a read loop, you might want the INPUT variable to have the special end-of-data code as its default value. That way the person using your program would not have to type in a funny looking number when he was finished with your program. Preceding the INPUT statement with a LET statement which gives the variable a default value would let him quit by simply pressing the return key.

```
30 PRINT"RADIUS (PRESS ' ENTER' TO QUIT)";
35 LET R = -999
40 INPUT R
45 IF R = -999 THEN 90
   etc.
```

Assigning a default value (with a LET statement) to a variable before INPUTting it can also be useful by providing shortcuts to people who frequently use a fancy program in a "normal" way. For instance, you might write a program to print term papers which allowed you to decide how wide the margins should be and how many lines the computer would print on each page. This would require variables for the number of spaces in the left hand margin (LM), the number of spaces in the right hand margin (RM), and the number of lines per page (NL). Most of the time, you would be happy with one-inch margins all the way around the paper. That could be accomplished for double-spaced typing on standard paper by letting LM = 10, RM = 10, and NL = 27. If you included these default values in your program, then you could order the normal printing by quickly pressing the return key three times. You would only have to think about the enter specific values when you wanted the program to print your report in an unusual format.

Taking the extra time to write LET statements, which give default values to variables the program will INPUT, is one small thing that makes the difference between a decent program and an outstanding one.

Chapter 8

Common Subroutines and Functions

Some program statement series are used repeatedly in many different programs. These statements satisfy common needs like rounding numbers, printing even columns on reports, or selecting random numbers for use in computer games. Writing out the whole group of statements every time you needed to do one of these common things in a program would require a lot of tedious effort and would make your programs very long and hard to read.

BASIC provides two tools that can eliminate repetitious writing of statements and shorten your programs: functions and subroutines. A *subroutine* is a series of statements written once in a program which can then be used in many different parts of the program without rewriting. A *function* is an abbreviation for a process that can be inserted in the middle of a statement. These definitions may not sound meaningful in isolation, but they will become clear once you examine them in detail.

FUNCTIONS

A mathematical function is a rule for converting one number into another number. A simple example is the absolute value function. The absolute value of a number is the distance between that number and zero. Both 5 and –5 have absolute values of 5. The mathematical rule for this function is:

If N is less than zero, the absolute value of N is –1 * N

Otherwise the absolute value of N is N.

To use the absolute value function in BASIC, you have to refer to it by its abbreviation ABS followed by parentheses containing the number for which you want to find the absolute value. Thus, ABS(18) means the absolute value of 18; ABS(X) means the absolute value of the number stored in variable X. A function is not a complete BASIC command. It appears as part of an expression in a statement like: 300 PRINT ABS(N) or 460 LET X = ABS(G - A) * 5. The parentheses following a function name can enclose any valid BASIC expression, variable name, or numeric constant. You can even nest functions inside each other. LET A = ABS(B - ABS(C - ABS(I))) is a valid BASIC statement, though you are usually better off using simpler expressions.

The absolute value function is most commonly used when calculating differences. If you wrote a program that determined the number of days between two dates without an absolute value function, it would produce a negative number when the earlier date was entered before the later date. If you described the difference as the absolute value of the result of the subtraction, then you would not have to worry about the order for inputting dates. Another use of the absolute value occurs in number guessing games where the winner is the one guessing closest (either higher or lower) to the correct answer. The following statements find which of two numbers (N1 and N2) is closest to the computers answer (A):

```
200 IF ABS(N1 - A) > ABS (N2 - A) THEN 270
210 IF ABS(N1 - A) < ABS(N2 - A) THEN 240
220 PRINT "IT's A TIE."
230 GOTO 300
240 PRINT "PLAYER # 1 IS CLOSEST"
250 GOTO 300
270 PRINT "PLAYER # 2 IS CLOSEST"
300  (continue with the program)
```

BASIC functions are always typed in the form: Abbreviation(expression). *This is one of the few cases in BASIC where blank spaces make a difference*. If you type ABS(X) instead of ABS(X), the computer may decide that you are talking about a variable named "ABS" instead of the function ABS( ). Never leave a space between the abbreviation for a function and the left parenthesis.

The square root function appears in many statistical and distance calculations. The square root of a number is the number which can be multiplied by itself to get the original number. In other words, if N = X * X, then X is the square root of N. A few real numbers have square roots that are whole numbers (0 = 0 * 0; 1 = 1 * 1; 4 = 2 * 2; 9 = 3 * 3; etc.). With most numbers, the square root does not work out to an even decimal fraction, so the computer provides a close approximation. If you command your computer to PRINT SQR(5) * SQR(5) it might give an answer of 4.99999 instead of 5 because it rounds off its answers for the square root function before multiplying. Negative numbers do not have real square roots. If you multiply a negative number by itself, you will get a positive answer. If you multiply a positive number by itself, you also get a positive number. So if you try to find a number that can be the square root of a negative number, you won't make any progress, and neither will your computer. Commanding

Table 8-1. Mathematical Functions.

Abbrev.	Function	Explanation and Examples
ABS	Absolute Value	The distance between a number and zero. Ex.: ABS(−5)=5; ABS(9)=9.
ATN	Arctangent	Trigonometry: inverse of the tangent function. Ex.: ATN(1)=0.785399; ATN(1.55741)=1 (answers in radians).
COS	Cosine	One of the main trigonometry functions. Ex.: COS(1)=0.540302; COS(90)=−0.448069 (using radians).
EXP	Exponential	EXP(N) = e ↑ N, where e is the base for natural logarithms. (The value of e is approximately 2.71828.) This is the inverse of the LOG function. Ex.: EXP(5)=148.413; EXP(2.99573)=20.
INT	Integer Truncate	The largest integer that is not greater than the given number. This function rounds down to the nearest whole number. Ex.: INT(3.9)=3; INT(−7.2)=−8; INT(5)=5.
LOG	Logarithm	The natural logarithm (base e) of a number. The inverse of the EXP function. Cannot be used with negative numbers. Ex.: LOG(148.413)=5; LOG(20)=2.99573.

RND(0)	Random Number	Picks a "random" number between zero and one. Each decimal value is equally likely to appear. When a program using RND(0) is run several times, the results will probably be different each time. Ex.: RND(0)=.539631; RND(0)=.9)=.905 RND(0)=.046387.
SGN	Sign	The answer tells if a number is positive, negative or zero, ignoring the absolute value. If N = 0 then SGN(N) = 0. If N > 0 then SGN(N) = +1. If N < 0 then SGN(N) = −1.
SIN	Sine	One of the main functions of trigonometry. Ex.: SIN(1)=0.841471; SIN(10)=−0.544021 (using radians).
SQR	Square Root	The answer multiplied by itself will give the original number. The starting number must be positive. The answer will also be positive. Ex.: SQR(25)=5; SQR(144)=12.
TAN	Tangent	The last of the three main trigonometry functions. Ex.: TAN(0.785399)=1; TAN(1)=1.55741.

your computer to find the square root of a negative number will produce an error message.

The BASIC abbreviation for the square root function is SQR. Some versions of BASIC also include abbreviations for a number of complex mathematical functions used in trigonometry and science computations. The more common functions are listed in Table 8-1. If some of the definitions do not make sense to you, don't worry. Many of the functions apply only to special types of problems. You could complete a successful programming career without ever including a COS function in any of your programs. These functions are included in the BASIC language for those people who need to use them to solve their problems.

The integer function (INT) is useful in many business and personal programs. It converts decimal numbers into simple integers (or whole numbers). You use the integer function for rounding, but it is not exactly the same as rounding. The integer function always rounds down. INT(4.9) = 4. INT(4.0)=4.INT(–4)=–4.INT(–4.2)=–5. For positive numbers, this is the same as throwing away the decimal fraction completely. Rounding down for negative numbers looks a little different because it produces a number with a larger absolute value. If you remember that –40 degrees is a lower (colder) temperature than –10, you should have little trouble remembering how integer rounding-down works.

Normal rounding calls for all fractions of one-half or more to be rounded up to the next higher integer and all fractions less than one-half to be rounded down. You can accomplish this by adding one-half (or .5) to a number before you round it down with the integer function. INT(4.9 + .5) = INT(5.4) =5. INT(4.4 + .5) = INT(4.9) = 4. The following statement will round the value of the variable N to the nearest whole number: LET N = INT(N + .5).

Other uses of the integer function include determining whether a number is odd or even and checking input values to make sure they are whole numbers. The integer function does not change the value of any whole number. X will equal INT(X) whenever X is a whole number. The following statements could be used in a food-ordering program to stop an order for half of a hot dog from getting past the computer:

```
300 PRINT"HOW MANY DO YOU WANT";
310 INPUT H
320 IF H = INT(H) THEN 350
330 PRINT"YOU MUST ORDER WHOLE ITEMS!"
340 GOTO 300
350  (continue with program)
```

Finding even numbers uses division. Every even number is divisible by two (without any fractional remainder). Thus, E / 2 is an integer if E is an even number. This can be tested by a BASIC statement like: IF E / 2 = INT(E / 2) THEN PRINT"EVEN" ELSE PRINT"ODD".

RANDOM NUMBERS

The random number function (RND(0)) is in a class by itself. All other functions give predictable results: SQR(9) is always 3. The random number function is unpredictable. The value of RND(0) will be different nearly every time you use it.

Many games and real-life situations involve an element of chance or unpredictability. Throwing dice, dealing cards, and trying to choose the fastest checkout line in a supermarket all require some blind luck. If you want to simulate any of these situations with a computer program, you need to use a random number function.

The defining characteristic of a random number function is that the result of any single use is unpredictable, but the distribution of a large number of uses is predictable. If you throw a die a single time, you have no way of knowing in advance what the result will be (other than that it will be a number between 1 and 6). However, you could be confident that if you threw the die ten thousand times that it would come up 6 approximately one-sixth of the time.

The RND(0) function always produces a number between zero and one. All the decimal values from 0.000001 through 0.999999 are equally likely to turn up, but seeing the results of the computer doing RND(0) ten times would not give any clues to what the result of the next time would be.

Nonetheless, RND(0) is a true function. If your computer started with the same hidden number (called the *seed*) each time it ran a program with a number of uses of RND(0), then it would produce identical results. Most computers use a part of memory that changes rapidly (like the internal clock that counts fractions of a second) as a seed for their random number function. That way the computer will behave differently each time you run your program. Some versions of BASIC allow you to control the seed with a special command.

To get an idea of what the random number function does, run the following short program on your computer several times in succession:

```
10 FOR I = 1 TO 20
20 PRINT RND(0),
30 NEXT I
40 END
```

You can use the random number function to decide whether or not the computer should take a given action by comparing the result of RND(0) to the percentage odds you choose for that action. If you want to mimic flipping a coin where there is a 50 percent chance of getting a "tails" and a 50 percent chance of a "heads," then you would compare RND(0) to .50, as shown:

```
50 LET R = RND(0)
60 IF R < .50 THEN 80
70 LET C$="HEADS"
75 GOTO 90
```

```
80 LET C$="TAILS"
90 PRINT "THE TOSS IS " ;C$
```

If you wanted to use a weighted coin that came up heads 90 percent of the time, you would only need to change the .50 in line 60 to .90.

The other common way of using the random number function is to make any one of a series of numbers equally likely to appear. If you are writing a program that "throws" dice, you want the computer to pick a number from one to six for each die. Since RND(0) always produces a decimal number less than one, multiplying RND(0) by six would give you an answer between zero and six. But it would still include decimal fractions. You could get rid of the fractions with the integer function (INT), which would round the answers down to 0, 1, 2, 3, 4, or 5. There is no zero on dice, so you have to add 1 to make sure that the final answer is 1, 2, 3, 4, 5, or 6. For a pair of dice, these steps would be repeated as shown in Fig. 8-1 and the following statements:

```
500 LET D1 = 6 * RND(0)
510 LET D1 = INT(D1) + 1
530 LET D2 = 6 * RND(0)
540 LET D2 = INT(D2) + 1
550 LET S  = D1 + D2
```

You can follow similar steps (changing only the multiplier) to have the computer pick a number from 1 to any upper limit you choose. Some versions of BASIC include the option of using RND(N) where N is any whole number greater than one. RND(N) gives the same results as: INT(N * RND(0)) + 1, and it is definitely easier to type.

SPECIAL COMPUTER FUNCTIONS

In addition to mathematical functions, most versions of BASIC include several functions related to the computer codes and strings of symbols. Unfortunately, this is one of the areas where there is the least standardization between different computer systems. Table 8-2 summarizes the more common special computer functions. Your computer may include many others, such as functions that give musical tones or change colors on the screen. You will have to read your manual for your specific computer to learn these more specialized functions. Also, it is quite possible that at least one of the functions listed here will not work on your machine.

The ASC function gives the *ASCII* (American Standard Code for Information Interchange) code number for a symbol (or the first symbol in a string variable). This allows you to perform arithmetic manipulations on letters. One use is to change letters from uppercase to lower case. Using string variables to hold a message, you would have to write a long series of IF . . . THEN statements (a case structure) to change "A" to "a", "B" to "b", etc. However, the ASCII code for each lowercase letter is exactly thirty-two more than its uppercase counterpart. So you could change all uppercase letters to the lowercase codes with the single statement: LET C = ASC(L$) + 32.

To print the result as a letter and not as a code number, you would use the CHR$ function. CHR$, the CHaRacter function, is the inverse of the ASC function. It turns ASCII code numbers into symbols for printing. Continuing the example with the statement PRINT CHR$(C); would cause your computer to print the actual lowercase letter. (This example assumes that your computer does print both upper- and lowercase letters; many

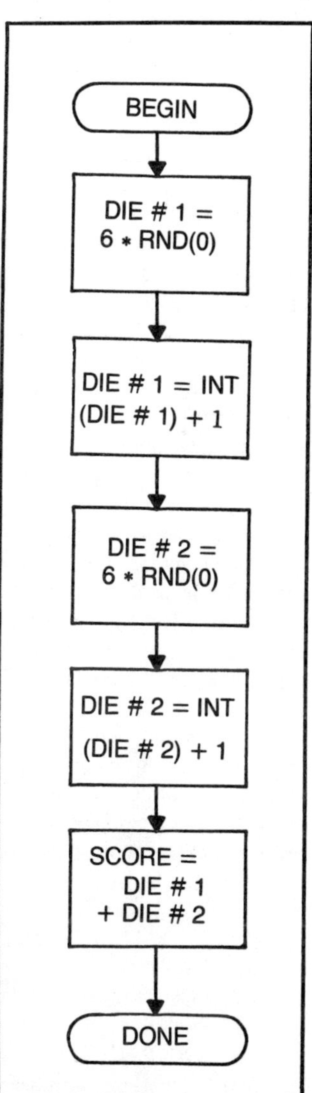

Fig. 8-1. Throwing a pair of dice.

computers print only uppercase letters, so this example may not work.

Other uses of the ASC and CHR$ functions include creating and deciphering secret codes and translating a key on your keyboard so it will print a different symbol. The translation feature is commonly used when a computer is hooked up to a printer with special characters (such as the British pound sign, or the symbol for copyright) which do not appear on the standard typewriter keyboard. The CHR$ function also provides you with the only way to print quotation marks (") in normal BASIC. Whenever BASIC sees a quotation mark in a PRINT statement or as part of an INPUT string, it interprets it to be the string delimiter (which is not printed as part of the string). The ASCII code for quotation marks is thirty-four. So, telling your computer to: PRINT CHR$(34); will cause it to print the quotes symbol.

The LEFT$ and RIGHT$ functions allow you to pay attention to only part of a string. Each of these functions require two *arguments* (the technical name for the expressions inside the parentheses) with a comma between them. The first argument is the string (or the name of the string variable) in which you are interested. The second argument is the number of symbols in that string that the computer will use. LEFT$ uses the first symbols (starting at the left) of the string. RIGHT$ uses the last symbols (starting from the right).

The LEFT$ function can make your input of strings more flexible. There are many cases where you can allow people to spell out their choices or abbreviate them in response to an INPUT question. With the LEFT$ command, you can check only the first letter of their answer to make the computer's decision. For example, you may have written a program that includes the question: INPUT "DO YOU WANT ANOTHER CARD"; A$. The most common negative reply would be "NO", but some players might reasonably answer nope, not now, *nunca, nein,* or even *nyet.* Testing for IF A$ = "NO" THEN 800 would not accept any of these alternatives. Treating any response starting with an "N" as a negative would take care of all of these answers. That could be accomplished with the statement: IF LEFT$(A$,1)="N" THEN 800.

The length function, LEN, tells how many characters are in a string. This can be useful if you are printing reports and want to know if a string variable will fit on the end of a line or needs to start on the next line. For example, the common text of a message might take up the first fifty spaces on a line, to be followed by a person's name, stored in N$. If the name is more than ten letters long, it won't fit within your margins, so you type:

```
900 IF LEN(N$) > 10 THEN 930
910 PRINT N$
920 GOTO 960
930 PRINT
940 PRINT N$;   (start of next line)
960    (continue with program)
```

Table 8-2. Special Computer Functions.

Format	Function
ASC(S$)	Gives the ASCII code number for the first symbol in the string S$. Ex.: ASC("A")=65; ASC(" ")=32; ASC("1")=49.
CHR$(N)	Gives the string symbol for the ASCII code number N. N has to be less than 256, and numbers above 127 will give different results on different computers. Ex: CHR$(65)="A"; CHR$(49)="1".
LEFT$(S$,N)	Gives the first (leftmost) N symbols in the string S$. Ex.: LEFT$("YES",1EFT$(" LEFT$("DECEMBER",3)="DEC".
LEN(S$)	The length of the string gives the number of letters and other symbols in the string S$. Ex.: LEN("YES")=3; LEN("DECEMBER")=8.
RIGHT$(S$,N)	Gives the last (rightmost) N symbols in the string S$. Ex.: RIGHT$("YES",1)="S"; RIGHT$("NOT ME!",5)="T ME!".
TAB(N)	Skips to column number N for printing. Ex.: PRINT TAB(10);"NO" leaves 10 blank spaces at the start of the line then prints "NO". PRINT N$; TAB(30);A$ could be used to print a report of names and addresses as two columns on the page or screen.

The LEN, LEFT$, and RIGHT$ functions can be used together to split strings into two parts and still print both parts. You might want to leave the first letter of each word as uppercase and convert all the rest of the letters to lowercase. (This would require repeatedly splitting the first letter off from the remaining letters and manipulating the first letter with the ASC function). Or you could write a pig-Latin translator based on the following simplified process:

```
200 PRINT "ENTER AN ENGLISH WORD";
210 INPUT A$
220 IF LEN(A$) < 2 THEN 300
230 LET F$ = LEFT$(A$,1)
240 LET R$ = RIGHT$(A$, LEN(A$)-1)
250 PRINT "IN PIG LATIN, YOUR WORD IS: ";
260 PRINT R$; F$; "AY"
270 GOTO 200
300 PRINT "PIG LATIN DOES NOT CHANGE WORDS WITH
    LESS THAN TWO LETTERS."
310 END
```

The final function listed in Table 8-2 is the most widely used. The TABulate function works like the TAB settings on a typewriter. It makes the computer skip ahead to a specific printing column.

The column number for printing the next character is enclosed in the parentheses following the TAB abbreviation. This function can be used only as part of PRINT statements, and the number of spaces for TABbing is limited by the normal line size for the particular computer. If you have already passed the column requested by the TAB function, the computer will continue printing without leaving any additional spaces.

```
20 PRINT TAB(20) "THIS IS A TITLE"
30 PRINT "WASHINGTON"; TAB(16); "FIRST PRESIDENT"
40 PRINT "ADAMS"; TAB(16); "SECOND PRESIDENT"
50 PRINT "THOMAS ALVIN EDISON"; TAB(16); "INVENTOR"
```

Line 20 uses the TAB function for indenting or centering a title. Lines 30 through 50 show how TAB is used for printing a list with more than one column. In line 60, the word "INVENTOR" would actually be printed starting in column 20 instead of column 16 because the long name at the start of the line goes past the TAB requested.

SUBROUTINES

A subroutine is a little program within a program. The "sub" part of the name indicates that subroutines are under the main program, on the lower levels of the program design. A subroutine will generally appear as a single box (something to be done) on one of the higher levels of your flowchart. The "routine" part of the name indicates that subroutines are often used to perform common, routine processes that may be repeated several times in a program.

Subroutines are similar to functions in that they provide common processes which can be referred to (or "called") several times in a program by using a short command. For functions, the calling command is the abbreviation for the function name. For subroutines, the calling command is the word GOSUB followed by a line number. The GOSUB command tells the computer to GO do the SUBroutine that starts at the specified line number, then come back and continue with the next statement.

Unlike functions that are built into the BASIC language, you have to write your own subroutines. This means that you can write subroutines that do anything you can design with BASIC statements. The only special command you need to write a subroutine is the RETURN command. The RETURN command tells the computer that it has reached the end of a subroutine. It causes the computer to return to the command following GOSUB that sent it to the subroutine.

The following program illustrates the mechanics of using the GOSUB and RETURN commands to control the use of a subroutine. It also shows the advantage of writing a special process as a subroutine once in a program, then using it several times. If you change the program so the computer pauses for a count of 500 or 1500, this advantage should become readily apparent.

```
100 PRINT "THIS PROGRAM USES A SUBROUTINE"
110 GOSUB 900
120 PRINT "TO MAKE THE COMPUTER PAUSE"
130 GOSUB 900
140 PRINT "AFTER PRINTING EACH LINE"
150 GOSUB 900
160 PRINT "SO YOU WILL HAVE TIME TO READ IT"
170 GOSUB 900
180 PRINT "BEFORE THE NEXT LINE APPEARS"
190 GOSUB 900
200 PRINT
210 PRINT "WITHOUT THE GOSUB COMMAND"
220 GOSUB 900
230 PRINT "THE FOR . . . NEXT LOOP CONTROLLING THE
      PAUSE"
240 GOSUB 900
250 PRINT "WOULD HAVE TO HAVE BEEN TYPED 10 TIMES."
260 GOSUB 900
270 PRINT "WHAT'S WORSE, TO CHANGE THE SPEED OF
      PRINTING"
280 GOSUB 900
290 PRINT "YOU WOULD HAVE TO RE-TYPE 10 LINES IN-
      STEAD OF 1."
300 GOSUB 900
310 PRINT
320 END
```

```
900 FOR P = 1 TO 1000
910 NEXT
920 RETURN
```

If a computer encounters a RETURN statement when it is not performing a GOSUB command, it will issue an error message because it will not know where to return. The END command in line 320 keeps the computer from proceeding into the subroutine statements at the end of the main program. Without that END, the computer would fall-through the sequential statements until it reached the RETURN and stopped with an error message.

When you write subroutines in BASIC, they should be isolated from the rest of the program so the computer can only run into their statements as the result of a GOSUB command. Also, each subroutine should have only one entry point (the starting line number) and only one exit point (the RETURN statement).

A program can include as many different subroutines as you choose to write. One subroutine can include a GOSUB command to perform another subroutine. But, the programmer must be careful when nesting subroutines this way not to accidentally create an endless loop of subroutines calling each other. No programmer would ever write a useless pair of subroutines like:

```
900 GOSUB 950
910 RETURN
950 GOSUB 900
960 RETURN
```

The computer would flip back and forth between lines 900 and 950 without ever reaching a return statement to get back to the main program. However, if you do not map out your program designs before writing your statements, it is easy to include statements inside subroutines that will produce the same results as this absurd example.

One of the most common subroutines for business programs provides rounding to the nearest cent. When discount prices and taxes are computed using percentages, they will often create answers that involve a fraction of a cent. Yet payments must always be in whole cents. Figure 8-2 is the flowchart for a dollars and cents rounding program. You have already used the INT function to round to the nearest whole number. The nearest whole number in prices is dollars, so before rounding you must change the units to cents (box 900). Then you can add one-half unit and round down (boxes 910 and 915). Finally you have to change the units back to dollars (box 930).

If you included this subroutine in a program, it could be used any time you wanted to round the value in the variable N to the nearest cent. The subroutine would not round a value in a variable named A, or T or anything but N. So each use of the subroutine would have to be preceded by a LET N= statement storing the value to be rounded in the variable used by the subroutine.

The program that ends this chapter uses the rounding subroutine three times: Lines 140-160 round the entered price and compares the result to the actual input to make sure that the entry did not include a fraction of a cent. Line 550 rounds the cash discount, and line 600 rounds the sales tax (computed at 6 percent of the subtotal). Remember the importance of error testing in INPUT loops and notice the use of default values (lines 100 and 510) as you try this program, or alter it to make it better fit your own needs.

```
 10 PRINT TAB(8);"CASH REGISTER"
 20 PRINT
 30 LET S = 0
100 LET P = 0
110 PRINT"PRICE (PRESS ENTER WHEN DONE)";
120 INPUT P
130 IF P <= 0 THEN 500   (end of data)
140 LET N = P
150 GOSUB 900
160 IF N = P THEN 190   (input is ok.)
```

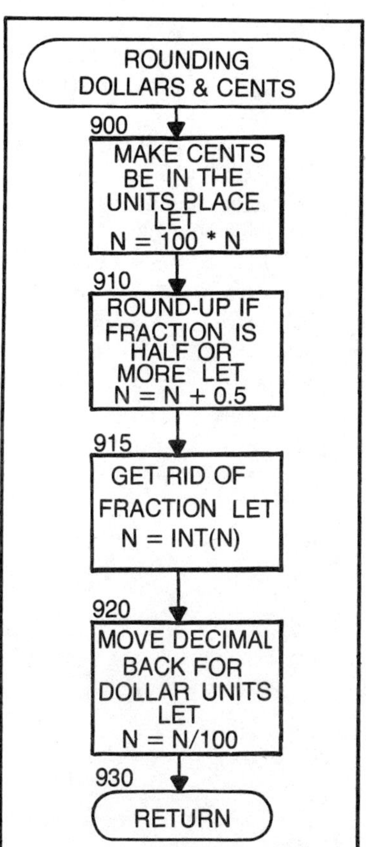

Fig. 8-2. Subroutine for rounding dollars and cents.

```
170 PRINT "PRICE MUST BE IN DOLLARS & CENTS."
180 GOTO 100
190 LET S = S + P   (add to subtotal)
200 GOTO 100
(end of order—time to handle totals)
500 PRINT "THE SUBTOTAL IS: $"; S
510 LET D = 0   (default is no discount)
520 PRINT "DISCOUNT PERCENT (IF ANY)";
530 INPUT D
540 IF D < 0 OR D > 20 THEN 700 (bad discount)
545 LET N = S * D/100   (/100 converts % to decimal)
550 GOSUB 900
560 LET S = S – N   (subtract discount from total)
570 IF N = 0 THEN 590
580 PRINT "YOUR DISCOUNT IS: "; N
585 PRINT "NEW SUBTOTAL IS: $"; S
590 LET N = .06 * S   (compute tax)
600 GOSUB 900
610 PRINT "SALES TAX ADDS: "; N
620 PRINT "GRAND TOTAL IS: $"; S + N
630 END
700 PRINT "DISCOUNT RATE MUST BE BETWEEN 0 & 20 %."
710 GOTO 510
(rounding subroutine)
900 LET N = 100 * N
910 LET N = N + 0.5
915 LET N = INT(N)
920 LET N = N / 100
930 RETURN
```

Chapter 9

Putting It All Together

Previous chapters covered a wide variety of programming tools. You have become at least vaguely familiar with the most common BASIC commands, with using flowcharts to map out program designs, and with programming structures for constructing high-quality programs. Now it is time to put these tools together in a professional approach to programming.

Professional programming is not the same thing as paid programming. Many people, hired as paid programmers, fail to produce professional-quality programs. Many top-quality programs are produced by people who write programs as a hobby or as a minor part of their jobs. The criteria that distinguish professional programs from experimental or "quick-and-dirty" programs are measures of long-range quality:

1. A professional program will not produce erroneous results. The minimum requirement for any good program is that it produces the correct result. A quick-and-dirty program may produce the correct results when it receives normal input values. A quality program will also handle exceptional data and identify errors instead of preceeding to produce nonsensical results from bad input.

2. A professional program is flexible. It is designed to handle a general family of related problems, not just a specific instance. The design also makes it easy for the author or another programmer to modify the program when the rules of the problem change. For example, an educational program to drill students about the names of the presidents should allow a new name to be added (every four years or so) without any major effort.

3. A professional program is easy to read. Anybody who understands the problem the program is supposed to solve and who knows the fundamentals of the computer language should be able to understand what the

computer will do by simply reading the program. Unnecessary complexity in a program is a sign of programmer's fuzzy thinking. The best programs are not "clever;" they are so clear that you wonder "why didn't I think of that?"

4. Finally, A professional program uses the computer to its best advantage. If speed of operation is most important to the problem, then the programmer will spend the extra effort (and cost and computer memory) to make the program run as fast as possible. If the available memory is small, then the programmer will change his design to cut down on the memory requirements (at the expense of flexibility and speed of operation). The professional programmer does not force the people using his program to change their priorities to fit his program. He designs his program to fit their priorities.

Using the computer to its best advantage requires the in-depth knowledge of an experienced practitioner. The first three criteria are the foundation of good applications programming. They can, and should, be represented by your first computer programs.

LIFE CYCLE OF A PROGRAM

A computer program has a life of its own with five distinct stages: definition, design, translation, testing, and maintenance. The definition and design stages are like the formative years of a child. If they are given sufficient attention and care, then the adolescent stages of translation and testing will be short and relatively painless. If the early stages are ignored, then the tasks of translating the program into computer statements and testing for proper results are apt to be confused and prolonged to the extent that the program never enjoys a productive adulthood as a maintained program.

Definition of a program involves describing its purpose and its limits. The stage is often called the requirements analysis. When it is finished, you know what the program needs to do in order to achieve its purpose. The definition describes *what* the program will do. It should be completed before you worry about *how* the program will work.

Design of a program involves developing a working plan for accomplishing the already defined purpose. In large projects the design stage is usually divided into a systems analysis phase and a program specification phase. The systems analysis phase produces an overall strategic plan, complete with a schedule and costs. Since a large project involves several related programs, the systems analysis also describes what each specific program will do and how the different programs will fit together. This phase has minimal relevance to small projects. The program specification phase of design is critically important to nearly all programming projects. This phase produces the map showing exactly how the program will work. The map will often be in the form of a top-level flowchart and as many lower-level flowcharts as necessary to make each step in the program clear. The map will be accompanied by a data dictionary explaining the meaning of each variable in the program.

Translation of a program involves converting the written design into statements in a computer language. This is the stage that most people think of as programming. Yet, it normally requires between one-sixth and one-third of the programming effort. If the design stage has been done well, then the translation stage is an almost mechanical task of coding commands for the computer.

Testing a program involves hunting for errors and correcting them. Testing may reveal mistakes made during the translation stage, but it also may identify problems which were overlooked in the design. Anything that prevents a program from fulfilling its defined purpose should be straightened out before testing is completed. Now, programmers tend to be proud people who do not like to admit they make many mistakes. They like to describe the problems with their programs as *bugs* that crept into the program from the outside. Fixing a program so that it will work right is called *debugging.* Designing a program thoroughly enough that you don't leave any holes for bugs to creep in is called professional programming.

Once a program has been fully tested, it starts to save people time and effort. It is trusted (sometimes more than it should be) to produce correct results. The success and value of the completed program can be evaluated by comparing it to its original definition. A good program accomplishes its purpose, whatever that purpose may be.

Maintenance of a program involves keeping it active and useful. Maintenance may be as simple as keeping a good copy of the program and its instructions available for use. It may also require making changes to the program to keep it useful when conditions affecting its purpose change. Or, a program may be changed to enhance its use with new ideas. You cannot accurately predict the maintenance that one of your programs will need, but in our rapidly changing world you can expect that some maintenance effort will be needed to keep your program useful for more than a couple of years. Again, a thorough job of program design will make it much easier to keep a program up to date with later maintenance changes.

DEFINING THE PROBLEM

Finding the definition of a problem is easy in schools. The teacher gives out an assignment and that is the problem. The assignment tells you exactly what you need to accomplish.

Most real programming problems are not handed to programmers as clearly described assignments. They start as vague ideas: "Can the computer do . . . ?" "There's a problem with accounting (or inventory control, or some other aspect of a business); let's see if the programmer can help straighten it out." "I'm getting tired of spending so much time preparing these reports. Can't the computer help me?" None of these starting points really tell what must be done.

Many programmers have sat down to discuss a problem with somebody once and then have gone off to write a program to solve that problem. Several weeks or months later they have returned to show off their solution to the problem. The usual response is something like "That's not what I meant at all. Your program won't do me any good." The programmer gets irate because the program does exactly what he heard the other person say he needed during the original conversation. In reality, the other person only had described the general nature of his problem because he was not familiar enough with computers to understand how to describe his problem in precise enough terms to be translated directly into computer statements. The programmer was not familiar enough with the particular type of problem to recognize all the complications that might arise. He only knew what he thought he heard the other person say.

Good problem definition takes time and effort. You must explore the problem and think of all the difficulties that might arise. You need to convert general ideas into specific requirements. If part of the problem includes printing results on a video screen or on paper, you should make a realistic mock-up showing sample results. Sometimes people don't know what they want until they see it.

Most important, whenever you are going to write a program for someone else to use, thoroughly review your definition of the problem with the people who are going to use it. Do not tell them, "This is what the computer can do for you." Instead, ask "Is this what you really want?"; "Are there any changes that would make the results better or easier to understand?" You may get requests for things that you can't make the computer do. You and the user may have to make compromises or leave part of the problem unsolved, but at least you will know that when you complete your program it will be something the other person actually wants to use. If you discover that the other person wants the impossible or does not know what he wants (and both situations do arise in real life), then you can stop working on the problem before you have wasted too much time and effort.

This chapter will trace the full development of a useful program. The general purpose of the program will be to determine how much money you would accumulate by putting money into a savings account every month. The money in the account will earn interest. That interest is calculated by multiplying the balance in the account by the interest rate. The total savings will equal the sum of all the money you deposit plus all the interest.

You may close the book now and go write a program that will accomplish that general purpose. Your program will probably be a good program, but you will have to make a number of assumptions about the detailed requirements of the problem. How often is the interest computed and added to the balance? What is the interest rate? Can the interest rate change from year to year? Will the amount of money deposited be the same each month? The answers to each of these questions will change the definition of the problem.

It is tempting to choose the answers that make it easiest to write a program. Why make more work for yourself than necessary? But if you oversimplify the problem, it will cease to be useful. If you write the program so that it only computes the results of depositing twenty dollars a month into an account that pays 5 percent interest annually for ten years, it will be of no use to anyone trying to consider alternatives.

You could decide to play it safe by making your program handle any possible version of the problem. That decision could make you spend so much time working out all the unusual possibilities that you could not complete the program on time. Also, allowing both the interest rate and the amount deposited to change every month would mean that the person using the program would have to enter those values for each month. A twenty-year savings plan would require entering 240 deposits and 240 interest rates. Many people would not want to spend that much effort.

Figure 9-1 describes the purpose of the Savings Plan program. The definition of the problem is completed by defining the output and the input that will be used to meet the purpose.

The output description says that the program will tell only the total savings, the accumulated interest, and the total deposits at the end of the savings plan. Other definitions might require printing the balance at the end of each year, or showing the interest and deposits month by month. This definition does not specify the format of the output. You may assume that any readable presentation of the results is acceptable. If the appearance of the output is important, then a sample form must be part of the definition.

The input is defined to be the amount of monthly savings (the same for each month), the interest rate (one rate for the life of the plan), and the number of years in the savings plan. To use this program, you will only have to enter three numbers. Those three inputs will let you see the results of a wide range of possible savings alternatives. This definition should make the program both easy to use and reasonably useful.

The definition is not complete until all the decisions about what the program will do have been made. You will need to decide how often to compute the interest: daily, monthly, quarterly, or annually. That decision will affect the total amount of interest. Since the deposits are made monthly, it seems reasonable to compute the interest at the end of each month. This choice also simplifies the program because the balance won't change between interest payments.

What values are acceptable as input for the interest rate, monthly deposits, and number of years of savings? The editing criteria used to prevent keying errors from fouling up the answers should be part of the definition. For this problem, you may restrict the number of years to a lifetime—between 1 and 75 years—and not allow any fraction of a year. The minimum deposit is one dollar (zero or negative amounts do not provide savings) and obviously cannot include a fraction of a cent.

The interest rate is the item most likely to be entered wrong because it can be expressed as either a decimal fraction or a percentage. The decimal fraction would use a number only one-hundredth the size of the

Purpose—To calculate the amount of money saved by depositing a certain amount of money into a savings account each month for several years.
Output—Total balance at the end of the savings plan, with accumulated interest and the total amount actually deposited.
Input—Amount of monthly deposits, interest rate, and number of years in the savings plan.
Limitations—Amount of deposit must be at least one dollar per month. Interest rate is annual percentage. It must be between 1 percent and 50 percent. Rates may include a fraction of a percent (like 5.75 percent).

The savings plan must last a whole number of years, at least one and not more than 75 years. Interest is to be compounded monthly at the end of each month.

The deposit is to be made at the first of each month. Money amounts (deposits and interest) must be paid in dollars and cents. Fractions of a cent are not allowed.

Fig. 9-1. Program definition for Savings Plan program.

equivalent percentage. To keep the figures realistic, the program requesting interest rates as percentages should accept only values greater than one. (This will identify any interest rate entered as a decimal fraction to be an error.) Also, interest rates of 50 percent or more can be eliminated as totally unrealistic.

Spending this much time developing a detailed definition may seem to make the problem more complicated. Yet the decisions that were made as part of this definition would have to be made before the program was completed. Making the definitions precise before you start writing the program gives you a chance to be sure those decisions will be agreed upon. You and whoever you are writing the program for will have the same understanding of the problem.

The written definition becomes the standard for judging the final product. The definition for a large project may be a long printed report that is formally approved by a committee before any money is allocated for programmers. The definition for a small project may be a single page of notes you write for yourself. In either case, the definition stage of a programming project is necessary. You should always know where you are trying to go before you work hard trying to get there.

DESIGNING THE PROGRAM

The design phase is the most creative part of a programming project. What needs to be accomplished has already been defined (often by someone else). Now, the programmer has to use his ingenuity to figure out how to make the computer satisfy those needs. There is never a single right answer to a design problem. Twenty different programmers might produce a dozen different designs to solve the same problem. As long as they met all the requirements of the definition phase, the different designs would be right answers.

Design involves developing both *process* and *data* relationships. *Process* is the series of steps that will eventually be translated into statements of a computer language. *Data* includes the variables and specific values the program will use. Flowcharts are used to describe process. A data dictionay is used to describe the data relationships.

In designing a program from the top down, you should start with the definition of the problem and sketch a simple plan of the major tasks. The Savings Plan program will require three major steps: (1) getting the input values, (2) calculating the change in the total each month, and (3) printing the results at the end of the savings period. These three steps are shown in Fig. 9-2. This flowchart also adds a choice at the end to decide whether the person wants to see the results of a different savings plan or quit. This added option makes the top level of the flowchart look like a simple loop.

The problem definition also provides the start of the data dictionary. You know the program will need variables to hold the required input values for the amount deposited each month, the annual interest rate, and the number of years in the savings plan. The output definition adds variables to hold the balance in the savings account, the total amount deposited, and the total accumulated interest. The form of the data dictionary can be a simple list of the variable names that will be used in the program, a short description of what they are used for, and a statement of the types of units used (dollars or cents; feet, meters or miles; etc.). The start of the data dictionary for the savings program might look like:

AM Amount deposited each month (in dollars)
IR Annual interest rate (in percent)
YR Number of years in savings plan (whole years)
B Balance in savings account (in dollars)
TD Total deposited (in dollars)
TI Total interest accumulated (in dollars)

When the top level of the design seems clear, then each of the major tasks can be expanded. The monthly calculations are the center of the whole program, so that is a good candidate for the next design effort. The monthly deposit is made at the first of each month. It should be added to the balance—step 1 of the next level of flowcharting. The interest is calculated at the end of the month. In step 2 the amount of interest will equal the interest rate multiplied by the balance in the account. One small problem: the interest rate for a month is not the same as the annual interest rate. Add a new variable for monthly interest to the data dictionary. The last thing that has to be done each month is to add the interest to the balance. Then the next month the whole process will be repeated. The repetition can be handled by a loop. The flowchart for this series of thoughts is shown in Fig. 9-3.

The data dictionary expands as the flowchart expands. The monthly calculations will use an interest rate that is one-twelfth the annual interest rate. A variable will be needed to hold the amount of interest computed each month. Controlling the loop requires knowing the total number of months (twelve times the number of years) and the use of a variable to count the number of times the loop is used. The new entries in the dictionary might look like:

IM Interest rate by the month (annual rate / 12)
IA Interest amount each month (in dollars and cents)

M Number of months of savings (number of years * 12)
CT Counter for loop

Completing the second-level design requires expanding the *Get Input* and *Print Results* boxes of the top-level flowchart. You will also need to add some steps to prepare the variables for the monthly calculations. The balance of the account has to start at zero (before the first deposit). The number of months and the monthly interest rate have to be calculated. A completed flowchart for the entire savings plan is shown in Fig. 9-4. No new entries have been added to the data dictionary by this expansion.

This design looks complete enough that you could translate it into a BASIC program. However, the object is not just to produce a program, but to satisfy all the requirements of the definition. The purpose of the program

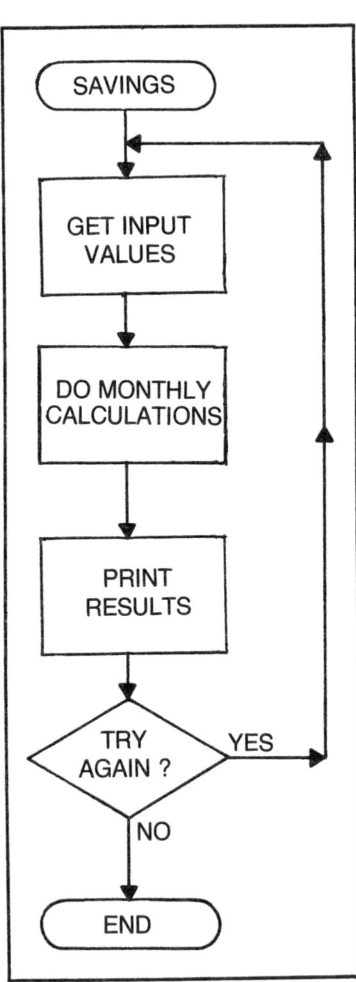

Fig. 9-2. Top-level flowchart for Savings program.

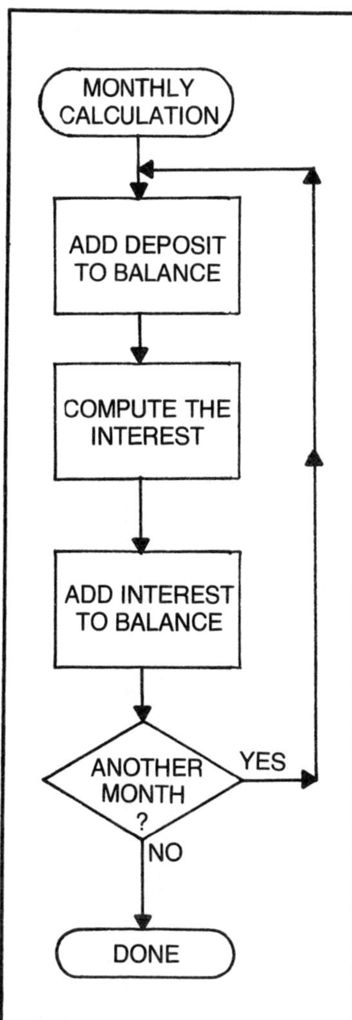

Fig. 9-3. Monthly calculations flowchart.

was to calculate the amount of money saved by depositing a certain amount into a savings account each month for several years. The output was supposed to be the total balance with accumulated interest and the total amount deposited. So far, so good. The design matches the definition of the problem. The user gets to choose the amount to deposit, the interest rate, and the number of years. The input has to satisfy certain requirements.

Wait a minute. The flowchart does not make sure that the amount deposited will be at least one dollar, that the interest rate will be between 1 and 50 percent or that a whole number of years will be used. The design needs to be improved to cover the defined requirements.

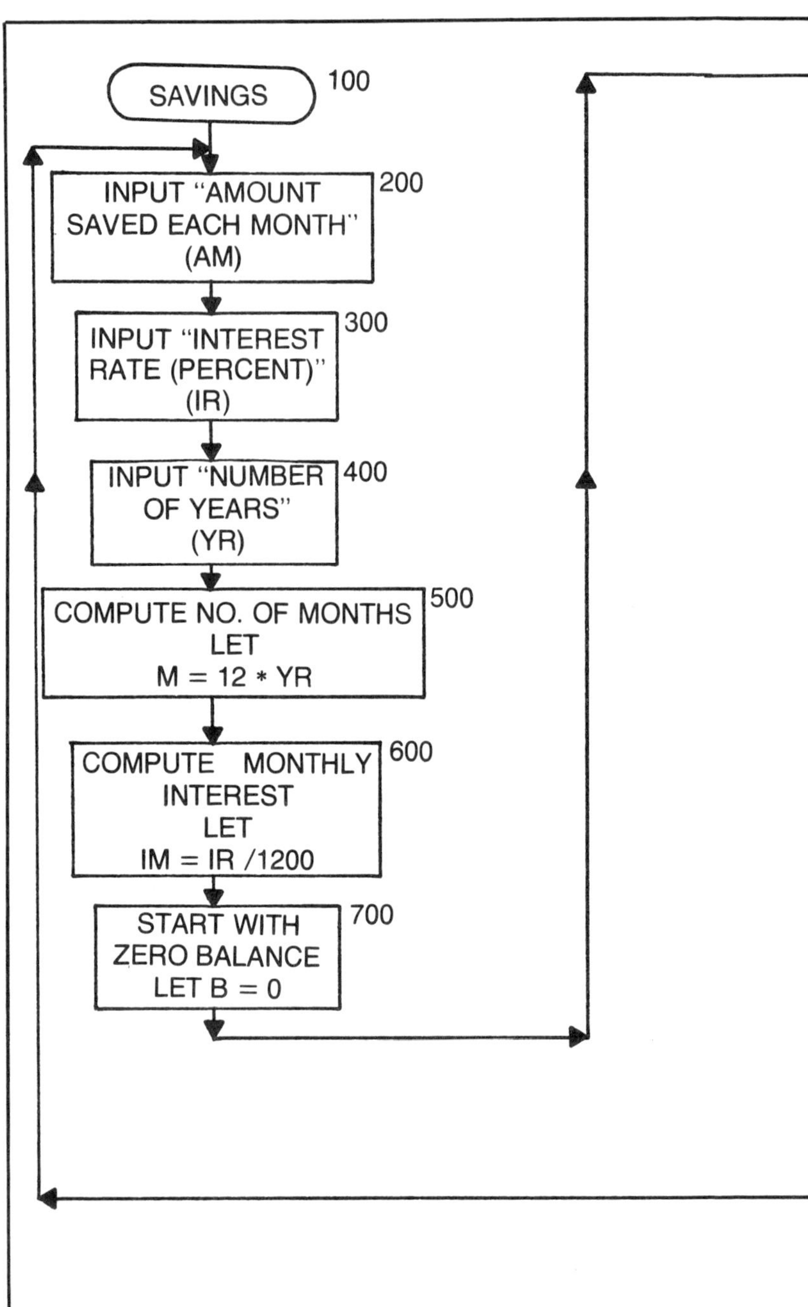

Fig. 9-4. Expanded flowchart for Savings Plan program.

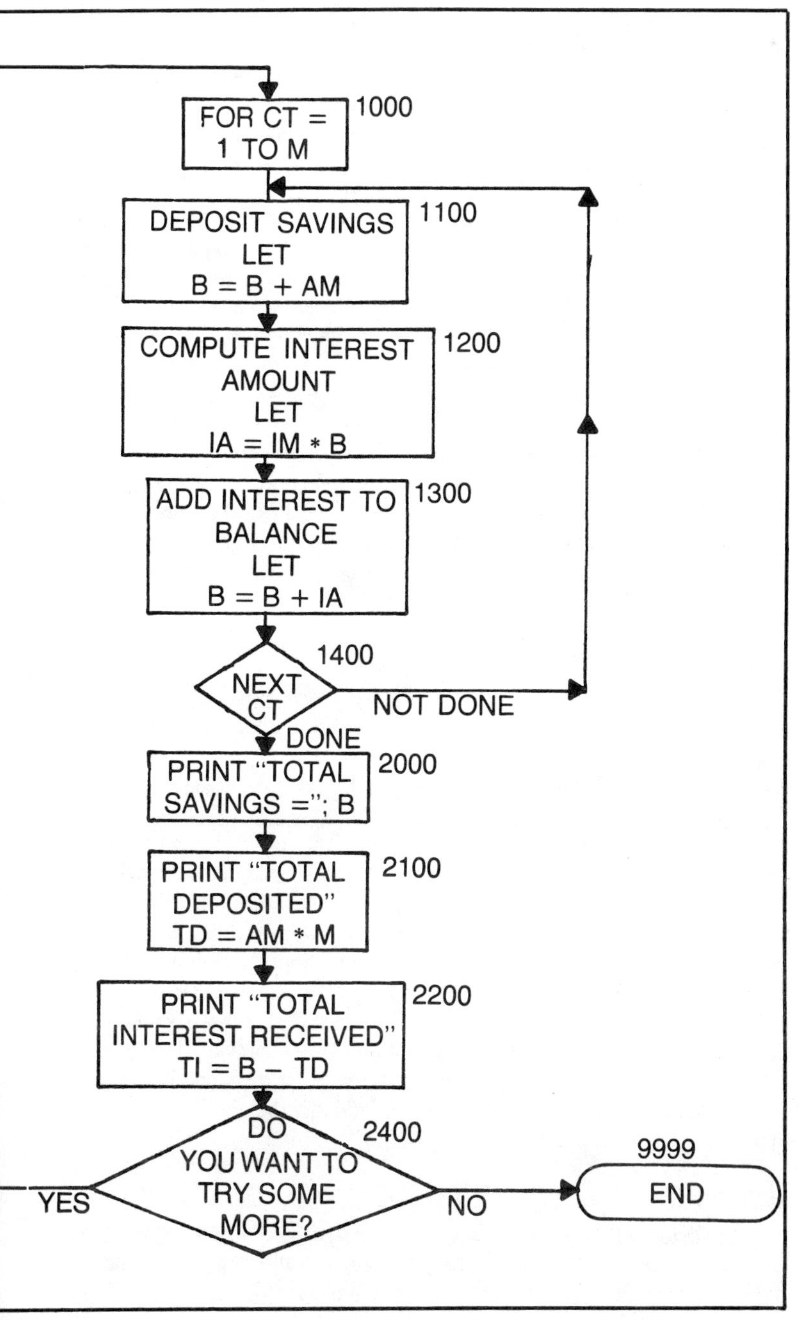
FOR CT =
1 TO M
1000
DEPOSIT SAVINGS
LET
B = B + AM
1100
COMPUTE INTEREST
AMOUNT
LET
IA = IM * B
1200
ADD INTEREST TO
BALANCE
LET
B = B + IA
1300
NEXT
CT
1400
NOT DONE
DONE
PRINT "TOTAL
SAVINGS ="; B
2000
PRINT "TOTAL
DEPOSITED"
TD = AM * M
2100
PRINT "TOTAL
INTEREST RECEIVED"
TI = B – TD
2200
DO
YOU WANT TO
TRY SOME
MORE?
2400
YES
NO
9999
END

The missing requirements can easily be added to the design by changing the three input boxes into input loops that test for good values. This expansion is simple enough that it does not require an additional flowchart. The flowchart does not have to include every statement to be used in the final program. It does have to be complete enough so it is obvious to you that you can follow the design to write a program that correctly meets all of the requirements of the definition of your program.

The design phase often takes more time and effort than the translation phase. In a large project, the design phase will result in a notebook full of process and data descriptions. In a small project, a single flowchart with a list of variables may suffice. In either case, you should be able to read the design and understand how to convert it into a computer program and how it satisfies every part of the definition.

The first draft of a design often turns out to be unsatisfactory. You will discover difficulties you had not thought of before when you start mapping out a solution to a problem. If one design starts becoming too complicated or cannot meet all of the requirements of the definition, throw it away and start over. Your first effort will not be wasted. You will have gained a better understanding of the problem which should make your next attempt work better. It is much easier to change a design on paper than it is to try to revise a program based on an inadequate design.

TRANSLATING THE DESIGN INTO A PROGRAM

Translating a program from a good design into the statements of a program is a fairly mechanical task. The programmer's job is similar to that of a scholar translating a book from one language to another. The design describes the program in a combination of English, mathematical equations, and graphic symbols. The computer can only understand a program written in BASIC or some other computer language. The programmer needs to code the program design into the computer without changing its meaning.

The first step in translating a program into BASIC is often writing line numbers next to each box in the flowchart. This helps establish the organization of the program and identify the major sections. The line numbers should be spaced far enough apart that you can type a number of statements for each box. The line numbers added to Fig. 9-4 show the three sections of the top-level flowchart. The *Get data* section has line numbers less than a thousand. The one-thousand line numbers are used for the monthly calculations, while the two-thousand line numbers identify the *Print results* section.

REMARKS

The main audience for the computer language version of your program is the computer. Nevertheless, some human beings will read the computer code. The program should be written so that it is easy for people as well as computers to understand.

Including comments or remarks between computer statements can make it much easier for someone else to follow a program listing you've written. BASIC includes a special command, REM (short for remark), for inserting remarks into a program. When the computer sees the REM command, it ignores the rest of the statement and proceeds to the next statement. But when another programmer sees a REM command in a program, he should know that it contains a message or title that helps explain the program.

The first lines in a program usually should be remarks identifying the name of the program, the name of the author or designer, and the date it was written. This information allows you to match a program listing with any written documentation on its design and use. If the program is copyrighted, then the copyright notice should also appear as an opening remark. The opening remarks for many programs will be as simple as:

```
10 REM SAVINGS PLAN
20 REM BY R. GALBRAITH   JULY, 1981
```

Other remarks are put in a program as titles for main sections and subroutines. These help people understand what each part of the program does. A series of asterisks or dashes in a remark line helps make it stand out from the rest of the program, so that you can quickly spot the beginning of sections and subroutines. For example:

```
 199 REM *** INPUT LOOPS ***
 499 REM *** INTEREST CALCULATIONS ***
 199 REM *** DISPLAY RESULTS ***
5000 REM *** ROUNDING TO CENTS SUBROUTINE ***
5050 REM ---------------------------------
```

Some versions of BASIC use the apostrophe (') as an abbreviation for REM. These versions allow remarks to appear on the same line as another statement. Anything appearing after the apostrophe (unless the apostrophe is part of a string value) is treated as a remark by the computer. Thus, the line GOSUB 5000 'ROUNDING, would be interpreted by the computer as identical to: GOSUB 5000 without the attached comment.

The use of remarks along with spacing within your statements will go a long way towards making your programs understandable. The remarks and any extra spaces do take up space in the computer's memory, so don't go overboard explaining each line. No amount of explaining will make up for a poor design, and a good design does not need too many remarks to make it understandable.

FOLLOWING THE FLOWCHART

The main task of translation involves converting each block on the flowchart (or other design plan) into one or more BASIC statements. You can generally start at the beginning and proceed in order until the end. However, there is no reason you could not start with any block you want and translate the blocks in any order. As long as you number the statements

```
10   REM  SAVINGS PLAN
20   REM  BY R. GALBRAITH    JULY, 1981
100    FOR CT = 1 TO 6
110    PRINT
120    NEXT
130    PRINT TAB(10);"SAVINGS PLAN"
140    PRINT "THIS PROGRAM CALCULATES HOW MUCH MONEY YOU WOULD HAVE"
150    PRINT "IF YOU DEPOSITED AN AMOUNT OF MONEY INTO AN INTEREST PAY
       ING"
160    PRINT "ACCOUNT ON THE FIRST OF EACH MONTH FOR SEVERAL YEARS."
170    PRINT
199  REM *** INPUT LOOPS ***
200    PRINT"HOW MUCH DO YOU WANT TO DEPOSIT EACH MONTH";
210    INPUT AM
220    IF AM  >= 1 THEN 250
230    PRINT"THE MINIMUM DEPOSIT IS ONE DOLLAR."
240    GOTO 200
250    LET N = AM * 100
260    IF N = INT(N) THEN 300
270    PRINT"YOU CAN'T DEPOSIT A FRACTION OF A CENT."
280    GOTO200
300    PRINT"WHAT INTEREST RATE WILL YOU RECEIVE";
310    INPUT IR
320    IF IR > 1 AND IR < 50  THEN 400
330    PRINT"NOBODY PAYS THAT KIND OF INTEREST."
340    PRINT"NORMAL RATES ARE BETWEEN 5 AND 20 PERCENT."
350    GOTO 300
400    PRINT"HOW MANY YEARS WILL YOU SAVE";
410    INPUT YR
420    IF YR = INT(YR) THEN 450
430    PRINT"ENTER A WHOLE NUMBER OF YEARS, PLEASE."
440    GOTO 400
450    IF YR >= 1 THEN 480
```

Fig. 9-5. Savings Plan program listing.

```
460     PRINT"THAT IS ABSURD.  USE A POSITIVE NUMBER OF YEARS."
470     GOTO 400
480     IF YR < 75 THEN 500
490     PRINT"YOU WON'T LIVE THAT LONG -- USE A NUMBER LESS THAN 75."
495     GOTO 400
499 REM *** CALCULATIONS ***
500     LET M = 12 * YR
600     LET IM = IR / 1200
700     LET B = 0
800     PRINT
810     PRINT
820     PRINT"THE CALCULATIONS WILL BE COMPLETED IN A MOMENT."
1000    FOR CT = 1 TO M
1100    LET B = B + AM
1200    LET N = IM * B
1210    GOSUB 5000      'ROUNDING
1220    LET IA = N
1300    LET B = B + IA
1400    NEXT CT
1999 REM *** DISPLAY RESULTS ***
2000    PRINT
2010    PRINT"YOUR TOTAL SAVINGS WOULD BE:";TAB(40); B
2100    LET TD = AM * M
2110    PRINT"YOU WOULD HAVE DEPOSITED A TOTAL OF:";TAB(40); TD
2200    LET TI = B - TD
2210    PRINT"THE TOTAL INTEREST YOU EARNED WOULD BE:";TAB(40); TI
2300    PRINT
2310    PRINT
2400    PRINT"DO YOU WANT TO TRY A DIFFERENT SAVINGS PLAN (YES/NO)";
2410    INPUT A$
2420    IF A$ = "NO" THEN 9999
2430    IF A$ = "YES" THEN 2460
2440    PRINT"ANSWER EITHER 'YES' OR 'NO'";
```

```
2450     GOTO 2410
2460     PRINT
2470     PRINT
2480     GOTO 200
5000 REM *** ROUNDING TO CENTS SUBROUTINE ***
5010     LET N = 100 * N
5020     LET N = INT(N + .5)
5030     LET N = N / 100
5040     RETURN
5050 REM-----------------------------------------
9999     END
```

Fig. 9-5. Continued from page 119.

correctly and complete every block in the design, the statements will fit together in the end. You will probably discover that you have to leave blanks in some GOTO and GOSUB statements until you have written lines that establish the particular statement the program needs to GOTO.

Write your translation in pencil first. This allows you to read the entire program and correct any errors before they get into the computer. A few programmers are able to type their programs into the computer as they translate them. However, most people find they are more accurate and save time over the long run if they translate their programs on paper first and then type them into the computer as a separate step.

A complete translation of the Savings Plan program is listed in Fig. 9-5. You should be able to match it step by step with the flowchart in Fig. 9-4.

The first lines of the program display the name of the program and a brief explanation of its purpose. This allows the person using it to verify that they are running the program they want and informs them what the program will do even if they have not read anything about it. If the program were copyrighted, the opening display would include a copyright notice so the user would know it is illegal to make copies of the program for distribution.

The box to input the amount of deposit is translated into lines 200 through 280. The definition of the problem requires that the program ensure the amount is at least one dollar and does not include a fraction of a cent. After you have written a large number of input loops, these lines will be obvious and not require a design any more detailed than the single box. If you are not sure how to code the lines, you might want to make a more detailed flowchart first that shows each test of the input data (see Fig. 9-6). Determining whether the amount includes too many decimal places (frac-

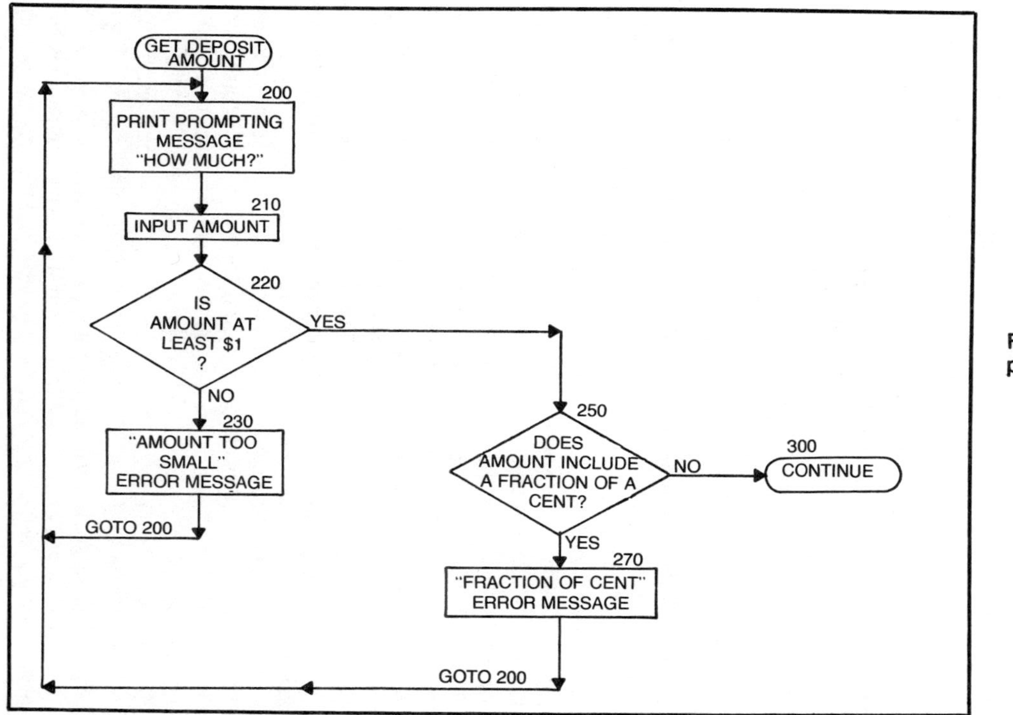

Fig. 9-6. Detailed flowchart for deposit input loop.

tions of a cent) requires multiplying the number by 100 to make cents the unit (line 250), then using the integer function to determine if the result is a whole number (line 260). This test adds a new variable (N) to the data dictionary.

The next two input boxes on the flowchart also translate into input loops. These are similar to the loop for the deposit amount. The boxes labeled 500 through 1100 each translate into a single matching BASIC statement.

Interest is added to savings accounts in one-cent units. The calculation in line 1200 will often produce results with fractions of a cent. The interest needs to be rounded before it is added to the balance. For now, you can enter a single GOSUB statement to handle the rounding, and write a note to yourself that you will need to write a dollars-and-cents rounding subroutine starting at line 5000. The subroutine can be written after the main program is completed.

Printing the results can be done with a straightforward translation of the flowchart. The boxes labeled 2100 and 2200 each translated into two statements, one to compute the value and one to print it.

The final decision translates into another input loop. This time the editing requirements are not specified by the design. You could easily check for the first letter only (using the LEFT$ function) and/or include a default value of either YES or NO to improve the program without violating the original definition.

To complete the program, it is necessary to add the rounding subroutine (lines 5000 through 5040) and the END statement for the program (line 9999). The rounding subroutine uses the same statements as the one discussed in Chapter 8.

The first run of the program might work (if you entered the statements accurately), but the output would not be attractive and easy to read. Also, the person might get impatient waiting for the program to finish the calculations if a large number of years were entered. Adding blank lines (800, 810, 2000, 2300, 2310, 2460, and 2470) can space out the displays and make them easier to read. Printing a warning message (line 820) before the computer enters a long group of calculations will reassure the user that nothing is wrong when the computer appears to do nothing for a while. These small program refinements are seldom included in the design but are added during the translation to improve the final program.

Save your program on a disk or cassette as soon as you have finished typing it in. If you try to run the program first, there is always the possibility that it will contain a mistake which erases the program from memory. Even if your program is perfect, static electricity may be somewhere in the computer system and might erase the program. Few things are more frustrating than spending an hour or more typing in a long program and then losing it because you forgot to save the program.

If you are working on a system with disks, saving a program is fast enough that you will probably not want to wait until the program is completed before you save it. After every ten minutes or so of typing, you can issue the command: SAVE "SAVINGS" (or whatever short name you choose for the program). Then if the computer runs into a problem, you can LOAD the first part of the program back in and never lose more than a few minutes worth of typing effort.

PROGRAM TESTING

Once you have typed a complete program into the computer, you need to test it to make sure it works properly. The best testing uses the capabilities of both the programmer and the computer.

You are probably not the world's greatest typist. You will likely make a mistake or two each time you type in a long program. The first step in testing is simply to proofread the program. It helps if you have a listing of the program printed on paper, but if your computer does not have a printer, you can accomplish the same result by listing a few lines at a time.

Read each line carefully, looking for any typing mistakes. Compare the program to the flowchart. You should be able to check off each box in your flowchart when you read the matching statements. If the statements do not match the design, then you probably either left out some lines or made a mistake in typing a line number (which would make the statement appear in the wrong part of the program).

Double check the decisions in the program. It is easy to reverse the logic of a comparison by typing the greater than sign (>) when you meant less than. Think through the "equals" case for number comparisons. Do you really mean less than (<) or not greater than (<=)? These comparisons cause problems in programs because many different English words are used for comparisons, and comparisons in English speech are often inprecise.

Try to be your own worst critic. Any trouble spots you find and eliminate from your program will be an error that nobody else sees. Testing for the strange things that might possibly go wrong before you claim that the program is finished will make other people learn to trust your programs. Programmers with good reputations probably make as many errors initially as programmers with bad reputations. The difference is that the more professional programmers avoid passing their mistakes on to the people who use their programs.

After you have studied your program and corrected any errors you spotted, it is time to run the program. Start your test runs using input values that are easy to calculate. That way you can do the calculations yourself to verify the computer's answer. Easy values for the savings plan would be a 100 dollar deposit, 12 percent interest (1 percent each month), and a 1 year term.

At the end of the first month, the balance would be $100 deposited plus $1 interest (multiplying by 1 percent is the same as dividing by 100). The second monthly deposit would increase the total to $201, which would earn $2.01 interest. Continue the calculations on a piece of paper. The twelfth month should start with a balance of $1168.25 and add a deposit of $100. The interest on the new balance is 12.68. The final total is $1280.93. The deposits total $1200, so the remaining 80.93 is the accumulated interest. Run the program to see if it produces the same results. If it does not, then you made a mistake in either the program or the calculations.

Many of the mistakes you can make in a program will produce a statement the computer cannot interpret. Whenever the computer encounters such a statement, it will print an error message telling you what line number has the error and giving a clue as to what the error is. You can generally correct an error promptly after the computer has spotted it for you. Some programmers get lazy about their testing, expecting the computer to find the errors for them. This is an expensive and potentially dangerous practice, particularly in BASIC. The BASIC language is generally interpretive, which means that the computer pays attention to the content of a statement each time it tries to execute that statement. Each time you run a test of most programs, only some of the statements get executed. Every place your program has a choice (such as an IF . . . THEN statement), the test may take only one of the paths. The computer will never notice any of the statements on the path not taken.

You cannot be sure your program works correctly until you have tested all the paths. The flowchart should help you identify the test values you can use to try each path. The test should include absurd input values (like −200 for deposits, 500 percent interest, and −2 years) to make sure the input loops are treating bad values according to the program definition.

Program testing should be systematic. Try the important combinations, keeping track of successes and problems. A complex program may allow for too many options to test all possible combinations of options. You should still test each individual option at least once. You will probably never be absolutely sure that a complex program is completely free of problems. (Not even IBM will guarantee that its programs will work correctly for all possible combinations of values.) You should at least be willing to bet anybody that your tested program will work properly with the first values they try.

Testing is not a quick task. The testing phase of program development usually takes longer than the translation phase. It is not uncommon for testing to require more time than the definition, design, and translation phases combined. This is especially likely if not enough time was spent on the definition and design to make the program clearly understood.

ISOLATING PROBLEMS

Sooner or later, a test run of a program will demonstrate that there is a problem without showing you which statement or statements need to be changed. Even if the computer prints an error message saying that it ran into trouble in line 800, it does not necessarily mean that line 800 should be changed. The problem may have been created by a mistake in an earlier statement.

The computer will recognize an error when it runs into a NEXT command when it is not executing a loop that started with a FOR command. The mistake may be a NEXT command typed in the wrong place, or it could be caused by forgetting to type in the matching FOR statement several lines earlier. The same problem could be caused by a GOTO or IF . . . THEN statement anywhere in the program that directed the computer to enter into the middle of a loop. Similar problems can result in the computer detecting an error when it reaches a RETURN statement without having been sent there by a GOSUB command.

Other problems won't be identified by the computer at all. The program may run to completion satisfactorily but produce a wrong result. Your first try at the Savings Plan program might tell you that the result of depositing $100 a month at 12 percent interest for a year was a total balance of $101. Obviously the program did not do the calculations correctly. After you have checked to see that the LET statements seem correct, there are some less obvious errors to check:

1. The wrong variable name may be used in a LET or PRINT statement. Be especially careful with names containing I or 1 and O or 0.

2. A variable may not have been given the correct initial value (usually zero) before the program started adding to it.

3. A variable may have been given the correct initial value at the wrong time. For instance, if the statement LET B = 0 came between the FOR CT = 1 TO M and LET B = B + AM statements, the balance of the savings plan would start over with zero each month.

4. A loop is repeated either too many or too few times. Most often the number of repetitions will be off by one because of the vague meaning of words like "between." (Are the numbers 1 and 10 included when you ask for a number between one and ten?)

5. A variable is used to hold more than one value. When the same variable name is used with a second meaning, the value for the first meaning is lost. Another reference to the variable for the first meaning will produce a misleading result. This mistake occurs most often with variable names used as counters in both the main part of a program and a subroutine. The counting in the subroutine will change the value of the variable used by the main program after the return. The main defense against accidentally reusing a variable name for a different purpose is maintaining a complete data dictionary as you create your program.

Even if you are aware of the things that might be causing a particular problem, you might not be able to spot the mistake when you read the program listing. Everybody has a tendency to fill in the blanks when they are reading, especially if they already think they know what the statements say. Sometimes it is necessary to add special computer instructions to help isolate a problem in the middle of a large program.

The two most common types of instructions for isolating problems in a program are data dumps and program traces. A *data dump* displays values of variables at a specific point in a program. It dumps the content of some parts of the computer's memory onto the screen. A *program trace* causes a message to be printed each time a specific part of the program is executed so you can see the order in which different blocks are performed and count the number of times a loop is repeated. Both data dumps and program traces are commonly referred to as *debugging statements.*

Debugging statements are temporarily added to a program in places that you suspect might contain an error. After the program has been corrected, the debugging statements are deleted so they won't clutter up the final program.

If the Savings Plan program you type into your computer gives wrong results at the end, you might suspect that the monthly calculations are done the wrong number of times. You have no evidence from running the program because the calculational loop does not contain any PRINT or INPUT statements. Your suspicion could be confirmed or disproven if you added a new line 1001 PRINT"STARTING A MONTHLY CALCULATION" and ran the program again. By counting the number of times that message appeared, you would know exactly how many times the loop was repeated. Tracing statements are most often useful to check that subroutines are being entered and left in the correct sequence. You might discover that a perfectly good rounding subroutine is not helping your program because the computer never reaches a GOSUB command, or that a combination of IF . . . THEN and GOTO statements is causing the computer to completely skip some important statements.

A dump statement could be used to check the calculations inside the calculational loop. Adding statements 1002 PRINT B, AM and 1221 PRINT B, IA to the program would let you check the calculations month by month to spot any errors before they became compounded.

There comes a day in the life of every programmer (and it usually falls on a Friday), when he has a program that produces the wrong result but he can't for the life of him find an error in the program. He has tried everything he can think of. He has read the listing until he has it practically memorized. He has added traces and dumps in all the complicated parts of the program. Nothing seems to work. It is not time to resign and promise never to write another program. It is time to use the ultimate tool for program debugging: a fresh perspective.

You should develop the habit of reading other people's programs and having other people read your programs. It is an excellent way to learn different ways of solving problems. It also keeps you conscious of good programming practices. Share your successes, but also share your problems. Often the different viewpoint of another friendly programmer can help you over the rough spots in programming.

Whenever you run into a dead end while trying to solve a programming problem, ask for help. Tell the other person what the problem is and let him try to locate it. Do not tell him your ideas of where you think the error might be. Do not tell him which parts of the program you know are right. You have been concentrating on the trees so long that you may have overlooked the shape of the forest. A friend who brings a fresh perspective to the problem may ask different questions than the ones you have focused on. His different vantage point will often pinpoint the difficulty with your program in a surprisingly short time. Don't be embarrassed by his speed. The day will come when you spot in an instant an error he has been struggling with for hours in one of his own programs.

DOCUMENTATION

Developing a computer program requires a lot of time. By the time you finish defining, designing, translating, and testing a program to do a specific task on the computer, you probably could have completed the same task two or three times using paper, pencil, and a pocket calculator. Computer programs save time and effort when they are used repeatedly: tens, hundreds, or thousands of times.

You should do your best to make sure your programs will be used often. That requires having the program available and knowing how to use it. When you have just finished developing a program, it will be fresh in your mind. You will know where to find it, and you will probably be eager to show anyone who is interested (and some people who are not) how it works. Later, you will develop another program, and another, and another. After you have built a collection of one hundred or more programs, you will not be able to keep the details of all of them in your head. You will need an index to find specific programs, and you will need documentation to explain them.

Most large organizations have developed their own standard forms for documenting programs. Each completed program will be accompanied by a folder of technical documentation and operations documentation. *Technical documentation* is written to explain the program to other programmers (or to remind the original programmer of the details months or years later). *Operations documentation* is written for people who may not know programming to explain how to use the program.

Documentation does not have to be elaborate to be useful. A book is not needed to explain a one-page program. Some documentation is useful even if you are writing programs for your own use. Writing a couple of pages while a program is fresh on your mind can preserve your ideas and keep a program useful for years. An undocumented program is apt to be quickly lost and forgotten.

The technical documentation should not require extra effort after testing has been completed. The information a programmer needs to know to understand a program, and to figure out how to modify it or improve it later, should have been written during the definition and design phases. A complete program documentation package would consist of descriptions of the purpose, output and input, the data dictionary, the flowchart, and a listing of the program statements. For many BASIC programs, a single program summary sheet (Fig. 9-7) can include the program definition and the data dictionary. This sheet can also provide an index to where the program is stored. The form shows the short name used to save the

PROGRAM NAME: SAVINGS PLAN	**SHORT NAME:** SAVINGS **DATE WRITTEN:**

PURPOSE: TO CALCULATE THE AMOUNT OF MONEY SAVED BY DEPOSITING A CERTAIN AMOUNT OF MONEY INTO A SAVINGS ACCOUNT EACH MONTH FOR SEVERAL YEARS.

OUTPUT: TOTAL BALANCE WITH ACCUMULATED INTEREST AND TOTAL DEPOSITED

INPUT: AMOUNT OF MONTHLY SAVINGS. INTEREST RATE. NUMBER OF YEARS OF SAVINGS

VARIABLES:

ABBREV.	MEANING
AM	AMOUNT SAVED EACH MONTH
IR	INTEREST RATE (ANNUAL PERCENT)
YR	NUMBER OF YEARS OF REGULAR SAVING
M	NUMBER OF MONTHS OF REGULAR SAVING
IM	MONTHLY INTEREST RATE (DECIMAL)
B	BALANCE IN SAVINGS ACCOUNT
IA	INTEREST AMOUNT ADDED MONTHLY
TD	TOTAL DEPOSITED
TI	TOTAL INTEREST
CT	COUNTER FOR MONTHS
N	NUMBER, FOR ROUNDING

Fig. 9-7. Program summary sheet for Savings Plan program.

program on a disk file. If you are using cassettes, this could easily be changed to list the identification of the specific tape. If your programs are stored on a number of different disks, you might want to add the disk number to the summary. This one page, plus a one page flowchart (Fig. 9-4) may be adequate technical documentation for your purposes.

The operating instructions for some programs can be included in the program itself (as initial PRINT statements or an optional subroutine). More complicated programs require an instruction page or booklet to explain them. Most people feel more comfortable about using a program if they have read about it first. They would also like to have something handy to which they can refer if they get confused or want to understand the choices the program offers. Your programs will be used and trusted more if people feel comfortable running them. Whenever you write a program that you expect someone else to use, you should write at least a brief explanation to help them get the most out of your program. Good documentation will enhance the value of your programs.

A program that is well defined, designed, translated, tested, and documented has reached maturity. It may enjoy a long and useful life. The completion of the major development stages does not necessarily mean a program is rigidly set forever. Even adults change with the times. Even mature programs can be improved. The small extra effort of filing your technical documentation will make the later tasks of changing and enhancing your programs much easier.

Chapter 10
Types of Values

Half the craft of programming consists of structuring computer processes. Sequences, alternation, loops, and subroutines are the primary building blocks for these processes. The other half of the programmer's craft is structuring data. Data structures can be as simple as a single variable or as complex as a large corporate data base. The primary building blocks for data structures are value types.

Different types of problems require different types of information. You should not respond to a true-false question with a long essay. The correct response is limited to one of two values. Multiple choice questions allow more answers, but you are still limited to a finite set of possible values. Fill-in-the-blank questions allow an infinite number of possible answers formed by putting almost any number of letters and spaces together to make words.

Even number problems have different sets of possible answers. Counting the number of times something is started limits you to positive whole numbers. Measuring distances often requires the use of fractions or decimals. Measurement is also different than counting: counting should produce an exact answer while measurements are just close approximations. Some number problems require the use of negative numbers (like debts in accounts). Negative numbers are meaningless in other contexts (how long is –10 feet?).

Each variable in a program can store one particular type of value. The programmer needs to define the appropriate type of value to give reasonable answers to his problem. Different programming languages allow different choices of data types. Many languages require that the acceptable values for each variable be described in the program before any process statements are written. BASIC does not require how to specify all variables and their types. It uses a default (single precision, floating decimal point) suitable for most number values. However, there are some problems where this standard data type is not reasonable and a different type should be used.

VALUES IN THE COMPUTER

The circuits that modern computers use to perform arithmetic and store values are essentially on/off switches. Each individual switch is called a *bit* because it contains a tiny bit of information. A bit can have only one of two values. If the switch is on, the value of the bit is 1 (or true). If the switch is off, its value is 0 (or false). Some computer languages include a data type that uses a single bit for true/false information. Standard BASIC does not.

Groups of switches are connected inside the computer to form larger units. The most widely used unit consists of eight bits and is commonly called a *byte* (Fig. 10-1). Each bit within these larger units has a place value. This is similar to the ones, tens, and hundreds places of the decimal system except that the place values are ones, twos, fours, eights, etc. The eight bits in a byte can have any one of 256 different values.

The 256 different values in a byte are used as codes for letters and other symbols. A variety of different coding schemes are used on computers. The ASCII (American Standard Code for Information Interchange) system defines the meaning of codes 0 through 127. Most microcomputers use the ASCII codes plus special definitions (graphics and nonstandard symbols) for codes 128 through 255. Other common coding systems are binary coded decimal (BCD) and IBM's Extended Binary Coded Decimal Interchange Code (EBCDIC). A data type that interprets a byte (or other unit) as the code for a set of symbols is a *character* data type. Standard BASIC uses characters only as part of strings.

A byte is not a very useful unit for number variables. Few people would be satisfied with a computer that would only handle whole numbers between 0 and 255. Most programs require number types that can support a larger number of values. This requires several bytes to be strung together. Two bytes can provide 65,536 different possible values. (That is 256 ↑ 2.) Four bytes provide over four billion possible values (256 ↑ 4 = 4,294, 967,296). So, a reasonably small amount of computer memory can be used to hold very large numbers.

Many (but not all) versions of BASIC provide for three different data types to represent numbers inside the computer. These primary data types are integers, floating point decimals, and double precision floating point decimals.

Integers

Integers are positive and negative whole numbers. You can reach any integer by starting at zero and either repeatedly adding or subtracting one. Integers can be used for counting and for any arithmetic not involving fractions or decimals. BASIC generally stores an integer variable as two bytes (or sixteen bits). One bit is used for the sign. That bit is turned on (value = 1) for a negative number and is turned off (value = 0) for a positive number. The remaining 15 bits can store any whole number between 0 and 32,767.

Integer arithmetic is simpler than arithmetic requiring decimals. Therefore using the integer data type for variables will let the computer run your programs more quickly. This is especially true for the variables used as counters inside of loops. Integers also require less room in the computer's memory than other data types. The savings in memory is usually less important than the savings in time, but occasionally it becomes crucial to fitting a complex program into a microcomputer.

You can use integer variables for true/false situations or for multiple choices, as well as for counting numbers. Since neither of these situations allow as many possible values as integers, you should include a test in any input loop to make sure users entered only acceptable values (like 1 for true and 0 for false). You cannot use integer variables for any calculations that require fractions or decimals. The computer would round each value down to an integer, just like when you use the INT function. You also cannot use an integer variable to hold a number larger than 32,767 (in most BASIC systems) or smaller than −32,768. For larger absolute values and fractions, you must use a different data type.

BASIC needs an instruction from the programmer before it will define a variable to an integer type. Generally this can be done with a DEFINT (DEFine INTeger) command. The DEFINT command has to be one of the first lines in the program so the computer will know how to set space aside for the variable before it starts doing any calculations. The DEFINT command is followed by one letter, or several letters separated by commas. It makes the computer treat any variable whose name starts with the specified letter as a variable. In a program starting with "10 DEFINT N", the variables named N, N1, N9, NA, NZ, etc., would all have the integer data type. (N$ would still be treated as a string because of the dollar sign suffix.) The command: DEFINT I,K,J would cause all variables whose names begin with I or J or K to be defined as integers.

Some forms of BASIC allow you to define a variable to have the integer data type by adding a suffix. This works exactly like using the dollar symbol ($) for string variables. The percent sign may (or may not) declare a variable to be an integer. A two-line program will show you if your computer uses a percent-sign (%) suffix to identify integer variables:

```
10 LET X% = 10 / 3
20 PRINT X%
```

An integer variable will produce a result of 3 instead of 3.33333. Assuming your computer does use the integer type this way, you must be careful to include the suffix each time you refer to the variable. BASIC will consider X% and X to be two distinct variables stored in different parts of the computer memory. The command PRINT X would not produce the same result as PRINT X%.

Some BASIC dialects do not allow you to use the integer data type (with either DEFINT or a suffix). Other BASIC dialects assume that all numeric variables have an integer value. To make the best use of the BASIC on your machine, you need to learn some of the specific options written for your computer.

Floating Decimal Point Numbers

The default data type for variables in BASIC is floating decimal point. This data type uses one group of bits to store the digits of the value in a manner similar to integers. This part is called the *mantissa*. A second group of bits, the *exponent*, is used to determine where the decimal point belongs. The values 12.0000 and 12000.0 would have the same mantissa, but different exponents are responsible for the decimal point floating from one place in the number to another. One bit of the mantissa and one bit of the exponent are used for the sign. A negative sign in the mantissa means that the number is less than zero. A negative sign in the exponent means that the absolute value of the number is less than 1.

The floating point representation allows a wide range of different values to be stored in a small amount of computer memory (typically four bytes). It is always possible to dream up a number that will be too large to be stored in a floating point variable. The limit is different on different computer systems. Most BASIC floating point variables have a maximum exponent size somewhere between 36 and 99. They could not calculate a number like (20↑ 20)↑20. However, the exponent for a trillion is only 12, so you are not going to run into many problems with answers too large for the standard floating point data type on your computer.

The number of bits in the mantissa is more likely to cause you difficulty. The standard floating point mantissa uses enough bits to hold six decimal digits. Any calculations involving more digits will only produce approximate results. Any extra digits will be lost as rounding errors. If you used standard floating point variables in an accounting program, individual values between $10,000.00 and 999,999.90 would be accurate to the nearest dollar, but not to the nearest cent. Six digit accuracy is sufficient for many applications, but no rounding errors would be acceptable in a bank.

The following program will illustrate the weakness of limited precision arithmetic. If you started with $999,999 in the bank and added a thousand pennies (one at a time), you would have a total of $1,000,009. However, one cent is eight digits away from the hundred thousand dollar digit, so the one cent additions do not affect the six digit mantissa. Most computers will tell you that the answer for those additions is to leave the total of the original $999,999.

```
 10 REM ROUNDING ERROR DEMONSTRATION
100 LET T = 999999
```

```
110 LET C = .01
120 FOR I = 1 TO 1000
130 LET T = T + C
140 NEXT
150 PRINT T
160 END
```

(Note: you could probably speed up this program by defining I to be an integer. Try a line like: 20 DEFINT I.)

Double Precision Numbers

A computer could be programmed to produce results with almost any number of accurate digits. The mantissa used in the floating point number would have to be expanded to enough bits to store the largest required number. Using eight bytes for a floating point number instead of the usual four provides fourteen to sixteen digit accuracy (depending on how many bits are saved for the mantissa). Fourteen digit accuracy will keep track of amounts up to a trillion dollars accurate to the penny. This level of precision is referred to as double precision because each value requires twice as much storage room in the computer's memory as the standard single precision floating point numbers.

Many dialects of BASIC include a double-precision data type. A DEFDBL (DEFine DouBLe) command works the same way as the DEFINT command to instruct the computer to treat certain variables as double precision data types. If your BASIC uses suffixes to assign data types, then the pound sign (#) probably signifies double precision.

You may be tempted to define the variables in your programs to be double precision types. After all, why not use the best? Most computers do computations in eight, sixteen, or thirty-two bit units (one, two, or four bytes). Using double precision numbers creates a lot of extra effort for the computer. This means that using double precision numbers when you do not need them could make your program take more than twice as long to run as it would with standard variables. Also, the extra bytes of memory required for double-precision variables could create difficulties in some situations.

The effect of using different data types can best be illustrated by a program containing arithmetic loops. Run the following program the way it is written. Note how many seconds it takes to be completed. Add a line defining all variables to be double precision (if your computer allows the DEFDBL command): 30 DEFDBL A,B,C. (N is not included because many versions of BASIC will not allow double-precision variables to be the counter in a FOR . . . NEXT loop.) Run the program again. Some of the results will show more decimal places, but it takes considerably longer to run the program. Changing all the variables to integers (30 DEFINT A,B,C,N) speeds up the program, but produces wrong answers after division.

```
 10 REM DEMONSTRATION OF DATA TYPES
 30 REM STANDARD FLOATING POINT IS THE DEFAULT
 50 LET A = 10
 60 LET B = 7
100 LET C = A / B
110 PRINT "10/7 ="; C
200 FOR N = 1 TO 4000
210 LET A = A + B
220 NEXT
230 PRINT "TOTAL IS"; A
300 LET C = C / 10
310 LET C = C * 7
320 LET C = C * 10
330 PRINT "TEN IS"; C
999 END
```

As a general rule, you will want to use the simplest data type adequate for the problem you need to solve. Integers are the best type to use whenever you can be sure that the values will never include fractions or numbers greater than 32,000 or less than −32,000. Double precision floating point variables should be used only when you need more than six digits to describe the value accurately. The rest of the time, the normal BASIC single precision floating decimal point data type will be your choice.

STRINGS OF CHARACTERS

You have already made some use of string variables. They store words and names. The name is based on the definition of a string as a bunch of characters strung together like beads on a necklace. In all dialects of BASIC, a dollar sign ($) suffix is used to identify a variable as having a string data type.

String variables are more complicated than any of the number variable types. A number variable always uses the same amount of computer memory. That allows the computer to assign a certain group of bytes to the variable for the entire program. A string variable might begin with no characters (the null value) and then receive a short value (like "BOB"). The same variable might later be changed to have a longer value ("GEORGE WASHINGTON CARVER") and then switched back to a shorter value ("JR"). The computer has to figure out how to keep track of the variable and assign enough memory to store its value. One possible way of doing this would be to assign a certain number of bytes (say 64) to each string variable. The solution is not generally used because if the number of bytes were large it would waste too much room inside the computer. Few computers have enough memory to spare to allow you to use two hundred bytes just to store the word "NO." If the number of bytes assigned to each string were small (for example, 16) to save space, then the programs could not handle reasonably long names like GEORGE WASHINGTON CARVER.

A few dialects of BASIC (notably Hewlett-Packard's) require the programmer to specify the maximum number of characters in each string variable. A variable that would only hold yes/no answers could be assigned a maximum size of 3. The variable for a person's name might be assigned a maximum size of 25. The computer could then reserve an appropriate amount of memory for each variable. The programmer uses a DIM (for DIMension) command to specify the maximum size for each string variable. That maximum length is written inside brackets following the name of the variable. For example: DIM A$ [3], N$ [25], S$ [2] reserves three bytes of memory for string A$, twenty-five bytes for N$ and two bytes to store the value of S$. The DIM command must be used for each string variable before the program uses it to store any values.

The more common way for BASIC to store strings is to set aside a section of the computer's memory to store the values of the string variables in the program. The first byte in this area will hold the length of the first variable (the number of characters in its actual value). The computer uses this value to know how many bytes to include in that string and where it can start storing the next string. BASIC also maintains a directory of string variables that keeps track of the starting point in memory for each variable. If a string variable gets a new, longer value assigned, then BASIC will move the value to another part of memory so it will not overlap another string. The job of allocating enough memory for each string is done by the computer. The programmer does not have to worry about how much room each variable needs or where it is stored in memory.

This method of handling string variables limits the length of each string to a number between 0 and 255 (the numbers that can be represented in the single byte used for lengths). Also, if the length of string variables changes frequently inside a program, the operation of that program may be slowed down considerably because of the amount of work the computer has to do in moving the string variables around within the memory.

Most BASIC systems have a small amount of space reserved for strings. If your program uses a lot of string variables or long string values, you may need to change the default allocation. The CLEAR command is used to reserve space for string values. CLEAR 5000 would reserve five thousand bytes to hold the values of the string variables in the program. CLEAR 0 would not allow any space for a string variable. You only need to use a CLEAR statement in your program if the default value produces an error message that the computer is out of string space. When you use the CLEAR command, it should be the first statement in your program (other than REMarks). Otherwise the process of reserving memory might wipe out the results of any statements already executed.

String type values in a program must be enclosed inside quotation marks. The quotation mark delimiters are optional when responding to an INPUT command. If you type the quotation marks, they will not be stored as part of the value. However, they are necessary if you want to INPUT a value that includes any of the other BASIC delimiters: commas (,), colons

(:), or semicolons(;). Unless they are enclosed inside quotes, BASIC will assume they are delimiting the boundary between two different values. Some dialects of BASIC include a LINE INPUT command that will accept every typed character as part of the string value. The command is like the standard INPUT command except that it does not print a question mark (?) prompt and it allows delimiters to be part of the string value.

MIXING DATA TYPES

Using more than one data type for numbers can create problems. Comparing values in an IF . . . THEN statement might not produce the correct result because the integer representation for 24 does not look equal to the floating point representation of the same number. Neither representation looks like the characters "24."

Before any two values can be compared or used in the same arithmetic operation, they must have the same data type. BASIC will automatically convert values for the numeric data types (integer,,standard floating point, and double precision) to a common data type for arithmetic. This conversion limits the accuracy of the result to the least precise data type of any value used in a calculation. If you multiply a double precision value by a standard floating point value, only the first six digits of the result will be accurate. If you assign the result to a double precision variable, the computer may print a full sixteen digit result, but the last ten digits are apt to be wrong. Similarly using an integer variable I with a value of 4 and a standard floating point variable N with a value of 4.3, the computer would interpret the if clause of: IF I = N as being true.

The computer will allow you to mix numeric data types freely within your program. It leaves you the responsibility of choosing data types appropriately. If you do not accept that responsibility wisely, then mixing data types may cause your program to produce inaccurate results. Remember, every calculation is only as precise as its precise variable. If you use any integer data types in a calculation, the result is limited to integer accuracy. You can obtain true double precision results only if all the variables in your calculation have double precision values. This is an example of the old saying; a chain is only as strong as its weakest link.

Numbers can also be represented as strings. People usually type numbers as a string of digits. The computer then converts the string of digits (with a sign and decimal point) in your program or the response to an INPUT command into the appropriate format for the computer.

BASIC will not automatically convert the values of string variables into number values nor the values of numeric variable types into string values. Therefore your program cannot mix string and numeric data types in comparisons. IF N = A$ will produce an error. Also, you cannot perform any arithmetic operations on string variables. LET A = N + "2" will produce an error message.

Many versions of BASIC allow the programmer to convert data types using special functions. The function STR$(N) converts the value of the numeric variable into a string. If the value of N were two, the command LET X$ = STR$(N) would give X$ the value "2". The value function is the inverse of the string function. It converts a string data type into a numeric value. The command LET A = VAL(X$) would convert the value "2" back into a number and store it in variable A. If X$ had the value "ABC" instead of "2", then the VAL function obviously could not work. You should always test to make sure that a string represents a valid number before your program tries to convert it to a number.

CONSTANTS

Many programs use the same number values many times. They may contain loops that add one to a variable, or they may have several different statements using twelve as the number of months in the year, or 3.14159 as pi for calculations with circles. Each time BASIC encounters such a number typed into a program, it must convert that string of digits into another data type for calculations.

You can speed up the operations of your programs by using variable names to hold frequently used constants. This practice means the computer only has to convert the value once, when it is first assigned to a variable. The following program uses P for pi and U for the unit one.

```
10 REM ASSIGNING CONSTANTS FOR VARIABLES
20 LET P = 3.14159
```

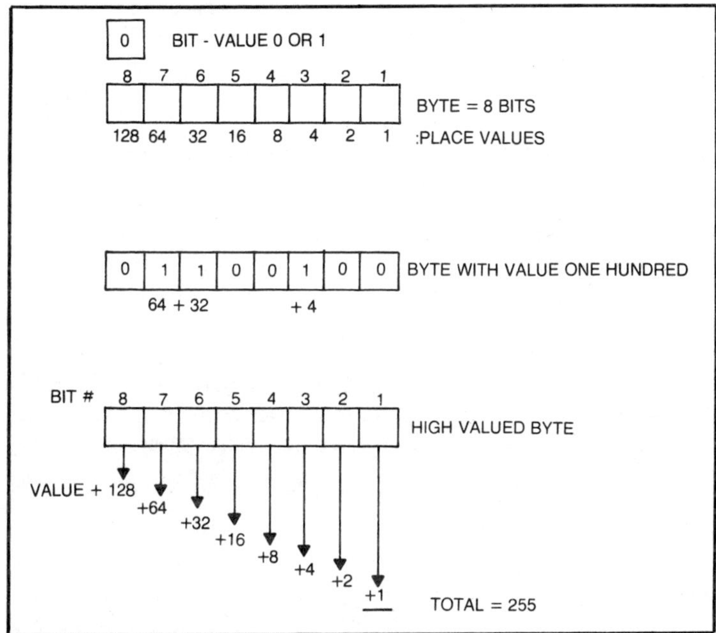

Fig. 10-1. A byte of data.

```
 30 LET U = 1
 50 LET T = 0
100 FOR N = 1 TO 5000
110 LET T = T + U
120 LET X = T * P
130 NEXT
200 PRINT T; "CALCULATIONS MADE"
210 END
```

Compare the time that program takes to run on your machine with the same program using typed constants in each line in the loop. The second version forces the computer to convert the strings "1" and "3.14159" into floating point numbers five thousand times. (Note: Printing the value of N at the end instead of the value of T would give the false report of 5001 calculations. Why? Review Chapter 6 if you are not sure.)

```
 10 REM USING CONSTANTS INSIDE A LOOP
150 LET T = 0
100 FOR N = 1 TO 5000
110 LET T = T + 1
120 LET X = 1 * 3.14159
130 NEXT
200 PRINT T; "CALCULATIONS COMPLETED."
210 END
```

Using variables to list the important constants once in a program is a good practice to follow. It saves the computer time in BASIC. It can also save the programmer time when a constant has to be changed. If your program is used for several years, there is a good chance some values you originally thought were constants will have to be changed. This includes such items as tax rates, the number of products your company sells, any dates used to validate input, etc. Using variables to store these values will allow you to update your program by changing a single LET statement located at the beginning of the program. That is much easier than trying to find and change all the statements containing the value .05 for sales tax rate (without changing any place where .05 refers to a 5 percent discount for early payment).

Understanding data types puts you one step beyond those who simply know enough to use the computer. It requires that you pay enough attention to what goes on inside the computer so you can control it and avoid being misled by results that appear to be more accurate than the precision of data allows.

Chapter 11

Tables of Values

Your mind is capable of dealing with large amounts of information at once because it organizes related items into larger structures. You do not remember the alphabet as twenty-six unrelated symbols. Your mind stores the letters as a single list starting with A. If you doubt this, try saying the letters of the alphabet starting with Z as rapidly as you can name the alphabet in the usual order.

Your programs can handle large numbers of individual variables by similarly grouping them into larger data structures. The most widely used group data structures are arrays and files. Arrays are discussed in this chapter. Files are examined in Chapters 12 and 13.

An *array* is an ordered collection of values (or variables for storing values). Each value in an array is called an *element* of the array. All elements in an array must be the same type—integer, standard floating point, double precision, or string. A list is a simple array. Lists are ordered so that there is a first element, followed by a second element, and so on, until the last element is reached. Each element on a list can be identified by a number indicating its position in the list.

You probably already use the element number to substitute for the name value of months in dates. Why write "September 25, 1981" when "9/25/81" conveys just as much meaning? The shortcut uses the common array of months:

Element #1 = JANUARY
Element #2 = FEBRUARY
Element #3 = MARCH
Element #4 = APRIL
Element #5 = MAY
Element #6 = JUNE

Element #7 = JULY
Element #8 = AUGUST
Element #9 = SEPTEMBER
Element #10 = OCTOBER
Element #11 = NOVEMBER
Element #12 = DECEMBER

BASIC arrays are specified by including element numbers inside parentheses as part of the variable name. Using M$ as the variable name for months, you would use M$(1) to store JANUARY and M$(12) to store the value DECEMBER. The data type for each element is determined by the first part of the array name. The dollar sign with the M identifies this array as a collection of strings. Integer and double precision arrays can be specified the same way as single integer and double precision variables. The default data type is the standard floating point number.

The value inside the parentheses is called the *subscript* of the array. The verbal description of an element in an array, say B(5), is commonly shortened to "B sub 5". Subscripts must be positive integers. You cannot find element number one-and-a-half or element number minus-three in a list. The negative subscript will produce an error message. A fractional subscript will be automatically rounded down by most versions of BASIC, so that asking for M$(2.5) would be treated by the computer as M$(2).

Subscripts for arrays can be any valid expression. Most often a counter variable-name will be used as the subscript. If the names of the months were stored in the M$(x) array, then all twelve names would be printed by the following loop:

```
300 FOR I = 1 TO 12
310 PRINT M$(I)
320 NEXT
```

More elaborate expressions can be used as subscripts if necessary. The computer will accept statements like PRINT M$(A*B +3 – C(I)/D), as long as the value of the expression inside the parentheses calculates out to be a positive number. Your programs will be easier to understand and will run faster on the computer if you keep the expressions simple. Using integer data type variables as subscripts will particularly speed up the computer's execution of your program.

BASIC reserves a set of contiguous memory cells for each array in your program. To do this, it must know at the start of the program how many elements will be needed for each array. These sets of memory compartments are reserved with the DIM (DIMension) command. The format of the DIM statement is the command word followed by a list of the names of the elements with the largest subscript for each array. DIM A(15), M$(12), X(2) would reserve enough space for all the elements of A( ) up to A(15), enough space for a directory of the twelve month names in M$( ) and for X(0), X(1), and X(2). Unlike most other computer languages, arrays in BASIC include an element number zero. When A( ) is dimensioned to 15, the sixteen memory compartments are reserved for elements A(0) through

A(15). This full memory is assigned even if your program only uses the particular variables A(5), A(10), and A(15). Once the DIM command has been issued, the size of the array is fixed. The computer will not allow it to expand. The statement LET A(17) = 5 will produce an error message unless the A( ) was given a dimension of at least seventeen.

Every array has a maximum size. The maximum size is specified in the DIM statement. The individual elements of an array are identified by the array name and a subscript. The subscript in BASIC must be at least zero and cannot be greater than the maximum size.

LOADING TABLES

In most BASIC dialects the DIM statement will initialize the value of each element in a numeric array to zero. (String arrays are initialized to length equal zero.) This is handy if the values in the array will be calculated within the program.

Often, you will want to use an array to hold a table of constant values, like the names and number of days in each month. In this case, your program must include instructions to load each of the values into memory. After dimensioning M$(12) for the names and D(12) for the number of days, you could assign the values with a tedious series of LET statements:

```
 10 DIM M$(12), D(12)
100 LET M$(1) = "JANUARY"
110 LET D(1) = 31
120 LET M$(2) = "FEBRUARY"
130 LET D(2) = 28
etc.
```

The same result can be accomplished with much less typing by using a READ loop (Fig. 11-1):

```
 10 DIM M$(12), D(12)
100 FOR N = 1 TO 12
110 READ M$(N), D(N)
120 NEXT
130 DATA JANUARY,31,FEBRUARY,28,MARCH,31,APRIL,30
140 DATA MAY,31,JUNE,30,JULY,31,AUGUST,31
150 DATA SEPTEMBER,30, OCTOBER,31, NOVEMBER,30,
    DECEMBER,31
```

READ loops are very convenient for moving fixed values into arrays. In some programming situations, you won't know the values for the array or even the number of elements in the array until the program is run. An example of this situation is a game that can be played by many players at once. In that situation, you can dimension and load the array dynamically as part of the program:

```
10 PRINT"HOW MANY PEOPLE ARE GOING TO PLAY";
20 INPUT P
30 IF P > 0 THEN 50
40 PRINT"THE GAME REQUIRES AT LEAST ONE PLAYER."
```

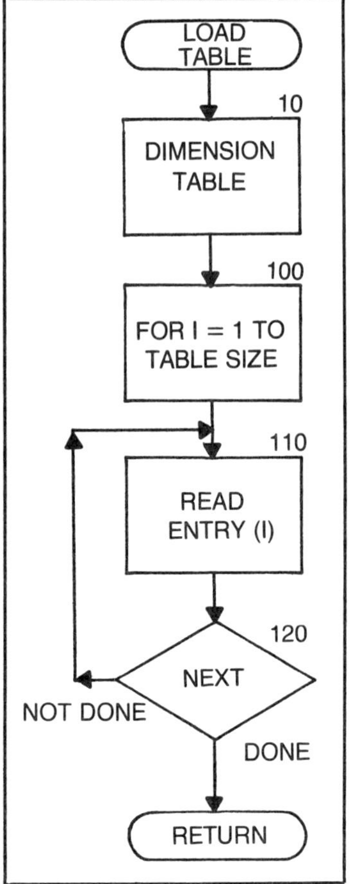

Fig. 11-1. Loading a table into memory.

```
 45 GOTO 10
 50 IF P = INT(P) THEN 70
 60 PRINT"ENTER A WHOLE NUMBER OF PEOPLE !!"
 65 GOTO 10
 70 IF P < = 100 THEN 100
 80 PRINT"TAKE TURNS. NO MORE THAN 100 AT A TIME."
 85 GOTO 10
100 DIM N$(P)
110 FOR I = 1 TO P
120 PRINT"WHAT IS THE NAME OF PLAYER #";I;
130 INPUT N$(I)
140 NEXT
```

Most of the statements (30 through 85) in this section are used to ensure that the size given for the array will be a reasonable, positive integer. Once the initial setup has been completed, the program will be able to prompt each player by name at the appropriate points in the game by printing N$(1) where the value of I identifies the current player.

PROGRAMMING WITH ARRAYS

Arrays require some extra statements at the beginning of a program. You must define the specific data structure to the computer before you use it. This requires specifying the size and dimensioning the array. For tables, each value must be loaded into the proper element of the array (generally with a FOR . . . NEXT loop). String arrays will often require the use of a CLEAR statement to reserve enough space for the string values.

The extra statements needed to set up the array are often offset by reducing the number of statements needed to process the separate data items. Often the use of more complex data structures will allow the programmer to write a program that is easier to follow and to modify.

The advantages and disadvantages of arrays can be seen by comparing two versions of the same general program. This program is defined to serve as a cash register for a small snack bar (Fig. 11-2.) As a quantity of each item on the menu is specified, the program is to automatically add the cost to the total for the order. When the customer says he does not want anything else, the program computes the sales tax and asks for payment of the grand total.

Both versions of the program use the same top-level design (Fig.11-3). The main structure of the program is an order-taking loop that displays the menu, asks for choice of item, and, when a valid item is chosen, asks for the number of units. The program then adds the price for the chosen items and arrives at the total cost for the order. This loop is repeated until the customer chooses no more items. The final sequence in the program computes the tax (rounded to the nearest cent) and prints the totals.

The program listing titled Snackbar (Fig. 11-4) is a straightforward implementation of this design written by an eight-year-old student. It lacks any REM statements because of the large burden of typing any extra statements would require under the hunt-and-peck method of typing. Otherwise, it is a good and effective program. The purpose of the definition is satisfied. All input values are tested for reasonableness. (If you study the statements carefully, you may be able to recognize two ways that an unreasonable person could foul up the results. Neither error would result from any accidental entry, so the program would be quite suitable for use by employees.)

The second version of the program, Snack2 (Fig. 11-5), uses one table to hold the list of items on the menu (F$ - for Foods) and another table for their prices (P). Excluding the REMarks statements in Snack2, both programs have the same number of statements.

Statements 20 through 170 in Snack2 set up the tables using N as the number of items on the menu, data statements to specify the values of food names and prices, and a READ loop to load the tables. These statements have no counterpart in the Snackbar version.

PROGRAM NAME: CASH REGISTER FOR A SNACKBAR

SHORT NAME: SNACKBAR

DATE WRITTEN: JUNE 1981

PURPOSE: TO TOTAL THE COST OF ITEMS PURCHASED AT A SNACKBAR, INCLUDING SALES TAX OF 5%. CHECKS TO MAKE SURE ONLY REASONABLE ORDERS ARE ACCEPTED.

OUTPUT: MENU WITH PRICE OF EACH ITEM
TOTAL COST OF ORDER WITHOUT TAX, THE AMOUNT OF TAX, AND THE GRAND TOTAL

INPUT: WHICH ITEMS ARE INCLUDED IN THE ORDER AND HOW MANY OF EACH ARE WANTED

VARIABLES:

ABBREV.	MEANING
W	WHAT ITEM IS BEING ORDERED
H	HOW MANY UNITS OF THAT ITEM IN THE ORDER
TC	TOTAL COST OF ORDER (WITHOUT TAX)
T	TAX AMOUNT
GT	GRAND TOTAL (WITH TAX)
I	INTEGER COUNTER FOR LOOPS

MENU:

1	SMALL DRINKS	40¢ each
2	LARGE DRINKS	75¢ each
3	SNOW CONES	35¢ each
4	POPCORN	25¢ per bag
5	CANDY BARS	30¢ each

Fig. 11-2. Definition of snackbar problem.

Printing the menu requires nine statements in Snack2 (lines 200-260) and thirteen statements in Snackbar. The significant difference is that the tables allow the use of a three-statement FOR . . . NEXT loop in place of individual lines to print each item. This difference would increase in favor of using the array if there were more items on the menu.

After the customer's input values have been checked, Snack2 is able to use the value for What-item as the subscript for the price table. A single line (560) is adequate to calculate the additional cost of H units of any item on the menu. A second line (570) prints a verification of the amount ordered.

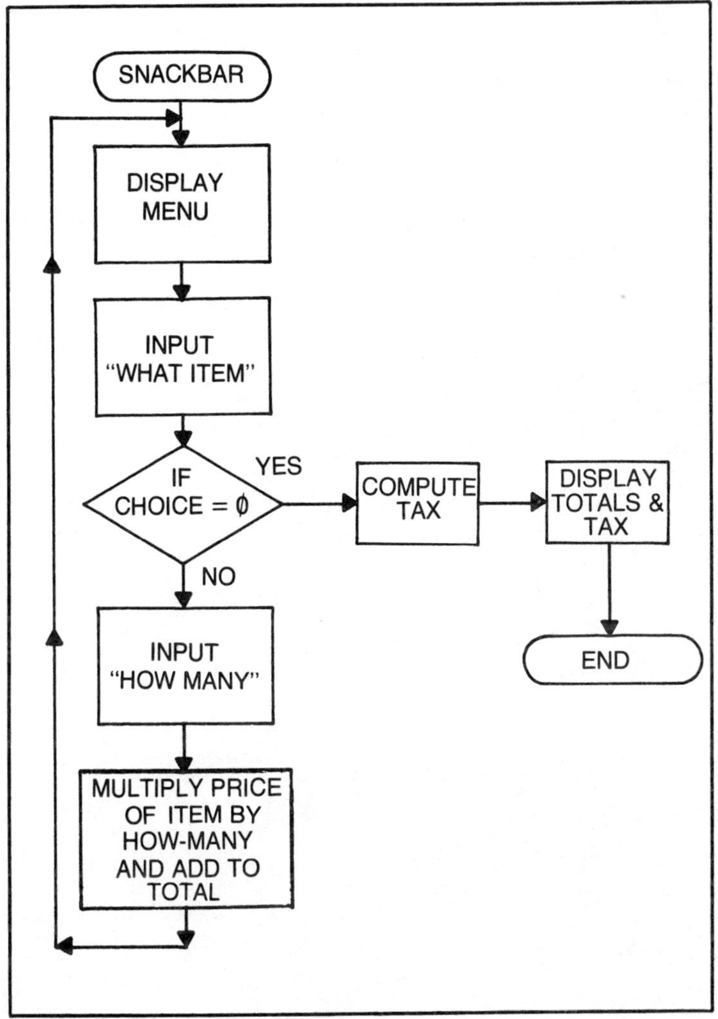

Fig. 11-3. General design of Snackbar program.

```
1       LET TC=0
5       FOR I = 1 TO 10
6       PRINT
7       NEXT I
10      PRINT"              $ SNACKBAR $"
13      PRINT"          1- SMALL DRINKS (.40)"
14      PRINT"          2- LARGE DRINKS (.75)"
15      PRINT"          3- SNOW CONES   (.35)"
16      PRINT"          4- POPCORN      (.25)"
17      PRINT"          5- CANDY BARS   (.30)"
18      PRINT"                BUTTER ON POPCORN IS FREE"
20      PRINT
21      PRINT"       HELP YOURSELF IF YOU WANT EXTRAS"
22      PRINT
23      PRINT"   WHAT DO YOU WANT (ENTER 0 FOR NOTHING ELSE)";
25      INPUT W
50      IF W=0 THEN 1000
55      PRINT"HOW MANY ";
60      INPUT H
65      IF H<0 THEN 150
70      IF H>100 THEN 200
75      IF W=1 THEN 250
80      IF W=2 THEN 300
85      IF W=3 THEN 350
90      IF W=4 THEN 400
95      IF W=5 THEN 450
100     PRINT"ORDER BY NUMBER:1-5"
102     GOTO 15
150     PRINT"HEY,YOU CAN'T ORDER LESS THAN 0"
160     GOTO15
200     PRINT" IF YOU ORDER MORE THAN 100 AT A TIME THEN YOU'LL HAVE
        TO PAY ME $1000 EXTRA FOR EACH ITEM"
210     GOTO15
250     LET TC=TC+.40 * H
260     GOTO15
300     LET TC=TC+.75 * H
310     GOTO15
350     LET TC=TC+.35 * H
360     GOTO15
```

```
400    LET TC=TC+.25 * H
410    GOTO15
450    LET TC=TC+.30 * H
460    GOTO15
1000   LET T=.05*TC
1010   LET T=T*100
1020   LET T=INT(T+.5)
1030   LET T=T/100
1050   LET GT=T+TC
1060   PRINT"YOU OWE ME $";TC;"PLUS $";T;"TAX."
1100   PRINT"THAT WILL BE $";GT
1150   PRINT
1160   PRINT
10000  END
```

Fig. 11-4. Snackbar program listing.

Without the arrays, the Snackbar version must use a case structure to calculate the cost of the ordered items. This requires five IF . . . THEN selection statements (75-95), five calculations (250, 300, 350, 400, and 450) and five closing GOTO statements. Printing a verification of the cost as each item is ordered would require an additional PRINT statement matching each calculation. Case structures always require a relatively large number of statements. An array often allows a case structure to be replaced by a simple sequence, thereby simplifying a program.

Suppose you are operating a snack bar. Inflation forces you to raise some of your prices (an unfortunately frequent event). Which version of the program would be easier to change? In Snackbar, you would have to change a print statement in the menu and a calculational statement somewhere in the middle of the program for each item with a price change. If you are not a superior typist, you might make a typing error that would cause your program to charge customers a different price than the one displayed on the menu. If you were using Snack2, you would only have to change a DATA statement at the beginning of the program. The menu and the cost calculation would then be automatically changed by the array logic.

Your snackbar is a success. You want to expand your menu. With the array version of the program, you would need to change line 30 to reflect the new number of items on your menu and add data statements. (If you were wondering why a variable had been used to hold the number five instead of just typing "5" in the related statements—40, 150, 240, and 310—the reason should be obvious now.) Without the array, new menu lines and case structure statements would have to be added for each new item. To

```
10   REM   SNACK BAR
20      CLEAR 1000
30      LET N = 5
40      DIM F$(N), P(N)
90   REM      READ PRICES              ***
100     DATA SMALL DRINKS, .40, LARGE DRINKS, .75
110     DATA SNOW CONES, .35, POPCORN (BAGS), .25
120     DATA CANDY BARS, .30
150     FOR I = 1 TO N
160     READ F$(I),P(I)
170     NEXT I
180     LET TC = 0
190  REM      DISPLAY MENU             ***
200     FOR I = 1 TO 8
202     PRINT
204     NEXT I
210     PRINT TAB(10)"JULIE'S SNACK BAR"
220     PRINT
230     PRINT" 0 -- NOTHING MORE"
240     FOR I = 1 TO N
250     PRINT I; "-- ";F$(I); TAB(24);P(I)
260     NEXT I
270     PRINT "WHICH ITEM DO YOU WHAT";
280     INPUT W
290     IF W <> INT(W) THEN 320
300     IF W = 0 THEN 700
310     IF W > 0 AND W <= N THEN 400
320     PRINT"PICK ONE OF THE LISTED NUMBERS."
330     GOTO 270
400     PRINT"HOW MANY DO YOU WANT";
410     INPUT H
420     IF H = INT(H) THEN 450
430     PRINT"YOU HAVE TO ORDER A WHOLE NUMBER OF ITEMS !!"
```

```
440     GOTO400
450     IF H < 100 THEN 480
460     PRINT"BE REASONABLE.  THIS IS ONLY A SMALL SNACK BAR."
470     GOTO 400
480     IF H > 0 THEN 550
500     PRINT"STOP WASTING MY TIME WITH SILLY ORDERS !"
510     PRINT"THIS TIME ORDER RIGHT."
520     GOTO 210
560     LET TC = TC + H * P(W)
570     PRINT H;F$(W);" COST ";H * P(W)
580     IF TC > 500 THEN 650
590     PRINT"ANYTHING ELSE?"
600     GOTO 210
650     PRINT"SORRY, YOU HAVE BOUGHT ALL MY GOODIES."
660     GOTO 710
690  REM    GRAND TOTALS    ***
700     PRINT
710     PRINT"YOUR ORDER TOTALS:";TAB(24); TC
720     LET T = .05 * TC
730     LET T = INT(100 * T + .5) / 100
740     PRINT"SALES TAX ADDS:"; TAB(24); T
750     LET GT = TC + T
760     PRINT"PLEASE PAY:";TAB(24); GT
9960 REM  END OF THE PROGRAM ***
9999    END
```

Fig. 11-5. Snack 2 program listing.

appreciate the advantages of using the arrays, you should revise both versions of the program to add three items to the menu: hot dogs at .90, hamburgers at 1.00, and potato chips at .30 each.

The two possible difficulties with the Snackbar version have been cured in Snack2. Orders for a fraction of an item are eliminated by lines 420—440 in Snack2. A customer playing with the keyboard could keep Snackbar in the main loop forever. Line 580 in Snack2 forces the program to end eventually, even if the customer never specifies item 0.

SEARCHING A TABLE

Arrays are commonly used to match input data with specific values. This is one way to edit string variables to make sure that only correct values are entered. Looking up a specific value on a table is also the basis for many conversions or code translations.

To find whether or not a specific value is included in a table, you may compare the value with each element in the table. If the value equals the element, your search is done. Otherwise, you move on to the next element. If you run out of elements before you find a matching value, then you know the value is not on the table. This design for a table look-up is shown as a subroutine by Fig. 11-6. This design is called a linear search because it goes right down the line of elements in the array. There are other designs for searching arrays (notably the binary search which keeps splitting the array into halves), but they require arranging the elements of the array in special orders. The fancier searches take less time to find a value in a large table, but the simple linear search is best for small tables and will work with any array.

The table look-up routine can be demonstrated using the table of month names (M$). Assume that part of a program asks the user to input a

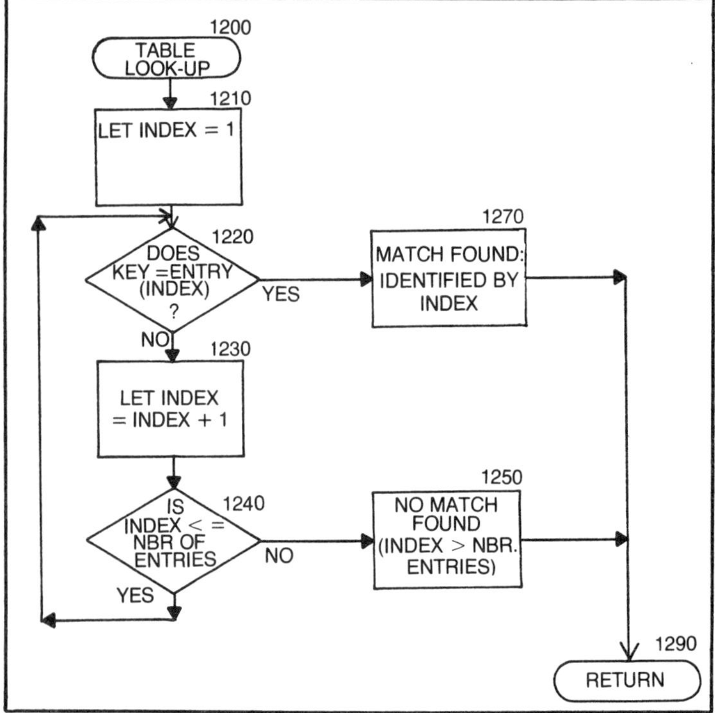

Fig. 11-6. Table look-up subroutine.

month as part of a birthdate for a horoscope or an invoice date for billing. The program needs to make sure that the input value is the name of a real month. If the month is good, then the program can calculate elapsed time using the number of the month. When the subroutine is completed, the value on the Index (I, used to subscript the array) will be the number corresponding to the correct month name. If the input value (or key, K$) is not the name of a month, then the value of the Index will be 13 at the end of the subroutine. The top level of the program will be able to check the value of the Index to decide if it needs to loop back for a corrected entry.

```
1200 REM -- TABLE LOOK-UP SUBROUTINE --
1210 LET I = 1
1220 IF K$ = M$(I) THEN 1270
1230 LET I = I + 1
1240 IF I < = 12 THEN 1220   'check next element
1250 PRINT K$;" IS NOT THE NAME OF A MONTH IN EN-
     GLISH."
1255 GOTO 1290
1270 PRINT K$;" IS MONTH #";I
1290 RETURN
```

Of course, this subroutine will not work unless you have first dimensioned and loaded the table M$. You should be able to write a program to calculate a person's age in months that uses this subroutine to translate the value of both the person's birth-month and the present month. The program will also require the current year and the year of the person's birth as input.

A METRIC/ENGLISH CONVERSION PROGRAM

The United States is becoming a nation with two systems for measuring almost everything. In addition to the old English (imperial) measurements of feet, miles, gallons, pounds, etc., measurements are expressed in the metric system. Making comparisons between measurements often requires looking up a conversion factor in a printed table and multiplying by the number of units to be converted. To convert from inches to centimeters, you first have to find out that each inch is the same as approximately 2.54 centimeters. Multiplication informs us that four inches is slightly more than ten centimeters. These conversions become tedious with a pencil and paper. If you were to put your conversion tables in a computer, you could use the computer's arithmetic speed to make conversions between metric and English units a snap.

The main idea of the conversion program is to ask a person to name a type of unit (either metric or English) along with the quantity of those units and have the computer display the equivalent measurement in the other system. Since the program will not include all the possible variations in units and their spellings, it will be a good idea to include a provision for listing all the units the program recognizes.

The conversion program will require three matching arrays: one for the names of the metric units (M$), one for the names of the English units

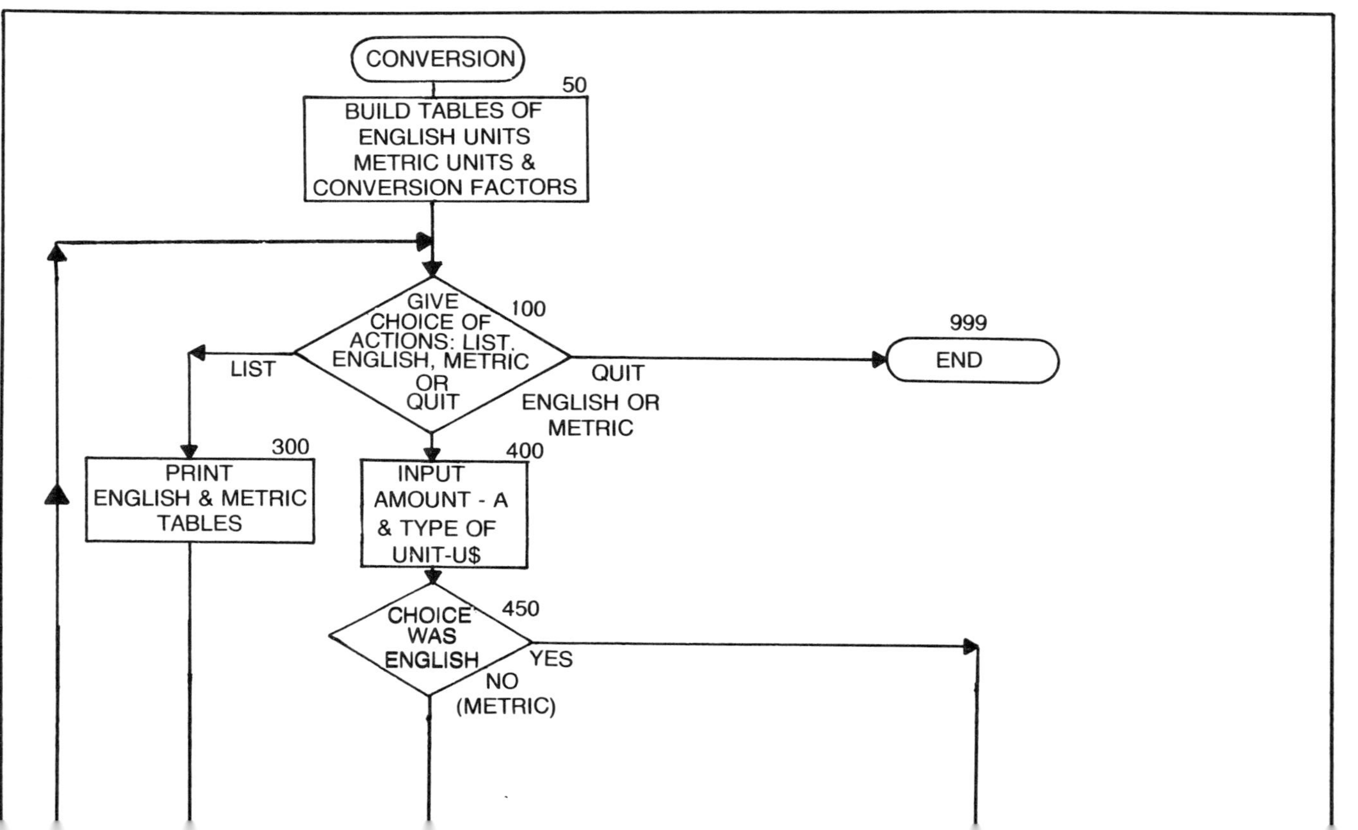

CONVERSION
50
BUILD TABLES OF ENGLISH UNITS METRIC UNITS & CONVERSION FACTORS
100
GIVE CHOICE OF ACTIONS: LIST, ENGLISH, METRIC OR QUIT
LIST
QUIT
ENGLISH OR METRIC
999
END
300
PRINT ENGLISH & METRIC TABLES
400
INPUT AMOUNT - A & TYPE OF UNIT-U$
450
CHOICE WAS ENGLISH
YES
NO (METRIC)

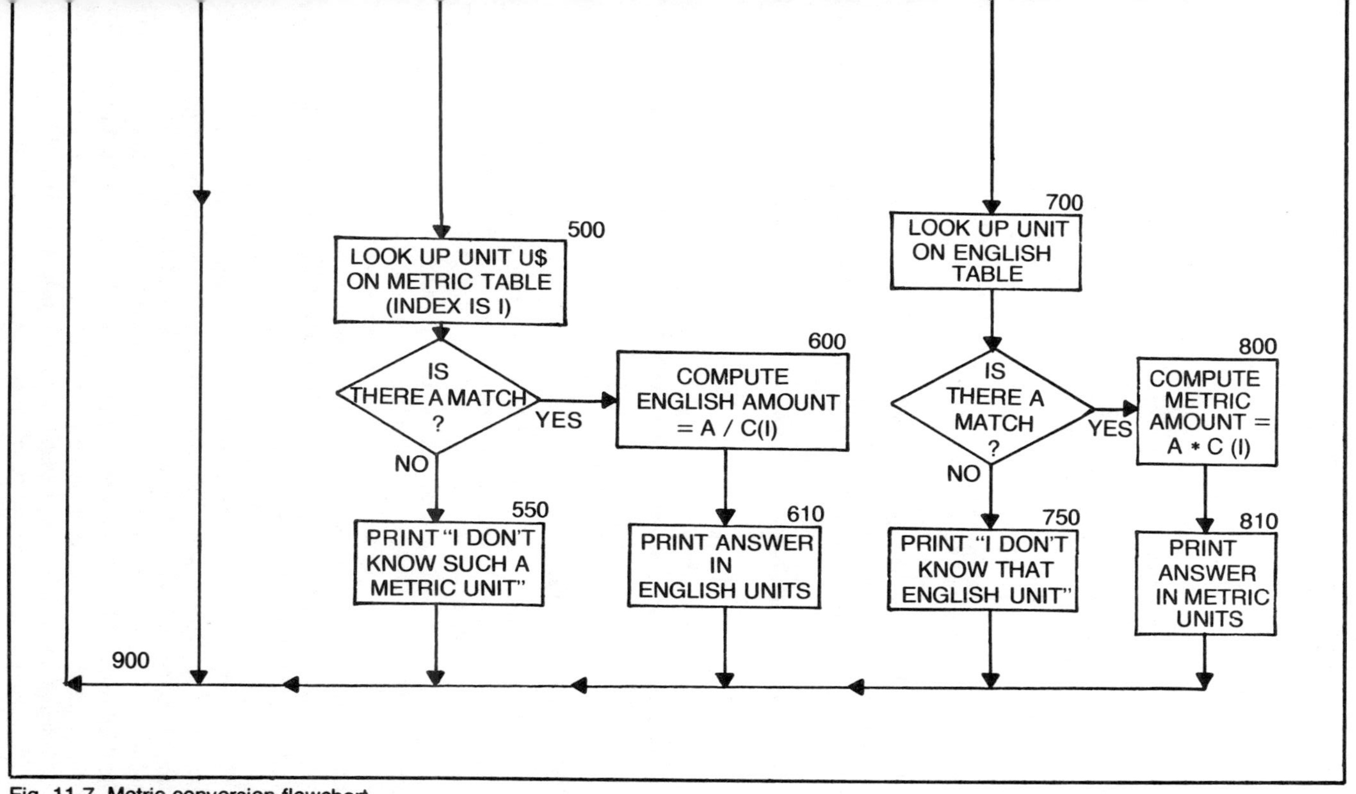

Fig. 11-7. Metric conversion flowchart.

(E$), and one for the conversion factors (C). If the conversion factors are chosen to be the number of metric units in each corresponding English unit, then converting from English to metric units will require multiplying by the conversion factor. Converting from metric to English can be accomplished by dividing by the same number.

Having selected the data structures, the program design can now be developed into a full top-level flowchart (Fig. 11-7). The first task will be to dimension and load the tables. The core of the program will be a loop, repeatedly giving the user the option of converting a specific unit (English or metric), seeing the list of available units, or stopping. If the program is run using a video display, there will probably need to be a pause at the bottom of the loop, so that printing the choices does not erase the information the user asked for. This pause is not diagrammed in the flowchart, but will be represented by line number 900 (indicated in the bottom left corner). The actual conversions will be accomplished by table look-ups using either the metric table (M$ at line 500) or the English table (E$ at line 700). The detailed flowchart for each of these tasks will resemble Fig. 11-6, using the input value of U$ as the Key and the variable 1 as the Index.

For the demonstration program, ten different pairs of equivalent units were chosen. The conversion factors were copied from a printed conversion table. Each matching set of values is typed on its own DATA statement (lines 72-90 in Fig. 11-8). The same program design could be used for any number of units, or for translating values between any two systems. The line numbers in the program listing match the numbers written by each box on the flowchart.

TWO-DIMENSIONAL ARRAYS

Think of mathematical tables you have seen: multiplication tables, income tax tables, the trigonometry tables in the back of math books, accountant's ledger sheets, etc. You are not visualizing a one-dimensional list. Most likely, you are thinking of a two-dimensional arrangement with rows and columns of numbers. Most people find it easy to organize data into two-dimensional arrays in their minds. This data structure is so common in mathematics that it has a special name, the *matrix.*

BASIC allows you to create matrices by DIMensioning arrays with two subscripts (separated by a comma). The first subscript is used to specify the row of the table. The second subscript specifies the column. Each element in a matrix is identified by a unique combination of a row number and a column number. The order in which the subscripts are written is important to handling matrices. As Fig. 11-9 illustrates, element M$(1,3) occupies a different place in the computer's memory than element M$(3,1). The third seat in the first row is not the same as the first seat in the third row (though they may have the same value at some point in time).

Loading values into a matrix usually involves a pair of nested FOR . . . NEXT loops. For each row (the outer loop), the value for each column is loaded (the inner loop) before proceeding to the next row. The following routine stores the standard multiplication table in memory:

```
100 DIM M(12,12)
200 FOR R = 1 TO 12
210 FOR C = 1 TO 12
220 LET M(R,C) = R * C   'Instead of a READ statement
230 NEXT C
240 NEXT R
```

Once the table has been created, any row or column can be treated like a one-dimensional array by keeping the value of one subscript the same while varying the other subscript:

```
300 PRINT "THE MULTIPLES OF 7 ARE:",
310 FOR C = 1 TO 12
320 PRINT M(7,C),
330 NEXT C
```

Individual elements can be treated as simple variables by specifying both subscripts. The calculations involving matrices match the operations you could do with a group of numbers written in rows and columns on a piece of paper.

Many versions of BASIC allow you to create arrays with three or more dimensions. However, these more complex data structures are not as widely used as lists and matrices because they do not match the way that people normally think. People occasionally think of information arranged in the three dimensions of space, but even that level of complexity is often confusing. It is hard to keep more than two levels of subscripts straight in your mind. Designing a program so all data can be stored and manipulated as part of a five-dimensional array (say, A(13,6,18,20,3)) may prove that you are clever, but it will not show that you are a good programmer. There is a big strain in keeping track of all those subscripts in order to understand what any statement in your program really means. Such a program would be a millstone around the neck of anybody who had to maintain or modify it. You should do your best to make sure that both your data structures and your process structures can be easily understood by normal people.

A BUDGET MATRIX

A Budget Planning program offers a good opportunity to use a matrix in a moderate size program. An annual budget can be written as a matrix with one line (row) for each budget category and one column for each month. Some of the rows would hold income items, like salary for an individual or sales for a business. Other rows would hold expense items, like utilities. The bottom row could be used to show the difference between the total of the income items and the total of the expense items. For a personal budget, the bottom line would represent the savings accumulated; the bottom line for a business is the net profit. To get a complete picture for the year, a thirteenth column could be used to hold the total of the twelve month columns.

```
10   REM   METRIC CONVERSIONS
20   REM   BY R. GALBRAITH,   AUGUST 1981
30      CLEAR 400
40      DIM M$(10), E$(10), C(10)
50      FOR I = 1 TO 10
60      READ M$(I), E$(I), C(I)
70      NEXT I
72      DATA CENTIMETER, INCH, 2.540
74      DATA METER, FOOT, 0.3048
76      DATA KILOMETER, MILE, 1.609
78      DATA LITER, GALLON, 3.786
80      DATA STERE, CU.YARD, 0.7646
82      DATA GRAM, OUNCE, 28.35
84      DATA KILOGRAM, POUND, 0.4536
86      DATA SQ.METER, SQ.FOOT, 0.0929
88      DATA HECTARE, ACRE, 0.4047
90      DATA SQ.KILOMETER, SQ.MILE, 2.590
100     FOR I = 1 TO 6
110     PRINT
120     NEXT I
130     PRINT"THIS PROGRAM GIVES YOU THE FOLLOWING CHOICES:"
140     PRINT"   1 -- CONVERT FROM METRIC TO ENGLISH"
150     PRINT"   2 -- CONVERT FROM ENGLISH TO METRIC"
160     PRINT"   3 -- DISPLAY THE CONVERSION TABLES"
170     PRINT"   4 -- END THE PROGRAM"
180     PRINT"WHICH DO YOU WISH TO DO";
190     INPUT C
200     IF C = 1 OR C = 2 THEN 400   'DO CONVERSION
210     IF C = 3 THEN 300            'DISPLAY TABLES
220     IF C = 4 THEN 999            'QUIT
230     PRINT"THE ONLY CHOICES ARE: 1, 2, 3, OR 4."
240     GOTO 180
300  REM  ** PRINT TABLES **
```

Fig. 11-8. Metric program listing.

```
305      PRINT
310      PRINT TAB(12);"CONVERSION TABLE"
315      PRINT
320      PRINT"  ENGLISH UNIT"; TAB(28);"METRIC UNIT"
330      FOR I = 1 TO 10
340      PRINT"1 "; E$(I); TAB(17);"= "; C(I); TAB(28); M$(I)
350      NEXT I
360      GOTO 900                        'PAUSE & RETURN
400   REM  ** AMOUNT & UNIT TO CONVERT **
410      PRINT"TYPE THE UNIT TO BE CONVERTED";
420      INPUT U$
430      PRINT"HOW MANY "; U$; " UNITS TO CONVERT";
440      INPUT A
450      PRINT
460      IF C = 2  THEN 700              'ENGLISH LOOK-UP
490   REM -- METRIC TABLE LOOK-UP
500      LET I = 1
510      IF U$ = M$(I) THEN 600        'MATCH FOUND
520      LET I = I + 1
530      IF I <= 10 THEN 510             'NO MATCH
550      PRINT"I DON'T RECOGNIZE THAT METRIC UNIT."
560      GOTO 900                        'PAUSE & RETURN
600      LET E = A / C(I)
610      PRINT"THAT IS EQUIVALENT TO: "; E; E$(I);" UNITS."
620      GOTO 900                        'PAUSE & RETURN
690   REM -- ENGLISH TABLE LOOK-UP
700      LET I = 1
710      IF U$ = E$(I) THEN 800         'MATCH FOUND
720      LET I = I + 1
730      IF I <= 10 THEN 710             'NO MATCH
750      PRINT"I DON'T RECOGNIZE THAT ENGLISH UNIT."
760      GOTO 900                        'PAUSE & RETURN
800      LET M = A * C(I)
```

```
810     PRINT"THAT IS EQUIVALENT TO: "; M; M$(1);"  UNITS."
820     GOTO 900
900  REM ** PAUSE & RETURN **
905     PRINT
910     PRINT"PRESS 'RETURN' TO CONTINUE";
920     INPUT A$
930     GOTO 100                      'RETURN TO MENU
999     END
```

Fig. 11-8. Continued from page 157.

Budgeting programs can become quite complex. The sample program is kept simple by limiting its scope to a personal budget with only a few rows. The purpose of this program (Fig. 11-10) will be to help individuals plan their personal budgets by estimating their income and expenses for major items. The program will allow the user to revise his estimates for any item until he is satisfied with the overall budget. The output for the program will be the bottom-line savings for the year, and a display of the entire budget. Standard video displays and many small printers do not have enough room to print thirteen columns of numbers along with titles on a single line. Therefore the display for the budget will have to be divided into sections. One way to accomplish this is to allow the user to choose which month or category he wants to have displayed. The computer would then print a list of the categories for the chosen month, or the amount for a given category during all of the months.

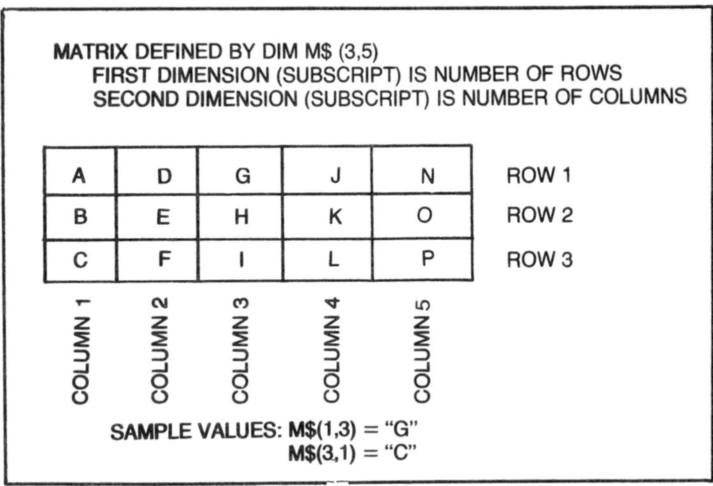

Fig. 11-9. Dimensions of a matrix.

PROGRAM NAME: BUDGET PLANNING

SHORT NAME: BUDGET

DATE WRITTEN: AUGUST 1981

PURPOSE: TO HELP INDIVIDUALS PLAN THEIR PERSONAL BUDGETS BY ALLOWING THEM TO ESTIMATE THEIR INCOMES AND REPEATEDLY, REVISE THEIR EXPENDITURE ESTIMATES UNTIL THEY BALANCE THEIR BUDGET WITH THE DESIRED AMOUNT OF SAVINGS.

OUTPUT: AMOUNT OF SAVINGS RESULTING FROM BUDGET (WITH A WARNING IF LESS THAN ZERO.)
DISPLAY OF BUDGET BY MONTH OR BY CATEGORY.

INPUT: BUDGET AMOUNTS FOR INCOME & EXPENSE CATEGORIES ON A MONTHLY OR ANNUAL BASIS

VARIABLES:

ABBREV.	MEANING
M	MONTH NUMBER
M$( )	TABLE OF MONTH NAMES
C	CATEGORY NUMBER
C$( )	TABLE OF CATEGORY TITLES
B(C,M)	MATRIX OF BUDGET AMOUNTS OF CATEGORY AND MONTH NOTE: MONTH 13 IS TOTAL FOR YEAR CATEGORY 13 IS NET SAVINGS CATEGORIES 1&2 ARE INCOME CATEGORIES 3-12 ARE EXPENSES
A	AMOUNT INPUT FOR BUDGET ENTRY

Fig. 11-10. Definition for Budget Planning program.

Since the program is for use by individuals, the input should be easy to enter, without any accounting knowledge on the port of the user. For the first estimate, the user should be asked to enter a budget amount for each category. Some items, like mortgage payments, will likely be the same amount for each month. The input process should allow the person to enter an amount once and use it each month. When revising estimates, the user should be able to change either the entry for a single month or all of the entries for any budget category.

In designing the program, the plan should allow for any number of budget categories. Whatever categories are included in a budget could be handled by building a table of category titles (C$) and indexing it with an integer variable (C). The month names are known. They can be stored in an array (M$) with an added thirteenth entry for the annual total. This table will be indexed by a second integer variable (M). The main data structure in the program will be a matrix holding the budget amounts (B(C,M)). The category index (C) will match the rows in the matrix with the appropriate category title in C$. The second subscript matches the month names with the columns in the matrix. A separate variable (A) will be needed for the amounts entered by the program's user. Other variables may be needed to control loops and choices in the program. They can be added at later stages in the design.

The process of the program will need to begin by setting up the arrays with DIMension statements and table loading loops. The user will then enter the budget estimates for each category. The task of entering budget amounts for a particular category can be defined as a subroutine (to be designed in detail later). Entering the amounts for all of the categories (except the bottom line) will be accomplished by a FOR . . . NEXT loop that changes the category number used in the "Enter Budget Amount" subroutine. After the loop is completed, the program will be able to compute the savings under the budget. Since this might be a complicated task, it is left as a single subroutine box in the top-level design.

Once the initial budget has been completed, the user will be asked to decide whether he wants to revise the budget or see a display of the budget by month or by category. To avoid an endless loop, the user will also be given the choice of ending the program. This section of the program can be written as a menu and an input loop (to make sure the user enters one of the valid choices).

If the user chooses to change the budget, he will be asked to identify the budget category he wants to change. Then he will need to enter the revised budget amounts for that category. If the "Enter Budget Amount" subroutine were designed carefully, it could be used for both the initial entry of estimates and for entering revised amounts. This will save the effort of writing two separate routines. The top-level flowchart (Fig. 11-11) now contains two identical boxes that refer to the same subroutine. After the budget has been revised, the bottom-line savings will have to be recomputed before the user returns to the menu. This could be accomplished either by repeating the "Compute Savings" subroutine and returning to the menu or by looping back to the "Compute Savings" box on the flowchart. Many professionals would prefer the first method because it makes the structure of the top-level flowchart simpler and more balanced. The second method is used in the sample. It saves a single GOSUB statement in the program, which is almost a totally irrelevant advantage.

If the user chooses to have his budget displayed by category, he will have to specify the category (chosen from a list of those available). Then the program will be able to print the budget amounts for that category showing every month. Similarly, if he chooses to have his budget for a month

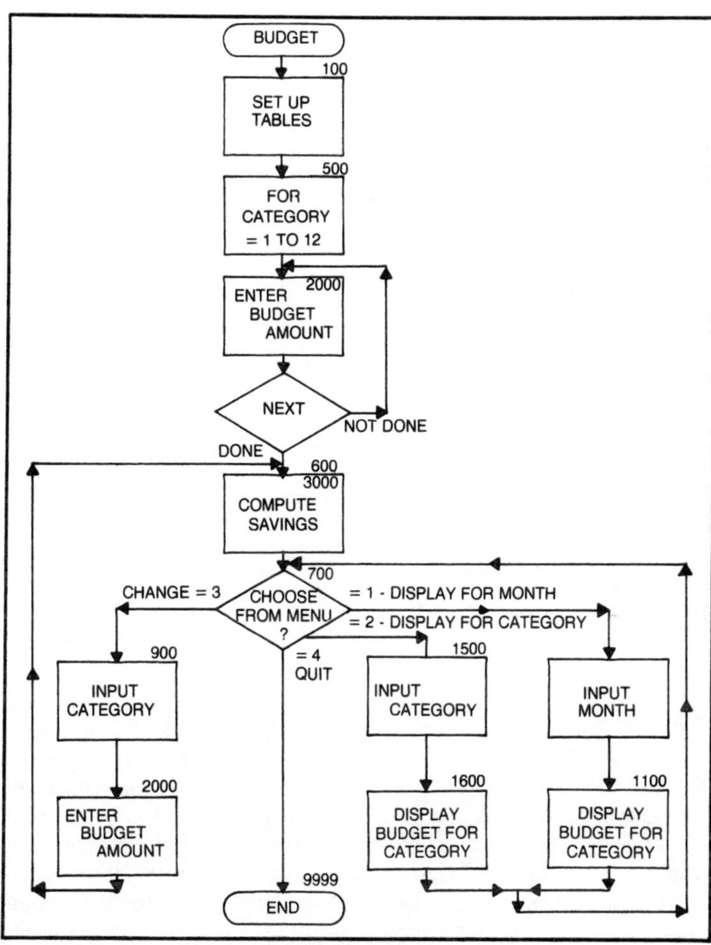

Fig. 11-11. Top-level design for Budget-Planning program.

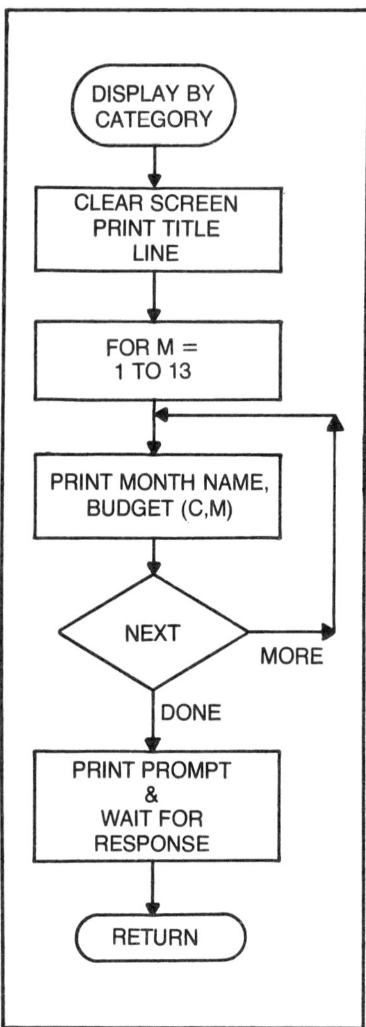

Fig. 11-12. Detailed flowchart for displaying budget.

displayed, he will have to specify which month. The program can then list the amounts for each category for the chosen month. The process for displaying the budget by month or by category will be essentially the same. The design for both can be shown by a single detailed flowchart (Fig. 11-12). Several blank lines will be printed to set the display off the previous displays. A title line should be included to specify what part of the budget is being displayed. Having completed these preliminaries, the heart of the process is a FOR . . . NEXT loop that uses the selected category or month for one subscript and varies the other subscript to print every budget entry (along with a title) in the selected row or column of the budget matrix. At the end of the display, the program should pause so the user can read the display at his own pace before returning to the menu.

At this point in the design, you could write the BASIC statements for the top-level of the program. The subroutine to enter budget amounts and the subroutine to compute savings have not been designed yet. Instead of writing the statements for those codes, the top-level of the program will simply include a GOSUB statement in each place that one of these subroutines appears in the design. If you can contain your impatience to start

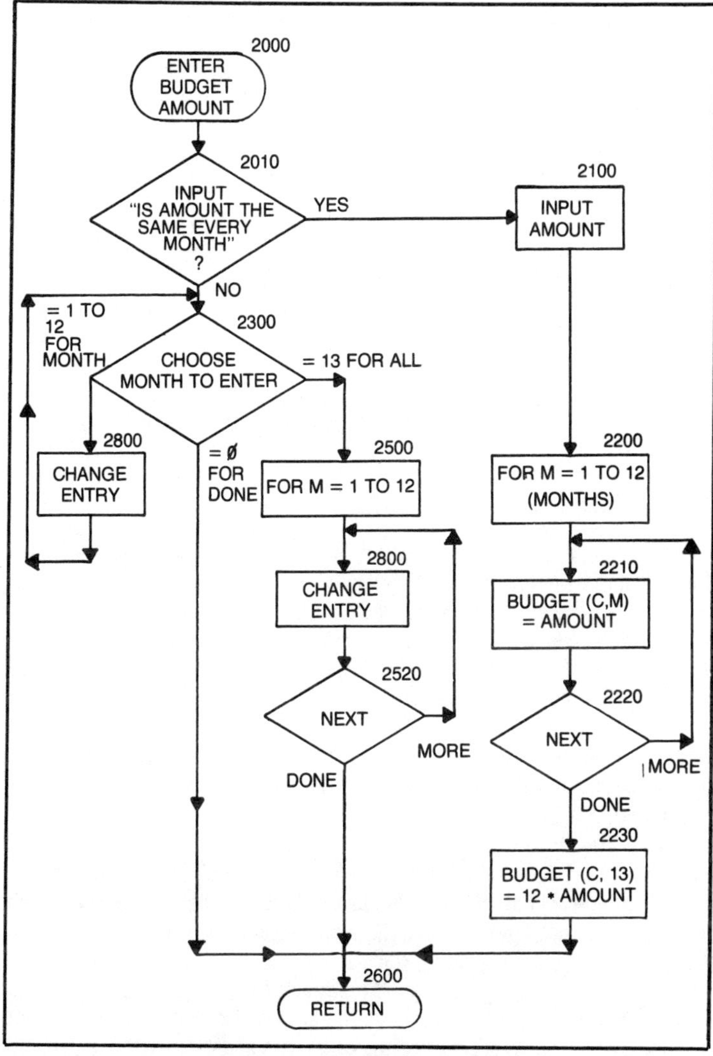

Fig. 11-13. Subroutine to enter budget amounts.

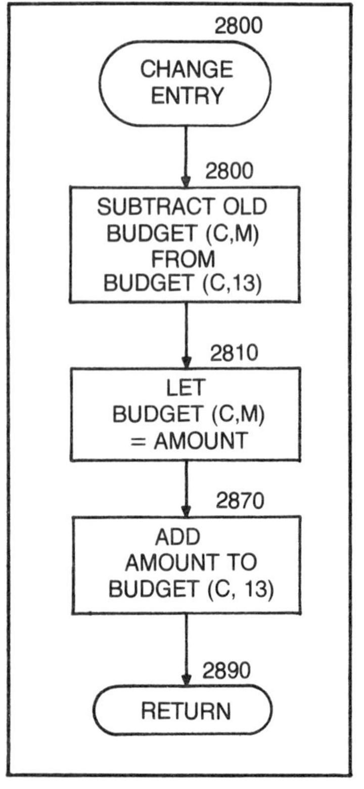

Fig. 11-14. Subroutine to change a budget entry.

putting the program into the computer, it is better to complete the design of the subroutines before starting to write the BASIC statements.

The subroutine to enter budget amounts needs to include several options. First, the user should be able to specify that the same amount is to be used for all the months. (Remember, the category has been determined before the subroutine is started.) If the amount varies, the user should be able to loop through all months (especially for the first estimates), entering a different amount each time. Alternatively, the user should be able to choose a particular month and enter its amount (especially while revising estimates) (Fig. 11-13).

If the amount is to be the same for each month, then a loop varying the month index (M) from one through twelve will let you put the input amount in each column of the chosen row in the budget matrix. The thirteenth column should hold the total for the year. That amount (B(C,13)) will be twelve times the amount input for a month.

If the user chooses to enter the amount for a single month, a small subroutine will be needed to change the amount for that specific element and also for the annual total. Entering different values for each month could be accomplished by repeating that same subroutine for all twelve months

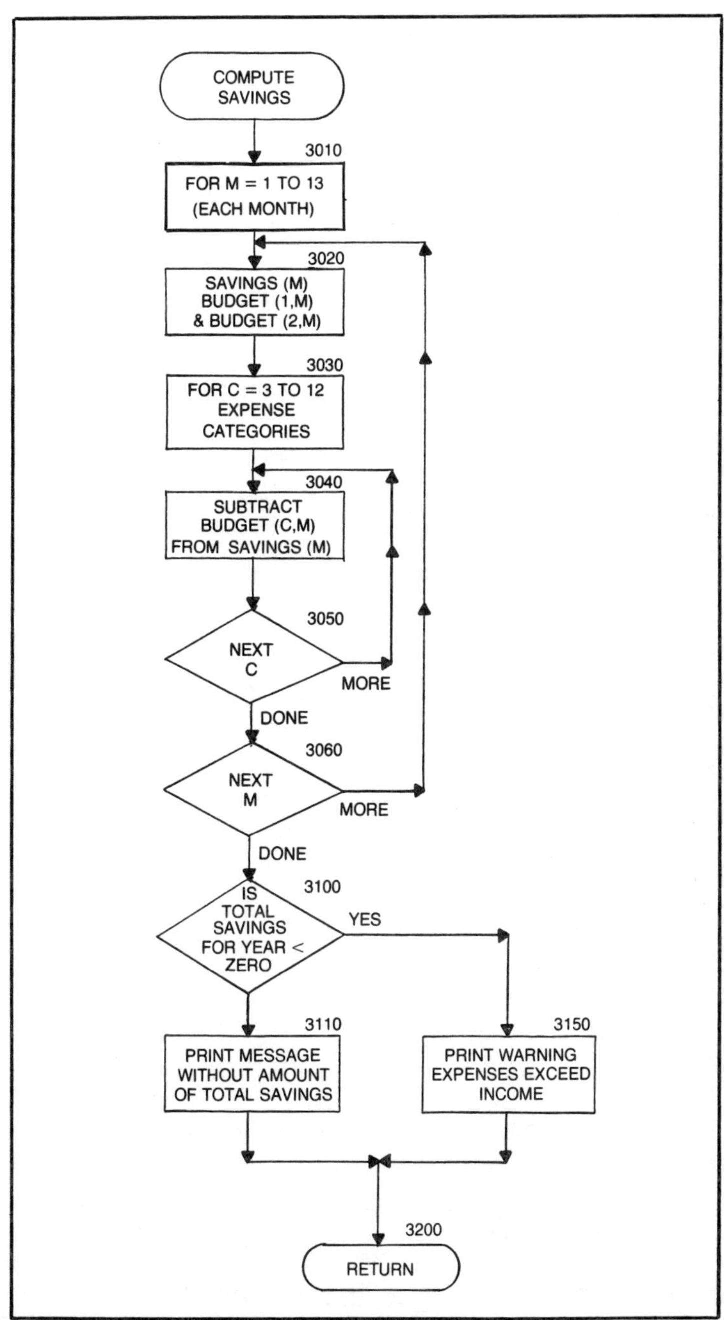

Fig. 11-15. Subroutine to compute savings.

```
10   REM  BUDGET PLANNING
20   REM  BY R. GALBRAITH,    AUGUST 1981
30      CLEAR 300
40      DIM M$(13)          'ARRAY FOR MONTH NAMES
50      DIM C$(13)          'ARRAY FOR CATEGORY TITLES
60      DIM B(13,13)        'MATRIX FOR BUDGET AMOUNTS
70      FOR I = 1 TO 6
80      PRINT
90      NEXT I
100     PRINT TAB(10);"BUDGET PLANNING PROGRAM"
110  REM -- LOAD MONTH TABLE --
120     FOR M = 1 TO 13
130     READ M$(M)
140     NEXT M
150     DATA JANUARY, FEBRUARY, MARCH, APRIL, MAY
160     DATA JUNE, JULY, AUGUST, SEPTEMBER, OCTOBER
170     DATA NOVEMBER, DECEMBER, TOTAL YEAR
180  REM -- LOAD CATEGORY TABLE --
190     FOR C = 1 TO 13
200     READ C$(C)
210     NEXT C
220     DATA SALARY, OTHER INCOME, HOUSING, UTILITIES, FOOD
230     DATA CLOTHING, TRANSPORTATION, MEDICAL, INSURANCE, RECREATIO
        N
240     DATA GIFTS/DONATIONS, OTHER EXPENSES, SAVINGS
250  REM -- INITIALIZE BUDGET TO ZERO --
260     FOR C = 1 TO 13
270     FOR M = 1 TO 13
280     LET B(C,M) = 0
290     NEXT M
300     NEXT C
400  REM -- INSTRUCTIONS --
410     PRINT
420     PRINT"YOU ARE TO ESTIMATE YOUR INCOME & EXPENSES USING CATEG
        ORIES:"
430     FOR C = 1 TO 12
440     PRINT TAB(6); C;" -- ";C$(C)
450     NEXT C
460     PRINT"THE COMPUTER WILL CALCULATE YOUR SAVINGS, THEN LET YOU
         REFINE"
470     PRINT"YOUR BUDGET."
490  REM -- FIRST BUDGET ESTIMATES --
500     FOR C = 1 TO 12
520     PRINT"ESTIMATE FOR "; C$(C); "     ";
530     GOSUB 2000                    'ENTER BUDGET AMOUNT
```

Fig. 11-16. Budget program listing.

```
540    NEXT C
600    GOSUB 3000                    'COMPUTE SAVINGS
690  REM -- CHOOSE NEXT STEP --
700    PRINT
710    PRINT"CHOOSE: 1-- DISPLAY FOR MONTH;   2-- DISPLAY FOR CATEG
       ORY"
720    PRINT"        3-- REVISE BUDGET;       4-- QUIT"
730    PRINT"WHICH DO YOU WANT TO DO";
740    INPUT A
750    IF A = 1 THEN 1000
760    IF A = 2 THEN 1500
770    IF A = 3 THEN  900
780    IF A = 4 THEN 9999             'END
790    PRINT"CHOOSE BY NUMBER: 1, 2, 3, OR 4."
800    GOTO 730
890  REM -- CHANGE BUDGET --
900    PRINT
910    PRINT"BUDGET CATEGORIES"; TAB(30); "TOTAL AMOUNT"
920    FOR C = 1 TO 12
930    PRINT TAB(5); C; "-- "; C$(C); TAB(32); B(C,13)
940    NEXT C
950    PRINT"WHICH DO YOU WANT TO CHANGE";
960    INPUT C
970    IF C < 1 OR C > 12 THEN 990
980    GOSUB 2000                    'ENTER BUDGET AMOUNT
985    GOTO 600                      'COMPUTE SAVINGS
990    PRINT"CHOOSE A CATEGORY FROM 1 TO 12."
995    GOTO 950
1000 REM -- DISPLAY FOR MONTH --
1010   PRINT
1020   PRINT"DISPLAY FOR WHICH MONTH (1 - 12, OR 13 FOR TOTALS)";
1030   INPUT M
1040   IF M >= 1 AND M <= 13 THEN 1100
1050   PRINT"ENTER A NUMBER BETWEEN 1 & 13";
1060   GOTO 1030
1100   PRINT
1110   PRINT
1120   PRINT
1130   PRINT TAB(10);"BUDGET FOR: "; M$(M)
1140   FOR C = 1 TO 13
1150   PRINT C$(C); TAB(18); B(C,M)
1160   NEXT C
1170   PRINT TAB(8)"PRESS ENTER/RETURN TO CONTINUE";
1180   INPUT A$
```

```
1190    GOTO 700                    'RETURN TO OPTIONS
1500 REM -- DISPLAY FOR CATEGORY
1510    PRINT
1520    PRINT"CATEGORIES ARE:"
1530    FOR C = 1 TO 13
1540    PRINT TAB(5); C;"-- "; C$(C)
1550    NEXT C
1560    PRINT"WHICH CATEGORY DO YOU WANT DISPLAYED";
1570    INPUT C
1580    IF C >= 1 AND C <= 13 THEN 1600
1590    PRINT"ENTER A NUMBER BETWEEN 1 & 13."
1595    GOTO 1570
1600    PRINT
1610    PRINT
1620    PRINT
1630    PRINT TAB(10);"BUDGET FOR: "; C$(C)
1640    FOR M = 1 TO 12
1650    PRINT M$(M); TAB(18); B(C,M)
1660    NEXT M
1670    PRINT TAB(16);"-----------"
1680    PRINT M$(13); TAB(18); B(C,13)
1690    PRINT TAB(8);"PRESS ENTER/RETURN TO CONTINUE";
1700    INPUT A$
1710    GOTO 700                    'RETURN TO OPTIONS
2000 REM ---- ENTER BUDGET AMOUNT ----
2010    PRINT"IS THE AMOUNT THE SAME EVERY MONTH";
2020    INPUT A$
2030    IF A$ = "YES" THEN 2100
2040    IF A$ = "NO"  THEN 2300
2050    PRINT "ANSWER  'YES'  OR  'NO'."
2060    GOTO 2010
2090 REM -----
2100    PRINT"ENTER THE AMOUNT PER MONTH";
2110    INPUT A
2120    IF A >= 0 THEN 2200
2130    PRINT "NO NEGATIVE NUMBERS, PLEASE."
2140    GOTO 2100
2200    FOR M = 1 TO 12
2210    LET B(C,M) = A
2220    NEXT M
2230    LET B(C,13) = 12 * A
2240    GOTO 2600                   'RETURN
2250 REM -----
2300    PRINT
```

Fig. 11-16. Continued from page 167.

```
2305    PRINT"CHOOSE THE MONTH TO ENTER (OR ENTER 13 FOR ALL MONTHS)
        "
2310    PRINT"WHICH MONTH -- OR 0 IF DONE";
2320    INPUT M
2330    IF M = 0 THEN 2600              'RETURN
2340    IF M = 13 THEN 2500
2350    IF M >= 1 AND M <= 12 THEN 2380
2360    PRINT "MONTHS ARE NUMBERED 1 - 12."
2370    GOTO 2310
2380    GOSUB 2800                      'CHANGE ENTRY
2390    GOTO 2310                       'ANOTHER MONTH?
2490 REM -- ALL MONTHS
2500    FOR M = 1 TO 12
2510    GOSUB 2800                      'CHANGE ENTRY
2520    NEXT M
2600    RETURN
2790 REM ---- CHANGE ENTRY ----
2800    LET B(C,13) = B(C,13) - B(C,M)
2810    PRINT"AMOUNT FOR "; C$(C);" DURING "; M$(M);
2820    INPUT A
2830    IF A >= 0 THEN 2860
2840    PRINT "ENTER A POSITIVE AMOUNT";
2850    GOTO 2820
2860    LET B(C,M) = A
2870    LET B(C,13) = B(C,13) + A
2880    RETURN
2890 REM ----------
3000 REM ---- COMPUTE SAVINGS ----
3010    FOR M = 1 TO 13
3020    LET B(13,M) = B(1,M) + B(2,M)
3030    FOR C = 3 TO 12
3040    LET B(13,M) = B(13,M) - B(C,M)
3050    NEXT C
3060    NEXT M
3100    IF B(13,13) < 0  THEN 3150       'DEFICIT BUDGET
3110    PRINT
3120    PRINT"YOUR BUDGET PROVIDES"; B(13,13); "DOLLARS IN ANNUAL SA
        VINGS."
3130    GOTO 3200
3150    PRINT
3160    PRINT"***  WARNING  ***"
3170    PRINT"YOUR BUDGETED EXPENSES EXCEED YOUR INCOME BY  $"; ABS(
        B(13,13))
3180    PRINT"***  REVISE YOUR BUDGET  ***"
```

```
3200     PRINT
3210     RETURN
3220 REM ----------
9999     END
```

Fig. 11-16. Continued from page 169.

inside a loop. Either way, you will have determined both the category number and month number before you call (or GOSUB) the subroutine to change an entry.

The obvious part of the change entry routine is a statement LETting the appropriate budget entry equal the input amount. Next, the total for the category has to be adjusted. You could add the amounts for all twelve months together with a loop, which is somewhat time-consuming. If you were working the problem on paper, you would probably add the difference between the new estimate and the old entry to the old total. The program can imitate that by first subtracting the old budget entry for the month from the old total. After the entry has been changed, the new amount can be added back to the total. Adjusting the total with this method requires only two arithmetic operations (one subtraction and one addition) instead of the twelve additions involved in recreating the total with a loop (Fig. 11-14).

The only step remaining to complete the program design is to decide how to compute the savings. The general idea is to add the income items and subtract the expense items. Whatever amount is left will be the savings. If the resulting amount is less than zero, then the person has a deficit budget. Unless the person using the program thinks he is a government, he will have to revise his plans to live within his means.

You have to know which categories are income items and which are expenses before you can complete the specifications for the subroutine. The demonstration Budget program uses only two income categories: take-home salary and other income. These will be rows 1 and 2 in the matrix. Ten common household expense categories are provided: housing (rent or mortgage payments), utilities (gas, electricity, and telephone), food, clothing, transportation (gasoline, car payments, and maintenance and/or commuting costs), medical, insurance premiums, recreation (entertainment and vacations), gifts/donations (for those tax deductions), and other expenses. These fill rows three through twelve of the matrix. That leaves the thirteenth row to hold the amount of savings (Fig. 11-15).

With these decisions made, the heart of the compute savings subroutine becomes a loop that is repeated for each column (month and total) in the matrix. The two income items are added together. Then, an inner loop subtracts each of the expense categories (3-12) from the total. After both loops have been completed, the result is tested to determine whether to print the amount of savings or to print a warning showing the amount of deficit spending in the budget. The subroutine ends with a statement returning to the main program.

Translating the design into a complete program is a rather straightforward operation. You do need to be careful to type the subscripts correctly. Writing the actual line numbers on the flowcharts (as was done in the illustrations) helps keep the GOTO and GOSUB statements straight (Fig. 11-16).

This program is considerably longer than any of the previous programs in this book. It is still not a long program by commercial standards. It is long enough that the advantages of using REMark statements and subroutines should be obvious when you read it and match the statements with the design. When you enter it into your computer, you will need to devise tests to check that each of the options on the flowchart work correctly.

You may have found that the use of arrays and the budget matrix make the program hard for you to read and understand. That should not be a concern if this is your first experience with matrices. You can reassure yourself of the value of arrays by trying to write a program that uses only simple variables to produce the same results as the Budget program. Avoiding the use of arrays will make your program use at least ten times as many statements.

Chapter 12

Using Data Files

Most business computers spend very little time computing. The majority of the work done on business computers involves maintaining files of information. Typically a company will file all of its bills, checks, personnel information on employees, customer mailing lists, and inventory lists of equipment in its computer. The programs that work with this information act more like an efficient clerk with a large number of filing cabinets than like a scientist or mathematician with a calculating machine.

Even a small microcomputer can store and retrieve a tremendous number of symbols using peripheral storage devices such as disk drives and tape recorders. However, there are definite limits to how many variables even the largest computer can reasonably process at the same time. Therefore, the crucial design problem for handling large volumes of information in a computer is how to organize the data into meaningful units small enough to process easily and large enough to be useful.

FILES AND RECORDS

A *file* is a collection of information on any subject. A file is typically stored in a peripheral storage device (tape or disk for computer files, cabinets or shelves for paper files). A file does not have a defined size. It can grow larger as the information is added and it can shrink as information is deleted. A file can be completely empty (having no information) or it can be as large as your storage space allows. Computer files with millions of items of information are not uncommon.

The usefulness of a file is determined at least as much by how it is organized as by what information it contains. A file that consists of all of the mail you have ever received stuffed into a large box is less useful than a smaller file of all of the bills you have received arranged in the order in which you have to pay them.

The main unit for organizing information in files is the *record*. A record is a collection of information that describes an individual or logical unit. All information about the same unit should be stored in the same record (or group of records) and the information on a particular record should describe the same unit. A recipe file has one record for each recipe. Each recipe record has the name of a particular dish, a list of ingredients, and the cooking instructions for that dish; it will not include the ingredients or instructions for any other dish. Occasionally, some strange information (like a scribbled phone number) may appear on a record where it does not belong. Such information does not help one use the file and may be confusing. The technical data-processing term for information stored in a record or file where it does not belong is "garbage." Good computer filing systems are designed to prevent garbage from getting stored.

A record can be as simple as an index card which lists a single name and phone number, or as complicated as a family doctor's record with sections identifying the family, insurance information, medical history of each family member, a list of all charges and payments, and pages of illegible notes written by the doctor. There are computer techniques to handle records with variable options (like the doctor's record), but those techniques are beyond the scope of this book.

Most computer files can be designed to use fixed format records. A fixed format record is like a form. Blank spaces (or variables) are set aside to hold specific pieces of information (values) in specific places. The same information (name, address, etc.) is in the same place on every copy of the form.

The card catalog in a library is an example of a file that uses fixed format records. Actually, library catalogs contain three types of records (author cards, title cards, and subject cards), but records of the same type have the same format. Figure 12-1 shows the format for an author card. The top left-hand corner contains a call number (the code libraries use to locate the book on their shelves). The top line contains the name of the author of a book. The other lines contain the title, publisher, city of publication, copyright year, and a list of subjects covered by the book. This information can be conveyed without labeling the items on each card as long as you know the general format describing where each item is listed. There will be a different author card for each book in the library, but the format for each will be exactly the same. The title and subject cards have their own format, which is slightly different than the format for the author card, but as long as you know which record format you are looking at you should have no trouble reading the card.

Most computer files use unlabeled records, like the library catalog cards. Only the data values are stored on tape or disk. This saves both time and space in reading and writing records. The format of the record is described within the computer programs. If several different record types

EXAMPLE:

```
834.234  Galbraith, Richard

         COMPUTER PROGRAMMING: Starting with the BASICs
         TAB Books,     Blue Ridge Summit, PA
         1981

         Computers, BASIC Language
```

RECORD FORMAT:

```
Call-Nbr. Author's Name
          Title of Book
          Publisher Name     City
          Copyright Year

          Subjects
```

Fig. 12-1. Author record in a library card file.

are stored in the same file, each record must contain a value (usually the first item in the record) which tells which type of record it is. Otherwise, the program would not be able to interpret the information in the record properly. Whenever feasible, it is best to use the same record format for each record in a single file.

One of the first steps in designing any computer filing system is to write a record description. A record description should specify what unit is used for each record. Is there one record for each person, or one record for each month, or one for each person each month? Any one of those definitions might be used to file mortgage payment records. You might have one record showing all payments made by an individual. You might prefer to look at all payments for a given month at the same time. Or, you might want to have a separate record for each payment received. The remainder of the record description is a data dictionary listing the data items (and the variable name that will represent them) in the order in which they appear on the record.

A record can contain any combination of lower level data types. Some of the items on a record might be strings, others might be integers, and still others floating-point numbers. A record can also contain one- or two-dimensional arrays. The designer is free to build records in any format that makes sense to him. The only restriction is that each item or array in the record should describe the unit defined for that record.

MEMBERSHIP FILING SYSTEM

The main points of computer file processing can be illustrated by a program that solves a fairly common and simple problem. The purpose of the program will be to keep track of the members of a club or other organization. The program will use a membership file which contains one record for each member. The main program must add new records to the file (when a new member joins), change the information on existing records (when a member moves), delete records (when a member quits), and display information about a specific member. Since the file will be stored on tape or disk, other programs may use the same file to print mailing labels for the organization's newsletter or print lists of members who are behind in paying their dues.

You can assume that the organization already has a membership file, with information written on 3-by-5 cards as in Fig. 12-2. The top section of the membership card can be represented by a series of string variables for last name, first name, street address, city, state, ZIP code, and the area code and phone number. (The R prefix was chosen for the variable names to show that they are part of Record, but any legal BASIC variable names could be used.) It is possible to use number variable types for the ZIP code and phone number. However, if the ZIP code were defined to be a number, then the code 07612 would be printed as 7612 (dropping the leading zero). A seven-digit phone number might be subject to rounding errors, plus using the string data type allows the dash to be included as part of the number. It

SAMPLE CARD:

```
Smith, Robert          (602) 555-8100
123 W. Main
Phoenix, AZ 85001

Joined: 6-76           ASSOCIATE
Paid thru: 12-82         # 40576
```

BASIC RECORD DESCRIPTION:

Variable	Item
R1$	Last Name
R2$	First Name
R3$	Street Address
R4$	City
R5$	State
R6$	ZIP Code
R7$	Phone Area Code
R8$	Phone Number
R9$	Membership Type
S1	Date Joined
S2	Dues Paid Through Date
S3	Membership Number

Fig. 12-2. Membership card and record description.

is often best to define large number codes (like social security numbers) to be values of string variables and restrict the use of number variables types to items you might conceivably use in arithmetic.

The bottom lines of the membership card contain the type of membership (life, regular, associate, and student—or whatever categories the particular club uses), the membership number assigned to the individual, the date the member first joined the club, and the date for which his dues are currently paid up. The type of membership is obviously a string variable. The membership number is defined to be a standard number variable. If you want to get fancy, you can have your program automatically assign membership numbers to new members by adding one to the last number assigned. Formatting the dates requires some extra thought.

Dates can be defined in a number of ways. The international standard for dates is the form: CCYY-MM-DD (century, year, month, and day). This format is convenient for arranging dates in order or comparing dates to see which is larger. Without the dashes, each date could be a single number variable. Americans are generally more used to the Gregorian format: MM/DD/YY (month, day, and year). This format is more difficult for computers to work with because 120180 is a larger number than 011585 even though the second number represents a much later date. Nevertheless, if you are writing programs for Americans, you will probably want to have the dates look right to your users. One compromise is to use separate variables for the month, day, and year of each date. Then you can arrange them any way you want.

In the sample, you only need to worry about the month and the year. A single decimal number, with the integer part representing the month and the fractional part representing the year, can be used for each of these dates. If the dates have to be compared, the month and year can be separated using some arithmetic and the INTeger function. If S1 is one of these dates, the month (M) will equal INT(S1). The year (Y) will equal 100 * (S1 – M). Of course, the decimal date will print 6.82 instead of 6/82, but it is easier to type month and year.

Now that the format for the record has been determined, you need to decide how the file will be stored, on tape or disk (or even punched cards).

STORING A COMPUTER FILE

Unfortunately, BASIC does not include a standard method of storing and reading files. The specific commands you use and the physical arrangement of the information in the computer and its peripherals will depend on the particular brand of system you are working with and whether you are using tape or disks for your files. The following discussion covers the most common variations. The sample BASIC routines are written to work with Microsoft BASIC as implemented on Radio Shack® computers. The same ideas and designs are used in time-sharing systems (such as Hewlett-Packard) and other microcomputer BASICs (such as Applesoft).

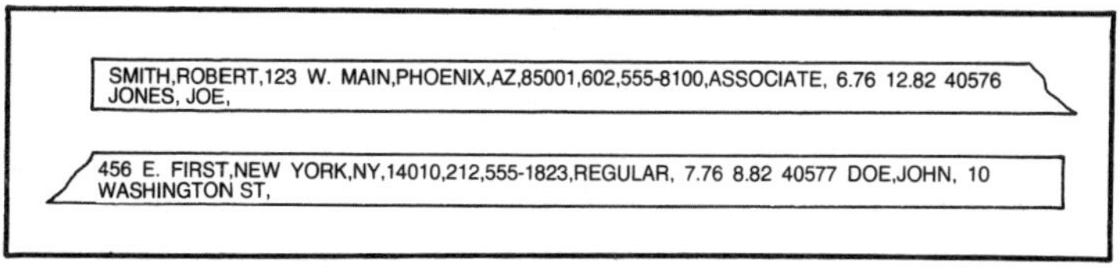

SMITH,ROBERT,123 W. MAIN,PHOENIX,AZ,85001,602,555-8100,ASSOCIATE, 6.76 12.82 40576
JONES, JOE,

456 E. FIRST,NEW YORK,NY,14010,212,555-1823,REGULAR, 7.76 8.82 40577 DOE,JOHN, 10
WASHINGTON ST,

Fig. 12-3. Records stored sequentially on tape.

But a few of the specific command words have to be changed to match the local dialects of these other manufacturers. The differences were not created by the manufacturers to confuse programmers or to make it more difficult for their customers to switch to other machines. When BASIC was originally created, it was designed for use by college engineering students. The authors did not give the students the ability to use large data files. Later, several different authors devised ways to improve BASIC, giving it file commands. The revisionists tried to stay consistent with the spirit of standard BASIC. However, since different programmers do not think exactly alike, the improvements to BASIC came out looking slightly different from each other.

The most common way to store data records in a computer system is in a *sequential* file. Figure 12-3 illustrates the format of part of a sequential file stored on tape. The various data items are written in a sequence, one right after the other. The items for the first record are stored together, followed by the items for the second record, etc. In BASIC, the items are separated by commas (or other delimiters), so the computer will be able to tell where one item ends and the next begins. There is no information on the file itself that tells how many items belong to each record, or what any item means. That information must be part of the record description the programmer builds into each program that uses the file.

There will be gaps of blank spaces on the tape or disk files. Each time the computer reads or writes information on a tape, the motor of the recorder has to start moving the tape. It takes a fraction of a second for the tape to set up to normal speed, which requires that a fraction of an inch of tape be left blank before each segment of data. Disks are divided into segments called *sectors*. On most microcomputer systems, each sector contains 256 bytes (characters). The computer actually moves information to and from disks a sector at a time. In a sequential file, the division between sectors may come in the middle of the record. The computer does not know or care where the record ends until it is told by an instruction in the program.

One side effect of having gaps within files is that there is no way for the computer to know it has reached the end of the file. The blank space after the last record will look just like a big gap. Every sequential file needs to have a special end of file record. Some systems automatically provide a standard EOF (end-of-file) marker. BASIC generally requires that the programmer define and write his own end-of-file record. This is similar to the special end-of-data value you used in READ loops in Chapter 7. If your file has a string variable, it can be given the value "END-OF-FILE" for the final record. If all of your variables are numeric, then a value like −99999 can be used to indicate the end of the file. In either case, the end-of-file record in BASIC should have the same format (number of values of each data type) as a regular record, because your program will not be able to test to see if it has reached the end of the file until after it has read the last record into memory.

ASSIGNING FILES TO PROGRAMS

A computer program cannot use the information in a file while it is stored on a peripheral tape or disk. The information must first be read into the computer's memory. The BASIC commands for copying information from a peripheral file into memory all use a file number followed by a list of variables which hold the copied values in memory. Some systems require a preliminary command to set aside temporary space to receive messages from the peripheral files. This preliminary command may be part of the operating system. Radio Shack's Disk BASIC asks for the number of files when it loads BASIC into the machine. The answer provides the number of files allowed for any programs run in BASIC. Other systems, like Hewlett-Packard's BASIC, require a FILES command at the beginning of each program that uses disk files.

In a few cases, the computer will know which file you want to use directly from the file number. Cassette systems frequently have a special file number reserved for each tape recorder. Any time you refer to that file number, the computer will automatically look at whatever tape is in that recorder. The standard tape recorder in Radio Shack's computers always has file number −1.

If your system does not automatically assign file numbers, then your program must include a command that matches each file number with the peripheral file you want to use. Disk files always require some type of assignment command. Hewlett-Packard BASIC uses the command: ASSIGN File-name, File-number, Response-Code. The file-name is the name given to the file when it is stored on disk. This name is stored in the disk directory, just like the short program names you use when you SAVE or LOAD a program. The file-number is the small integer that the rest of the commands in the program will use to refer to the file. It is usually best to assign your files starting with 1 and to number consecutively for however many files your program needs. The file numbers are used only inside a particular program. The file named MEMBERS might be assigned to file number 1 in one program and file number 3 in another program. The response-code is a variable that can be tested to see whether or not the computer found the requested file name in the directory when it started the ASSIGN command. If the named file does not exist on the disk, any attempt to read the file is doomed to fail. If your program is writing information to a file, the response-code can tell you whether it will be erasing an old file with the same or creating a totally new file. The following code might be used in a Hewlett-Packard program:

```
10 FILES *                                    'standard assignment
20 ASSIGN "MEMBERS",1,R
30 IF R = 0 THEN 100                          'file not on directory
40 PRINT"MEMBERS FILE IS ALREADY ON DISK."
50 PRINT"DO YOU WANT TO REPLACE IT (1 FOR YES)";
60 INPUT A
70 IF A = 1 THEN 100
80 PRINT"CANNOT CONTINUE WITH PROGRAM"
90 END
100 REM CONTINUE WITH PROGRAM
```

Microsoft BASIC uses an OPEN command instead of the ASSIGN command. The format is: OPEN Type$, File-number, File-name. The Type$ value specifies whether the program will use the file as input or output. The file-number and file-names have the same meaning as in the ASSIGN version of the command.

The value "I" for Type$ tells the computer that the program will read the information from an existing file. If the named file does not already exist in the disk directory, the BASIC will print an error message. Also, your program will not be able to write information on a file opened for input.

The value "O" for Type$ tells the computer to prepare to write information on the disk. If the named file is already on the disk, the new information will be written in the same place as the old file, erasing whatever was stored there. If there is no file on the directory with the requested name, then the computer will set up a new file. If the disks do not have room for a new file, the system will print an error message.

You cannot have the same sequential file open for both input and output at the same time. Instead, you need to open the old file for input and a new file for output, which will give you a different copy of the input file. After you are finished, you can get rid of the extra copy of the file with a KILL command. KILL file-name will release a data file from disk exactly like KILL program-name removes a program from disk.

Any file that has been OPENed for use should be CLOSEd after the program is finished with it. The CLOSE command releases the file from the assigned file-number and updates the directory on disk. If a file is not closed after it is changed, the computer may not be able to find it on disk the next time you try to use it. The CLOSE statement is simply the word CLOSE followed by the file-number to be closed. If no file-number is specified, then all of the open files will be closed.

READING A FILE

The INPUT# command reads information from a file into the computer's memory. The verb INPUT# is followed by the assigned file-number and a list of variables which will hold the values copied from the input file.

Commas are used to separate the file number and each of the variables. The statement INPUT#1A,B,C would copy three standard number items from file number 1 into the variables A, B, and C. The program could then use the variables with the file information just like any other program variables in BASIC statements. If the statement were repeated, the next three items on file #1 would be copied into the same variables, replacing the first set of values.

The data types in the INPUT# statements have to match the data types of the values in the file. Otherwise, an error message will be printed, abruptly ending the program. The normal way to keep the INPUT# formats matched with the data on the file is to read an entire record at a time. For large records this might require two or more consecutive INPUT# commands, but reading a whole record allows the program to use the record description to keep the values straight. The following statement would read a record from the "MEMBER" file assigned to file # 1:

```
200 INPUT#1,R1$,R2$,R3$,R4$,R5$,R6$,R7$,R8$,R9$,S1,S2,S3
```

Hewlett-Packard BASIC uses the verb READ# instead of INPUT#. Otherwise, its file reading command works exactly like the sample explained above.

The illustration statements allow only a single record to be processed in the computer at a time. As soon as a second record is read (or input) into memory, the values of the first record are lost. Since the file is stored sequentially, the program cannot go back and look at the first record again unless the file is closed and reopened to start at the beginning. Processing a file this way requires some special planning during the design. The complete design for sequential processing is presented in Chapter 13.

If the file is small enough so that all records can be stored in memory at the same time, then programming to use the file becomes much more flexible. The remainder of this chapter will assume that the club has so few members that the membership records will fit into your computer's memory.

To store the records in memory, the program will require enough variables to hold the values on the file. The easiest way to do this is to use arrays in place of each item on the record description. Each record can be given a number as it is read, and that number can be used as a subscript for all the arrays. Figure 12-4 shows how the MEMBER file might be stored in a group of twelve arrays. The initial statements in the program would have to have CLEARed enough string space and DIMensioned all the arrays to reserve space for the largest number of records that could be in the file.

When an array is used to store the records in memory, the entire input file can be copied into memory with a single routine at the start of the program. The design for this routine will be very similar to a loop used to load a table. The major difference is that you do not know ahead of time exactly how many records are in the file. That number will change every time a record is added or deleted. So, instead of using a FOR . . . NEXT loop, you have to count the records in the program and quit when you read

RECORD#	R1$	R2$	R3$	R4$	R5$
1	SMITH	ROBERT	123 W. MAIN	PHOENIX	AZ
2	JONES	JOE	456 E. FIRST	NEW YORK	NY
3	DOE	JOHN	10 WASHINGTON	SEATTLE	WA
.	.	.	.	.	.
.	.	.	.	.	.
.	.	.	.	.	.

RECORD#	R6$	R7$	R8$	R9$	S1	S2	S3
1	85001	602	555-8100	ASSOCIATE	12.82	6.76	40576
2	14010	212	555-1823	REGULAR	8.82	7.76	40577
3	95002	333	555-9023	REGULAR	9.83	8.79	42345
.	.	.	.	.	.	.	.
.	.	.	.	.	.	.	.
.	.	.	.	.	.	.	.

Fig. 12-4. Records stored in arrays.

the special end-of-file record. The design for a file reading loop is shown in Fig. 12-5. If you are using a tape system with an automatically assigned file number, then the OPEN and CLOSE boxes should not be included in your design.

This design adds to the count before each record is read. When the program discovers it has reached the end of the file, it has to subtract one back from the count. This appears awkward. Why not wait until after the record has been read to count it? It could be done if your BASIC allows zero as a subscript. The problem is that the INPUT# (or READ##) statement uses the record count as a subscript to determine which element of the array to use for the incoming record. Counting the record before reading it allows the first record to use element number 1 of each array, and so forth. Fixing the count to avoid counting the end-of-file marker as a real record only requires a single statement, which is not a high price to pay for having the records numbered in what most people consider to be the normal way.

Additional flexibility can be provided by using a string variable for the file name in the OPEN statement (Fig. 12-6). By having the user give the name of the file he wants to use for this run, the program can be used unaltered to maintain information on any number of different clubs. The ability to use the same programs for several different sets of data will make those programs more valuable, and will let you expand your computer use beyond your original requirements with no new programming work.

WRITING A FILE

When you finish running a program, the values of its variables are lost. To keep the information for later use, those values must be written on a data file. Values are stored on a peripheral device by the PRINT# command (or, in some dialects, the WRITE# verb). The PRINT# command requires the file-number of some file that has been assigned to an output device (either by the system or by an OPEN statement). The file number can be followed by any list of values, variables, and expressions that would be acceptable in a normal PRINT command. (Exception: The TAB(function may not be allowed when PRINTing to a data file.)

With tape systems, the PRINT# statement will look exactly like the INPUT# statement (except for the verb itself) that will be used to read the file later. On some disk systems there are several complications to be considered.

The PRINT# command may copy the values indicated by the variable names and expressions into the end of the sequential file in the same format that a plain PRINT command would copy them onto the video screen or printer. If the variable names are separated by commas, a number of unnecessary blanks would be written between the variables on the tape or disk. This does not cause serious problems, but it does waste space. Generally, it is best to use semicolons between the variables and expressions on a disk PRINT# statement because that avoids writing the extra blanks. The statement PRINT#1, A;B;C will store the values of the three

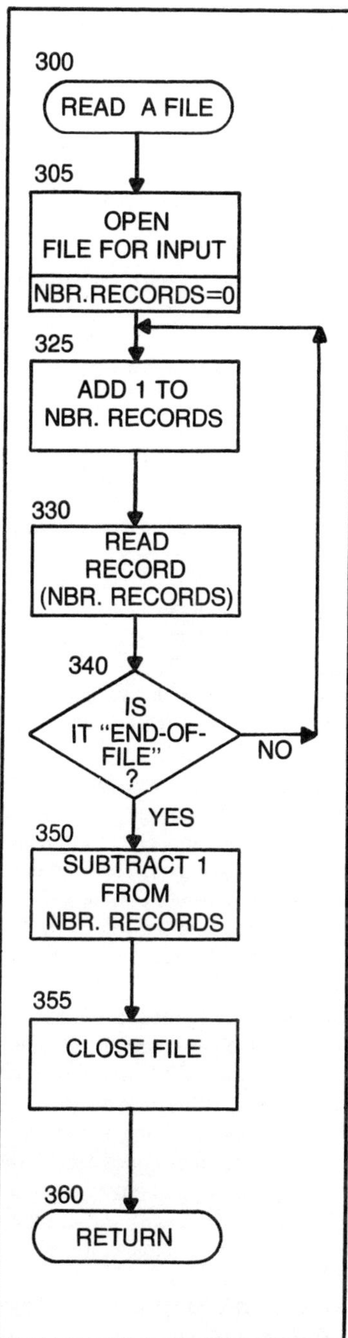

Fig. 12-5. Flowchart to read a file into arrays.

```
300 REM  ***  READ A DISK FILE  ***

305  PRINT "NAME OF FILE TO READ";

310  INPUT F$

315  OPEN "I",2,F$                  'Microsoft Disk File Assignmen
     t

320  LET N = 0                      'Initialize Record Count

325  LET N = N + 1

330  INPUT#2, R1$(N), R2$(N), R3$(N), R4$(N), R5$(N), R6$(N), R
     7$(N), R8$(N), R9$(N), S1(N), S2(N), S3(N)

340  IF R1$(N) <> "END-OF-FILE" THEN325

350  LET N = N - 1                  'Do not count END-OF-FILE reco
     rd

355  CLOSE 2

360  RETURN

365 REM---------------------------
```

Fig. 12-6. File-reading subroutine.

variables on the file. Repeating the statement without changing the values of the variables would result in a file with six entries; the sequence of the values of A, B, and C would be repeated twice.

The PRINT# statement does not automatically write any delimiters between variables. This does not cause any problems with number variables because all number values are normally printed with one blank space as the last character. When the computer reads the file with an INPUT# statement, it will be able to tell where each number variable ends by that final blank. String variables do create a problem. The statements PRINT#1, "JOHN";" PAUL" and PRINT#1, "JOHN PAUL" produce exactly the same image on tape or disk (at least in some versions of BASIC). If this is the case in your version of BASIC, then each string value needs to be followed by a comma written on the file. PRINT#1, A$;",";B$ will write the value of A$, followed by a comma and the value of B$. This format will be accepted by a later INPUT#1, A$,B$ statement. Without the comma in the PRINT# statement, the INPUT# statement would combine the values of both the original A$ and B$ into a longer string which would then be stored in A$. You may have to experiment a little with your system to see whether or not it requires the commas to be written. Writing unnecessary commas will be just as destructive as not including them where necessary. A file starting with the values: "JOHN,,PAUL,," would be treated by an INPUT#1, A$,B$ statement by storing the value JOHN in A$ and an empty string (printed as a blank) in B$ because each comma signals the end of a string.

Normally, each PRINT# statement will write one entire record to a file. The list of variables on the PRINT# statement should be the same as

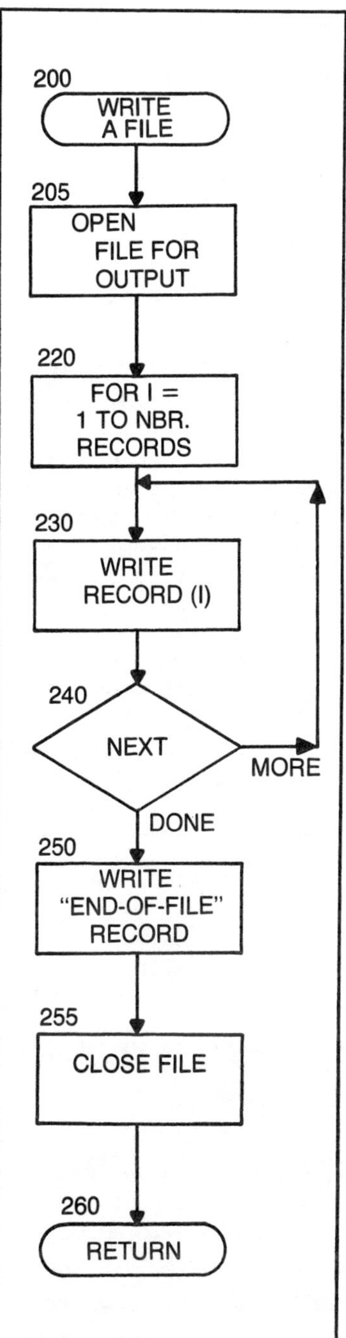

Fig. 12-7. Flowchart to write a file from arrays.

the record description used in reading the same file. This is not an absolute requirement of BASIC, but it makes it much easier to keep the items in each record straight in the programmer's mind. The command to write one record to the MEMBER file on a tape system that automatically provides the commas would look like:

```
200 PRINT#1, R1$, R2$, R3$, R4$, R5$, R6$, R7$, R8$,
    R9$,S1,S2,S3
```

On a disk system that does not automatically supply delimiters between string variables, the equivalent statement would be:

```
200 PRINT#1, R1$;“,”; R2$;“,”; R3$;“,”; R4$;“,”; R5$;“,”; R6$;“,”;
    R7$;“,”; R8$;“,”; R9;“,”; S1; S2; S3
```

When the regular records have been written, the BASIC program must write special end-of-file record. Without that record, any program that tries to use the file later will end up searching for the final record forever. The easiest way to write an end-of-file record is to LET the first variable in the regular PRINT# statement equal the special end-of-file value the programmer has chosen, then repeat the standard PRINT# command (which would not have to be rewritten if it were a subroutine). Alternately, you can write a separate end-of-file PRINT# statement with values for the variables in the record. A short final record produced by: PRINT#, “END-OF-FILE” would not work. The program that reads the file with an: INPUT#1, R1$, R2$, R3$, R4$, R5$, R6$, R7$, R8$, R9$, S1, S2, S3 would continue to try to find values for R2$ through S3 before your program was able to check to see that R1$ had the value: END-OF-FILE.

Figure 12-7 diagrams a subroutine used to write a file of records stored in a series of arrays in the computer's memory. The program will have to

```
200  REM  ***  WRITE DISK FILE  ***"

205  PRINT "NAME OF FILE TO WRITE";

210  INPUT F$

215  OPEN "O",1,F$          'Microsoft Disk File Assisnment

220  FOR I = 1 TO N         'All Records

225  PRINT#1, R1$(I);","; R2$(I);","; R3$(I);","; R4$(1);","; R
     5$(I);","; R6$(I);","; R7$(I);","; R8$(1);","; R9$(1);",";
      S1(I); S2(I); S3(I)

240  NEXT I

250  PRINT#1,"END-OF-FILE,"; "END,"; "END,"; "END,"; "END,"; "E
     ND,"; "END,"; "END,"; "END,"; 0; 0; 0

255  CLOSE 1

260  RETURN

265  REM ---------------------------
```

Fig. 12-8. File-writing subroutine.

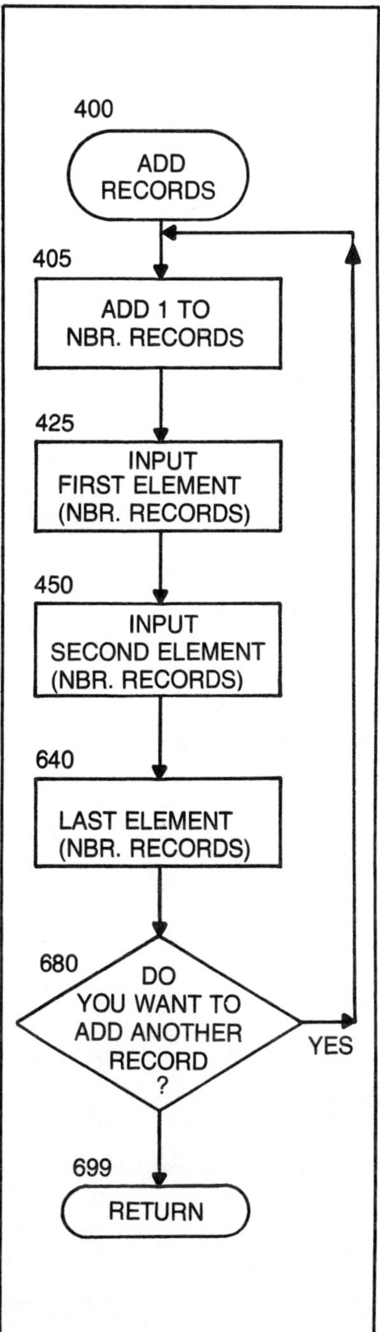

Fig. 12-9. Flowchart for adding records.

```
400  REM  ***  ADD RECORDS  ***
405      IF N < M  THEN 420            'Is the File Full?
410      PRINT"FILE IS FULL -- CANNOT ADD RECORDS"
415      GOTO 699                      'Exit -- Return
420      LET N = N + 1
425      PRINT"LAST NAME";

430      INPUT R1$(N)
435      IF LEN(R1$(N)) > 1 THEN 450
440      PRINT"NAME MUST HAVE AT LEAST TWO LETTERS."
445      GOTO 425
450      PRINT"FIRST NAME";
455      INPUT R2$(N)
460      PRINT"STREET ADDRESS";
465      INPUT R3$(N)
470      PRINT"CITY";
475      INPUT R4$(N)
480      PRINT"STATE";
485      INPUT R5$(N)
490      IF LEN(R5$(N)) = 2 THEN 505
495      PRINT"USE 2 LETTER POSTAL ABBREVIATION."
500      GOTO 480
505      PRINT"ZIP CODE";
510      INPUT R6$(N)
515      IF LEN(R6$(N)) = 5 THEN 530
520      PRINT"ZIP CODE MUST BE 5 DIGITS."
525      GOTO 505
530      PRINT"PHONE -- AREA CODE";
535      INPUT R7$(N)
540      IF LEN(R7$(N)) = 3 THEN 555
545      PRINT"AREA CODE HAS 3 DIGITS."
550      GOTO 530

555      PRINT"PHONE NUMBER";
560      INPUT R8$(N)
565      IF LEN(R8$(N)) = 8 THEN 580
570      PRINT"PHONE NUMBER SHOULD BE 8 CHARACTERS, COUNTING THE DA
         SH."
```

```
575     GOTO 555
580     PRINT"MEMBERSHIP TYPE";
585     INPUT R9$(N)
590     PRINT"MEMBERSHIP NUMBER";
592     INPUT S3(N)
594     IF S3(N) > S3(N-1) THEN 600
596     PRINT"THAT NUMBER HAS ALREADY BEEN USED."
598     GOTO 590
600     PRINT"DATE JOINED (MM.YY)";
605     INPUT S1(N)
610     IF S1(N) < 13 AND S1(N) >= 1 THEN 625
615     PRINT"MONTH MUST BE 1 TO 12."
620     GOTO 600
625     IF S1(N) <> INT(S1(N)) THEN 640
630     PRINT"ENTER YEAR AFTER THE DECIMAL POINT."
640     PRINT"DUES PAID THRU (MM.YY)";
645     INPUT S2(N)
650     IF S2(N) < 13 AND S2(N) >= 1  THEN 665
655     PRINT"MONTH MUST BE 1 TO 12."
660     GOTO 640
665     IF S2(N) <> INT(S2(N)) THEN 680
670     PRINT"ENTER YEAR AFTER THE DECIMAL POINT."
675     GOTO 640
680     LET A$ = "YES"                'Default is Add Another Record
685     PRINT"DO YOU WANT TO ADD ANOTHER RECORD (YES/NO)";
690     INPUT A$
692     IF A$ = "YES" THEN 405
698     RETURN
699 REM ----------------------
```

Fig. 12-10. Add records subroutine.

use some variable (N) to keep track of the number of records in the file. This allows the bulk of the work to be done with a simple FOR . . . NEXT loop that copies each element of the arrays in turn onto a peripheral file. After all the records have been copied, the special end-of-file record is written. On tape systems, the OPEN and CLOSE boxes may not be necessary. The statements for implementing this design using Microsoft Disk BASIC is shown in Fig. 12-8.

ADDING RECORDS TO THE FILE

A record can be added to a file stored in memory by a simple sequence. First, the number-of-records count needs to be increased by one so it will be the subscript of the first empty slot in the arrays. Next, a value for each item in the record is INPUT into the appropriate array variable. By adding an option at the end of the sequence which ask the user if he wants to enter another record, the ADD RECORDS subroutine becomes a loop that can be used to add as many records as wanted to the file (Fig. 12-9).

Actually, there is a limit to the number of records you will want to add to your file. If you try to add more records than the memory of the computer will hold, your program will die with an error message (destroying all the additions that you have made). You cannot make your computer hold an infinite number of records, but you can include a test in your program that will prevent an attempt to add too many records from causing a fatal error. If you compare the current number of records to the maximum number allowed by your DIMension statements, you can stop the user from adding more records than your program can handle (see lines 405—415 in Fig. 12-10). This will not solve the problem of handling the extra record. That will require starting a second file or changing the program. But at least it will keep all the records already entered from being wiped out.

The length of your ADD RECORDS routine will depend on how many items are on each record and how thoroughly you test the input values to make sure no bad data gets on your file. Figure 12-10 lists a subroutine that does a moderate amount of input validation for the twelve items in the Member record description. The order in which the items are entered in the subroutine should be the order that will make the most sense to the person who has to type the information. It does not have to match the order of the items in the record description. It is easier for you to design programs that are easy for people to use than it is for you to design people that can easily use complex programs.

With this design, you do not need a separate program or routine to create a file. If you choose not to read a file into memory, adding records will start a new file by adding records starting with record number one.

FINDING AND DISPLAYING A RECORD

Storing information in a computer file does not do you any good unless you have a way of retrieving the information when you want it. One reason for having a membership list on a computer is to find information on a particular member known either by name or membership number.

You can write a subroutine which will compare the values of any item in each record to a value specified by the user of the program. When the values match, you will have found the record you are looking for. The item you choose to match with the user's value is commonly called a *key field* for the record. The value the user is looking for is called the *search key* or key value. For the Member file, the last name of the member is an item that you would probably want to use as a key field. You could decide to use several different items in the same record as key fields, or you could create a key field combining several different items on each record. However, each key field would require its own matching subroutine. For the sake of simplicity, the sample program will only use the last name as the key for displaying a record.

When the records are stored in arrays, searching for a record requires a process very similar to looking up a value on a table. After the user has specified which record he wants by entering a value for the search key, the program starts with the first record and compares the value of the key field (subscripted by a counter variable) to the search key. If the values do not match, the search continues with the next record (Fig. 12-11). If the values

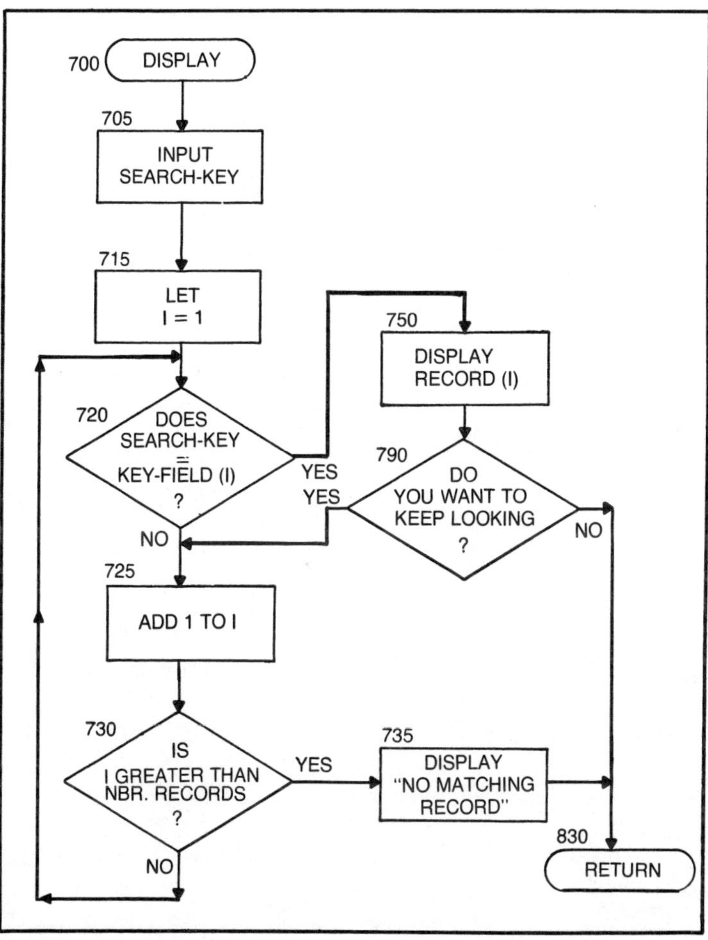

Fig. 12-11. Flowchart to find and display a record.

do match, then you can display the values of all of the items on that record with PRINT statements.

If the key is unique, that is if no two records have the same value for the key field, then the search can end as soon as a matching record is found. However, if more than one record could have the same value in the key field, then the first record that matches the search key may not be the record the user wants to see. The member's last name is not likely to be a unique key. Even a small club is likely to have two Smiths or a couple of brothers in its membership. Under these conditions, the search routine will need an option to continue to look for other records that match the same key. This option is provided by lines 790-820 in Fig. 12-12.

```
700  REM  *** FIND & DISPLAY A RECORD ***
705     PRINT"LAST NAME OF MEMBER";
710     INPUT K$                          'Search Key
715     LET I = 1
720     IF K$ = R1$(I) THEN 750
725     LET I = I + 1
730     IF I <= N THEN 720                'Loop for Search
735     PRINT"NO SUCH MEMBER ON FILE."
740     PRINT
745     GOTO 830                          'Exit -- RETURN
749  REM -- MATCH FOUND --
750     PRINT
755     PRINT R1$(I);", "; R2$(I); TAB(30);"("; R7$(I); ") "; R8$(
        I)
760     PRINT R3$(I)
765     PRINT R4$(I);",  "; R5$(I);"    ";R6$(I)
775     PRINT"   JOINED:"; S1(I); TAB(30); R9$(I)
780     PRINT"PAID THRU:"; S2(I); TAB(30);"$"; S3(I)
785     PRINT
790     LET A$ = "NO"                     'Default is stop search
795     PRINT"LOOK FOR ANOTHER MEMBER WITH SAME NAME";
800     INPUT A$
805     IF A$ = "YES" THEN 725
810     IF A$ = "NO"  THEN 830
815     PRINT"ANSWER  'YES'  OR  'NO'";
820     GOTO 800
830     RETURN
835  REM -----------------------
```

Fig. 12-12. Display record subroutine.

The search routine would not be completed without a test to see whether the end-of-file was reached without finding a matching record. In arrays, this can be done by comparing the counter variable to the number of records currently stored.

The display should be formatted to please the eye of the user. The format provided by lines 750-785 in Fig. 12-12 was designed to look like the original membership card shown in Fig. 12-2. You may want to modify these lines so the record looks better when displayed on your particular computer.

MODIFYING A RECORD

The membership records of some individuals will need to be changed from time to time. A member may move, which requires changing the address and phone number on his record. A member may change his/her name, most likely upon marriage. Most members will pay dues at least once in a while, which may coincide with a change in their type of membership. Some members will quit or die; their records should be deleted from the file.

The first step in any of these changes is to find the record that needs to be changed or deleted. Thus, the left side of the flowchart for a modification subroutine could be identical to the search and display subroutine (Figs. 12-11 and 12-13). The major difference between the two routines is that the modify routine has to do more work after the record has been found.

The sample modification routine uses the membership number as the search key. The membership number is unique; no two members can be given the same membership number. (To ensure this, the add-records routine checked to make sure that each membership number was larger than the previous one.) Using a unique key reduces the chances of accidentally changing the wrong record. It also simplifies the process slightly by eliminating the need for an option to search for another record once a match has been found.

In this design, a menu is displayed along with the record. The menu offers choices for changing three groups of items (address/phone, name, and dues paid/membership type). This division matches the three types of events discussed above as the logical causes for information to be changed. The actual changes can be accomplished with INPUT statements for the specific items in the record (identified by the matching subscript). After the change has been made, the program returns to the statements (lines 1050-1085) that display the record. This allows the user to verify that his change has been made correctly. It also allows the user to choose from the same menu again, making several changes to the same record without having to repeat the search.

Looping back to the menu requires that the menu offer the choice of accepting the record the way it is displayed and going to the exit point for the subroutine. The final choice in the menu is deleting the record. After the

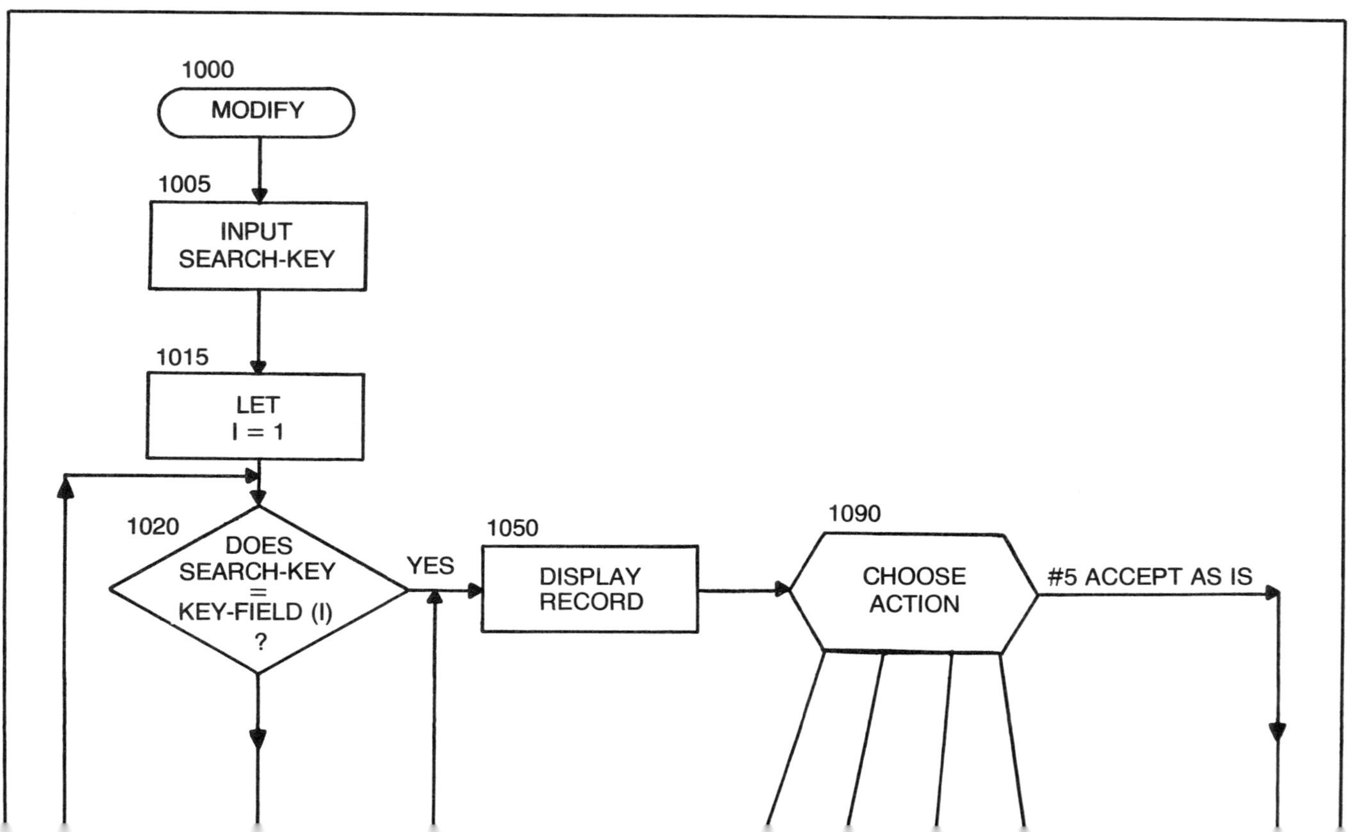
1000
MODIFY
1005
INPUT
SEARCH-KEY
1015
LET
I = 1
1020
DOES
SEARCH-KEY
=
KEY-FIELD (I)
?
YES
1050
DISPLAY
RECORD
1090
CHOOSE
ACTION
#5 ACCEPT AS IS

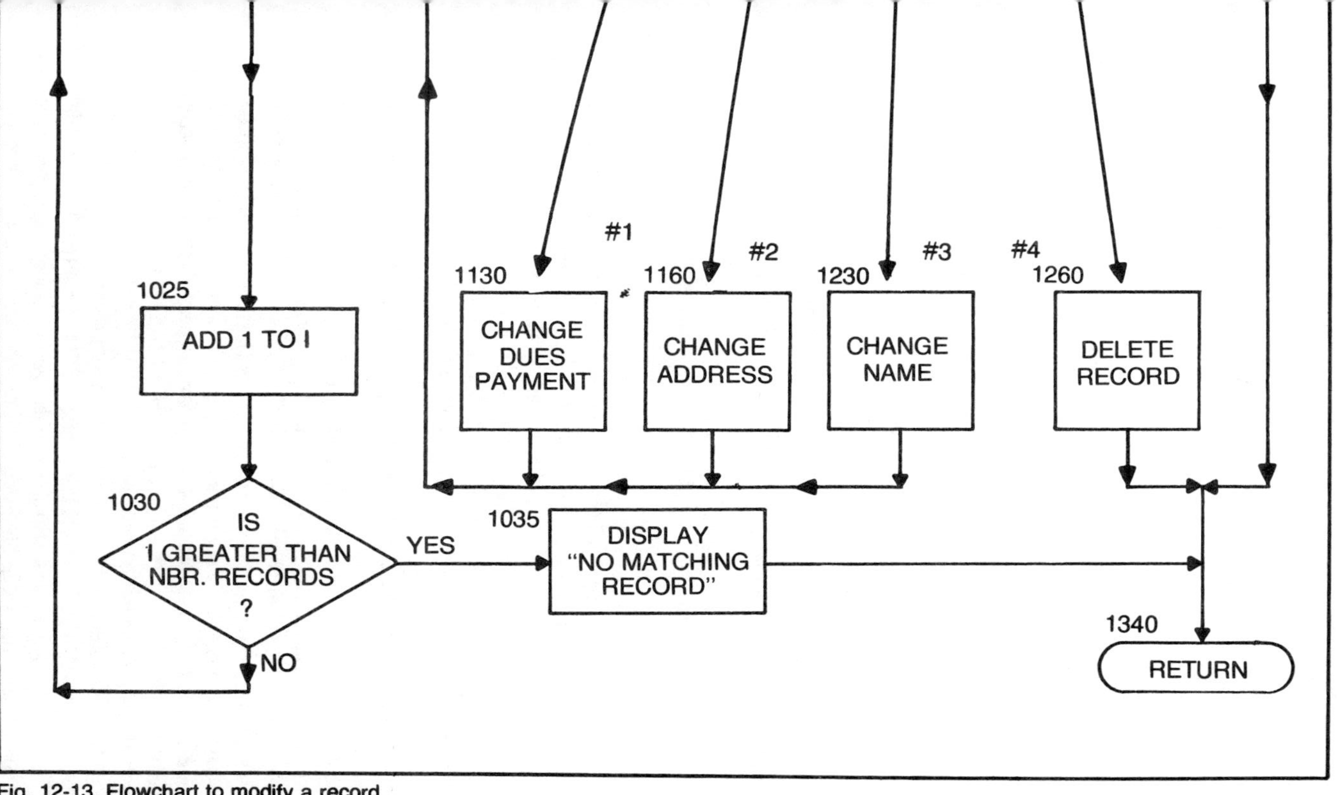

Fig. 12-13. Flowchart to modify a record.

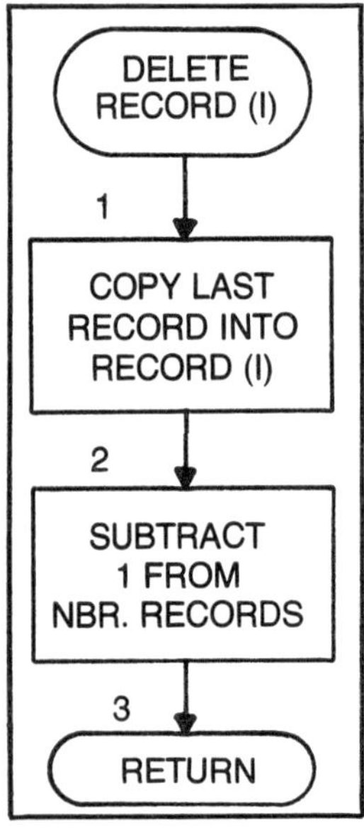

Fig. 12-14. Flowchart for a simple deletion.

record is deleted, it obviously cannot be displayed again. So the delete process is automatically followed by the subroutine exit.

DELETING A RECORD

You can delete a record from a manual card file by simply throwing away the card for that record. The file will then have one less card than it did before. Deleting a record from the middle of an array is slightly more complicated. You cannot just erase the right element in each array because the file uses the subscript of the array to count records. The computer would still count the blank entries as a record.

The easiest way to fill the blank space where a deleted record used to be is to replace each item in the old record with the same item for the last record on the file (Fig. 12-14). This will remove all evidence of the old record from the file. It will also leave you with two copies of the last record on the file. Next, you subtract one from the counter the program uses to count the total number of records in the file. This will make the computer think it has the right number of records. The old last record will be ignored, because the computer will stop looking at the arrays when it reaches the number of the ignored item because you have stored a duplicate in place of the deleted record. Figure 12-15 shows the contents of a five record file at each stage of the deletion process.

One side effect of this design for deleting records is that the order of the records is changed. The old last record is no longer at the end of the file. This may or may not cause a problem with your file. Assume that you were keeping the membership file in order of membership number. When you add a new member, you look at the last membership number in the file and assign the next number to the new member. If the old last record had been moved, you would end up with several members having the same number.

The process for deleting a record from a file without changing the order of the remaining records is similar to the process when you remove one slide from a slide projector and then, move each of the following slides forward one space so there will be no glaring blanks in the show. The record deletion process would replace the record to be deleted with a copy of the record following it. Then the next record in line would replace the duplicate record preceding it. The process would continue as illustrated by Fig. 12-16 until the last record was copied. Then the record count would be reduced by one to ignore the old (duplicate) copy of the last record. This tedious process can be accomplished with a loop (Fig. 12-17). If your file involves many records with several string variables, the copying may take a few minutes.

The entire subroutine for finding, then changing or deleting a record in a file, is listed below as Fig. 12-18. Lines 1265-1330 form the loop that copies records for a deletion.

TOP-LEVEL DRIVER

Normally, the first step in designing a program with several functions is to develop a top-level flowchart that shows how all the functions will fit together. This chapter started by separately examining each of the major file-handling functions. None of the subroutines that have been developed thus far would be a useful program by itself. They need to be combined.

The top-level design will not add any new ideas to your programming knowledge. It will essentially be a menu followed by a case structure to

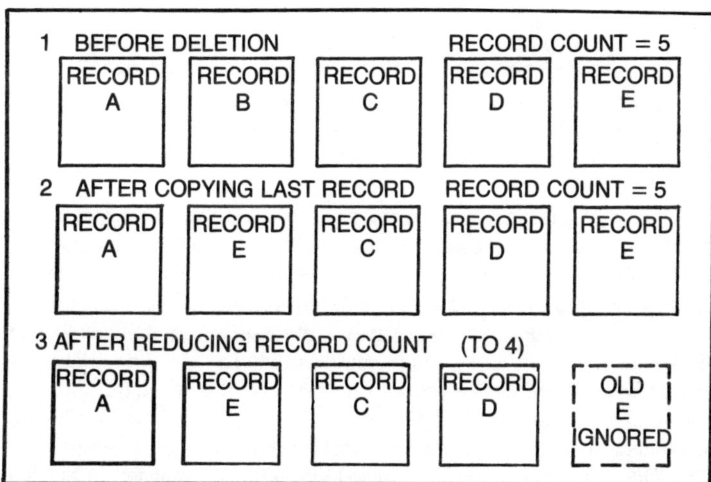

Fig. 12-15. A file during record deletion.

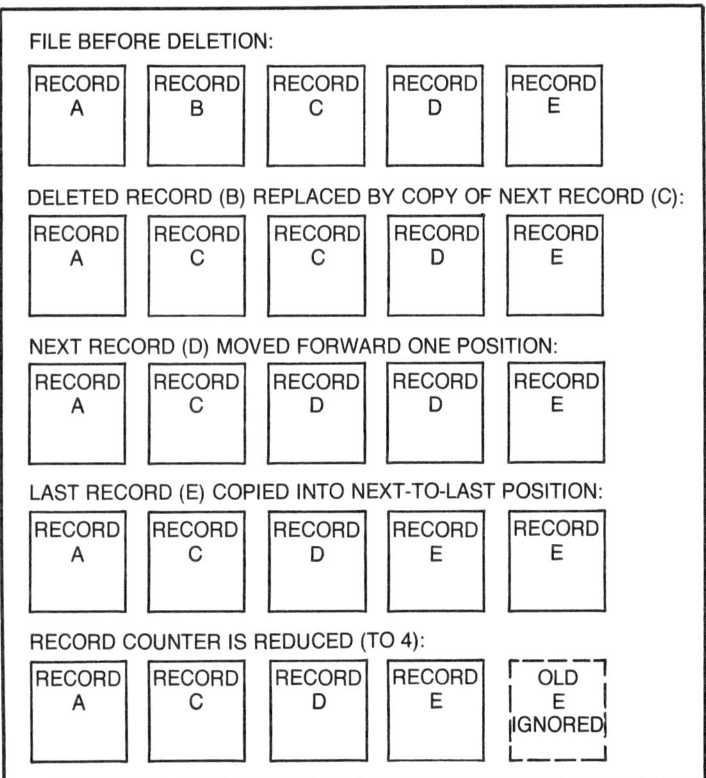

Fig. 12-16. Deletion without changing the order.

select the appropriate function. Since individual tasks have already been written as subroutines, the program that drives those functions will have to recognize that, after each subroutine is completed, the program will continue with the next line in sequence. This may make it a little harder to write the main program, but that is the price to be paid if you do not design the whole program from the top down.

The first lines in the main program (Fig. 12-19) will have to set aside memory space for all of the arrays that the file will use. Using a variable to specify the maximum number of records the arrays will hold (line 20) makes it much easier to change the size for different amounts of available memory. Once the file space has been set up, the program enters its main loop by displaying a menu listing all of the options (lines 35-90). An INPUT loop asks the user for his choice and tests to make sure it is one of the options in the program. The series of IF . . . THEN statements (lines 135-185) implement the case structure for selecting the requested subroutine.

The final subroutine (lines 1400-1455) prints a reminder that ending the program will erase all records currently in the computer and gives the user another chance to save his file on disk or tape. There are few things more frustrating to a person using a computer than for him to complete his work and then accidently erase everything he has entered in the computer. A good programmer will minimize the likelihood of such accidents.

Figure 12-20 closes the chapter with the complete Member file handling program. Most of the statements (lines 200-1350) have been listed earlier in the chapter. Remember, if you are not using a disk system with BASIC written by Microsoft, you will have to revise some of the lines in the subroutines that actually read and write your files.

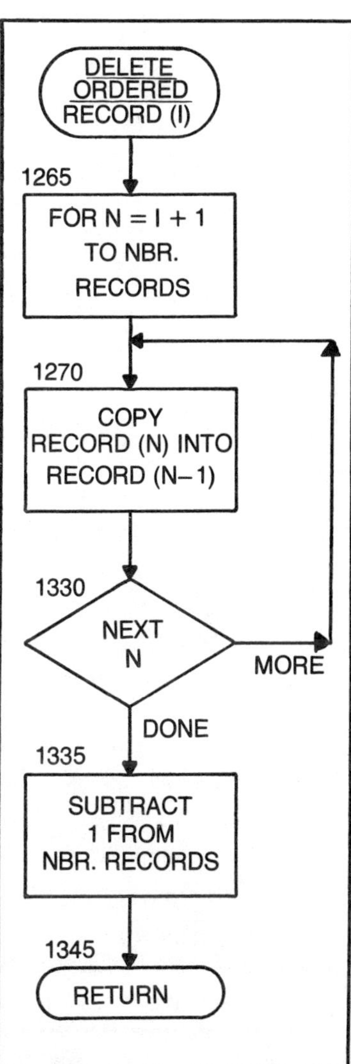

Fig. 12-17. Flowchart to preserve order while deleting.

```
1000 REM  *** MODIFY A RECORD  ***
1005     PRINT"MEMBERSHIP NUMBER TO FIND";
1010     INPUT K                        'Numeric Search Key
1015     LET I = 1
1020     IF K = S3(I) THEN 1050
1025     LET I = I + 1
1030     IF  I <= N   THEN 1020              'Continue Search
1035     PRINT"NO SUCH NUMBER ON FILE."
1040     PRINT
1045     GOTO 1340                           'Exit -- Return
1049 REM -- MATCH FOUND --
1050     PRINT
1055     PRINT R1$(I);", "; R2$(I); TAB(30);"("; R7$(I); ")  "; R8$
         (I)
1060     PRINT R3$(I)
1065     PRINT R4$(I);",  "; R5$(I);"   "; R6$(I)
1075     PRINT"   JOINED:"; S1(I); TAB(30); R9$(I)
1080     PRINT"PAID THRU:"; S2(I); TAB(30); S3(I)
1085     PRINT
1090     PRINT"OPTIONS: 1--CHANGE PAID STATUS    2--CHANGE ADDRESS/
         PHONE"
1095     PRINT"         3--CHANGE NAME           4--DELETE RECORD
1100     PRINT"         5--ACCEPT AS SHOWN"
1105     PRINT"CHOICE";
1110     INPUT A
1115     ON A GOTO  1130, 1160, 1230, 1260, 1345
1120     PRINT"CHOOSE BY NUMBER: 1, 2, 3, 4, OR 5";
1125     GOTO 1110
1130 REM -- CHANGE STATUS --
1135     PRINT"NEW PAID THRU DATE (MM.YY)";
1140     INPUT S2(I)
1145     PRINT"NEW MEMBERSHIP TYPE";
1150     INPUT R9$(I)
1155     GOTO 1050                      'Display Changed Record
1160 REM -- CHANGE ADDRESS/PHONE --
1165     PRINT"NEW STREET ADDRESS";
```

Fig. 12-18. Modify record subroutine.

```
1170    INPUT R3$(I)
1175    PRINT"NEW CITY";
1180    INPUT R4$(I)
1185    PRINT"NEW STATE";
1190    INPUT R5$(I)
1195    PRINT"NEW ZIP CODE";
1200    INPUT R6$(I)
1205    PRINT"PHONE AREA CODE";
1210    INPUT R7$(I)
1215    PRINT"NEW PHONE NUMBER";
1220    INPUT R8$(I)
1225    GOTO 1050                   'Display Changed Record
1230 REM -- CHANGE NAME --
1235    PRINT"NEW FIRST NAME";
1240    INPUT R2$(I)
1245    PRINT"NEW LAST NAME";
1250    INPUT R1$(I)
1255    GOTO 1050                   'Display Changed Record
1260 REM -- DELETE & PRESERVE ORDER --
1265    FOR C = I + 1 TO N          'Move all following record up
1270    LET R1$(C-1) = R1$(C)
1275    LET R2$(C-1) = R2$(C)
1280    LET R3$(C-1) = R3$(C)
1285    LET R4$(C-1) = R4$(C)
1290    LET R5$(C-1) = R5$(C)
1295    LET R6$(C-1) = R6$(C)
1300    LET R7$(C-1) = R7$(C)
1305    LET R8$(C-1) = R8$(C)
1310    LET R9$(C-1) = R9$(C)
1315    LET S1(C-1)  = S1(C)
1320    LET S2(C-1)  = S2(C)
1325    LET S3(C-1)  = S3(C)
1330    NEXT C
1335    LET N = N -1                'Reduce Record Count by 1
1340 REM  -- EXIT POINT --
1345    RETURN
1350 REM -----------------------
```

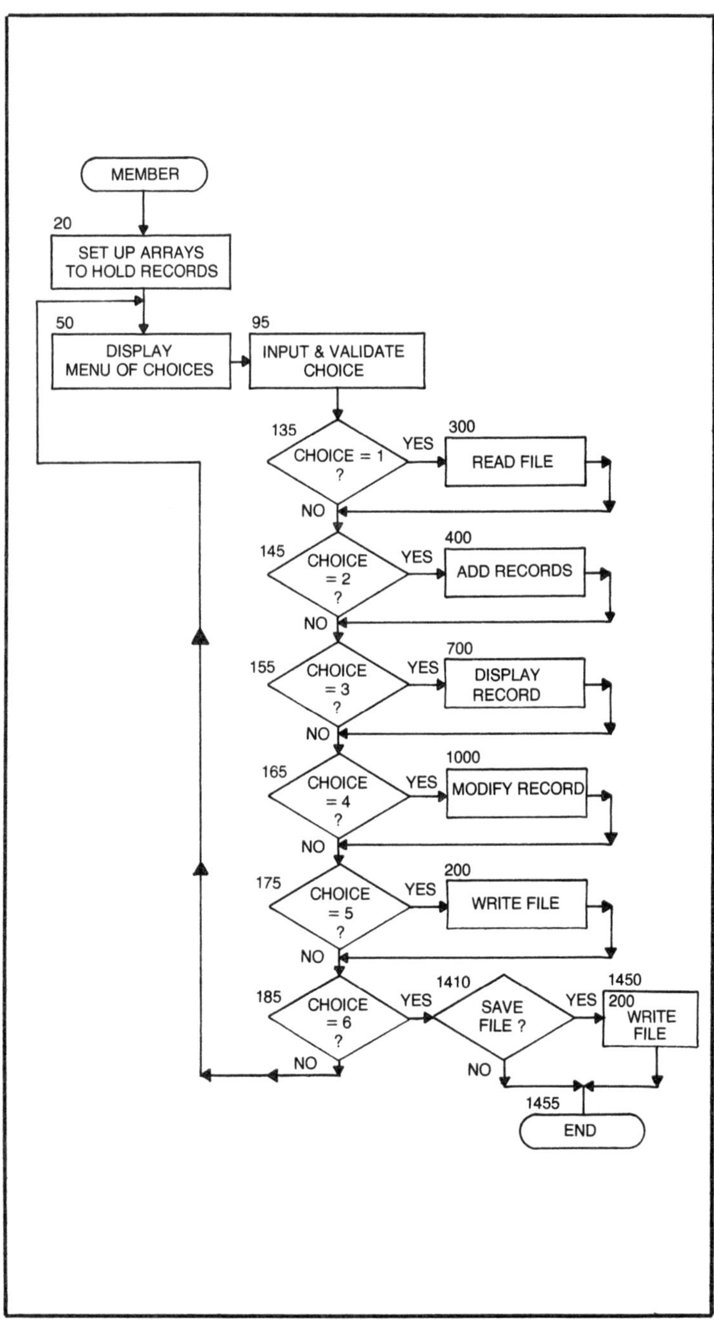

Fig. 12-19. Flowchart for top-level driver routine.

```
5    REM   MEMBERSHIP FILE SYSTEM
10   REM  by Richard Galbraith                 August. 1981
15      CLEAR 5000                                'Reserve String Space
20      LET M = 50                                'Max. Nbr. of Records
25      LET N = 0                                 'No Records at Start
30      DIM R1$(M), R2$(M), R3$(M), R4$(M), R5$(M), R6$(M), R7$(M)
        , R8$(M), R9$(M), S1(M), S2(M), S3(M)
35      FOR C = 1 TO 6                            'Print Blank Lines
40      PRINT
45      NEXT C
50      PRINT TAB(15);"MEMBERSHIP SYSTEM"
55      PRINT"FILE CURRENTLY HAS"; N;"RECORDS."
60      PRINT
65      PRINT TAB(5);"1 -- READ FILE FROM DISK"
70      PRINT TAB(5);"2 -- ADD RECORDS TO FILE"
75      PRINT TAB(5);"3 -- DISPLAY A RECORD (BASED ON NAME)"
80      PRINT TAB(5);"4 -- MODIFY A RECORD (BASED ON MEMBERSHIP #)
        "
85      PRINT TAB(5);"5 -- WRITE FILE TO DISK"
90      PRINT TAB(5);"6 -- END PROGRAM"
95      PRINT"CHOOSE ACTION (BY NUMBER)";
100     INPUT C
105     IF C > 0 AND C < 7  THEN 120
110     PRINT"ENTER A NUMBER BETWEEN 1 & 6";
115     GOTO 100
120     IF C = INT(C)  THEN 135
125     PRINT"ENTER A WHOLE NUMBER";
130     GOTO100
135     IF C <> 1 THEN 145
140     GOSUB 300                       'Read File
145     IF C <> 2 THEN 155
150     GOSUB 400                       'Add Records
155     IF C <> 3 THEN 165
160     GOSUB 700                       'Display Record
165     IF C <> 4 THEN 175
170     GOSUB 1000                      'Modify Record
```

Fig. 12-20. Complete member file processing program.

```
175     IF C <> 5 THEN 185

180     GOSUB 200                   'Write File

185     IF C = 6  THEN 1400         'End Program

190     PRINT

192     PRINT

194     GOTO 50

195  REM ------------------------

200  REM  ***  WRITE DISK FILE  ***"

205     PRINT "NAME OF FILE TO WRITE";

210     INPUT F$

215     OPEN "O",1,F$        'Microsoft Disk File Assignment

220     FOR I = 1 TO N       'All Records

225     PRINT#1, R1$(I);",";  R2$(I);",";  R3$(I);",";  R4$(I);",";  R
        5$(I);",";  R6$(I);",";  R7$(I);",";  R8$(I);",";  R9$(I);",";
         S1(I);  S2(I);  S3(I)
240     NEXT I

250     PRINT#1,"END-OF-FILE,";  "END,";  "END,";  "END,";  "END,";  "E
        ND,";  "END,";  "END,";  "END,";  0;  0;  0

255     CLOSE 1

260     RETURN

265  REM ---------------------------

300  REM  ***  READ A DISK FILE  ***

305     PRINT "NAME OF FILE TO READ";

310     INPUT F$

315     OPEN "I",2,F$               'Microsoft Disk File Assignmen
        t
320     LET N = 0                   'Initialize Record Count

325     LET N = N + 1

330     INPUT#2, R1$(N), R2$(N), R3$(N), R4$(N), R5$(N), R6$(N), R
        7$(N), R8$(N), R9$(N), S1(N), S2(N), S3(N)

340     IF R1$(N) <> "END-OF-FILE" THEN325

350     LET N = N - 1               'Do not count END-OF-FILE reco
        rd

355     CLOSE 2

360     RETURN

365  REM---------------------------

400  REM  ***  ADD RECORDS  ***

405     IF N < M  THEN 420          'Is the File Full?
410     PRINT"FILE IS FULL -- CANNOT ADD RECORDS"
```

Fig. 12-20. Continued from page 203.

```
415     GOTO 699                              'Exit -- Return
420     LET N = N + 1
425     PRINT"LAST NAME";
430     INPUT R1$(N)
435     IF LEN(R1$(N)) > 1 THEN 450
440     PRINT"NAME MUST HAVE AT LEAST TWO LETTERS."
445     GOTO 425
450     PRINT"FIRST NAME";
455     INPUT R2$(N)
460     PRINT"STREET ADDRESS";
465     INPUT R3$(N)
470     PRINT"CITY";
475     INPUT R4$(N)
480     PRINT"STATE";
485     INPUT R5$(N)
490     IF LEN(R5$(N)) = 2 THEN 505
495     PRINT"USE 2 LETTER POSTAL ABBREVIATION."
500     GOTO 480
505     PRINT"ZIP CODE";
510     INPUT R6$(N)
515     IF LEN(R6$(N)) = 5 THEN 530
520     PRINT"ZIP CODE MUST BE 5 DIGITS."
525     GOTO 505
530     PRINT"PHONE -- AREA CODE";
535     INPUT R7$(N)
540     IF LEN(R7$(N)) = 3 THEN 555
545     PRINT"AREA CODE HAS 3 DIGITS."
550     GOTO 530
555     PRINT"PHONE NUMBER";
560     INPUT R8$(N)
565     IF LEN(R8$(N)) = 8 THEN 580
570     PRINT"PHONE NUMBER SHOULD BE 8 CHARACTERS, COUNTING THE DA
        SH."
575     GOTO 555
580     PRINT"MEMBERSHIP TYPE";
585     INPUT R9$(N)
590     PRINT"MEMBERSHIP NUMBER";
```

```
592      INPUT S3(N)
594      IF S3(N) > S3(N-1) THEN 600
596      PRINT"THAT NUMBER HAS ALREADY BEEN USED."
598      GOTO 590
600      PRINT"DATE JOINED (MM.YY)";
605      INPUT S1(N)
610      IF S1(N) < 13 AND S1(N) >= 1 THEN 625
615      PRINT"MONTH MUST BE 1 TO 12."
620      GOTO 600
625      IF S1(N) <> INT(S1(N)) THEN 640
630      PRINT"ENTER YEAR AFTER THE DECIMAL POINT."
635      GOTO 600
640      PRINT"DUES PAID THRU (MM.YY)";
645      INPUT S2(N)
650      IF S2(N) < 13 AND S2(N) >= 1  THEN 665
655      PRINT"MONTH MUST BE 1 TO 12."
660      GOTO 640
665      IF S2(N) <> INT(S2(N)) THEN 680
670      PRINT"ENTER YEAR AFTER THE DECIMAL POINT."
675      GOTO 640
680      LET A$ = "YES"               'Default is Add Another Record
685      PRINT"DO YOU WANT TO ADD ANOTHER RECORD (YES/NO)";
690      INPUT A$
692      IF A$ = "YES" THEN 405
698      RETURN
699   REM ----------------------
700   REM  *** FIND & DISPLAY A RECORD ***
705      PRINT"LAST NAME OF MEMBER";
710      INPUT K$                     'Search Key
715      LET I = 1
720      IF K$ = R1$(I) THEN 750
725      LET I = I + 1
730      IF I <= N THEN 720           'Loop for Search
735      PRINT"NO SUCH MEMBER ON FILE."
740      PRINT
745      GOTO 830                     'Exit -- RETURN
```

Fig. 12-20. Continued from page 205.

```
749  REM -- MATCH FOUND --
750      PRINT
755      PRINT R1$(I);", "; R2$(I); TAB(30);"("; R7$(I); ") "; R8$(
         I)
760      PRINT R3$(I)
765      PRINT R4$(I);",  "; R5$(I);"   ";R6$(I)
775      PRINT"   JOINED:"; S1(I); TAB(30); R9$(I)
780      PRINT"PAID THRU:"; S2(I); TAB(30);"#"; S3(I)
785      PRINT
790      LET A$ = "NO"                 'Default is stop search
795      PRINT"LOOK FOR ANOTHER MEMBER WITH SAME NAME";
800      INPUT A$
805      IF A$ = "YES" THEN 725
810      IF A$ = "NO"  THEN 830
815      PRINT"ANSWER  'YES'  OR  'NO'";
820      GOTO 800
830      RETURN
835  REM ------------------------
1000 REM  *** MODIFY A RECORD  ***
1005     PRINT"MEMBERSHIP NUMBER TO FIND";
1010     INPUT K                       'Numeric Search Key
1015     LET I = 1
1020     IF K = S3(I) THEN 1050
1025     LET I = I + 1
1030     IF  I <= N   THEN 1020             'Continue Search
1035     PRINT"NO SUCH NUMBER ON FILE."
1040     PRINT
1045     GOTO 1340                          'Exit -- Return
1049 REM -- MATCH FOUND --
1050     PRINT
1055     PRINT R1$(I);", "; R2$(I); TAB(30);"("; R7$(I); ")  "; R8$
         (I)
1060     PRINT R3$(I)
1065     PRINT R4$(I);",  "; R5$(I);"   "; R6$(I)
1075     PRINT"   JOINED:"; S1(I); TAB(30); R9$(I)
1080     PRINT"PAID THRU:"; S2(I); TAB(30); S3(I)
1085     PRINT
```

```
1090    PRINT"OPTIONS: 1--CHANGE PAID STATUS    2--CHANGE ADDRESS/
        PHONE"
1095    PRINT"          3--CHANGE NAME          4--DELETE RECORD
1100    PRINT"          5--ACCEPT AS SHOWN"
1105    PRINT"CHOICE";
1110    INPUT A
1115    ON A GOTO  1130, 1160, 1230, 1260, 1345
1120    PRINT"CHOOSE BY NUMBER: 1, 2, 3, 4, OR 5";
1125    GOTO 1110
1130 REM -- CHANGE STATUS --
1135    PRINT"NEW PAID THRU DATE (MM.YY)";
1140    INPUT S2(I)
1145    PRINT"NEW MEMBERSHIP TYPE";
1150    INPUT R9$(I)
1155    GOTO 1050                    'Display Changed Record
1160 REM -- CHANGE ADDRESS/PHONE --
1165    PRINT"NEW STREET ADDRESS";
1170    INPUT R3$(I)
1175    PRINT"NEW CITY";
1180    INPUT R4$(I)
1185    PRINT"NEW STATE";
1190    INPUT R5$(I)
1195    PRINT"NEW ZIP CODE";
1200    INPUT R6$(I)
1205    PRINT"PHONE AREA CODE";
1210    INPUT R7$(I)
1215    PRINT"NEW PHONE NUMBER";
1220    INPUT R8$(I)
1225    GOTO 1050                    'Display Changed Record
1230 REM -- CHANGE NAME --
1235    PRINT"NEW FIRST NAME";
1240    INPUT R2$(I)
1245    PRINT"NEW LAST NAME";
1250    INPUT R1$(I)
1255    GOTO 1050                    'Display Changed Record
1260 REM -- DELETE & PRESERVE ORDER --
1265    FOR C = I + 1 TO N           'Move all following record up
```

Fig. 12-20. Continued from page 207.

```
1270     LET R1$(C-1) = R1$(C)

1275     LET R2$(C-1) = R2$(C)

1280     LET R3$(C-1) = R3$(C)
1285     LET R4$(C-1) = R4$(C)

1290     LET R5$(C-1) = R5$(C)

1295     LET R6$(C-1) = R6$(C)

1300     LET R7$(C-1) = R7$(C)
1305     LET R8$(C-1) = R8$(C)

1310     LET R9$(C-1) = R9$(C)
1315     LET S1(C-1)  = S1(C)

1320     LET S2(C-1)  = S2(C)

1325     LET S3(C-1)  = S3(C)

1330     NEXT C

1335     LET N = N -1                    'Reduce Record Count by 1

1340 REM  -- EXIT POINT --

1345     RETURN

1350 REM ----------------------
1355     RETURN

1400 REM  ***  END OF PROGRAM  ***

1405     PRINT

1410     PRINT"REMINDER:  IF YOU FORGOT TO WRITE THE FILE TO DISK"

1415     PRINT"             ALL OF YOUR CHANGES & ADDITIONS WILL BE L
         OST."

1420     PRINT"DO YOU WANT TO WRITE THE FILE NOW";
1425     INPUT A$

1430     IF A$ = "NO"  THEN 1455

1435     IF A$ = "YES" THEN 1450

1440     PRINT"PLEASE ANSWER  'YES'  OR  'NO'";
1445     GOTO 1425

1450     GOSUB 200                       'Write File
1455     PRINT "GOOD-BYE"
1460     PRINT
1465     END
1470 REM-------------------------
```

You may wish to modify this program for an organization of which you are a member. There are several improvements you might make. The values entered to change a record (lines 1135-1250) could be edited to make sure they are reasonable. The edits were left out of the sample to keep the printed listing short. Also, the record display should probably be a separate subroutine. That would eliminate having two sets of duplicate statements (lines 750-785 and lines 1050-1085). You may also be able to design other enhancements for your own version.

Chapter 13
Handling Large Files

Businesses often use files with thousands, or even millions, of records. It is impractical to store such large files in arrays. Small computers have only enough memory to store a few hundred moderately sized records at a time. Even the largest computers made today do not have enough memory to store a million tax-return records in arrays.

Large files are generally stored on peripheral devices. Disk files can hold much more information than the computer's central memory. Tape files, using many reels or cassettes, can handle a practically infinite number of records. The central processing unit never looks at all of the information in the file at once. Instead, the records can be copied into memory one at a time. The computer program can then do whatever the programmer has determined needs to be done with that record before the next record from the file replaces it in memory.

Most programs that use very large files are designed for *batch processing*. When you had a small file stored in memory, each time you wanted to change a record you had the program find that particular record and modify it. If you tried to use that same design with large sequential files, you would spend most of your time looking for the right record. The idea behind batch processing is to save up requests to change records (or display them) until you have a whole batch of them. If you arrange the requests in the same order as the records on the file, then you only have to search the entire file once to make every change on your list. If you wanted to change one hundred records one at a time, you would have to looking through the files one hundred times. But if your files were arranged alphabetically by name, and if also sorted the changes alphabetically, then you could make a single trip to the files and pick out the one hundred records in order.

In many businesses, several clerks spend all day preparing changes. One clerk may enter new charges while another clerk enters payments received from customers and a third clerk handles new accounts. At the end of the day, the changes entered by the clerks are sorted together. Each night the sorted batch is used to update the company's financial accounts. The next morning, the managers have a report from the computer showing the current information for their accounts.

There needs to be some way of telling what changes the computer program actually made. You would not want to have to print a copy of every record each time the file was updated and then compare the fat print-out to the previous fat print-out to see exactly what items had been changed. You also would not want an unnoticed change to be made that increased one employee's paycheck by a thousand dollars or cut your boss's paycheck accidentally. The normal way of verifying a large file update is to include an audit trail in the program to list every item added, changed, or deleted from the file, and also to print a summary at the end that shows how many records are included in each file and how many additions, deletions, and changes were made. This form of audit trail allows the results to be verified by comparing the printed report to the pile of requests for changes (transactions) without having to read through the entire file.

SEQUENTIAL UPDATE

Careful planning is needed to update a large sequential file in a single program. Some records will be added; others will be deleted or changed. Parts of the file will be left the same. The records on the file you want to change are written sequentially on a tape or disk. There is no way to fit an additional record between two records on the original tape. You cannot even change a record on the original tape, because the tape moves while you are reading the record. If you tried to write the changed record back on the same tape, you would be copying it on top of a different part of the tape. The old record would still be on the tape unchanged, plus the changed version would have wiped out the following record. The solution to this problem is to write out a whole new file each time you do a sequential update.

The standard sequential update design uses three files (Fig. 13-1). The requests for additions, deletions, and changes are batched together in one file, commonly called the transaction file. The computer program is expected to take action on each of these requests. The main file that holds all of the records, commonly called the *master* file, is read into the computer one record at a time. If none of the transactions affect the record currently in memory, it is copied to a new (or updated) master file. If one of the transactions changes the record, then those changes are made in memory before the record is copied to the new master file. After one record is copied, the next one is read into memory. When the records on the old master file have been read and changed or copied to the new master file, the process is complete. The new master will contain up-to-date information

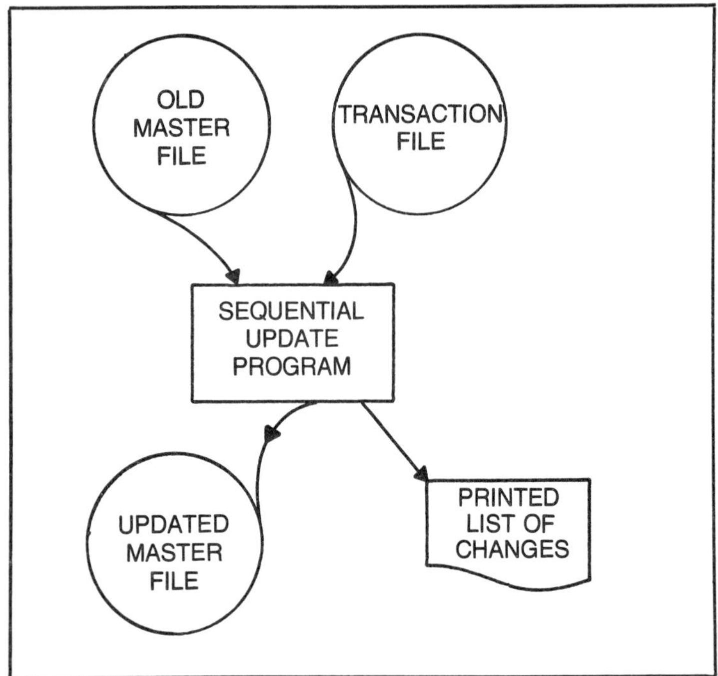

Fig. 13-1. Files for sequential processing.

for every record. The old master file and the transaction file are no longer needed.

In normal commercial practice, two or three old versions of the master file and transaction files are saved as protection against losing the current master file. If the tape or disk holding the current master file were damaged, the information on it could be recreated by using the saved transaction file to update the old version of the master file. Some provision for having back-up copies of important files is vital to every business data-processing plan. Even if you had a printed copy of the payroll information for each of the ten thousand employees of a large company, think of the cost and time it would take to type that information back into the computer. Also, think of how popular you would be if nobody got their paycheck on time because your computer files were not ready.

The sequential order of master file and transactions is vital. Some key item in each record is used to match the transaction requesting a change with the master record. Both files must be arranged so the records are arranged according to the value of that key element. If three successive records on a master file were for JONES, JACKSON, and JEKYLL while the transactions were properly ordered to change JACKSON, then JEKYLL, and JONES, the record for JONES would have already been copied to the new master while the computer was looking for JACKSON. The computer would have no way to go back and correct the record for JONES. The limitation of viewing only one record at a time from each file means that the computer has to assume the records are in proper order on the file.

Since only one record is visible at a time and the program cannot go back to a previous record, it is necessary to avoid having more than one record with the same value for the key on the master file. The computer must be able to tell which particular record to change from the key (without having someone pause to look at each record). Names are seldom satisfactory as keys for large sequential files. There is always the possibility that two people with the same name will have records on file. It is easier to ensure that each record will have a unique key if some specially created code, such as a social security number or account number, is used as the key. The common complaint about computers treating people as numbers is a by-product of making unique keys out of numbers. Computers do not really prefer to address people as numbers. They would be just as happy to use fingerprint codes or unpronouncable strings of letters or anything else that would have a different value for each record in their files.

The key in a sequential file should not be an item whose value can change. If you were to change the value of the key item in a file (as when JEKYLL changes his name to HYDE), the record would no longer be in its proper sequence. To maintain the file in sequential order (without resorting the records), you would need to add a record for HYDE and delete the record for JEKYLL as though they were two distinct records.

The rest of this chapter assumes you are working with a sequential file that has a numeric key item. The first record on the file will have the lowest value in the key item. Every following record will have a larger value in its key field than any preceding record.

The batch design can handle all changes to a file in a program that stores just three records in memory at a time, one for each file. The old record will hold the last record read from the input file. The work record will store the next record written to the updated output file. The third record in memory is a copy of the current transaction (change request). These records are shown in Fig. 13-2.

Since the main file is sequential, the key field in the work record will always be less than the key field in the old record. If the key in the transaction record matches the key in either the work record or the old record, then your program could make changes to the record in memory. If the transaction key is in between the values for the old and work records, then you could add a new record in sequence by writing a copy of the work record to the output file and moving the information on the transaction record to the work record. If the transaction key matches the old record, then the old record can be deleted by reading the next record from the input file into the old record (without copying the old record to the new file).

The transaction key will often have a larger value than the old record. This will be the case anytime you have not reached the desired part of the file. To move forward to the next record in the file, you would write a copy of the work record on the output file, move the old record to the work record, and read the next record from the input file. Each time you repeat this process, you move records from the input file into the computer's memory and onto the updated file. This will let you copy the parts of the input file not affected by any transactions unchanged on the output file.

If the value of the transaction key ever gets less than the key field in the work file, you have missed your chance. Either the transaction was out of sequence, i.e., its key is smaller than the key of the preceding transaction, or there is no record on the input file to match the key on that transaction. In either case, the program must reject the transaction as an error and go on to look at the next transaction.

Some special problems arise at either end of the sequential file. In the beginning, you do not know what record belongs in the work record. The first record written to the new file may be a copy of the first record on the input file, or it may be an addition from the first transaction. One way to start the program without any trouble is to read the first input record into the old record, read the first request on the transaction file into the transaction record, and put a fake "header" record in the work record. To guarantee that the records will appear in sequence, the key in the header record can be given the lowest possible value. If the keys on real records are all positive numbers and the lowest number allowed by your computer is negative, you will always be able to know whether the work record is a real record or the fake header. Similarly, the highest value that your computer allows can be used as the end-of-file value in your sequential files. This will keep the values of the old record and work record in sequence,

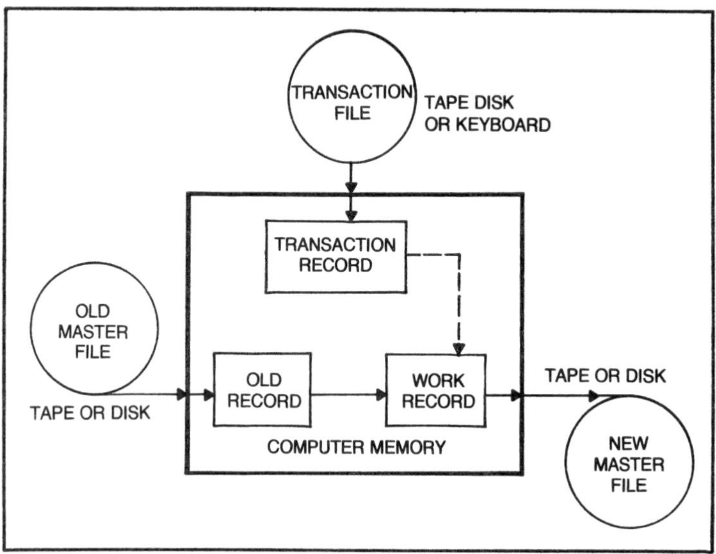

Fig. 13-2. Record storage during a sequential update.

even at the ends of the files. The program will still have to include some special checks to make sure it does not copy the fake header record as part of the updated file, nor tries to read another record from the input file after the end-of-file record has been copied into memory.

TOP-LEVEL DESIGN

As with most other programming problems, the sequential update is easier to understand if you work with an example. Suppose the organization you wrote the membership program for grew to a thousand members. Your computer can no longer hold the member's records in memory. It is time to write a sequential update program to handle the same information.

The data dictionary will be considerably different. No arrays or subscripts are needed. Instead, you will have variables named for each item in the transaction file, old file and new file. Figure 13-3 is a data dictionary which uses the same variable names for items in the old file that were used in the earlier Member program. The matching items in the new and transaction files have names with matching numbers. The names in the new file start with "U" (for update). The names for the transaction file start with

RECORD DESCRIPTIONS			
Transaction	**Old File**	**New File**	**Description Transaction Type**
C0$			
C1$	R1$	U1$	Last name
C2$	R2$	U2$	First name
C3$	R3$	U3$	Street address
C4$	R4$	U4$	City
C5$	R5$	U5$	State
C6$	R6$	U6$	ZIP code
C7$	R7$	U7$	Phone area code
C8$	R8$	U8$	Phone number
C9$	R9$	U9$	Membership type
D1	S1	T1	Date joined (MM.YY)
D2	S2	T2	Dues paid thru (MM.YY)
D3	S3	T3	Membership Nbr.*KEY FIELD*

COUNTERS

NI Number of records read from input file
NT Number of transactions read
NN Number of records written on new file
NA Number of records added
ND Number of records deleted
NC Number of change transactions processed
NR Number of transactions rejected as errors

OTHER

F1$ Name of input (old) file
F2$ Name of output (new) file
HV Highest value available on computer
LV Lowest value available on computer

Fig. 13-3. Data dictionary for membership update.

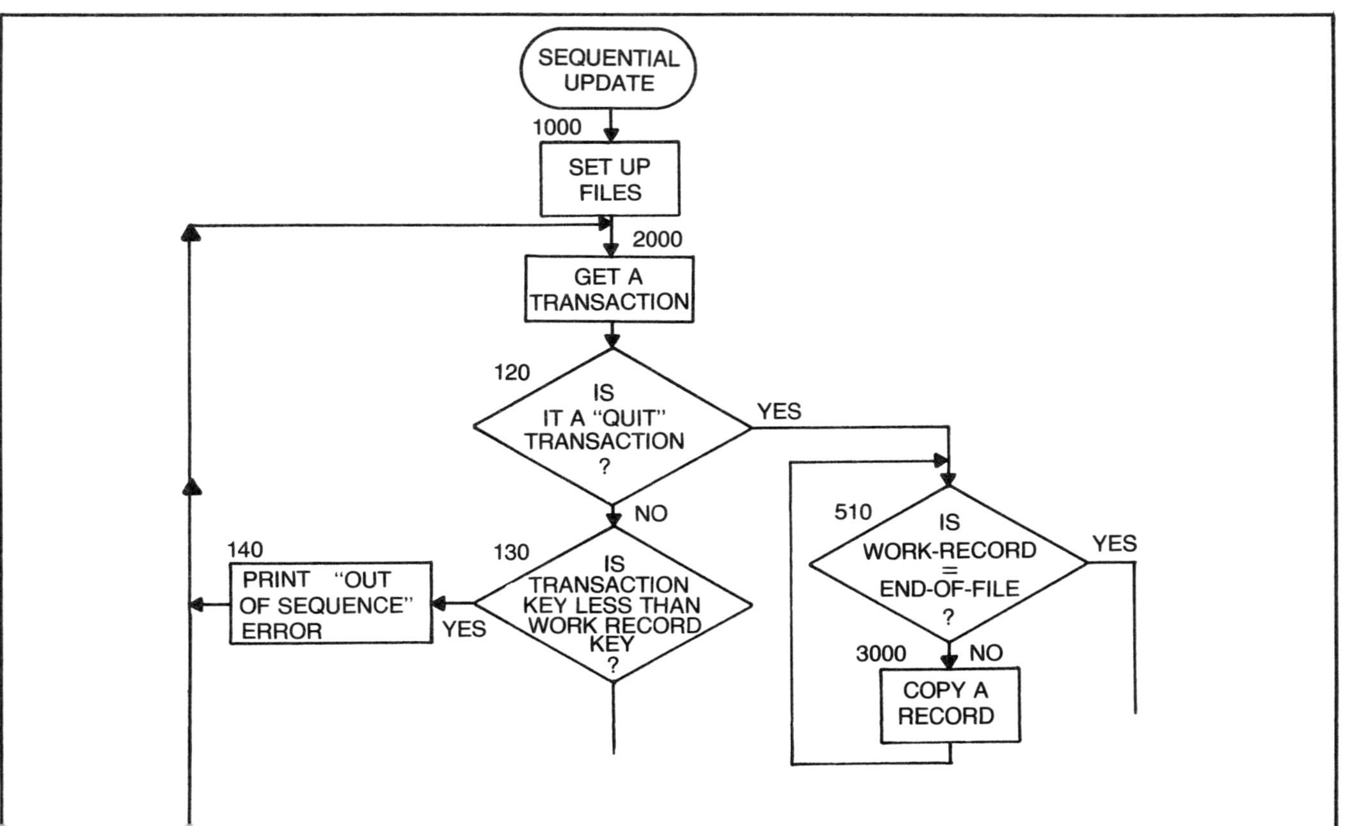
SEQUENTIAL UPDATE
1000
SET UP FILES
2000
GET A TRANSACTION
120
IS IT A "QUIT" TRANSACTION ?
YES
NO
510
IS WORK-RECORD = END-OF-FILE ?
YES
NO
3000
COPY A RECORD
130
IS TRANSACTION KEY LESS THAN WORK RECORD KEY ?
YES
140
PRINT "OUT OF SEQUENCE" ERROR

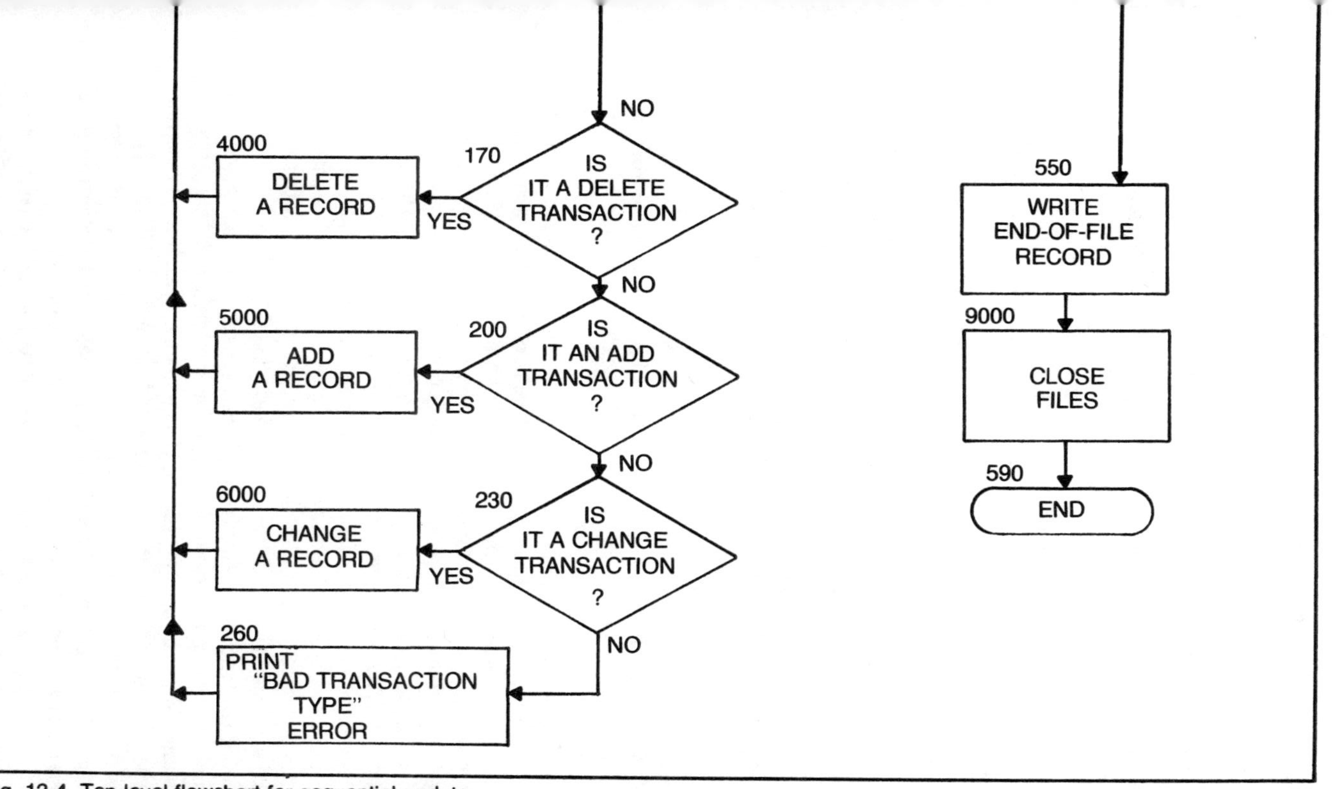

Fig. 13-4. Top-level flowchart for sequential update.

"C" (for change request). The transaction file has one additional item (CO$) which identifies the type of action requested (delete, add, or change). You could choose any names you like, but it does help if the variable names are chosen in a way that helps you keep track of which file each item belongs to and which items in different files have the same meaning.

The program will need variables to count everything that happens for the audit trail. Counters are provided for the number of records in each file; the number of addition, deletion, and change transactions processed; and the number of transactions rejected because of errors. Ideally, the number of rejected transactions will always be zero, because you would never make any mistakes in typing transactions. Nevertheless, your program should be designed to take care of the worst possibilities.

Other variables are included for the file names of the old and new files on disk. Each time the file is updated, you will probably want to give the updated file a slightly different name than before. One good idea is to include the date as part of the name. A file updated on July fourth might be named: MEMB0704. That way you could always tell which version of the file was the most recent just by looking at its name.

The highest possible value (HV) and lowest possible value (LV) are assigned to special variables for two reasons: It is easier to type HV the same way many places in a program than to type 1.70141E+38. The highest value possible on one computer might not be the same as the highest value on another computer. If the value is assigned to a variable at the beginning of the program, it will be much easier to change the program to work on a different computer than if you had to find (and change) the different statements that check for the high value code.

Programmers use several different designs for updating sequential files. The design developed in this book centers around a loop that determines what happens to each transaction. The body of the loop begins when a transaction is copied into memory. (You do not have to worry about the specific statements for getting the transaction into memory. That can be identified as a subroutine.) If it is a request to quit making changes (the end-of-file record for transactions), the program leaves the loop. If the membership number (key field) in the transaction is less than the key in the work record, then the transaction is out of sequence. The program cannot go backwards to look for a matching record, so it must reject the transaction and start the loop over for the next transaction (Fig. 13-4).

If the type of transaction is a delete, then the program would do a deletion subroutine before getting the next transaction. Different subroutines would be used for add and change transactions. If the transaction type were anything else, the program would not know what it was supposed to do with the record, so the transaction would have to be rejected. Regardless of the type of transaction, the program would be able to respond appropriately and then return to get the next transaction.

The program would not work if you started with the loop. Before it could match the transactions with the records in the master file, the files (on disk or tape) would have to be assigned to the program and the first records moved into memory. The specific steps required to set up the files for use will depend on the type of files (and the dialect of BASIC). At the top level, this initial process can be a simple subroutine box.

The program should not end as soon as the last transaction has been processed. There may be more records on the old file that have not been read or copied yet. If the program ENDed, all of those records at the end of the old file would be missing from the new file. Before stopping, the program should check to see if each record on the old file has been processed. That will be true only when the work record in memory holds the end-of-file record. As long as there are records left in memory, the program should repeat a little loop that copies a record to the new file and replaces it with one from the old file.

Finally, after the records from the old file have been processed, the program writes the special end-of-file record (not counted as a member record in the audit trial) and does a final subroutine to close the files and print the audit trail summary.

The top-level design of the update program can be directly translated into BASIC statements with the help of the data dictionary. You won't get very far if you try to run the program as listed in Fig. 13-5. The subroutines requested in lines 100,110, 180, 210, 240, 520, and 570 have not been written yet. The details needed to complete the program have been left for lower levels of the top-down design. At this point you are probably not sure how long each important subroutine will be. The GOSUB statements assign a starting line number to each subroutine that is a thousand numbers away from any other subroutine. So, there should be enough room to fit any reasonably sized subroutine in its assigned place.

You should pay particular attention to what happens at either end of every sequential file when you review the design for a sequential process. This flowchart recognizes that some special action is needed to "prime the pump" with the first records, even though the details have been left for a later planning step. No special action is needed at the beginning of the transaction file; the first record can be treated exactly like any other record.

More programming mistakes are made in handling the end-of-file records in sequential processing than in any other sections of the design. The earlier discussion explained the necessity of copying the remaining records from the old file if the end-of-the-transaction file is reached before the end-of-master file. The other question that needs to be answered is: what happens if you run out of records in the input file before you run out of transactions?

If the end-of-file record on the input file has a key field with the highest possible value for that field, then the value of the key in the transaction can never be greater than key in the last (end-of-file) record read from the input file. That means the final record will stay in memory until all possible transactions have been processed or rejected. You could not run out of input records while looking with one for a large enough key value to match a

```
10   REM    SEQUENTIAL FILE UPDATE
20   REM    by R. Galbraith        August, 1981
30      CLEAR 300                     'Reserve String Space
40      LET HV =  1.70141E+38          'Highest Value
50      LET LV = -1.70141E+38          'Lowest Value
100     GOSUB 1000                    'Set up Files
110     GOSUB 2000                    'Get Transaction
120     IF CO$ = "Q" THEN 500         'Quit?
130     IF D3 >= V3  THEN 170         'Trans.Key >= Work Record
140     PRINT "TRANSACTION FOR:"; D3; "OUT OF SEQUENCE -- REJECTED."
145     PRINT
150     LET NR = NR + 1               'Count Rejects
160     GOTO 110                      'Next Transaction
170      IF CO$ <> "D"  THEN 200
180     GOSUB 4000                    'Delete Record
190     GOTO  110                     'Next Transaction
200      IF CO$ <> "A"  THEN 230
210     GOSUB 5000                    'Add a Record
220     GOTO  110                     'Next Transaction
230      IF CO$ <> "C"  THEN 260
240     GOSUB 6000                    'Change Record
250     GOTO  110                     'Next Transaction
260     PRINT "TRANSACTION FOR:"; D3; "BAD TYPE CODE: "; CO$; " -- R
         EJECTED."
265     PRINT
270      LET NR = NR + 1              'Count Rejects
280      GOTO  110                    'Next Transaction
290  REM ------------------------
500  REM --- END OF TRANSACTIONS ---
510      IF V3 = HV  THEN 550         'End of File?
520     GOSUB 3000                    'Copy Record
530      GOTO  510                    'Repeat
550  REM -- END OF FILE
560      PRINT#2, "END-OF-FILE,"; "END,"; "END,"; "END,"; "END,"; "EN
          D,"; "END,"; "END,"; "END,"; HV; HV; HV
570      GOSUB 9000                   'Close Files & End
580      END
585  REM
590  REM ------------------------
```

Fig. 13-5. BASIC statements for the top level of Update.

transaction. If the end-of-file record on the sequential file did not include the highest possible key, it would be a simple matter to LET the key field in the old record equal the high-value whenever the program determined that it had reached the end-of-file.

While using special high-value records at the end of a file (and low-value header records at the start) can solve problems with matching transactions to the sequential keys on the master record, they should not be treated as regular records. Some extra statements will be needed in the "copy a record" subroutine to prevent the program from adding extra copies of the header and end-of-file records to the updated file.

DELETING AND ADDING RECORDS

Deleting a record is the simplest action in a sequential update. The only information needed in the transaction record is the key value (D3 membership number) of the record to be deleted (Fig. 13-6). When the matching value (S3) is stored in the old record in memory, that record can be wiped out by reading the next record from the old file. If the key in the transaction is less than the old record, then the program needs to copy a record on the master file and loop back to see if the next record is the one to be deleted. This process will be repeated until a match is found or until the program determines that there is no record on the file with a matching key. Since the master file is in sequence based on the key field, each time the loop is repeated the key value in the old record will get larger. If that value

```
4000 REM  ***  DELETE A RECORD  ***
4010      IF D3 = S3  THEN 4100                'Match Found
4020      IF D3 < S3  THEN 4200                'No Match
4030      GOSUB 3000                           'Get Next Record
4040       GOTO 4010                           'Repeat
4050 REM  ----
4100      PRINT "RECORD #:"; S3; "  FOR: "; R2$; " "; R1$; "--IS DELET
          ED."
4110      GOSUB 8000                           'Read On Top of Old Rec.
4112       IF S3 = HV  THEN 4120
4115      LET NI = NI + 1                      'Count Input
4120      LET ND = ND + 1                      'Count Deletes
4130      GOTO 4300                            'Exit
4140 REM  ----
4200      PRINT "NO MATCH FOR TRANSACTION #"; D3; "--- CANNOT DELETE."
4210      LET NR = NR + 1                      'Count Rejects
4300      RETURN
4310 REM -------------------------------
```

Fig. 13-6. BASIC statements to delete a record.

becomes larger than the key in the transaction record, there is no chance that the program will ever find a matching record on the file. At this point the transaction should be rejected as a mistake. This process is diagrammed in Fig. 13-7.

The flowchart for adding a new record (Fig. 13-8) looks very similar to the flowchart for deleting a record (Fig. 13-6). In both cases, the key in the transaction is checked to see if it matches one of the records in memory. If there is not a match, the program checks to see if the transaction key belongs before the old record. If the transaction belongs after the old record (higher in the sequence), then a record is copied and the tests for a match are repeated. You know the loop will have to end eventually because the end-of-file record will put the highest possible value in the old record, so the transaction key will have to come before the end-of-file.

The major difference between the two processes is what happens when a match is found. The deletion subroutine carries out its deletion if a match is found and rejects the transaction if there is no match. The addition subroutine must reject the transaction if it matches one of the records already on the file to avoid creating records with a duplicated key value.

When the program has determined that there is no matching record, it knows the transaction fits between the old record and the new record. (If the transaction key were less than the key in the work record, the computer would have noticed the "no match" situation before the previous old record had been moved to the work record. It may help to review Figure 13-2 to clarify what happens as records are copied within the computer.) It can now add the new record in its proper sequence by writing the work record to the new file and replacing the work record in memory with the items in the transaction. To keep the audit trail complete, the count of new records should be increased as soon as the work record has been written on disk or tape.

There are still a couple of things that can go wrong with this design. Special consideration is needed if you want to add a record at the beginning of the file. The transaction key will be less than the old record key before any records have been moved to the work record. The values in the work record will contain the fake header that does not represent any members belonging on the updated file. (Some sequential processing designs use the header record as a permanent part of the file, counting one more record than the actual number of members. That is an acceptable practice, but it is not necessary.) Line 5200 in Fig. 13-9 has the program skip the statements that write the work record on the new file only if it is the header record with the low-value key. Then, when the items on the transaction are copied into the work record, it becomes the first record on the new file.

The other problem arises when someone wants to add and delete records with the same key value during the same run of the program. If both the deletion and add subroutines checked for matches in the work record, you could add a record with one transaction, then turn around and delete it with the next record. You could not delete an old record and then add a new

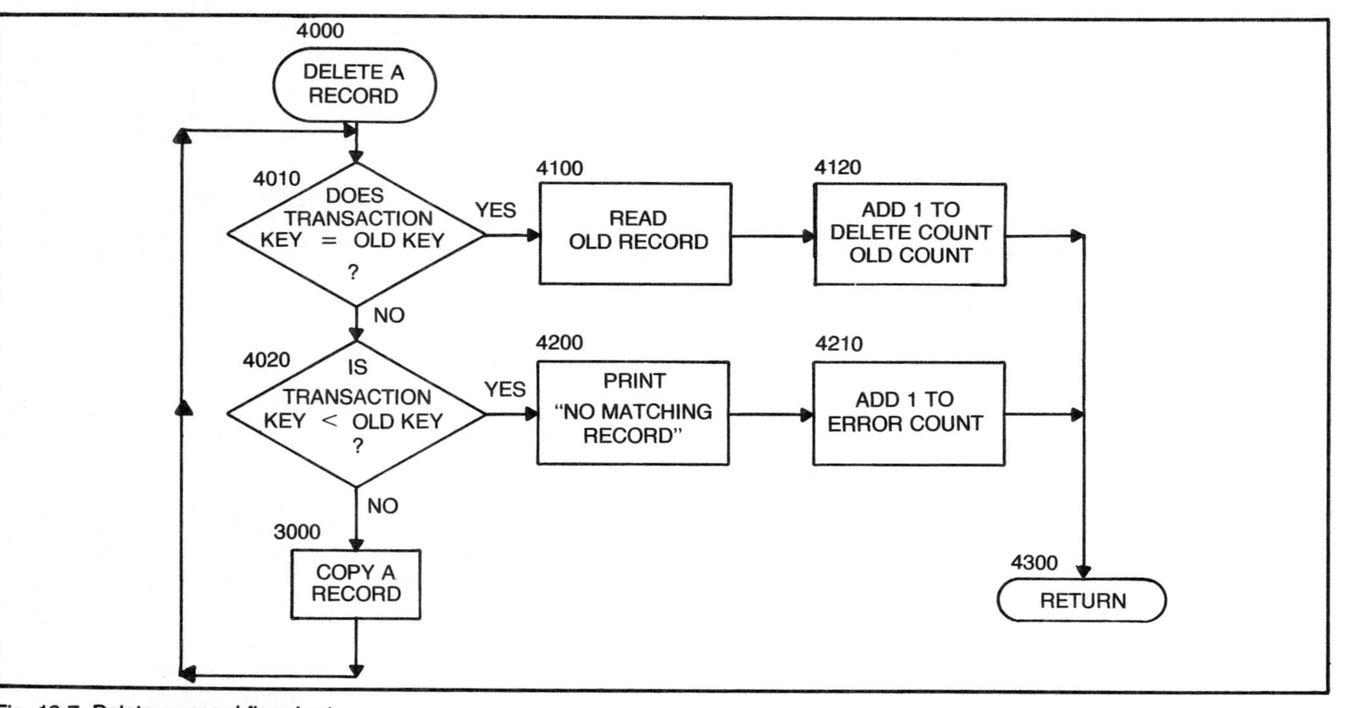

Fig. 13-7. Delete-a-record flowchart.

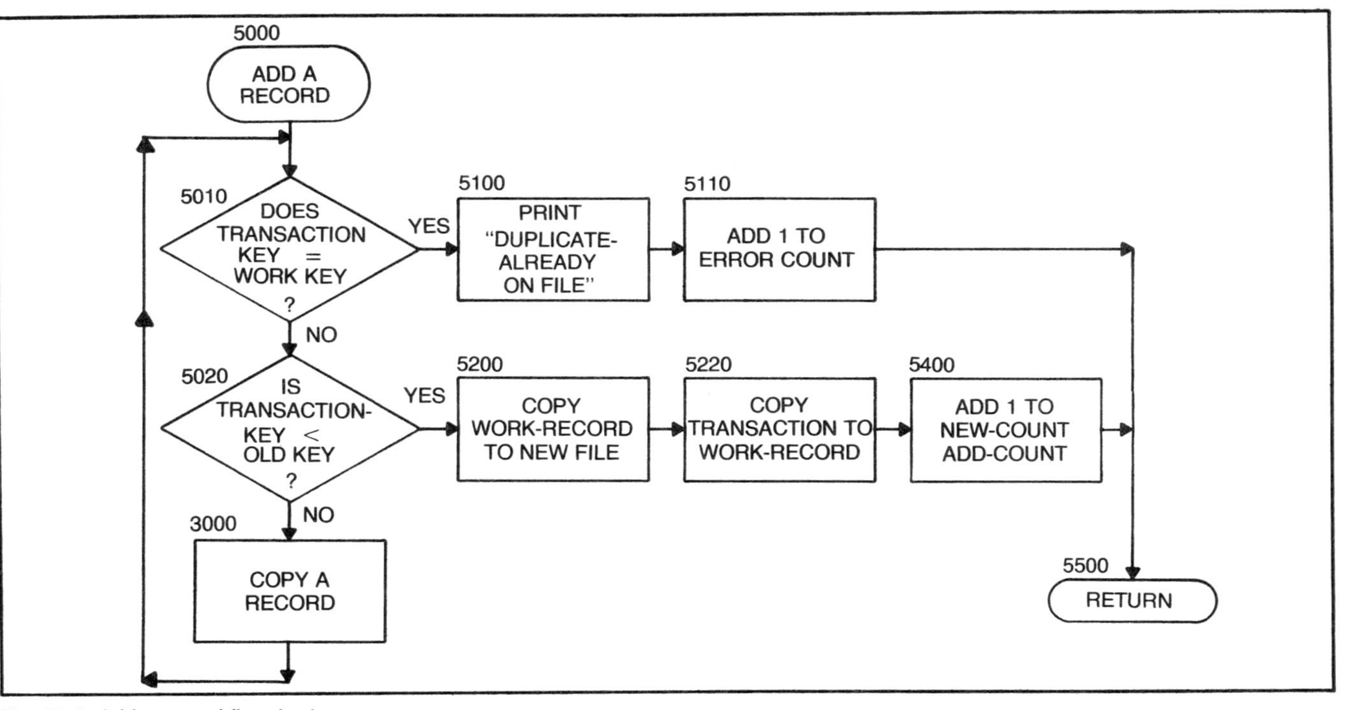

Fig. 13-8. Add-a-record flowchart.

```
5000 REM  ***  ADD A RECORD  ***
5010     IF D3 = V3  THEN 5100                    'Duplicate Found
5020     IF D3 < S3  THEN 5200                    'Add Between Records
5030     GOSUB 3000                               'Get Next Record
5040     GOTO  5010                               'Repeat
5050 REM   ----
5100     PRINT "DUPLICATE RECORD WITH #"; D3; "--- CANNOT ADD."
5110     LET NR = NR + 1                          'Count Rejects
5120     GOTO  5500                               'Exit
5130 REM   ----
5200     IF V3 = LV  THEN 5220                    'No Work Record
5210     GOSUB 8100                               'Write New Record
5215     LET NN = NN + 1                          'Count Output
5220     LET U1$ = C1$                      'Move Transaction to Work Rec.
5230     LET U2$ = C2$
5240     LET U3$ = C3$
5250     LET U4$ = C4$
5260     LET U5$ = C5$
5270     LET U6$ = C6$
5280     LET U7$ = C7$
5290     LET U8$ = C8$
5300     LET U9$ = C9$
5310     LET V1  = D1
5320     LET V2  = D2
5330     LET V3  = D3
5400     PRINT "RECORD #:"; V3;" FOR:"; U2$; " "; U1$;" --- IS ADD
         ED."
5420     LET NA = NA + 1                        'Count Adds
5500     RETURN
```

Fig. 13-9. BASIC statements to add a record.

record with the same key value. As soon as a record is deleted, its place is taken by the next record in the file. The add transaction would immediately be rejected (by lines 130-140 in Fig. 13-5) as being out of sequence. What's worse is that any addition belonging between the deleted record and the following record would also be rejected as out of sequence.

This design solves that problem by matching deletions with the old record. The key in the work record is left as it was, which will be a value less than the deleted record or any following transactions. If the next transaction wanted to add a new record to replace the one that had just been deleted, its key would fall between the work record and the new "old record." The add subroutine would work just fine. The only problem is that you could no longer add a record and immediately delete it. The added record would be stored in the work record and the key in the old record would be larger, signaling "no matching record" in the deletion subroutine. In many situations this is not a serious problem. It does not make sense to add a record and delete it immediately—unless there has been a mistake. The program will reject the attempted deletion and call attention to the error on the audit trail report. A clerk can then determine whether the deletion transaction or the add transaction (or both) contained the error, and can enter an appropriate correction.

If you really want to add and immediately delete a record in your version of the program, it can be done. But it requires a much more complicated design for both the deletion and add subroutines, particularly if you need to be able to add a replacement record with the same key value as a deleted record. In normal batch processing, all of the transactions from several clerks are sorted together by the computer before the update. The computer would have to have some way of knowing how to order transactions with the same key. You would have to design a method for telling the computer whether it should add then delete, or delete then add. Most systems prefer to follow the simple rule that any deletion will come first, then adds, and finally changes (so you can change a record that has just been added). The subroutines presented in this chapter are designed to work with this common rule.

CHANGING A RECORD

The subroutine to change some of the items on a record starts with the same type of loop as the delete and add subroutines. The first comparison checks for a matching key value in the work record. (If the comparison were made with the old record, the program would not be able to match a change request with a record that had just been added and stored in the work record.) If the keys do not match, the program checks to see if the desired record would have come before the old record. If so, the transaction has to be rejected because none of the remaining records could have a matching key value. (All of them will have larger keys.) If the transaction key is not less than the old record, there is still a chance of getting a matching key in the work record, so the copy-a-record subroutine is used and the loop is repeated (Fig. 13-10).

Once the transaction is matched with a work record, then the values of specific items in the work record can be changed. A transaction might want to change only a single item (such as the phone number) or any group of items. Usually at least some of the items are left unchanged. The value of the key item is never changed, because changing the key could destroy the sequential order of the file.

In the sample program, the transaction record has a variable for each item in the work record. Some systems use different change transactions to change different parts of the work record, particularly if the work record includes many items. Either way, the computer must decide what to do about each item on the transaction. Normally, if an item is left blank, the program will assume no change is desired; the value of the matching item in the work record is left unchanged. Anytime a variable on the transaction file has a value other than blank spaces, that value is copied into the work record, replacing the previous value. Once the value from the transaction has been copied into the work record, it is impossible to tell what value was in the work record. If the audit trail is going to show what was changed, then the message describing the previous and new values needs to be printed before the copying actually occurs (Fig. 13-11).

You may want to erase the value of a particular item in a record. Some member may have his telephone disconnected and his phone number should appear as a blank on the file. Entering a blank on the transaction would leave the phone number unchanged. That is fine, because you do not want to have to type in a value for every item each time a single item is changed. In the rare instances where you want to erase the value of an item, you should be willing to enter a special value like "DELETE", "ERASE", or "*". The asterisk (*) is commonly used as the code for blanking out an item because it only takes one keystroke and very few data items would accept it as a meaningful value in a real record. When the program encounters the special

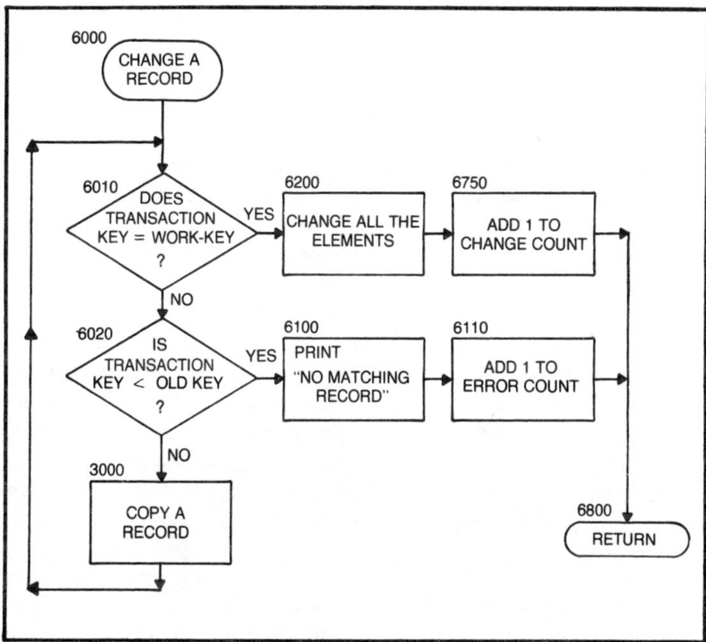

Fig. 13-10. Change-a-record flowchart.

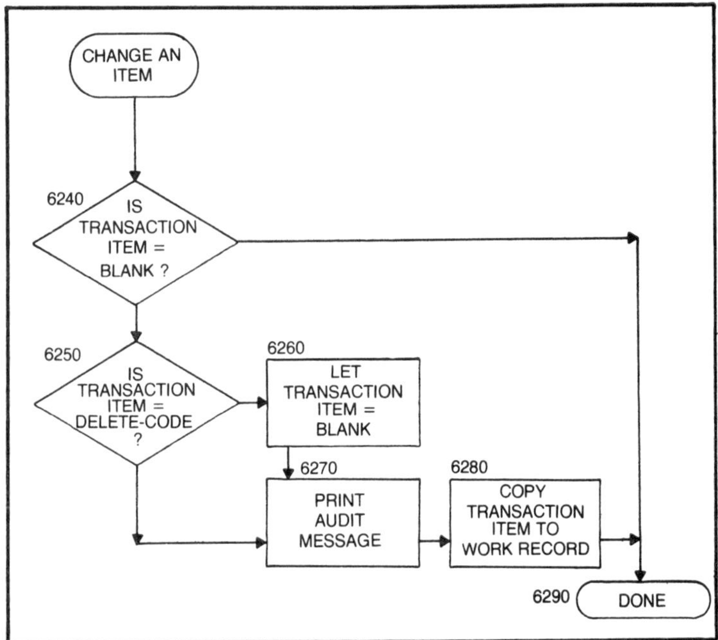

Fig. 13-11. Change-an-item flowchart.

deleting code, it can replace the code with a value of blanks before printing the audit message and changing the value in the work record.

Lines 6010-6040 in Fig. 13-12 implement the loop in Fig. 13-10. The copy-a-record box is left as a single GOSUB statement. The actual copy statements will be contained in a lower level subroutine that will be used by line 520 of the top level (Fig. 13-5) and the deletion and add routines as well as by the change subroutine. There is no sense in writing the same statements four times when once is enough. Lines 6100-6130 reject a transaction that does not match any record on the file.

Once a match is found, the record to be changed is identified for the audit trail (line 6200). Then a routine similar to Fig. 13-11 is included for each item on the record except the key (V3 on the work record). No provision is made for erasing the last name (U1$ in lines 6210-6230) because the original definition for the membership file stated that every member had to have a name. The other items allow erasure codes. The codes for the two date fields (lines 6640-6710) are different than the other fields because BASIC will not allow a number variable to be left blank. This code assumes that the process which created the transaction record used the lowest possible value (LV) as the default instead of a blank. This allows the field to be erased by changing it to zero.

None of the values in the transaction record have been checked to make sure they are reasonable. If the transaction said that a member's dues were paid through −45, the value on the master file would be changed to that absurd date. The validation statements were left out of the change and add subroutines to keep them short. This would be acceptable in business programming only if each item were checked for unreasonable values and any errors rejected at some earlier point. The transactions should be checked either in the get-transaction subroutine or by a separate program run before the update program.

The final lines in the subroutine (6750 and 6800) increase the count of changes for the audit trail and return the program to the top level to handle the next transaction. The number of changes in the audit trail will be a count of transactions that changed one or more items. It is not a count of the number of items changed. Remember: the purpose of the audit trail is to verify that the computer did everything it was supposed to. Normally there will be one piece of paper for each transaction. That one piece of paper (example: a change of address notice giving a new street address, city, state, and ZIP code) may cause several items to be changed. It is much easier to count the pieces of paper and compare the total to the changes reported on the audit trail than to read each piece of paper counting the items to be changed.

THE TRANSACTION FILE

You have several choices in designing the transaction file and the subroutine that will process it. The primary requirements are that each transaction will have been properly edited (to avoid putting bad information into the master file) before the "get-a-transaction" subroutine is completed and the transactions must be entered into the update program in sequential order.

In a large business environment, the editing and sorting into sequential order are apt to be done by different programs. Several different editing programs may be available for clerks to use when typing transactions into the computer from their boards. This will let any typing errors be corrected immediately, instead of correcting them the next day from the audit trail report. The edit programs will store the validated transaction records in small disk files. A BASIC edit program would consist of a series of INPUT loops that prompt for an item and loop back if an acceptable value is not entered (Fig. 13-13).

The transactions can be entered in the edit program in any order. Usually the sequence of the resulting file will be the order in which stacks of paper were handed to the clerk at the keyboard. A separate program can consolidate the records on the small files into a single file and then sort the records into sequential order from the lowest key value to the highest. If two or more records have the same key value, the program can arrange them with deletes first, adds next, and changes last. Sorting programs for commercial use are usually written in machine language rather than BASIC because they involve nested loops and frequent rearrangement of string space. Sorting programs can be written in BASIC (whole books are devoted

```
6000 REM  ***  CHANGE A RECORD  ***
6010     IF D3 = V3  THEN 6200                   'Match Found
6020     IF D3 < S3  THEN 6100                   'No Match
6030     GOSUB 3000                              'Get Next Record
6040     GOTO  6010                              'Repeat
6050 REM  ----
6100     PRINT "NO MATCH FOR TRANSACTION #"; D3; " --- CANNOT CHANGE.
         "
6110     LET NR = NR + 1                         'Count Rejects
6120     GOTO 6800                               'Exit
6130 REM  ----
6200     PRINT "CHANGES MADE IN RECORD #"; D3
6210     IF C1$ =""  THEN 6240
6220     PRINT "LAST NAME            FROM: "; U1$; TAB(44); "TO: "; C1
         $
6230     LET U1$ = C1$
6240     IF C2$ =""  THEN 6290                   'Item Not Changed
6250     IF C2$ <> "*" THEN 6270                 'Erase Item Value
6260     LET C2$ =""
6270     PRINT "FIRST NAME           FROM: "; U2$; TAB(44); "TO: "; C2
         $
6280     LET U2$ = C2$
6290     IF C3$ ="" THEN 6340
6300     IF C3$ <> "*" THEN 6320
6310     LET C3$ =""
6320     PRINT "STREET ADDRESS       FROM: "; U3$; TAB(43); " TO: "; C
         3$
6330     LET U3$ = C3$
6340     IF C4$ =""  THEN 6390
6350     IF C4$ <> "*" THEN 6370
6360     LET C4$ =""
6370     PRINT "CITY                 FROM: "; U4$; TAB(44); "TO: "; C4
         $
6380     LET U4$ = C4$
6390     IF C5$ ="" THEN 6440
6400     IF C5$ <> "*" THEN 6420
6410     LET C5$ =""
6420     PRINT "STATE                FROM: "; U5$; TAB(44); "TO: "; C5
         $
6430     LET U5$ = C5$
```

Fig. 13-12. BASIC statements to change a record.

```
6440    IF C6$ ="" THEN 6490
6450    IF C6$ <> "*" THEN 6470
6460    LET C6$ =""
6470    PRINT "ZIP CODE              FROM: "; U6$; TAB(44); "TO: "; C6
        $
6480    LET U6$ = C6$
6490    IF C7$ ="" THEN 6540
6500    IF C7$ <> "*" THEN 6520
6510    LET C7$ =""
6520    PRINT "PHONE AREA CODE       FROM: "; U7$; TAB(44); "TO: "; C7
        $
6530    LET U7$ = C7$
6540    IF C8$ =""  THEN 6590
6550    IF C8$ <> "*" THEN 6570
6560    LET C8$ =""
6570    PRINT "PHONE NUMBER          FROM: "; U8$; TAB(44); "TO: "; C8
        $
6580    LET U8$ = C8$
6590    IF C9$ =""  THEN 6640
6600    IF C9$ <> "*" THEN 6620
6610    LET C9$ =""
6620    PRINT "MEMBERSHIP TYPE       FROM: "; U9$; TAB(44); "TO: "; C9
        $
6630    LET U9$ = C9$
6640    IF D1 = LV THEN 6690
6650    PRINT "DATE JOINED           FROM:"; S1; TAB(44); "TO:"; D1
6660    LET S1 = D1
6690    IF D2 = LV  THEN 6740
6700    PRINT "DUES PAID THROUGH     FROM:"; S2; TAB(44); "TO:"; D2
6710    LET S2 = D2
6740    PRINT
6750    LET NC = NC + 1                      'Count Changes
6800    RETURN
6810 REM ------------------------------
```

to the subject), but the interpretive nature of BASIC means that a file which can be sorted in a couple of minutes with a machine language program takes more than 30 minutes to sort in BASIC.

If editing and sorting programs have been used, then the get-a-transaction subroutine in the update program could be written in three simple steps: (1) read the next record from the sorted transaction file; (2) if it is the end of the file, move the "quit" code to the transaction type field (C0$); (3) otherwise, add one to the count of transactions for the audit trail (NT). Standard practice in many companies calls for a fourth step of printing an exact copy of the transaction on the audit report as soon as it is read into memory.

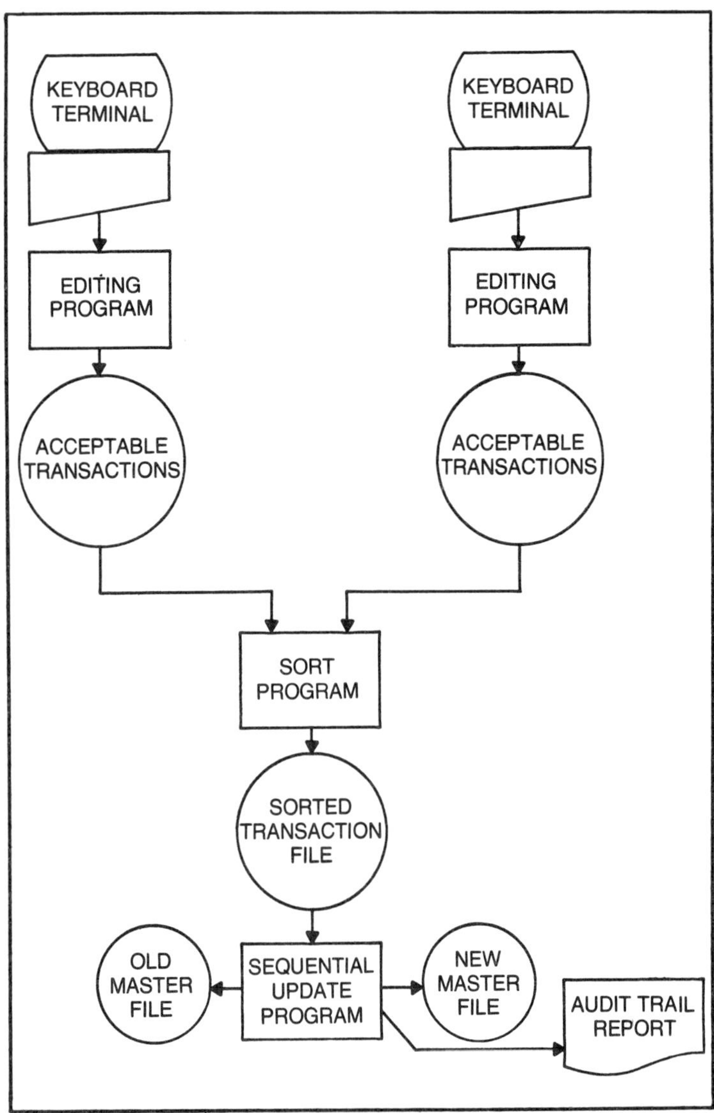

Fig. 13-13. Commercial batch processing.

Personal computers often have limited facilities for handling multiple files and sorting large files. The sequential update does require a minimum of two peripheral files (for the old and updated versions of the master file). If your microcomputer only has connections for two cassettes or if you are working with a single small disk drive, you may not be able to store the transaction file on a peripheral device.

The sample update program is designed to accept transactions from the keyboard during the update run. This means that a person must arrange the change requests (on paper) in sequential order before starting the program and must wait for prompts at the keyboard until the entire file has been updated. This design would not be practical if you had to make five hundred changes on a file with a million records, but it will work quite nicely for smaller jobs (Fig. 13-14).

The obvious way to get a transaction from the keyboard is to write a series of INPUT commands for the items in the record. That simple sequence could become frustrating to the person at the keyboard. The only items that need to be entered to delete a record are the transaction code for delete and the membership number (key field). Why should the program continue with prompts for the rest of the variables? Even worse, when you tell the computer that you want to quit, you don't want it to come back and ask you to enter a membership number, name, etc.

The person entering the transaction should not have to answer any more prompts than necessary. If he says he wants to quit, the program should know it is done with getting a transaction and go directly to the end of the subroutine. It should not even count the request to quit as a transaction (see lines 2020-2050 in Fig. 13-15). If the user says he wants to delete a record, then the program should skip to the end of the subroutine right after counting the transaction for the audit trail (line 2060) and getting the value for the key field (lines 2070-2100).

An add or change request needs to prompt for values for each of the items. If that makes typing too tedious, the change request can be split into different groups (as was done in Chapter 12) so that only a related group of items is requested. Of course, there is a trade-off between having to deal with too many items on one transaction and having too many different transactions. You have to be familiar with the specific job to determine the best way to design transactions for the user to enter.

The sample statements in Fig. 13-15 offer only the essentials of a get-a-transaction subroutine. For the sake of brevity (you may think this chapter is too long already), the input items are not checked for validity, If you decide to use this program in a practical application, you will want to add loops that force each input item to have a legitimate value. The statements that assign default values (like 2110, 2170, and 2440) are vital. If the user is changing one item and leaving the others alone, he will naturally press the Enter (or Return) key without typing a value for the times he does not want to change. Without the default values being assigned by the program, the variables in the transaction record would retain the values

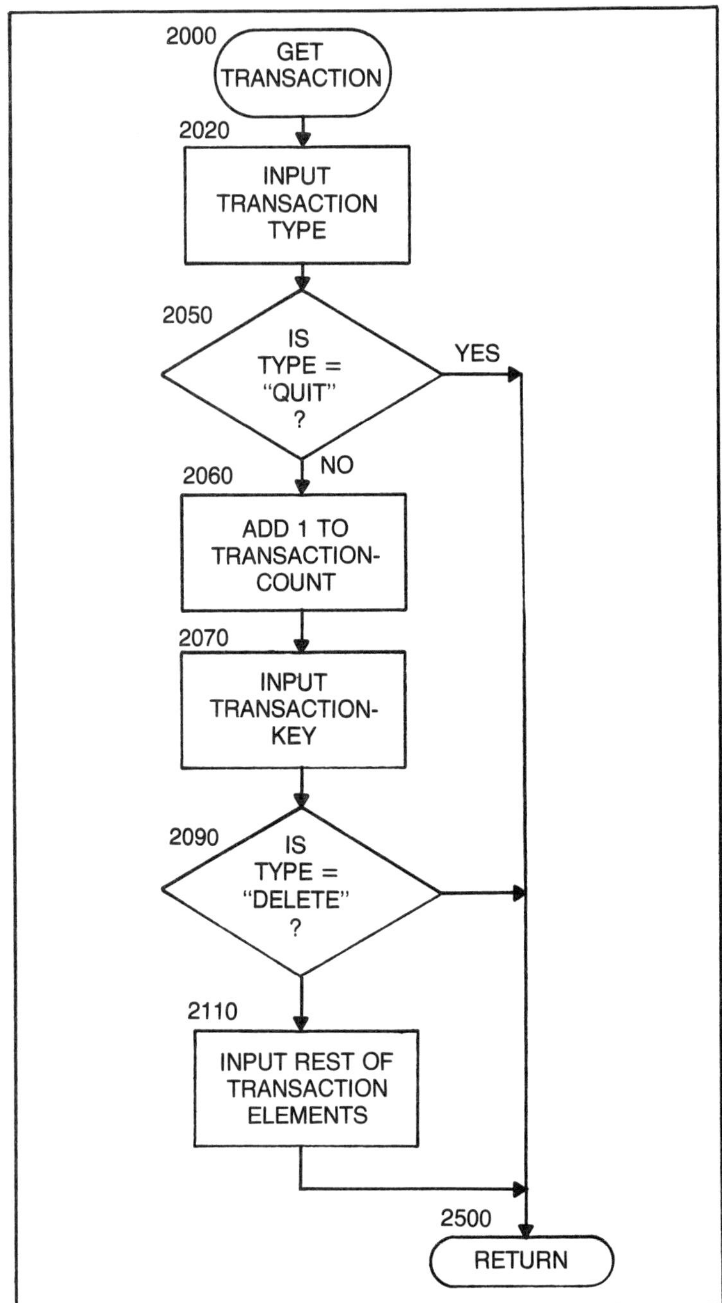

Fig. 13-14. Get-a-transaction flowchart.

from the previous record, which would lead to many unwanted changes. If you want to make sure a variable is blank, your program has to make it blank; doing nothing will let the memory location hold the value it previously contained.

HOUSEKEEPING FUNCTIONS

The major pieces of the sequential update have now been designed and discussed. All that remains to finish the program is to tidy up a few loose ends. The statements used to set up the files and terminate the program with neat-looking messages are often called the housekeeping sections. They are not very glamorous or complex, but they are as necessary to orderly data processing as dishwashing is to gourmet cooking.

The set-up subroutine prepares the computer's memory for the first transaction (Fig. 13-16). The first group of statements ensures that all variables used to count things start off at zero. Many versions of BASIC will do this automatically as part of the RUN command, but it does not hurt to be safe. Next, the old file has to be assigned as input to the program. The specific statements to do this will depend on your local dialect of BASIC. Lines 1100-1120 in Fig. 13-17 prompt for the name of a disk file and assign it the file number 1 in the Microsoft version of BASIC. On a cassette system, they might be replaced by a simple message asking the user to make sure the recorder was ready with the proper tape. A new file has to be assigned to hold the updated records. The necessary statements will be similar to the first file, except a different file name and file number (2 in the sample) will be used.

The initial values for the records stored in memory also need to be established. The work record starts with the lowest possible key (line 1190). Since this is the fake header record that acts as a place holder, the rest of the items can be on the updated file. The old record needs to hold the first real record on the master file. It is read from the old file with an INPUT#1 statement (written as a subroutine). If nothing exists on the old file except an end-of-file marker (an unlikely but possible event), then the key in the old record will hold the highest possible value. Otherwise, the program can count its first input record for the audit trail. The computer will now be ready to get down to business.

The next detail that needs to be completed is the task of copying a record. The design of several of the major subroutines called for copying the next record from the old file. The basic procedure was illustrated by Fig. 13-2, showing the movement of a record from the old file to the old record, then on to the work record and out to the new file. Now it is time to turn the general idea into specific statements. The potential pitfalls are accidentally erasing a record by pulling another record in its place before it has been copied, and accidentally copying the fake header record on the update file or trying to copy another record from the old file after you have reached its end. Figure 13-18 avoids those problems. The records are copied in order: the work record is added to the new file first, then the

```
2000 REM *** GET TRANSACTION ***
2010     PRINT
2020     PRINT"TYPE: ADD, CHANGE, DELETE, OR QUIT";
2030     INPUT C0$
2040     LET C0$ = LEFT$(C0$,1)      'Use First Letter Only
2050     IF  C0$ = "Q"  THEN 2500    'Exit
2060     LET NT = NT + 1             'Count Transactions
2070     PRINT "MEMBERSHIP #";
2080     INPUT D3
2090     IF  C0$ = "A" OR C0$ = "C" THEN 2110
2100     GOTO 2500                   'Exit
2110     LET C1$ = ""
2120     PRINT "LAST NAME";
2130     INPUT C1$
2140     IF LEN(C1$) > 1 OR C0$ = "C" THEN 2170
2150     PRINT "NAME REQUIRED TO ADD A RECORD"
2160     GOTO 2120
2170     LET C2$ =""
2180     PRINT "FIRST NAME";
2190     INPUT C2$
2200     LET C3$ =""
2210     PRINT"STREET ADDRESS";
2220     INPUT C3$
2230     LET C4$ =""
2240     PRINT "CITY";
2250     INPUT C4$
2260     LET C5$ =""
2270     PRINT "STATE";
2280     INPUT C5$
2290     LET C6$ =""
2300     PRINT "ZIP CODE";
```

Fig. 13-15. BASIC statements to get a transaction.

```
2310     INPUT C6$
2320     LET C7$ =""
2330     PRINT "PHONE AREA CODE";
2340     INPUT C7$
2350     LET C8$ =""
2360     PRINT "PHONE NUMBER";
2370     INPUT C8$
2380     LET C9$ =""
2390     PRINT "MEMBERSHIP TYPE";
2400     INPUT C9$
2410     LET D1 = LV
2420     PRINT "DATE JOINED";
2430     INPUT D1
2440     LET D2 = LV
2450     PRINT "DUES PAID THRU";
2460     INPUT D2
2500     PRINT
2510     RETURN
2520 REM ----------------------------------
```

values in the old record replace what had been in the work record, and finally the next record on the old file is brought into the computer's memory. The test in statement 3010 prevents the header record from being put on the new file. The test in statement 3200 causes the computer to skip looking for another record on the old file after it has reached the end-of-file (Fig. 13-19).

The actual INPUT# and PRINT# statements used to move records between peripheral files and memory are separated from the rest of the program as subroutines 8000 and 8100. These statements are displayed in Fig. 13-20. It may seem silly to write these two lines as separate subroutines. (Why bother with GOSUB, REMark and RETURN statements when only one statement does anything useful?) Keeping the statements that read and write records separate from the rest of the program makes them more visible and easy to compare. Since BASIC will make your program behave in strange and undesirable ways if the statement that reads a file does not describe the record exactly the same way as the statement

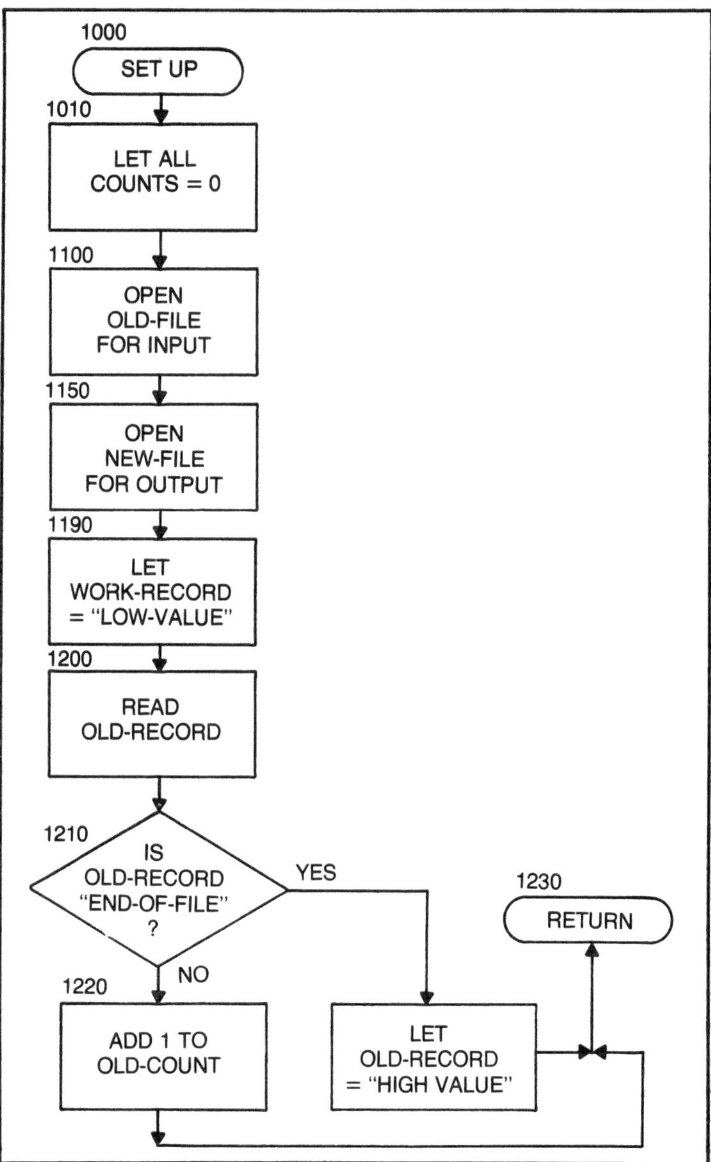

Fig. 13-16. Set-up flowchart.

that wrote the file, it is helpful to have the INPUT# statement listed close to the PRINT# statement so they can be compared. Standard practice in many programming offices requires that all statements which read or write any file in a program be grouped into one set of subroutines for this reason.

In order for the program to work properly, the file number in the INPUT# statement (line 8000) must match the file number in the statement (line 1120) that assigned the old file to the program. Similarly, the file number in the PRINT# statement (line 8100) must match the assigned output file (line 1170). The commas are specifically included in line 8100 because the sample program is written for a Microsoft disk system that does not automatically provide delimiters. In many other versions of BASIC the formats of the INPUT# and PRINT# statements would match exactly.

The read and write subroutines could be expanded to take care of some of the housekeeping and audit trail functions. Figure 13-21 diagrams a file reading subroutine that checks for the end-of-file and adds one to the count of input records after each real record is copied into memory. If this design had been used, then the higher level subroutines that set-up copy-a-record and delete-a-record would have been simpler. The end-of-file checks and audit trail counter were included in each of those subroutines to emphasize their importance. Normally it would be better to put them in the low-level read subroutine and not have to worry about them in the rest of the

```
1000 REM  *** SET UP FILES ***
1010      LET NI = 0                  '# Input Records
1020      LET NT = 0                  '# Transactions
1030      LET NN = 0                  '# New Records
1040      LET NA = 0                  '# Added Records
1050      LET ND = 0                  '# Deleted Records
1060      LET NC = 0                  '# Changes Made
1070      LET NR = 0                  '# Rejected Transactions
1100      PRINT "INPUT FILENAME";
1110      INPUT F1$                   'Old File
1120      OPEN "I", 1, F1$            'Disk File Open
1150      PRINT "OUTPUT FILENAME";
1160      INPUT F2$                   'New File
1170      OPEN "O", 2, F2$            'Disk File Open
1190      LET V3 = LV                 'Low Value Key in Work Record
1200      GOSUB 8000                  'Read Record
1210      IF S3 = HV THEN 1230        'End of File?
1220      LET NI = NI + 1             'Count Input
1230      RETURN
1240 REM ----------------------
```

Fig. 13-17. BASIC statements to set-up files.

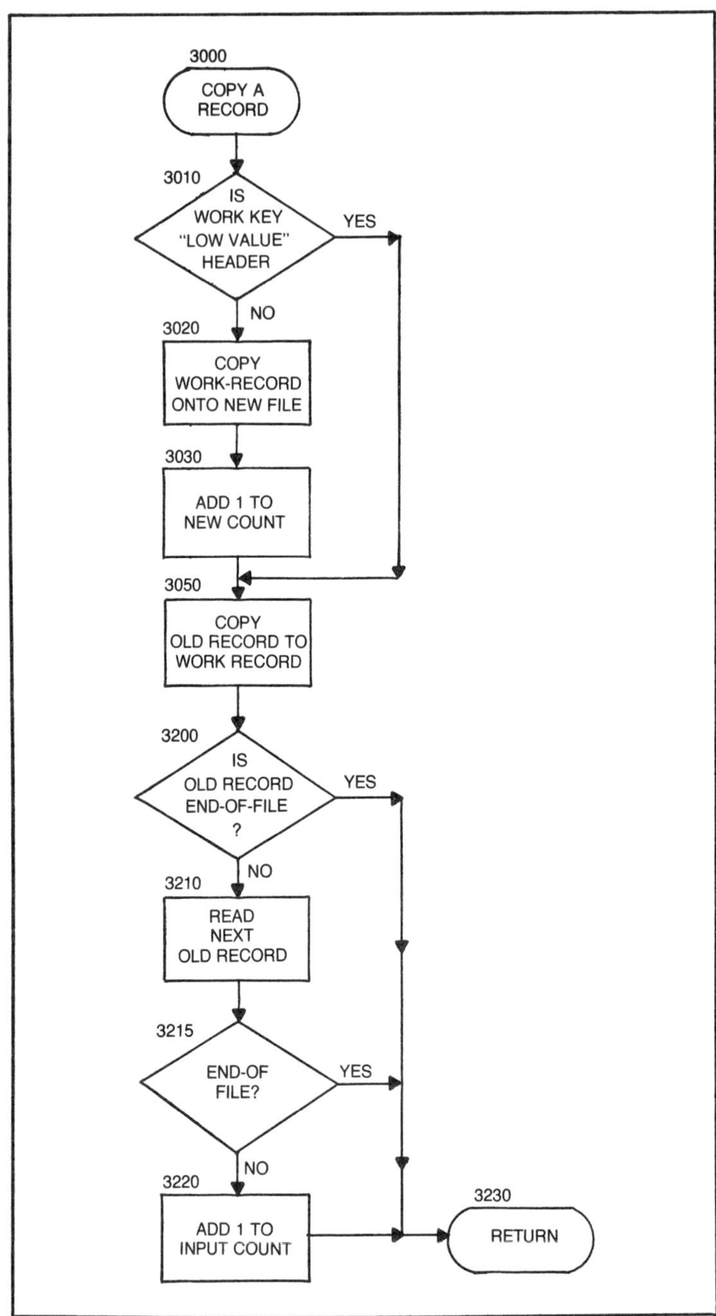

Fig. 13-18. Copy-a-record flowchart.

program. You should be able to design a similar write subroutine that takes care of the header record and output count.

WRAPPING IT UP

The closing subroutine is the last item needed to complete the update program. It needs to release the files assigned to the program, and print a summary of the audit trail. The first step is not required by all versions of BASIC. Some versions automatically close and release all files as part of the END command. However, if your version of BASIC does not provide automatic release, the failure to include CLOSE statements (lines 9010 and 9020) would make it impossible to read the information in your updated file for use at any later time.

The closing subroutine in the sample was given the starting line number of 9000 so it would appear at the tail end of a complete program

```
3000 REM  ***  COPY A RECORD  ***
3005     IF V3 = HV THEN 3230                    'Already at end
3010     IF V3 = LV  THEN 3050                   'No Work Record
3020     GOSUB 8100                              'Write New Record
3030     LET NN = NN + 1                         'Count Output
3050     LET U1$ = R1$                      'Copy Old Rec. to Work Rec.
3060     LET U2$ = R2$
3070     LET U3$ = R3$
3080     LET U4$ = R4$
3090     LET U5$ = R5$
3100     LET U6$ = R6$
3110     LET U7$ = R7$
3120     LET U8$ = R8$
3130     LET U9$ = R9$
3140     LET V1  = S1
3150     LET V2  = S2
3160     LET V3  = S3
3200     IF S3 = HV  THEN 3230              'End of File?
3210     GOSUB 8000                         'Read Next Old Record
3215     IF S3 = HV  THEN 3230              'End of File Yet?
3220     LET NI = NI + 1                    'Count Input
3230     RETURN
3240 REM ------------------------------.
```

Fig. 13-19. BASIC statements to copy a record.

```
7999 REM --- READ RECORD FROM OLD FILE ---
8000     INPUT#1, R1$, R2$, R3$, R4$, R5$, R6$, R7$, R8$, R9$, S1, S2
         , S3
8010     RETURN
8099 REM ---WRITE RECORD ON NEW FILE ---
8100     PRINT#2, U1$;",";U2$;",";U3$;",";U4$;",";U5$;",";U6$;",
         ";U7$;",";U8$;",";U9$;",";V1;V2;V3
8110     RETURN
8120 REM -----
```

Fig. 13-20. Read/write subroutines.

listing (Fig. 13-22). The design is a simple sequence of steps, so no flowchart was prepared. After the files are closed (lines 9010-9020), the counts from the audit trail are printed with appropriate titles (lines 9030-9100). This provides a quick summary of what was accomplished in the batch process just completed. It can also be used to spot problems with the program or certain transactions. If you start with the number of records on the input file, add the number of records added by the program and subtract the number of records deleted, the result should give you the number of records on the updated file. If it does not match the output count (line 9110), something obviously went wrong. Similar arithmetic can be used to make sure that the transaction records are properly accounted for (line 9120).

The whole program is now ready for testing. Do not trust this book or your typing ability. Try running the program several times with different types of transactions. You should always try to find out what might possibly be wrong with a program before you put your faith in it.

One of the first things you will discover when you try to test the UPDATE program is that you must have an old file before it can create a new file. The sequential update program is designed to be part of a data processing cycle. The cycle appears to have no beginning, but the first master file has to come from someplace. One way to create the first master file would be to temporarily revise (or *patch*) your program so it started off with a high-value key in the old record and never looked for an input file. This could be done by deleting line 1120 (the OPEN statement) and replacing lines 1200 through 1220 with a single statement giving the key item in the old record the highest possible value (1200 LET S3 = HV). After you created the original file, you would go back to the standard version of the program.

Large organizations tend to frown on people making temporary changes to their programs. They prefer the safety of having each program verified before it is put to use. In this environment, you would want to write a special little program to create an initial master file. A separate start-up program would also be desirable if you were writing programs for other people (who probably would not have hired you if they knew how to program themselves). The Initial program can be quite simple. All it has to do is assign a file to the program, write a single end-of-file record that matches the format used by the UPDATE program and close the file. Figure 13-23 accomplishes this task with ten statements, including remarks and an audit message.

When the file created by the INITIAL program is used as input for the UPDATE program, it immediately puts the high value end-of-file marker in the old record. The first real records can then be placed on the membership master file with a series of add transactions. (Note: if you change the value of numeric fields in the end-of-file record produced by the Member program from Chapter 12 to use the high value, you could start a file with the Member program and use it as input into the UPDATE program.)

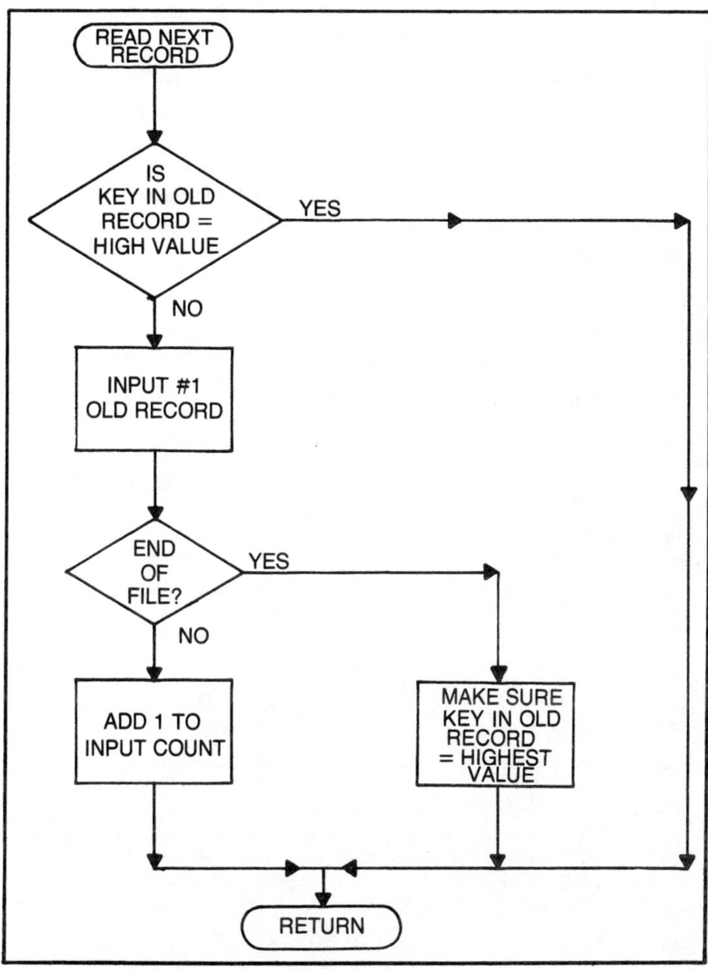

Fig. 13-21. Improved read subroutine.

```
10   REM    SEQUENTIAL FILE UPDATE
20   REM    by R. Galbraith        August, 1981
30       CLEAR 300                    'Reserve String Space
40       LET HV =  1.70141E+38        'Highest Value
50       LET LV = -1.70141E+38        'Lowest Value
100      GOSUB 1000                   'Set up Files
110      GOSUB 2000                   'Get Transaction
120      IF CO$ = "Q" THEN 500        'Quit?
130      IF D3 >= V3  THEN 170        'Trans.Key >= Work Record
140      PRINT "TRANSACTION FOR:"; D3; "OUT OF SEQUENCE -- REJECTED."
145      PRINT
150      LET NR = NR + 1              'Count Rejects
160      GOTO 110                     'Next Transaction
170      IF CO$ <> "D"  THEN 200
180      GOSUB 4000                   'Delete Record
190      GOTO  110                    'Next Transaction
200      IF CO$ <> "A"  THEN 230
210      GOSUB 5000                   'Add a Record
220      GOTO  110                    'Next Transaction
230      IF CO$ <> "C"  THEN 260
240      GOSUB 6000                   'Change Record
250      GOTO  110                    'Next Transaction
260      PRINT "TRANSACTION FOR:"; D3; "BAD TYPE CODE: "; CO$; " -- R
         EJECTED."
265      PRINT
270      LET NR = NR + 1              'Count Rejects
280      GOTO  110                    'Next Transaction
290  REM -----------------------
500  REM --- END OF TRANSACTIONS ---
510      IF V3 = HV  THEN 550         'End of File?
520      GOSUB 3000                   'Copy Record
530      GOTO  510                    'Repeat
550  REM -- END OF FILE
560      PRINT#2, "END-OF-FILE,"; "END,"; "END,"; "END,"; "END,"; "EN
         D,"; "END,"; "END,"; "END,"; HV; HV; HV
570      GOSUB 9000                   'Close Files & End
580      END
585  REM
```

Fig. 13-22. Update program listing.

```
590  REM -------------------------
595  REM
600  REM  *** SUBROUTINES FOLLOW ***
610  REM
1000 REM  *** SET UP FILES ***
1010     LET NI = 0                    '# Input Records
1020     LET NT = 0                    '# Transactions
1030     LET NN = 0                    '# New Records
1040     LET NA = 0                    '# Added Records
1050     LET ND = 0                    '# Deleted Records
1060     LET NC = 0                    '# Changes Made
1070     LET NR = 0                    '# Rejected Transactions
1100     PRINT "INPUT FILENAME";
1110     INPUT F1$                     'Old File
1120     OPEN "I", 1, F1$              'Disk File Open
1150     PRINT "OUTPUT FILENAME";
1160     INPUT F2$                     'New File
1170     OPEN "O", 2, F2$              'Disk File Open
1190     LET V3 = LV                   'Low Value Key in Work Record
1200     GOSUB 8000                    'Read Record
1210     IF S3 = HV THEN 1230          'End of File?
1220     LET NI = NI + 1               'Count Input
1230     RETURN
1240 REM -------------------------
2000 REM *** GET TRANSACTION ***
2010     PRINT
2020     PRINT"TYPE: ADD, CHANGE, DELETE, OR QUIT";
2030     INPUT CO$
2040     LET CO$ = LEFT$(CO$,1)        'Use First Letter Only
2050     IF  CO$ = "Q"  THEN 2500      'Exit
2060     LET NT = NT + 1               'Count Transactions
2070     PRINT "MEMBERSHIP #";
2080     INPUT D3
2090     IF  CO$ = "A" OR CO$ = "C" THEN 2110
2100     GOTO 2500                     'Exit
2110     LET C1$ = ""
2120     PRINT "LAST NAME";
```

```
2130 INPUT C1$
2140 IF LEN(C1$) > 1 OR C0$ = "C" THEN 2170
2150 PRINT "NAME REQUIRED TO ADD A RECORD"
2160 GOTO 2120
2170 LET C2$ =""
2180 PRINT "FIRST NAME";
2190 INPUT C2$
2200 LET C3$ =""
2210 PRINT"STREET ADDRESS";
2220 INPUT C3$
2230 LET C4$ =""
2240 PRINT "CITY";
2250 INPUT C4$
2260 LET C5$ =""
2270 PRINT "STATE";
2280 INPUT C5$
2290 LET C6$ =""
2300 PRINT "ZIP CODE";
2310 INPUT C6$
2320 LET C7$ =""
2330 PRINT "PHONE AREA CODE";
2340 INPUT C7$
2350 LET C8$ =""
2360 PRINT "PHONE NUMBER";
2370 INPUT C8$
2380 LET C9$ =""
2390 PRINT "MEMBERSHIP TYPE";
2400 INPUT C9$
2410 LET D1 = LV
2420 PRINT "DATE JOINED";
2430 INPUT D1
2440 LET D2 = LV
2450 PRINT "DUES PAID THRU";
2460 INPUT D2
2500 PRINT
2510 RETURN
```

Fig. 13-22. Continued from page 245.

```
3000 REM  ***  COPY A RECORD  ***
3005     IF V3 = HV THEN 3230                    'Already at end
3010     IF V3 = LV  THEN 3050                   'No Work Record
3020     GOSUB 8100                              'Write New Record
3030     LET NN = NN + 1                         'Count Output
3050     LET U1$ = R1$                 'Copy Old Rec. to Work Rec.
3060     LET U2$ = R2$
3070     LET U3$ = R3$
3080     LET U4$ = R4$
3090     LET U5$ = R5$
3100     LET U6$ = R6$
3110     LET U7$ = R7$
3120     LET U8$ = R8$
3130     LET U9$ = R9$
3140     LET V1  = S1
3150     LET V2  = S2
3160     LET V3  = S3
3200     IF S3 = HV  THEN 3230                   'End of File?
3210     GOSUB 8000                              'Read Next Old Record
3215     IF S3 = HV  THEN 3230                   'End of File Yet?
3220     LET NI = NI + 1                         'Count Input
3230     RETURN
3240 REM -------------------------------
4000 REM  ***  DELETE A RECORD  ***
4010     IF D3 = S3  THEN 4100                   'Match Found
4020     IF D3 < S3  THEN 4200                   'No Match
4030     GOSUB 3000                              'Get Next Record
4040     GOTO 4010                               'Repeat
4050 REM  ----
4100     PRINT "RECORD #:"; S3; "  FOR: "; R2$; " "; R1$; "--IS DELET
         ED."
4110     GOSUB 8000                              'Read On Top of Old Rec.
4112     IF S3 = HV  THEN 4120
4115     LET NI = NI + 1                         'Count Input
4120     LET ND = ND + 1                         'Count Deletes
4130     GOTO 4300                               'Exit
4140 REM  ----
4200     PRINT "NO MATCH FOR TRANSACTION #"; D3; "--- CANNOT DELETE."
```

```
4210    LET NR = NR + 1                          'Count Rejects
4300    RETURN
4310 REM -------------------------------
5000 REM  ***  ADD A RECORD  ***
5010    IF D3 = V3  THEN 5100                    'Duplicate Found
5020    IF D3 < S3  THEN 5200                    'Add Between Records
5030    GOSUB 3000                               'Get Next Record
5040    GOTO  5010                               'Repeat
5050 REM   ----
5100    PRINT "DUPLICATE RECORD WITH #"; D3; "--- CANNOT ADD."
5110    LET NR = NR + 1                          'Count Rejects
5120    GOTO  5500                               'Exit
5130 REM   ----
5200    IF V3 = LV  THEN 5220                    'No Work Record
5210    GOSUB 8100                               'Write New Record
5215    LET NN = NN + 1                          'Count Output
5220    LET U1$ = C1$                 'Move Transaction to Work Rec.
5230    LET U2$ = C2$
5240    LET U3$ = C3$
5250    LET U4$ = C4$
5260    LET U5$ = C5$
5270    LET U6$ = C6$
5280    LET U7$ = C7$
5290    LET U8$ = C8$
5300    LET U9$ = C9$
5310    LET V1  = D1
5320    LET V2  = D2
5330    LET V3  = D3
5400    PRINT "RECORD #:"; V3; " FOR: "; U2$; " "; U1$; " --- IS ADD
         ED."
5420    LET NA = NA + 1                          'Count Adds
5500    RETURN
5510 REM -------------------------------
6000 REM  ***  CHANGE A RECORD  ***
6010    IF D3 = V3  THEN 6200                    'Match Found
6020    IF D3 < S3  THEN 6100                    'No Match
6030    GOSUB 3000                               'Get Next Record
6040    GOTO  6010                               'Repeat
```

Fig. 13-22. Continued from page 247.

```
6050 REM   ----
6100    PRINT "NO MATCH FOR TRANSACTION #"; D3; " --- CANNOT CHANGE.
        "
6110    LET NR = NR + 1                          'Count Rejects
6120    GOTO 6800                                'Exit
6130 REM  ----
6200    PRINT "CHANGES MADE IN RECORD #"; D3
6210    IF C1$ =""  THEN 6240
6220    PRINT "LAST NAME            FROM: "; U1$; TAB(44); "TO: "; C1
        $
6230    LET U1$ = C1$
6240    IF C2$ =""  THEN 6290                    'Item Not Changed
6250    IF C2$ <> "*" THEN 6270                  'Erase Item Value
6260    LET C2$ =""
6270    PRINT "FIRST NAME           FROM: "; U2$; TAB(44); "TO: "; C2
        $
6280    LET U2$ = C2$
6290    IF C3$ ="" THEN 6340
6300    IF C3$ <> "*" THEN 6320
6310    LET C3$ =""
6320    PRINT "STREET ADDRESS       FROM: "; U3$; TAB(43); " TO: "; C
        3$
6330    LET U3$ = C3$
6340    IF C4$ =""  THEN 6390
6350    IF C4$ <> "*" THEN 6370
6360    LET C4$ =""
6370    PRINT "CITY                 FROM: "; U4$; TAB(44); "TO: "; C4
        $
6380    LET U4$ = C4$
6390    IF C5$ ="" THEN 6440
6400    IF C5$ <> "*" THEN 6420
6410    LET C5$ =""
6420    PRINT "STATE                FROM: "; U5$; TAB(44); "TO: "; C5
        $
6430    LET U5$ = C5$
6440    IF C6$ ="" THEN 6490
6450    IF C6$ <> "*" THEN 6470
6460    LET C6$ =""
6470    PRINT "ZIP CODE             FROM: "; U6$; TAB(44); "TO: "; C6
        $
6480    LET U6$ = C6$
```

```
6490    IF C7$ ="" THEN 6540
6500    IF C7$ <> "*" THEN 6520
6510    LET C7$ =""
6520    PRINT "PHONE AREA CODE      FROM: "; U7$; TAB(44); "TO: "; C7
        $
6530    LET U7$ = C7$
6540    IF C8$ =""  THEN 6590
6550    IF C8$ <> "*" THEN 6570
6560    LET C8$ =""
6570    PRINT "PHONE NUMBER         FROM: "; U8$; TAB(44); "TO: "; C8
        $
6580    LET U8$ = C8$
6590    IF C9$ =""  THEN 6640
6600    IF C9$ <> "*" THEN 6620
6610    LET C9$ =""
6620    PRINT "MEMBERSHIP TYPE      FROM: "; U9$; TAB(44); "TO: "; C9
        $
6630    LET U9$ = C9$
6640    IF D1 = LV THEN 6690
6650    PRINT "DATE JOINED          FROM:"; S1; TAB(44); "TO:"; D1
6660    LET S1 = D1
6690    IF D2 = LV  THEN 6740
6700    PRINT "DUES PAID THROUGH    FROM:"; S2; TAB(44); "TO:"; D2
6710    LET S2 = D2
6740    PRINT
6750    LET NC = NC + 1                      'Count Changes
6800    RETURN
6810 REM ------------------------------
7999 REM --- READ RECORD FROM OLD FILE ---
8000    INPUT#1, R1$, R2$, R3$, R4$, R5$, R6$, R7$, R8$, R9$, S1, S2
        , S3
8010    RETURN
8099 REM ---WRITE RECORD ON NEW FILE ---
8100    PRINT#2, U1$;",";U2$;",";U3$;",";U4$;",";U5$;",";U6$;",
        "; U7$;",";U8$;",";U9$;","; V1; V2; V3
8110    RETURN
8120 REM -----
9000 REM  *** CLOSE FILES & AUDIT TRAIL ***
9010    CLOSE 1
9020    CLOSE 2
```

Fig. 13-22. Continued from page 249.

```
9030    PRINT
9040    PRINT
9050    PRINT TAB(15);"SUMMARY OF UPDATE"
9060    PRINT NT;"TRANSACTIONS READ", NR;"TRANSACTIONS REJECTED"
9070    PRINT NA;"RECORDS ADDED     ", NC;"CHANGES MADE"
9080    PRINT ND;"RECORDS DELETED"
9090    PRINT NI;"RECORDS ON  INPUT FILE:", F1$
9100    PRINT NN;"RECORDS ON OUTPUT FILE:", F2$
9110    IF NN = NI + NA - ND   THEN 9130
9120    PRINT "*** WARNING: OUTPUT COUNT DOES NOT BALANCE ***"
9130    IF NT = NR + NA + NC + ND   THEN 9150
9140    PRINT "*** WARNING: TRANSACTION COUNTS DO NOT BALANCE ***"
9150    RETURN
9160 REM ----------------------------------------------------
```

You will probably need to work with the Update program and see the effects of various simplifications and improvements you think might work. Do not feel intimidated if you do not completely understand it on the first reading. The sequential update process is the most complicated of the standard types of business data processing programs. It is also one of the most commonly used program designs and the central component in many important computer applications. For these reasons, it is worth spending some time studying this chapter and working with the program until you feel confident about how it works.

```
10  REM  INITIALIZE SEQUENTIAL FILE
20  REM  by R. Galbraith       August, 1981
40     LET HV = 1.70141E+38                    'Highest Value
100    PRINT "NAME OF FILE TO INITIALIZE";
110    INPUT F2$
120    OPEN "O", 2, F2$                        'Open File for Output
130    PRINT#2, "END-OF-FILE,"; "END,"; "END,"; "END,"; "END,"; "EN
       D,"; "END,"; "END,"; "END,"; HV; HV; HV
140    CLOSE 2
150    PRINT F2$; " HAS BEEN INITIALIZED WITH AN END-OF-FILE RECORD
       ."
160    END
```

Fig. 13-23. Initial file program.

Chapter 14
Getting the Most Out of the Computer

The discussions in this book have not paid too much attention to the appearance of the output produced by the programs. For the most part, answers were simply PRINTed along with a message explaining their meaning. When you ran a program, the results were not expected to look pretty; they were just expected to be correct.

Most people prefer to look at things that are nicely arranged. This applies to computer output and members of the opposite sex as well as to art. You will want to spend a significant part of your programming efforts making sure the reports and displays your programs produce are attractive and easy to use. Well-designed output helps people get the most information out of their computers, and is also the most noticeable part of your programs. Nobody who sits down and runs your program is going to notice how clever your statements are, but everybody *will* notice what the displays on the video screen and the printed output look like.

Even though the appearance of the output is important, there are several good reasons for not emphasizing it in the earlier chapters.

1. Attractive output will not save a bad program. Unless your program is logically designed to produce correct answers and eliminate invalid input, the accuracy of its output cannot be trusted. The primary emphasis in programming must be on accuracy. Outward appearance is the frosting on the cake.

2. Like frosting, attractive output can be arranged at the end of the project. Once you know a program works correctly, you can always go back and improve the appearance of the output by rewriting a few PRINT statements and/or adding graphic subroutines.

3. This book was written for people using a wide variety of computer systems. The most attractive arrangement of information on a 132-column print-out would not fit on a 40-column video screen. Because of the wide variety of output peripherals, this book cannot cover the specific options for all common systems. This chapter will present some considerations for producing different types of output. You will have to experiment on your own computer to fine tune these ideas and create programs people love to watch.

REPORT PROGRAMS

Once information is stored in a computer file, people will think of lots of different reports they would like to have the computer create for them. First you want the computer to do the things that used to require hours of clerical drudgery. Later, you get ideas for having the computer dig helpful information out of the files that was too much bother to collect by hand.

Most of the reports produced by computers fall into one of three categories. They provide information on selected cases: whose accounts are overdrawn, which prisoners are scheduled for release this week, or which members should get reminders to pay their dues this month? They print information in a special format: labels for bulk mailings, payroll checks, or government forms. Or, they produce statistical summaries of the information in the file: how many employees are members of each ethnic minority, what is the average age of each group of employees, or how many members have joined during each of the last six months?

Designs for each of these three main types of reports will be illustrated with sample programs which use the membership file written by either the Member program from Chapter 12 or the Update program from Chapter 13.

A SELECTED LIST

Your organization has an annual banquet. As part of the ceremony, each new member is introduced and awards are given to those members who have just completed five, ten, twenty, or thirty years of service. You do not want to be embarrassed by leaving anyone out, so you write a computer program to list each member who should receive special recognition.

This problem definition is a typical request for a selected list of records from a computer file. The needed information (names of members and the date each joined the organization) is already in the computer. To produce a list of the specific members, the program will have to be fed the current year (so it can compute how long each person has been a member), then it can start reading through the file until it finds a record that matches the selection criteria or reaches the end of the file. When it finds the record of a member who deserves recognition, it can print the appropriate information and return to look for another record. When it reaches the end of the file, it can close by printing a short audit trail of the number of records read and the number selected for the report. This top-level design is shown in Fig. 14-1.

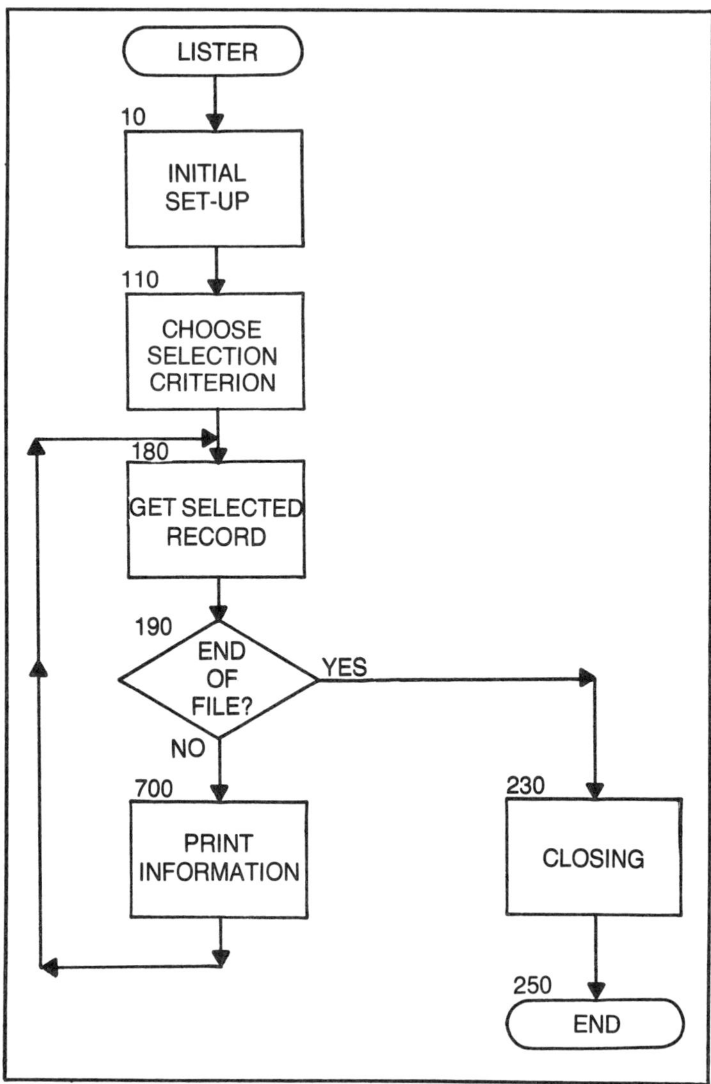

Fig. 14-1. Design for printing a selected list.

The general outline of the program is simple. Making sure that the output looks good adds complications. The different groups (new members, five year awards, etc) should appear as distinct groups, with a title at the beginning and a count of members at the end. Figure 14-2 provides a brief illustration of how the report might appear. The divisions between the groups are referred to as *control breaks* because they control the printer at the breaks between groups. This form of output is certainly more attractive than a long list of all the names of members who fit into any of the groups. (The problem of having January, 1980 print as 1.8 instead of 1.80 can be corrected by techniques described later.) If you have a large organization, the list of new members may take several pages. The report will look better if it leaves a margin at the bottom of each page and prints a title at the top of the next page before continuing the list. Your report program should provide for *page breaks* as well as group control breaks.

Page breaks require the use of an additional variable (LC for line counter) to keep track of how many lines have been printed on each page. Every time the program prints information, the line counter is increased by the number of lines printed. The current program prints a single line for each record, so the line counter is increased by one for each PRINT statement. If the list were double-spaced, the blank line between records would also be counted. The program should check to see if the page is full each time the line counter is changed. Unless the page is full, the program has completed its printing subroutine and can return to processing records (Fig. 14-3). When the page is full, the program will print any desired page footing (a message at the bottom of each page), prepare for the next page by starting the line count over (LETting it equal the number of lines at the top of the next page), and print the header or title on the top of the next page before it returns from the subroutine.

Your program can tell when a page is full by comparing the line counter (LC) to the maximum number of lines allowed on a page. Since the maximum number of lines is apt to vary depending on what size of paper you are using or whether your "page" is the number of lines that can fit on your video at one time. Typewriters and most computer printers print six lines for every inch. Standard (8½-by-11-inch) typing paper can hold 66 lines.

```
              MEMBERSHIP LONGEVITY LIST

      MEMBERS WITH 5 YEARS OF SERVICE
BOB SMITH                          JOINED: 8.75
JIM JONES                          JOINED: 1.75
ROBERT ANDREW VAN DER HUESENBURGHJOINED:9.75
       5 YEAR GROUP HAS 3 MEMBERS


      MEMBERS WITH 0 YEARS OF SERVICE
GEORGE WASHINGTON                  JOINED: 1.8
THOMAS JEFFERSON                   JOINED: 3.8
       0 YEAR GROUP HAS 2 MEMBERS


 6 RECORDS READ FROM FILE: TEST
 5 RECORDS INCLUDED ON REPORT
```

Fig. 14-2. Sample selected list report.

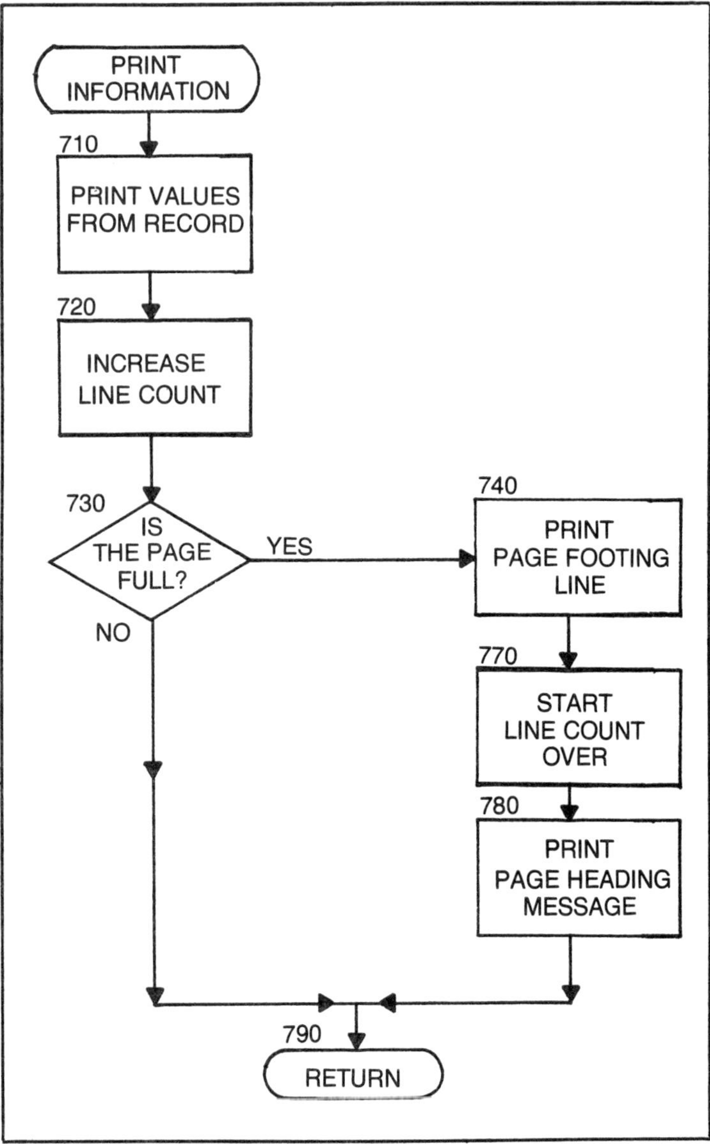

Fig. 14-3. Flowchart for printing with page breaks.

However, you need to make allowances for margins at the top and bottom of each page. You also need to leave room for the page footing, since it is not printed until after the program has determined that the page is full. Allowing one-inch margins at the top and bottom of the page (6 lines each) and two lines to print a page footing would give a maximum line count of 52.

Producing the same report on a sixteen line video would require a maximum line count of 14 (with no margins and two lines for the footing). Since this value can change so drastically, it is a good idea to store it in a variable at the beginning of your program, where it is easy to see and change. In the sample program, the maximum lines per page is a variable named LM.

The program also has to take appropriate action between pages. If you are printing on continuous paper (rolls or perforated fan-fold sheets), the program should print enough blank lines for the margins at the bottom of one page and the top of the next, then continue with the report. If you are printing on single sheets of paper or displaying the report on a video screen, you want the program to pause and give you a chance to put the next sheet of paper into the printer or read the information on the screen. In these cases, a prompt to press the Enter/Return key when ready and an INPUT statement will provide the user with the ability to control the output speed. This is the option used in the sample program.

The amount of information on the page heading and page footings will depend on the specific program. In many cases, the page heading can be a single line and the page footing can be omitted entirely. For other reports, you may use a number of lines at the top of each page to print the title of the report, the page number (which would use another counter variable), the date the report was printed and titles for each column of information. The page footing may contain totals for the page, the page number, or standard messages.

Selecting the right records and deciding when to make control breaks can both be done as part of the get-record subroutine. Each time a record is read into memory, the program needs to see if it has reached the end of the file or has another record to add to the input count (NI). Then the values in the record are compared to the selection criteria to determine if the record should be saved for printing. If not, the program loops back to read the next record (Fig. 14-4). Selected records are counted for the report and used to check for a control break.

A control break occurs whenever a selected record belongs to a different group than the preceding record. All the members of each group in the sample report will have joined in the same year. As long as the year for one record matches the value of the year in the previous year, no break has occurred. The only difficulty is that when the computer reads a record, it erases the values from the previous record. A direct comparison of one record with its predecessor is not possible. Instead, the value of the year for the current group needs to be held in a separate variable (HY for Hold Year in this case). Now the computer can tell when it has reached the break between two groups by comparing the year in each record to the value in the "hold" variable.

The end of the file obviously marks the end of the last group. So, when the end-of-file record has been read, the program wants to force a control break to be detected before returning to the top-level of the program and

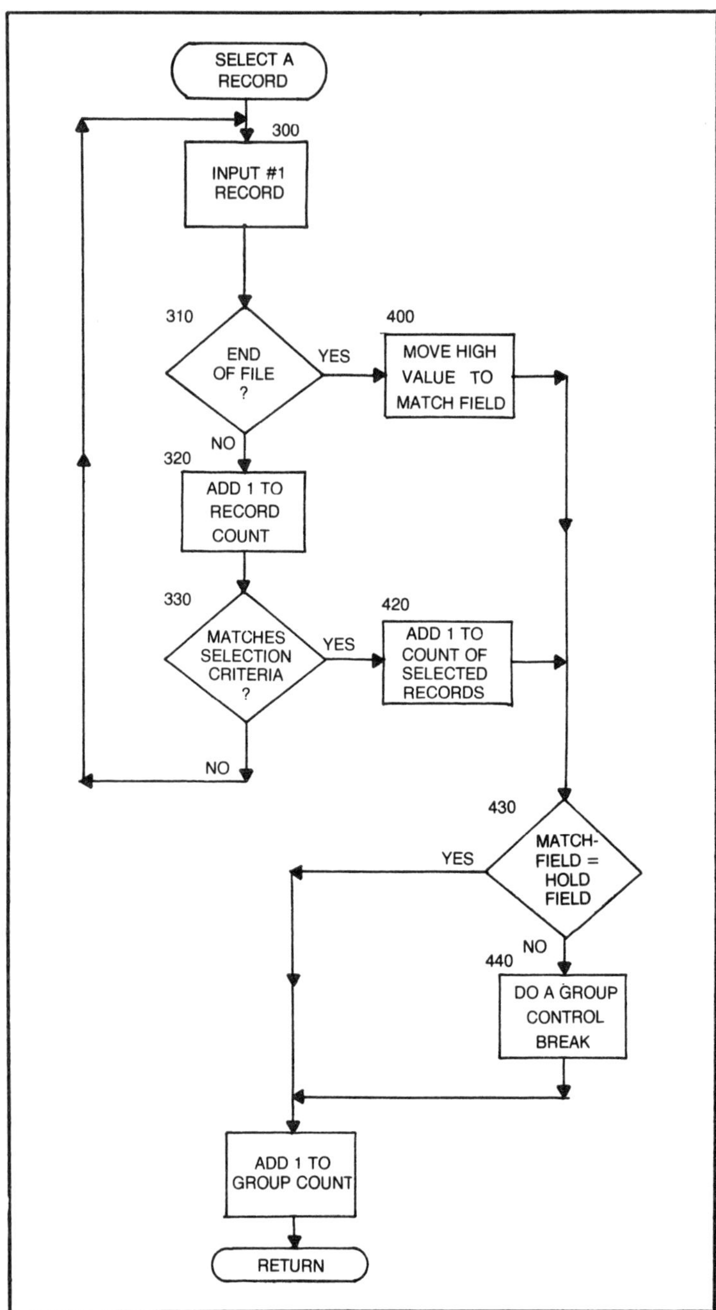

Fig. 14-4. Flowchart for record selection subroutine.

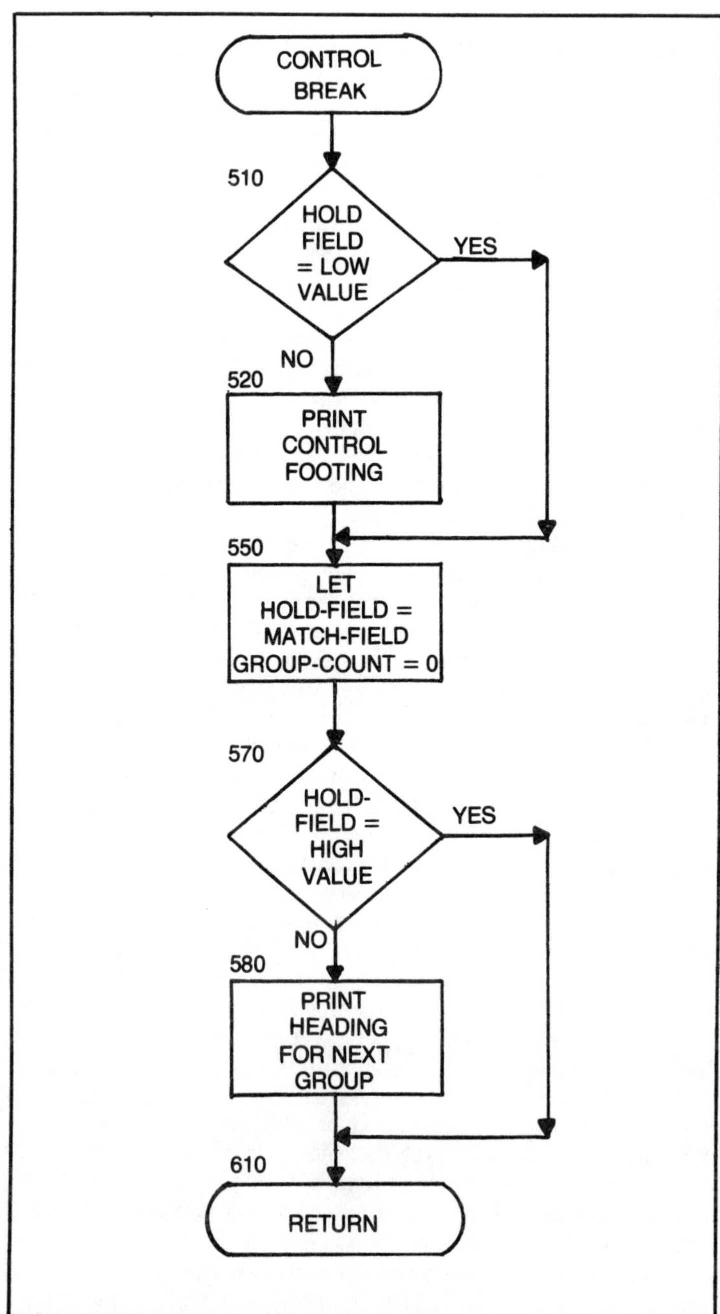

Fig. 14-5. Flowchart for a group control break.

closing the files. This special control break can be generated by moving the highest possible value (HV) to the record item compared to the hold variable. This will convince the program that a control break has occurred and force it to print the appropriate control footing. The control break subroutine will also have to check for the highest-value code so that it does not print an extra group heading at the end of the report (box 570 in Fig. 14-5).

The first record presents another problem. You do not necessarily know what the appropriate hold-value will be for the first group. If you automatically printed a heading for the group of members with thirty years of service, you might be left with an empty group. The group heading cannot be accurately printed until you have seen the values in the first selected record. You can begin the program by giving the hold variable a special code (like the lowest possible value, LV). Then the first selected record will cause a control break. You do not want to print a group footing yet (because you have not printed the records for the first group), so your control break subroutine includes a special check (line 510) to skip the footing if the hold variable contains the low-value code.

The general logic of a control break subroutine (Fig. 14-5) is to finish the old group (usually by printing a control footing that states how many records are in that group), preparing the program for a new group (by changing the value of the hold variable to match the record just read and by re-initializing the count of records in the group—NG—to a value of zero), and finally printing the heading for the new group. If you are not going to start each group on a new page, then the number of lines used to print the control footing and control heading need to be added to the line counter. If the new group is going to start a new page, then the program needs to print the appropriate number of blank lines or prompt for the new page and start the line count fresh with the heading.

Control breaks only work if the records are in the proper sequential order on the file. Otherwise, you would not have printed the records belonging in the first group before you read the first record in the next group. Many systems will use a sort program before each *select/print* program to make sure the records are in the proper sequence. Other systems will divide the task into three programs (or major subroutines) that first select records from the master file, second sort the selected records, and third print the report. The sample program assumes the membership file is already in the proper order. The sequential update kept the records in the order of membership numbers; it is assumed that membership numbers were assigned to members in chronological order when they joined. If this assumption is not true, the Lister program might produce reports showing several different small groups of new members in between groups of members with longer service.

Translating the flowcharts into an actual program that prints a list for *longevity* recognition (Fig. 14-6) is not trivial. Lines 10-270 implement the top-level flowchart (Fig. 14-1). Lines 25 (clearing all variables to zero and reserving 300 bytes of string space) and 250 (closing the file) may not be necessary in your version of BASIC. Also, the statements that assign the input file (lines 70-90) may have to be altered.

The "get record subroutine" (lines 290-470) may need some explanation. The input record description (line 300) includes all variables on the membership record even though this program only pays attention to the first and last names (R2$ and R1$) and the date joined (S1). The complete record must be described so that it matches the format of the record written by the program that created the file (Member or Update).

In some programs, only a single IF statement is needed to decide whether a record is selected or not. In this case the process is more complicated. The records need to be matched based on the year the member joined, but the date is stored with the month as the whole number part and the year as the decimal part of the variable. Separating the year (SY) from the rest of the value requires subtracting the month part of the value (INT(S1)) from the variable and then multiplying by 100 to move the decimal over two places (line 33). Since BASIC uses floating point arithmetic, any arithmetic done on fractions may produce a small rounding error. Such an error could prevent the calculated year from exactly matching the value for the selection year (YR). Line 335 rounds the calculated year (SY) to the nearest integer to avoid that danger.

Lines 340 through 380 check to see if the record falls into any of the selected groups. The absolute value function is included in checking for longevity to prevent problems from occurring at the turn of the century. In 1990, the ten-year group will be identified by a joining date in '80 (90 – 80 equals 10 in line 360). However, in 2005 the matching formula would produce: 05 – 95 = –10. Hence, the absolute value function protects the longevity of the program.

The control break and printing subroutines are simple illustrations of the designs presented in Fig. 14-5 and 14-3. You should be able to understand them without too much difficulty.

PRINTING MAILING LABELS

One of the more common uses for computers is to print mailing labels. Your organization probably sends out a newsletter or notices of special events. Since the names and addresses of the members are already stored in a computer file, it should be a simple task to print that information on gummed labels that can be stuck on envelopes or magazines.

Mailing labels are generally about two-and-five eighths inches long and one inch high. The output for your printing program must be designed carefully so the information fits on the label with no overlap. The vertical spacing is simple. You will print the name on the first line, the street address on the second line, and the city, state and ZIP code on a third line. Since there are six lines per inch, you need to print three blank lines before the next name to keep the printing lined up on the one-inch high labels.

```
10   REM  LIST FOR LONGEVITY RECOGNITION

20   REM  by Richard Galbraith                   August, 1981

25      CLEAR 300                                  'Reserve String Space

30      LET HV =  1.70141E+38                      'Highest Value

35      LET LV = -1.70141E+38                      'Lowest Value

40      LET LM =  14                               'Line Maximum

50      LET HY = LV                                'Initialize Hold Value
55      PRINT

60      PRINT TAB(10);"MEMBERSHIP LONGEVITY LIST"

65      PRINT

70      PRINT"ENTER FILE NAME";
80      INPUT F$

90      OPEN "I", I, F$

100     PRINT

110     PRINT"ENTER CURRENT YEAR";
120     INPUT YR

130     IF YR < 100 THEN 180

140     IF YR >=  0 THEN 180

150     IF YR = INT(YR) THEN 180
160     PRINT"YEAR MUST BE 2 DIGIT POSITIVE INTEGER."

170     GOTO 100

180     GOSUB 300                                 'Get Record

190     IF R1$ = "END-OF-FILE" THEN 230           'Finished

200     GOSUB 700                                 'Print Information

210     GOTO 180                                  'Next Record

220  REM -----

230     PRINT N1; "RECORDS READ FROM FILE: "; F$

240     PRINT NS; "RECORDS INCLUDED ON REPORT"

250     CLOSE

260     END

270  REM ---------------------------------

290  REM ***  GET RECORD SUBROUTINE  ***

300     INPUT#1, R1$, R2$, R3$, R4$, R5$, R6$, R7$, R8$, R9$, S1, S2
        ,S3

310     IF R1$ = "END-OF-FILE" THEN 400           'Final Control

320     LET N1 = N1 + 1                           'Count Input Recor
        ds

330     LET SY = 100 * (S1 - INT(S1))             'Get Year in Date Joined
```

Fig. 14-6. Lister program listing.

```
335     LET SY = INT(SY +.5)                    'Round to Integer
340     IF SY = YR          THEN 420            'New Member
350     IFABS(YR - SY) =  5 THEN 420            '5 Year Award
360     IF ABS(YR - SY) = 10 THEN 420           '10 Year Award
370     IF ABS(YR - SY) = 20 THEN 420           '20 Year Award
380     IF ABS(YR - 30) = 30 THEN 420           '30 Year Award
390     GOTO 300                                'Record Not Selected
400     LET SY = HV                             'End-of-File Value
410     GOTO 450                                'Control Break
420     LET NS = NS + 1                         'Count Selected Records
430     IF SY = HY  THEN 460                    'Same Group ?
450     GOSUB 500                               'Do Control Break
460     LET NG = NG + 1                         'Count Records in Group
470     RETURN
480   REM ------------
500   REM  ***  CONTROL BREAK SUBROUTINE
510     IF HY = LV   THEN 550                   'Starting First Group
520     PRINT TAB(5); ABS(YR - HY); "YEAR GROUP HAS"; NG; "MEMBERS"
530     PRINT TAB(15);"PRESS 'ENTER' TO CONTINUE";
540     INPUT A$
550     LET HY = SY                             'Change Hold Group
560     LET NG = 0                              'Number in New Group
570     IF SY = HV THEN 600                     'No Next Group
580     PRINT
582     PRINT
584     PRINT
590     PRINT TAB(5);"MEMBERS WITH"; ABS(YR - HY);"YEARS OF SERVICE"
600     LET LC = 1                              'Start of Page
610     RETURN
620   REM-----------
700   REM  ***  PRINTING SUBROUTINE  ***
710     PRINT R2$;" "; R1$; TAB(30);"JOINED:"; S1
720     LET LC = LC + 1                         'Count Lines Printed
730     IF LC < LM  THEN 790                    'More Room on Page
740     PRINT TAB(10);"PRESS 'ENTER' FOR NEXT PAGE";
750     INPUT A$
760     PRINT
```

```
762     PRINT
764     PRINT
770     LET LC = 1                              'Start New Page
780     PRINT TAB(5); ABS(YR - HY); "YEAR GROUP (CONTINUED)"
790     RETURN
800  REM -------------------------------------------------------
```

Fig. 14-6. Continued from page 263.

Suppose the cheapest way to buy gummed labels is in fanfold boxes of standard 8½-by-11-inch sheets. The fanfold makes your job easier because you do not have to count lines to make page breaks between sheets. The standard width creates a new problem. Three labels fit across the page. Instead of reading one record and printing one label, the program will have to print three labels at a time, as shown in Fig. 14-7.

The program needs to collect information from several (three) different records in a *buffer* before printing. A buffer is simply a part of memory set aside to hold a group of values that will be sent to, or received from,a peripheral device at one time.If you are working on a microcomputer with a disk, you may have noticed that the disk is not turned on each time your program reaches a PRINT# or INPUT#. The computer uses a buffer (often 256 bytes or characters long) to hold information for the disk drive. The PRINT# command stores information in the buffer. Only after the computer has collected enough information to fill the entire buffer does it take the time to actually turn on the disk and write the information on its magnetic surface. The buffer allows the computer to work faster, since it does not have to stop as often to wait for the disk.

You can create your own buffers by assigning some variables to hold information that you are saving to print. For the Label program, you might use arrays with a DIMensioned size of three to hold the information for the three labels that print across a page. You will need at least one array for each line. The sample program uses N$(I) for the first (name) line, A$(I) for the second (address) line, and C$(I) for the final (city) line.

The flowchart design for using a print buffer is similar to the design for a page break (Fig. 14-8). Each time you read a record from the file, you add 1 to the subscript that serves as the counter for the buffer selector. Then,

```
BOB SMITH                 JIM JONES                 K VAN DER HUESENBURGH
123 W. MAIN               456 E. FIRST              999 N. FOURTH
PHOENIX, AZ  85005        MESA, AZ  85202           BLUE RIDGE SUMM, PA  17099


GEORGE WASHINGTON         THOMAS JEFFERSON
546 S. HAMPTON            1900 PENNSYLVANIA AVE.
MOUNT VERNON, VA  20123   WASHINGTON, DC  19001


 5 LABELS PRINTED.
```

Fig. 14-7. Sample mailing labels.

instead of a PRINT command, you use LET statements to move the information to the appropriate elements in the array. The information from the first record will be stored in element number 1 of each array (N$, A$ and C$). The buffer is not full until information has been moved into all three elements of the arrays. So, the program will loop back to get the second and third records. When the third elements of the arrays have been filled, then it is time to print all three labels. The top line will contain all three names (N$(1), N$(2) and N$(3)). The next PRINT statement will put all three street addresses on the next line, etc. After each row of labels has been printed, the subscript needs to be reset to zero, so the next record you read will start in the first position of the next row.

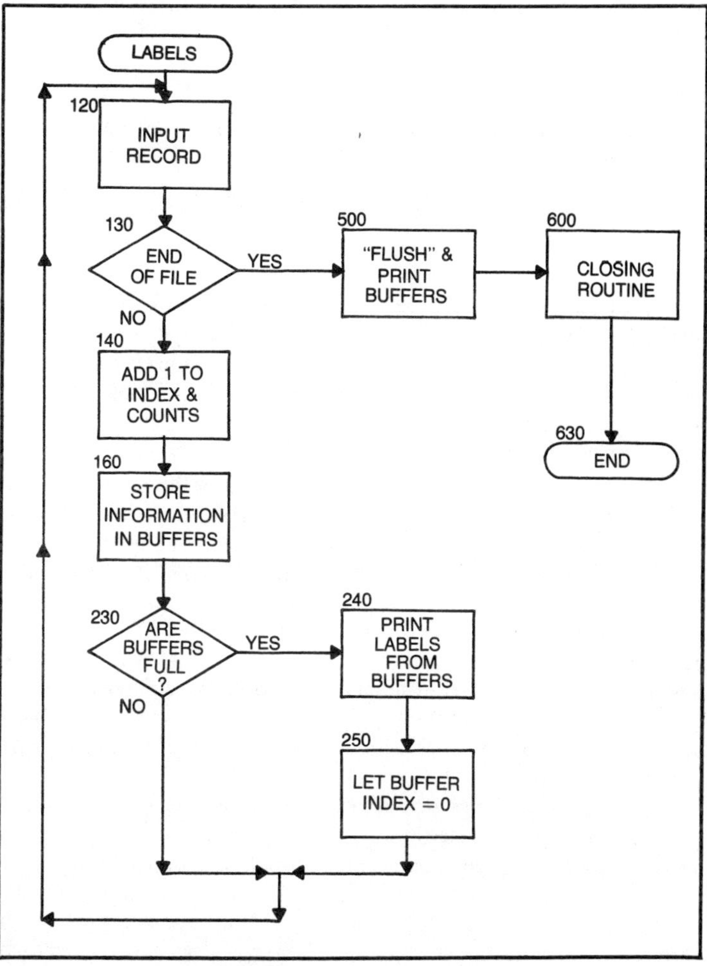

Fig. 14-8. Flowchart for printing labels.

If you are lucky, you will reach the end of the file right after you print a row of labels. More likely, the end of the file will come when the information for the last record or two is sitting in the buffer. Before closing the files, you will want to print the final labels. If your program just repeated the label printing subroutine, you would get duplicate labels for whoever occupied the last position on the previous row. Unless you move new values into an element of an array, it retains the value from the previous statements. Your program can "flush" the old values out of the buffer by moving blank spaces to the elements that follow your last record. If you only had one label stored in the buffer (subscript = 1), then you would move blanks to both the second and third labels before printing. If two labels were stored in the buffer, then you would move blanks only to the third label. (If three labels had been stored in the buffer, they would have been printed already, so you could skip the whole process of flushing and printing the contents of the buffer.)

CONCATENATION

You have studied the design of the Label program enough by now to discover that it still has an unsolved problem. Only one variable has been assigned to hold the member's name on the label, yet two different variables hold his first and last name on the record. How are you going to fit both values into one variable? Also, how are you going to fit the city (R3$), state (R4$), and ZIP code (R5$) into the single label variable (C$(I))?

The solution is *concatenation*, which is a fancy word for shoving two strings together to make a longer string. BASIC uses the plus sign (+) for concatenation, so it looks suspiciously like addition. However, the results of concatenation are quite different from addition. PRINT 3 + 3 performs addition and prints 6. PRINT "3" + "3" (using string values) performs concatenation and prints 33.

The most common problem with concatenation is the failure to include spaces where you want them. If R2$ holds the first name "BOB" and R1$ holds the last name "WHITE", then R2$ + R1$ would produce "BOBWHITE". To get a more readable name of "BOB WHITE", you would have to put a string with a value of space (" ") between R2$ and R1$. The appropriate expression for the member's name would be: R2$ + " " + R1$. This is the value stored in the name line of the labels (N$) by line 160 of the labels program (Fig. 14-9). The city line (C$ in line 220) is created by concatenating the name of the city (R3$), followed by a comma and blank space (", "), then the state abbreviation (R5$), two more blanks, and finally the ZIP code (R6$).

The concatenation of strings results in longer strings. There is no guarantee that a long name (like Robert Van Der Huesenburg) or a long address (like Blue Ridge Summit, Pennsylvania 17214) will fit on a small label. Most computer printers fit ten characters (letters and spaces) on each horizontal inch. A label 2⅝ inches wide will hold a maximum of twenty-six characters. If any of the strings in the buffer is longer than twenty-six characters long, it will run over onto the next label across the page, ruining a whole row of labels. Your program can use the LENgth function to make sure the strings are not too long. Line 50 of the LABELS program stores the width of each label (the number of characters that will fit across) in a variable (W). After the names are concatenated into N$(I), line 170 checks to see if the resulting name is too long. If the name is longer than the width, line 180 concatenates only the initial of the first name (LEFT$(R2$,1)) with the last name to make a shorter line for the label. (Note: If you are using a BASIC that requires strings to be DIMensioned, then the first letter of the string R2$ would be R2$(1,1) - for one letter starting at the first position. The LEFT$ function is not part of every version of BASIC.)

A different approach was used in lines 200-220 to make sure that the city line is not too long. The state (R4$) is a two-letter postal abbreviation and the ZIP code (R5$) is always five digits; the comma and blank spaces use a total of four characters. That leaves fifteen (W – 11) characters for the city name. A long city name can be detected (line 200) and if necessary, abbreviated (line 210), before it is concatenated with the rest of the variables (line 220). This procedure assumes that your update program edited the input values to make sure all state names on the file are only two letters long and the ZIP code on every record is also a valid value.

The complete Labels program is fairly short. The entire program can be represented with a one-page flowchart. It also contains more remarks (including the messages following the apostrophes at the end of most lines). You may want to read through once without looking at the remarks or the flowchart and then read it again while referring to the flowchart (Fig. 14-8) and reading all the remarks (Fig. 14-9). If you like the documentation when you see it in the book, use it when you write your own programs. You are not saving time when you leave out remarks. The extra time it takes to understand the program months later when you want to improve it or explain it to someone else will invariably be greater than the extra typing time the remarks would have required.

AGGREGATE COUNTS

The third common type of report program is used to produce aggregate counts (and other statistics) that summarize information from all records on the file. Assume that your organization has four different types of members (students, associate, regular, and life). Figure 14-10 is a sample of a report that shows the number of members of each type and the number who pay their dues each month. You may think of more useful items to count and produce a better report for yourself, but you should be able to use the same programming structures.

Statistical summary programs usually rely on arrays to accumulate counts (and/or totals for averaging). The report shown in Fig. 14-10 would use two arrays of counters, one (M) for the months and the other (T) for the types. Each time a record is read, the program would determine the month (from S2) that annual dues should be paid and add 1 to the count in that element of the month's array. Similarly, 1 would be added to the count that

```
10  REM LABELS (3 ACROSS)
20  REM by Richard Galbraith          August, 1981
30    CLEAR 300                                  'Reserve String Space
40    DIM N$(3), A$(3), C$(3)                    'Set Up Buffers
50    LET W = 26                                 'Width of Label
60    LET I = 0                                  'Initialize Index
70    PRINT"ENTER NAME OF FILES FOR LABELS";
80    INPUT F$
90    OPEN "I", 1, F$
100   PRINT"PRESS 'ENTER' WHEN LABELS ARE IN PRINTER";
110   INPUT A$
120   INPUT#1, R1$, R2$, R3$, R4$, R5$, R6$, R7$, R8$, R9$, S1, S2,
      S3
130   IF R1$ = "END-OF-FILE" THEN 500
140   LET NR = NR + 1                            'Count Records
150   LET I = I + 1                              'Increase Index
160   LET N$(I) = R2$ + " "+ R1$                 'Full Name
170   IF LEN(N$(I)) < W THEN 190                 'Fits on Label
180   LET N$(I) = LEFT$(R2$, 1) + " "+ R1$       'Use First Initial
190   LET A$(I) = R3$                            'Street Address
200   IF LEN(R4$) < W - 11 THEN 220              'Lons City Name?
210   LET R4$ = LEFT$(R4$, W - 11)               'Abbreviate
220   LET C$(I) = R4$ +", "+ R5$ +" "+ R6$       'City /State /ZIP
230   IF I < 3 THEN 120                          'Get Next Record
240   GOSUB 300                   'Print Labels when Buffers are Full
250   LET I = 0                                  'Restart Index
260   GOTO 120                                   'Get Next Record
270 REM -----
300   REM *** PRINT LABELS SUBROUTINE ***
310   PRINT N$(1); TAB(W+1); N$(2); TAB(2*W+1); N$(3)
320   PRINT A$(1); TAB(W+1); A$(2); TAB(2*W + 1); A$(3)
330   PRINT C$(1); TAB(W+1); C$(2); TAB(2*W +1); C$(3)
340   PRINT                                      'Blanks to Next Label
350   PRINT
360   PRINT
370   RETURN
380   REM -----
500 REM *** END OF FILE ***
```

Fig. 14-9. Labels program listing.

```
510  IF I = 0 THEN 600                  'Buffer Already Empty
520  IF I = 2 THEN 560                  '2 Records in Buffer
530  LET N$(2) = " "                    'Blank 2nd Label Across
540  LET A$(2) = " "
550  LET C$(2) = " "
560  LET N$(3) = " "                    'Blank 3rd Label Across
570  LET A$(3) = " "
580  LET C$(3) = " "
590  GOSUB 300                          'Print Remainins Labels
600  CLOSE
610  PRINT
620  PRINT NR; "LABELS PRINTED."        'Short Audio Trail
630  END
640  REM ------------------------------------------------------------
```

matched the membership type on that record, and also to the count of the total number of records (NR). When the program reached the end of the file, the counts needed to print the report would be stored in the arrays, ready for printing.

The aggregate counts program will have two main sections (Fig. 14-11). The first main section is a loop that reads records and adds to the counters until the end of the file. The second section prints the report from the information stored in the arrays. If any statistical calculations (such as dividing the count for each type by the total number of records to get percents) are needed, they would be included in the second section.

```
        COUNT OF MEMBERS BY DUES-MONTH AND TYPE
                 MONTH
2                JAN            1        TYPE
0                FEB            1        ASSOCIATE
1                MAR            0        REGULAR
0                APR            1        STUDENT
1                MAY            3        LIFE
0                JUN                     INVALID
0                JUL
1                AUG
1                SEP
0                OCT
0                NOV
0                DEC
0                ERROR
       6 TOTAL MEMBERS ON FILE.
```

Fig. 14-10. Simple aggregate counts report.

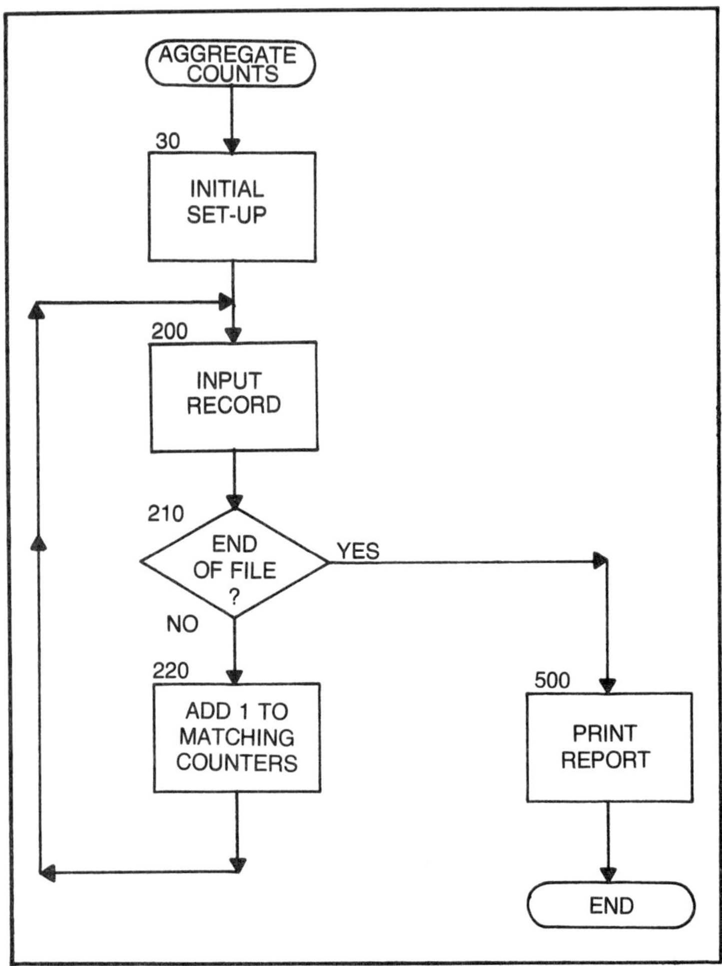

Fig. 14-11. Flowchart for aggregate counts report.

The Counts program (Fig. 14-12) will create the report formatted as shown in Fig. 14-10. This design should refresh your memory of the use of arrays and tables (from Chapter 11). In addition to the two arrays of counters, the program uses matching tables to print the titles of the months and membership types. In all cases, the arrays include an extra element at the end to handle any records that do not have a valid value for the month or membership type (R9$) variables. This is important. Without the statements that fit any invalid month values into M(13)—lines 240 and 250—and leave the subscript at 5 when the membership type in the records fails to find a match on the title table look-up—lines 280-310—the program would come to an abrupt halt with an error message if even one of the records on the file had a mistake in either of those fields. Allowing for bad values lets the program continue and produce the report.

The set-up portion of the program (lines 30-180) makes sure that the counters start at zero, loads the title tables with the desired values, and assigns the input file. The loop that reads and counts occupies lines 200-320.

The final section closes the file (line 510) and prints the report. The body of the report is divided into two FOR . . . NEXT loops. The first five lines have values for both months and membership types. Since there are more months than types of membership, the remaining months have to be reported with a second loop that does not refer to the type arrays.

FANCY PRINTING OF NUMBERS

Normally BASIC prints numbers without any commas and does not bother to align the decimal points in a column of numbers. Some versions of BASIC allow you to overcome this limitation by using an *image* of the way you want numbers to be printed. Images are strings of symbols that describe the way a number will look in a report. The normal symbols in an image are:

Number or digit (# or D). Each symbol is the place holder for one digit of the number.

Decimal point (.). Allows you to specify how many digits will be printed after the decimal point. The number will automatically be rounded to the specified level.

Comma (,). Shows where to place commas between digits.

Minus sign (–). Can be used to have the minus sign printed in front of the number (for science) or following the last digit (for accounting reports). If the image does not include a minus sign, the absolute value will be printed.

Dollar signs ($$). Used at the front of an image to indicate that a dollar sign should be printed immediately before the first nonzero digit.

The image "$$###,###,##" could be used to round a value to the nearest cent and print the result with a leading dollar sign. Figure 14-13 shows how a column of values would appear if printed using normal BASIC and two different images. This sample demonstrates the need to specify your images carefully. If you do not allow enough digits in your image, BASIC will not give you any warning, it will simply throw away the part of the number too big to fit in your image. Thus a value of 1.01E+6 (or 1,010,000) would be reduced to ten thousand by an image that did not include a millions place holder. Also, the failure to include a minus sign in your image could produce erroneous results.

The rounding provided by an image is limited to the printed value. The value stored in the variable is not rounded, so if you have the computer print the total of a column of numbers (added and then rounded), the result may not exactly match the total of the printed values (rounded by an image).

```
10   REM  AGGREGATE COUNTS
20   REM  by Richard Galbraith                 August, 1981
30      CLEAR 300
40      DIM M(13), MT$(13), T(5), TT$(5)       'Counters & Titles
50      FOR I = 1 TO 13
60      LET M(I) = 0                           'Initial Month Counts
70      READ MT$(I)                            'Month Title Table
80      NEXT I
90      DATA JAN,FEB,MAR,APR,MAY,JUN,JUL,AUG,SEP,OCT,NOV,DEC,ERROR
100     FOR I = 1 TO 5
110     LET T(I) = 0                           'Initial Type Counts
120     READ TT$(I)                            'Type Title Table
130     NEXT I
140     DATA ASSOCIATE, REGULAR, STUDENT, LIFE, INVALID
150     PRINT "ENTER FILE NAME FOR MEMBERSHIP COUNTS";
160     INPUT F$
170     OPEN "I", 1, F$
180     PRINT "READING FILE . . ."
190  REM ----
200     INPUT#1, R1$, R2$, R3$, R4$, R5$, R6$, R7$, R8$, R9$, S1, S2
        , S3
210     IF R1$ = "END-OF-FILE"  THEN 500       'Print Report
220     LET NR = NR + 1                        'Total Count
230     LET SM = INT(S2)                       'Month in Dues Date
240     IF SM > 0 AND SM < 13 THEN 260         'Valid Month
250     LET SM = 13                            'Code for Error
260     LET M(SM) = M(SM) + 1                  'Add 1 to Right Count
270     LET I = 1
280     IF R9$ = TT$(I) THEN 310               'Matching Type
290     LET I = I + 1                          'Check Next Type
300     IF I < 5  THEN 280
310     LET T(I) = T(I) + 1                    'Add 1 to Right Count
320     GOTO 200                               'Read Next Record
330  REM -----
500  REM  -- ALL RECORDS HAVE BEEN COUNTED --
510     CLOSE 1                                'Close Disk File
520     PRINT
```

Fig. 14-12. Counts program listing.

```
530       PRINT
540       PRINT TAB(10);"COUNT OF MEMBERS BY DUES-MONTH AND TYPE"
550       PRINT ,"MONTH",,"TYPE"
560       FOR I = 1 TO 5                          'Number of Types
570       PRINT M(I), MT$(I), T(I), TT$(I)
580       NEXT I
590       FOR I = 6 TO 13                         'Rest of Months
600       PRINT M(I), MT$(I)
610       NEXT I
620       PRINT TAB(20); NR; "TOTAL MEMBERS ON FILE."
630       END
640   REM ---------------------------------------------------------
```

Images are specified in two different ways in BASIC statements. The method you use will depend on the version of BASIC you have. Both methods include the word USING in a print statement. One method includes the image string (followed by a semicolon ;) between the USING command and the expression to be printed. The command: PRINT USING "$$###,##"; P would print the value stored in the variable P using the dollars-and-cents image. The other method uses separate statements to hold the image and the print command. An example of the second method is:

```
200 PRINT USING 205; P
205 IMAGE $$DDD.DD
```

In the second method, the IMAGE command works like the DATA command in identifying the use of the information on the rest of the line. The same IMAGE could be referred to in the line number following the USING command in several different PRINT statements. The IMAGE statement can be used to describe the format of an entire line of print, including different image strings for every value on the line.

The use of images (if your computer system supports them) provides a professional looking touch to reports generated with BASIC. It takes some

Normal BASIC	$$###,###.## Image	##,###.###- Image
12345.678	$12,345.68	12,345.678
22	$22.00	22.000
-5678.9	-$5,678.90	5,678.900-
200300	$200,300.00	200,300.000
1.01E+06	$010,000.00	010,000.000

Fig. 14-13. The effect of images on printed values.

extra effort to produce the polished results that will make your programs outstanding.

GRAPHICS

Most microcomputer versions of BASIC allow you to produce graphic output. With the graphics commands you can display pictures (sometimes in color) or mathematical graphs on the video screen. You can even create animation for video games. Unfortunately, the specific graphic commands vary drastically from computer to computer. The more common graphics commands are included in the BASIC dictionary (Appendix D). You will need to check the reference manuals for your particular computer to see which ones apply to your system.

The graphics commands are based on the same general ideas. The video screen is divided into hundreds of small spots (called pixels). Each spot can be identified by its position in a matrix. Usually the upper left corner of the screen is the starting point (0,0). The first subscript (X coordinate in normal geometry) specifies the horizontal position of the spot. The second subscript (Y coordinate) specifies the vertical position (how far down). Any pixel on the screen can be located by its X and Y values. Figure 14-14 illustrates the location of pixels on a small screen.

The graphics commands determined which pixels are turned on (lit) and which are turned off (dark). The single spot in the lower left-hand corner could be turned on by a command like SET(0,12) or PLOT 0,12. The horizontal line could be drawn by a FOR . . . NEXT loop like FOR X = 3 TO 15 : PLOT X, 2 : NEXT or by a single line drawing command that identified the line as X varying from 3 to 15 while Y is 2. Similarly, the vertical line is the result of varying Y (from 4 to 8) while X stays at 20.

With a little experimentation and planning with graph paper, you will soon get the hang of the graphics commands on your computer and be able to liven up your programs with handsome displays. Do not get carried away with building elaborate displays for all your programs. Let your graphics abilities be one more tool in your programming tool kit. Use all of your tools to meet the requirements of the problem you are working with. But, remember to pick your tools based on the needs defined by the purpose of the program. Never sacrifice the original purpose in an attempt to show off your ability with a particular tool.

THE END OF THE BEGINNING

As you reach the end of this book, you are just beginning to learn about computer programming and electronic data processing. Programming is an ever-changing field. It has emerged as a separate occupation only in the current generation. Hundreds of different programming languages have been created in that time. Many of those languages have already become totally obsolete. Advances in computers and their software appear annually, and will continue to do so in the forseeable future. You will need to continue your learning just to keep from falling behind.

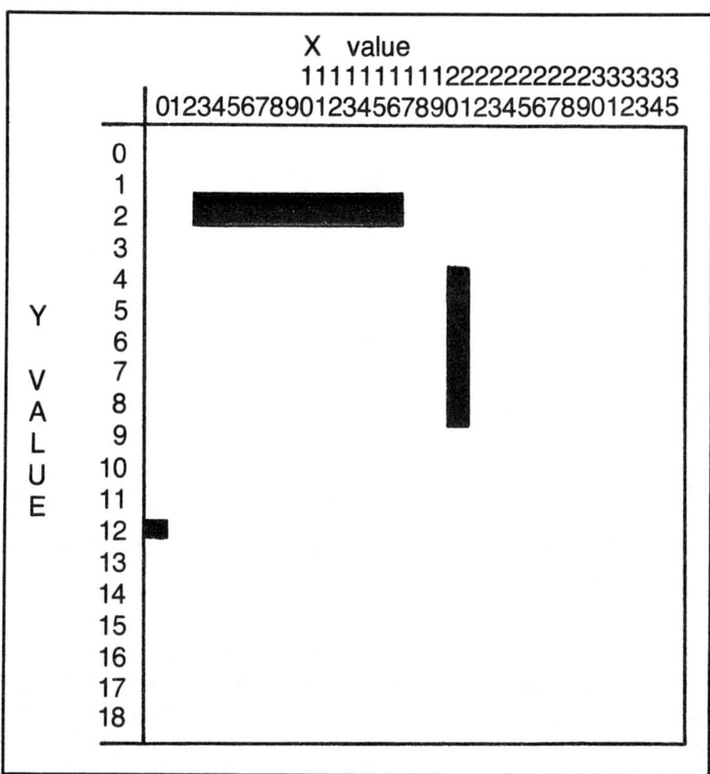

Fig. 14-14. Pixels on a small video screen.

While computers and the details of programming languages seem to be changing constantly, some aspects of programming have stayed the same. All digital computers and programming languages are based on the same mathematical principles and logical structures. Programmers in any language have to make similar provisions to check for valid data values, end-of-file conditions, and the other problem areas discussed in this book.

Most of the senior programmers today learned the fundamentals of programming while writing assembly-language programs. Their knowledge was easily transferred to writing programs in the newer languages of FORTRAN, COBOL, and BASIC. If you paid close attention to the fundamental ideas while you read this book, you should be able to apply them in writing programs for whatever computers and programming languages become available during the next thirty years.

Appendix A

Ideas for Programming Practice

Sometimes the most difficult part of writing is thinking of a good topic. You may find one of the most difficult parts of practicing your new programming skills is thinking of good problems to solve with the computer. The following list of suggestions may help you get started. The suggestions are grouped by the chapters in which the specific BASIC commands or structures appropriate for each problem are introduced. No programming problems are listed for Chapters 1 and 2, because the first BASIC commands are not introduced until Chapter 3.

CHAPTER 3

1. What different answers can you get by adding pairs of parentheses to the following statement:

   PRINT 1 + 7 * 6 / 3 – 5 ↑ 4 / 2

2. Use a LET statement to calculate the number of times your heart beats every day (assume a normal heart rate of 72 beats per minute). Use PRINT statements to display the answer and to calculate the number of times your heart will beat next year.

3. What is the largest number that BASIC will handle on your computer? (Try multiplication and/or exponentiation calculations to see what sized answers cause the computer to give you an error message.)

CHAPTER 4

4. Write a program that converts a temperature from degrees Fahrenheit to degrees Centigrade. The formula is: Centigrade = (Fahrenheit * 5 / 9) –32. Write a second program to convert from Centi-

grade to Fahrenheit. Does the second program always produce an answer exactly matching the value you started with in the first program?

5. Write a program that will print your name in large block letters. Example:

```
R R R R           0 0 0        B B B B
R       R       0       0      B       B
R R R R         0       0      B B B B
R       R       0       0      B       B
R         R       0 0 0        B B B B
```

6. Write a program that prints a meaningful message one word at a time. Add GOTO statements that completely change the meaning of the message.

CHAPTER 5

7. Write a flowchart for getting your computer ready for use in running a BASIC program.

8. Create a design for the decisions a baseball batter might have to make during a single pitch.

9. Draw a flowchart for getting an elephant into your bedroom.

CHAPTER 6

10. Assume a child is given an allowance that amounts to ten cents per week for every year of age. (He would get 90 cents each week when he is nine, one dollar a week when he is ten, etc.) Write a program that will print his total allowance for each year from his first birthday until he is fifteen. First, write it as a sequence of statements. Second, write it again using a loop with an IF . . . THEN statement. Third, write a final version using a FOR . . . NEXT loop.

11. A hard rubber ball bounces back to two-thirds of the previous height when dropped. If it were dropped from nine feet up, it would bounce six feet high on the first bounce (⅔ of 9) and 4 feet high (⅔ of 6) on the second bounce. If you dropped it from the top of the World Trade Center (about 1100 feet high), how many times would it bounce before it stopped going more than two feet high?

12. How many people would you have to have in a group before there would be a fifty-fifty chance that two of them would have the same birthday? (Hint: As you collect people in a room, the first one has a particular birthday. The second person would have 364 chances out of 365 of having a different birthday. The odds for the third person not matching either of the first two is 363/365. The combined odds of no matching birthdays for three people is (364/365) * (363/365). For four people the odds would be 364/365 * (363/365) * (362/365). Continue the pattern until the product is less than one-half.

13. How many ways can you make change for one dollar using quarters, dimes and nickels? (Use nested FOR . . . NEXT loops.)

CHAPTER 7

14. Write a program that will accept any four numbers on a DATA statement and print them out in order, from smallest to highest.

15. Find the sum and average of any group of numbers. (Use an INPUT loop with an end-of-data flag.)

16. Write a program that asks for a person's birthday (month and day), ensures it is a legitimate date, then prints a silly horoscope message. (Use a case structure to select the horoscope sign for each date.)

17. Write one program that can change temperatures from Centigrade to Fahrenheit, or Fahrenheit to Centigrade, and speeds from miles per hours to kilometers per hours, or kilometers per hour to miles per hour. Use a menu to select the desired calculation.

CHAPTER 8

18. To create addition flash cards, have the computer randomly select pairs of whole numbers. Print the numbers as an addition problem and ask for the answer. If the answer is right, print a nice, fancy message. If the answer is wrong, print the correct answer. After twenty problems, print a score card showing the number and percent answered correctly.

19. Write a number guessing game for two players. The computer picks a whole number from 1 to 100. Each player gets to guess. Whoever is closest wins. To make it more interesting, have the program call the players by name, keep count of the number of times each player wins and print a score card after 10 rounds, award three extra points if a player guesses the number exactly, and make sure that the second player does not guess the same number as the first player.

CHAPTER 9

20. Design and write a program that calculates the interest on a loan repaid in monthly installments. Input values should include the initial amount of the loan, the annual interest rate, and the amount of the monthly payment. Output should include the amount of interest and remaining debt each month, the number of months it will take to pay off the loan, the total amount of payments and total interest.

CHAPTER 10

21. Revise your number guessing game (suggestion # 19) so that two to ten players can play at once. Use arrays for their names, guesses on the current round and total points scored.

22. Represent a chess board as an eight by eight matrix. Write a program that will let a player place a queen or a knight on any square and have the computer respond by showing all of the squares that the piece (queen or knight) could reach on the next move.

CHAPTERS 12-14

23. Create a computerized system to keep track of all your books (with

author, title, date, publisher and main topics), or records (with title, artist, label, date and musical category), or household inventory (with item, date acquired, cost, and location for insurance purposes). Your system should include good update capability and several useful reports.

24. Think of ways to use programs in areas of your special interest and knowledge. The most useful programs reflect a combination of skill in programming and a thorough understanding of the problem area where the program is used.

Appendix B
Stages of Program Development

1. DEFINITION

Determine WHAT the program is going to do. This includes:

PURPOSE: Why the program is written. A brief description of what the program should accomplish.

OUTPUT: What the program will produce. A description of report and video display format and contents.

INPUT: What information is needed to use the program. A description of the data the user will be asked to provide.

2. DESIGN

Determine HOW the computer can satisfy the defined requirements. Details include:

PROCESS Structures: A map of the steps in the program. Normally a top-level flowchart, with as many supporting pages as necessary to describe the calculations and subroutines.

DATA Structures: A data dictionary defining all the variables and record formats the program will use.

3. TRANSLATION

Translate the design into a form the computer can handle. The boxes on the flowchart(s) are converted into BASIC statements and are given line numbers. Normally, the translation is done on paper first, then typed into the computer and saved on disk or tape.

4. TESTING

Make sure that the program in the computer does what it is supposed to do:

DESK CHECK: Read the program listing, looking for typographical errors or statements that do not fit the design flowchart and data dictionary.

VERIFY CALCULATIONS: Work the answers (output) out by hand for a couple of easy sets of input and compare with the results produced by the program.

LOOK FOR TROUBLE: Try running the program with strange values for input. Is there any combination of input that the program cannot handle properly?

TRY EVERY CHOICE: Make sure that your tests include every branch in the flowchart. Otherwise, there may be an undetected error in a statement on the path not taken.

ISOLATE ANY PROBLEMS: Add temporary trace & debug statements to print information that will help you see exactly what the program is doing and which line may be causing the bad output.

5. MAINTENANCE

Keep the program useful. Maintain it in a form that is easy for other people to understand. Provide clear instructions for its use. Keep the design documentation to make it easier to add improvements or make changes to the program.

(For Details, review Chapter 9.)

Appendix C
BASIC Grammar

The BASIC language has rules of grammar and parts of speech that parallel the grammer of natural languages, like English. This summary presents the elements of BASIC grammar starting with the smallest units and working up to the more complex structures. The corresponding English units are noted in parentheses.

SYMBOLS

character—Any symbol that is represented by a code number in the computer's memory. In most computers, each character uses one byte of memory (which provides for 256 possible different characters).
letters (Alphabet)—The characters A through Z. BASIC only recognizes uppercase letters in its defined words and variable names.
digits—The characters 0 through 9. Used to display numbers, digits cannot be the first character in a BASIC word or variable name.
punctuation—Characters that have special grammatical functions:

- **decimal point** (.)—Can only be used as part of a number.
- **comma** (,)—Used to separate items in a list, such as values for a DATA or PRINT statement.
- **semicolon** (;)—Used only in PRINT statements, replaces a comma when no space is desired between items.
- **colon** (:)—Used in some versions of BASIC to separate statements written on the same line.
- **backslash** (\)—Used in some other versions of BASIC to separate statements written on the same line.
- **quotes** (" ")—Used to mark the beginning and end of a string value.

parentheses ( )—Used to group items. Whatever is inside the pair of parentheses is treated as a single unit. The argument (input value) for a function must always be enclosed in parentheses.

apostrophe (')—In some versions, abbreviation for REM. The computer treats this symbol as the end of a line, so everything that follows it is a remark for human readers only.

question mark (?)—In some versions, abbreviation for PRINT.

operators—Characters that represent arithmetic operations; must be placed between two values.

plus (+)—Addition of numbers or concatenation of strings. (This character can also be the positive sign at the beginning of a number or its exponent.)

minus (–)—Subtraction of numbers. (This character can also be the negative sign at the beginning of a number or its exponent.)

asterisk (*)—Multiplication of numbers.

slash (/)—Division of numbers—as in fractions.

up-arrow (↑or ∧)—Exponentiation,or raising a number to a power. In some versions, a double asterisk (**) is used instead of the up-arrow.

comparators—Characters that represent a comparison between two values:

equal (=)—This symbol is also used in LET statements to indicate what value is to be stored in a variable.

less than (<)

greater than (>)

not equal—In some versions the number sign (#) is used; this is represented by the pair less than and greater than symbols (< >). Other pairs of comparators are used for Not Less Than (> =) and Not Greater Than (< =).

display characters—Lower case letters and graphic symbols that may be used as part of string values. These have no defined grammatical function in BASIC.

Control characters: characters associated with keys that control the action of the computer, such as the RETURN or ENTER key, backspace or left-arrow (←), etc.

WORDS

commands (verbs)—Words that tell the computer to take an action—do something words.

values (nouns)—Specific numbers or strings.

string—An ordered arrangement of characters.

integer—A number composed only of digits and possibly a sign. Integers cannot include decimal points and are limited in size (typically, an integer must be between –32768 and +32767).

floating point number—A number that can include a decimal point and exponent in addition to a sign and digits. If the exponent is written, it consists of the letter E followed by an integer.

double precision number—A floating point number that stores more decimal digits than a standard floating point number.
line number—A special whole number that identifies the location of a statement within a program.
variables (pronouns)—Memory locations that can contain values. Variable names must start with a letter and are typically limited to one or two characters in length. (The second character can be a digit or—in some versions—a second letter.) The type (gender) of a variable must match the type of value it holds (like "she" can only be used for feminine nouns and "they" can only be used for plural nouns). String variables are usually identified by a dollar sign ($) suffix.
logical operators (conjunctions)—Used to combine conditions. The only common logical operators are AND and OR.
other reserved words (prepositions)—Used to clarify some commands. Particular uses are to identify a location on a video screen (AT or @), a range of values (TO) or a synonym (AS).

PHRASES

expression—Anything that can be evaluated to determine a specific numeric value. Can be a value, a variable, or a combination of values, variables, functions (a type of command), operators and parenthesis.
condition—A comparison or combination of comparisons that can be evaluated to determine whether it is True (value 1 or −1 depending on the version of BASIC) or False (value 0).
array—A data structure that acts as a variable holding an organized group of values. Each value can be identified by its position within the array (using whole number subscripts).
list—An ordered group of variables, strings or expressions separated from each other by commas (or in some cases semi-colons). Each item in a list is treated as a separate unit.

SENTENCES

statement—A complete command to the computer. Every statement begins with a command word (verb). In the case of LET statements, many versions allow the command to be implicit (not written). The rest of the statement must follow the grammar associated with the specific command. (See the dictionary in Appendix D for details.)

PARAGRAPHS

line—A line number followed by at least one statement. Many versions of BASIC allow several statements (sentences) to be included on one line, as long as they are separated by colons or back-slashes. Nevertheless, most lines will contain a single statement.

subroutine—A logical group of lines processed as a single unit. A subroutine should have a single starting point (first line) and a single exit point (last line).

ESSAYS

program—A complete arrangement of statements (sentences) which satisfies its purpose when RUN (read) by itself.

Appendix D

BASIC Dictionary

This dictionary lists most of the commands used by the various versions of BASIC. Many of these words may not be included in your computer system, but they may still help you understand programs that were written for different computers. The core set of BASIC reserved words are underlined.

Many BASIC words must be followed by specific items of information (expressions, line numbers, file names, etc.). In the following, optional items are shown inside of brackets: [ ].

ABS(expression)—Absolute Value function, evaluates the unsigned value of the expression—the distance from zero. The result is a positive number.

AND—Condition AND condition, combines two conditions. The result is true only if both conditions are true; otherwise the result is false.

APPEND# file-number—Prepares a sequential disk file to have additional records added to the records already on file.

AS—Integer AS variable, assigns a variable name to a portion of a random access record.

ASC (character)—ASCII function, finds the American Standard Code for Information Interchange for a string character.

ASSIGN# file-number, file-name—Makes a specific file available for use in a program.

ATN (expression)—Finds the value of the trigonometric ArcTaNgent function. The inverse of the TAN function.

AT position—Specifies a specific position on a video screen. The position may be X and Y coordinates or a single integer, depending on the version of BASIC.

AUTO [line-number, increase]—Automatically provides line numbers while you are entering a program. AUTO 30,5 would provide 30 for the first line, 35 for the second, etc.

BACKSPACE# file-number—Backs up a disk file one position, so you could read or write the same record again. This command is not available on most systems.

BASIC—Beginners All-purpose Symbolic Instruction Code. As a command, BASIC tells the operating system to load the BASIC translator and start running it.

BREAK—Pressing this key interrupts whatever the BASIC program is doing and leaves the computer ready for another command. (Synonym: INTERRUPT.)

BYE—Signs off from a time-sharing system. Your terminal will be disconnected from the computer.

CALL file-name—Causes the named program to be loaded, then the program goes to the first statement of the called program.

CDBL(expression)—Converts the value of the expression to a double-precision value.

CHAIN file-name—Causes the named program to automatically follow the current program.

CHR$ (expression) —Finds the character (symbol) that has the ASCII value of the expression.

CINT (expression) —Converts the value of the expression to integer representation.

CLEAR [integer]—Clears all variables. Number-type variables are given the value of zero. If an integer follows the command, it specifies the number of bytes reserved for the values of string variables.

**CLK$**—Clock variable; its value is a string representing the current time (synonym: TIME$.)

CLOAD [program-name]—Loads a program from a cassette tape. If the program-name is not specified, the first program on the tape will be loaded.

CLOAD?—Compares the program in memory with a program read from a cassette. A warning message is displayed if the two do not match.

CLOSE [file-number]—Releases a file from a program (and updates the disk directory). If no file-number is specified, all assigned files are released.

CLS—CLears the Screen of a video display. (Synonym: HOME.)

CMD string—Issues an operating system command from BASIC.

COLOR codes—Specifies the colors that will be used in a video display.

COMMON list of variables—Specifies variables that are shared with CALLed or CHAINed programs.

CONT or CONTINUE—Used to continue a program from the point of interruption (usually follows use of the BREAK key).

COS (expression)—Finds the value of the trigonometric COSine function for the expression.

COT (expression)—Finds the value of the trigonometric COTangent function for the expression.
COR—Carriage Return Key; ends a keyboard message. (Synonyms: ENTER, RETURN.)
CSAVE file-name—Copies the program in memory onto a cassette tape, identifying it with the file-name.
CSNG (expression)—Converts the value of the expression to a single-precision floating-point representation.
CVD (string)—Converts a string into a double-precision value. Reverses the action of a MKD$ function.
CVI (string)—Converts a string into an integer value. Reverses the action of a MKI$ function.
CVS (expression)—Converts a string into a standard floating-point value. Reverses the action of a MKS$ function.

DATA list of values—Defines all the items in the list of values to be DATA for the program to use with READ commands.
DAT$—Date variable, stores the value of the current date as a string.
DEF DBL list of letters—Defines all the variables whose names start with the listed letters to be double-precision data types.
DEF FNx (variable = expression)—Defines a new function that can be used anywhere in the program. The new function is referred to as FNx, where 'x' can be any letter.
DEF INT list of letters—Defines all variables whose names start with the listed letters to be integer data types.
DEF SNG list of letters—Defines all variables whose names start with the listed letters to be standard floating-point data types.
DEF STR list of letters—Defines all variables whose names start with the listed letters to be string data types.
DEF USRn = address—Defines the starting address for a user-created machine language subroutine. The digit 'n' is used to identify different subroutines.
DEL or DELETE line number – line number—Deletes all program statements within the specified range of line numbers.
DIM array (integer) [list of arrays]—Defines the size (largest acceptable subscript) for an array or list of arrays.
DONE—Tells the operating system that you are done with BASIC but does not disconnect your terminal. (Synonyms: SYSTEM, CMD"S".)
DRAW shape-code AT position—Displays a shape (previously stored in memory) at the specified location on the video screen.

EDIT line-number—Starts a subroutine that lets you alter the contents of the specified line-number without retyping the whole line.

ELSE—Specifies the action to be taken when the condition in an IF statement is false. The complete statement would be: IF condition THEN command or line-number ELSE different command or line-number.
END—Ends a program and leaves BASIC ready for another command.
END# file-number—A special condition that is true only when the end of the specified file has been reached. Eliminates the need for a special end-of-file record on a sequential file.
ENTER—Key used to end a keyboard message and activate action by the central processor. (Synonyms: RETURN key, CR key.)
EOF (file-number)—A special end-of-file condition. See END#.
ERASE list of arrays—Releases memory space used for the listed arrays. Used to save computer memory or to allow the DIMension of an array to be changed.
ERROR—A special condition that is true only when the BASIC translator detects an error. Used to direct the program to replace the normal error-message with a subroutine specified by an ON ERROR GOTO line-number statement.
ERL—Variable whose value is the line-number where an error was detected.
ERR—Variable whose value identifies the type of error that was detected.
EXP (expression)—Inverse of the LOG function; finds the exponential value for the expression. The result is the mathematical constant e raised to the power defined by the expression.

FIELD# file-number, length AS variable, . . . —Defines a random-access record to be composed of a group of fields, each of which contains a string value of the specified length.
FILES list of file-names—Assigns a group of files for use in a program. The first file named will be referred to as file-name 1, etc.
FIX (expression)—Truncates the value of the expression to an integer. For positive numbers, the result is the same as the INTeger function. For negative numbers, FIX rounds up (FIX(−2.9) = − 2).
FLASH—Causes the display on the video screen to flash on and off.
FNx (expression)—A user-defined function. The result is determined by the formula in a preceding DEF FNx statement.
FNEND—In systems that allow the definition of a function (DEF FNx) to occupy several lines, FNEND indicates the end of the routine that defines the function.
FOR variable = expression TO expression [STEP expression]—The start of a loop that gives the named variable the initial value of the first expression and continues until the value of that variable exceeds the value of the second expression. If a STEP value is specified, that value is added to the value of the variable each time the loop is repeated. Without a STEP value, 1 is added to the variable each time through the loop. Loops that

begin with FOR must end with a NEXT statement.

FRE (variable)—Finds the amount a free space left in memory. If the variable is a number type, the result is the number of bytes not reserved for any purpose. If the variable is a string type, the result is the number of bytes reserved for strings that have not been assigned to specific variables.

GET file-name—Used on some systems instead of LOAD, copies a program into memory from disk.

GET string-variable—Gets the value of the key currently depressed on the keyboard. Somewhat like INPUT, except there is no prompt or display and the result is a single character. (Synonym: INKEY$.)

GET# file-number, list of variables—Used on some systems instead of INPUT#, reads values from a sequential file.

GET# file-number, record-number—Copies the specified record from a random-access file into memory.

GOSUB line-number—Causes the computer to execute the subroutine starting at the specified line-number. The statement following the GOSUB command will be executed after the computer reaches the RETURN command at the end of the subroutine.

GOTO line-number—Causes the computer to continue running the program with the specified line.

GR—Causes the computer to shift to low-resolution GRaphics display on the video screen.

HCOLOR = code—Specifies the color to be used in a high-resolution graphics display.

HEX$ (number)—Converts the number to its HEXadecimal (base 16) representation.

HGR and HGR2—Causes the computer to shift to an optional high-resolution graphics display.

HIMEM: address—Specifies the highest memory address that will be available to a BASIC program. (Allows memory to be reserved for machine language routines.)

HLIN X1, X2 AT Y—Draws a Horizontal LINe from X coordinate X1 to coordinate X2 with the vertical coordinate having the constant value Y.

HOME—Clears the screen and returns the cursor to its home position in the upper left-hand corner of the screen. (Synonym: CLS.)

HPLOT position—Causes High-resolution PLOTting at the specified position on the screen.

HTAB column-number—Moves the cursor horizontally on the screen to the specified column.

IF condition THEN line-number—Core version of the IF statement, specifies the next line that will be executed if the condition is true. If the condition is false, the computer drops through to the following statement.

IF condition [THEN] command [ELSE command]—Expanded version of the IF statement, causes any command following the condition to be obeyed only if the condition is true. The command following the ELSE word is obeyed only when the condition is false.

IMAGE format—Specifies the format for printing a line. Associated with a PRINT USING command.

IN# device-number—Specifies which peripheral device will be used for INPUT statements.

INKEY$—The value of this variable is the character associated with the key currently depressed on the keyboard.

INP (port-number)—Finds the value of the code arriving from a peripheral device at the specified port.

INPUT ["message";] list of variables—Prompts for a value to be entered at the keyboard for each listed variable. If a message is specified, it is printed as part of the prompt.

INPUT# file-number, list of variables—Copies values from the specified sequential file into the listed variables.

INPUT$ length # device-number—Inputs a string with the specified length from the specified peripheral device. This is an expanded version of the INKEY$ variable.

INSTR (string, search-string)—A specialized function used to locate occurrences of the search-string within larger strings.

INSTR$ (length)—Variable used to input a string of the specified length from the keyboard. The ENTER or RETURN key is not used and the value is not automatically displayed. Similar to INPUT$ and INKEY$.

INT (expression)—Rounds the value of the expression down to an integer.

INTERRUPT—Key that interrupts the BASIC translator and leaves the computer ready for a new command. (Synonym: BREAK.)

INVERSE—Reverses the colors on the video display (black letters on a white background, instead of white on black).

JOY (device-number)—Finds the value for the position of the JOYstick attached to the port for the specified device-number.

KILL file-name—Deletes the specified file from the disk directory and frees the space it used for other files.

LEFT$ (string, length)—Picks off the first letters of a string. The resulting value has the specified length and is composed of the LEFTmost characters in the original string.

LEN (string)—Finds the number of characters (LENgth) in the string.

LET variable = expression—Stores the value of the expression in the specified variable.

LINE INPUT string-variable—A special version of INPUT, includes all punctuation characters typed before the ENTER or RETURN key as part of the value of the input variable. Allows keyboard entry of quotes and commas.
LIST [line-number - line-number]—Prints (or displays a list of the program stored in memory. If line numbers are specified, only the statements within that range of line numbers are listed.
LLIST [line-number - line-number]—Lists the program on a line printer (instead of the screen display provided by LIST).
LPRINT list of expressions—Prints the values of the listed expressions on a line printer (in the same format that PRINT displays them on a screen).
LOAD file-name—Copies a program into memory from disk. (Some systems use GET as a synonym for LOAD.)
LOC (file-number)—Gives the location of the end of a random access file.
LOF (file-number)—Gives the number of records in a file (the Logical end-Of-File).
LOG (expression)—Finds the natural LOGarithm (base e) of the expression. This is the inverse of the EXP function.
LOMEM: address—Specifies the lowest memory address available for a BASIC program. (Allows space to be reserved for machine language routines or extensions of the operating system.)
LPOS (number)—Gives the TAB setting (horizontal column number) for the last character sent to the line printer.
LSET field-variable = string—Copies the string into the specified field starting from the left. Any room left in the field is filled with blank characters.

MAT array—Causes a command to apply to all elements of an array at once. Used for MATrix arithmetic.
MEM—Variable whose value is the number of bytes of available (unassigned) MEMory.
MERGE file-name—Merges the lines in the specified program (or subroutine) from a disk file with the program already in memory.
MID$ (string, position, length)—Extracts a shorter string of specified length from the MIDdle of the original string, starting with the character in the specified position.
MKD$(double-precision expression)—Converts a double-precision value into a string for storage in a field of a random-access record. The inverse of the CVD function.
MKI$(integer expression)—Converts an integer value into a string for storage in a field of a random-access record. The inverse of the CVI function.
MKS$(expression)—Converts a standard floating-point value into a

string for storage in a field of a random-access record. The inverse of the CVS function.
MOD—The remainder operator in integer division. Examples: 5 MOD 4 = 1, 8 MOD 3 = 2.
MORE# file-number—A special condition that is true if there are more records left on the specified sequential file. The opposite of END# or EOF#.

NAME file-name AS new-name—Changes the name of a file (or program) stored on disk.
NEW—Clears the memory for a new program, erasing whatever program lines had been stored in memory.
NEXT (variable)—Ends a loop that starts with a FOR statement. Increments the value of the variable and determines whether to repeat the loop or drop through to the next line because the upper limit for the variable has been exceeded. If a variable is specified, it must match the variable in the FOR statement.
NORMAL—Changes the video screen back to normal display, ending the INVERSE and/or FLASH displays.
NOT condition—Reverses the value of the condition from true to false, or from false to true.
NOTRACE—Stops the display or displays that trace the execution of a program. (Synonym: TROFF.)
NULL integer—Specifies the number of null output characters to be generated to allow a peripheral device to keep up with the computer.

OCT$(number)—Converts a number to its OCTal (base 8) representation.
OLD file-name—Copies an old program into memory. (Synonyms: LOAD, GET.)
ON expression GOSUB list of line-numbers—Selects the subroutine to be executed based on the integer value of the expression. The first subroutine is performed if the expression has a value of 1, etc.
ON expression GOTO list of line-numbers—Selects the next statement to be obeyed based on the integer value of the expression. If the value of the expression is 2, the program skips to the second line-number on the list, etc.
ON ERR GOTO or ON ERROR GOTO line-number—Specifies the start of a routine to be executed if a BASIC error is detected. The routine replaces the normal error message.
OPEN mode, file-number, file-name—Assigns a number to a file for use in a program. The mode identifies whether the file is available for sequential input ("I"), sequential output ("O") or random access ("R").

Other versions of BASIC use a combination of ASSIGN, FILES, APPEND, IN#, PR#, and SCRATCH# statements for similar functions.
OPTION BASE integer—Specifies the lowest acceptable value for array subscripts. Designed to save memory space when zero is not used as a subscript value.
OR—Combines conditions. Condition OR condition is true when either condition is true. The combination is false only when both conditions are false.
OUT port-number, expression—Sends the value of the expression to a peripheral device through the specified port.
OUTPUT "message", position, color—Displays the message in the specified position of the video screen with the lettering in the indicated color.

PAUSE integer—Causes the computer to pause for a length of time determined by the integer before continuing. Can be replaced by an empty FOR . . . NEXT loop.
PDL(port)—Sets a value from the game paddle attached to the specified port.
PEEK (address)—Finds the value (as an integer code) stored in memory at the specified address.
PLOT position [,color—Turns on a pixel at the given position on the video screen. (Synonym: SET or RESET.)
POINT (position)—Determines whether the pixel at the position is off (value zero), or on.
POKE address, expression—Stores the integer value of the expression in the specified address in memory.
POP—Deletes an address from the return stack. Ends a subroutine without going back to the statement that followed the GOSUB command. (Except in special circumstances, the POP command will not be used in a well-structured program.)
POS (expression)—Gives the location (column number) of the cursor where the next character will be displayed.
PR# port-number—Directs all output from PRINT commands to the peripheral device attached to the specified port.
PRINT list of expressions—Prints (or displays on a video screen) the values of the expressions in the list. The format is controlled by the punctuation (commas and semicolons) or by an image specified by the USING keyword.
PRINT@or PRINT AT position, list of expressions—Version of the PRINT statement that starts the display at the specified position on the video screen.
PRINT# file-number, list of expressions—Copies the values of the listed expression onto the specified sequential file.

PUT# file-number, record-number—Stores (writes) a record in a random-access file.
RANDOMIZE or RANDOM [seed]—Initializes the random number generator. If a seed is used, the sequence of random numbers produced by different runs of the program can be replicated by starting each run with the same seed value.
READ list of variables—Copies values from DATA statements into the listed variables.
READ# file-number, list of variables—Copies values from a sequential file into the listed variables. (Synonym: INPUT#.)
RECALL array—Copies all the values of a stored array from a disk file into memory.
REM remarks—Tells the computer to ignore the rest of the line because it contains explanatory notes for humans. (Synonym: the aspostrophe '.)
RENUM [starting-line, ending-line, increment]—Changes the line numbering in a program. Allows you to insert more lines in the middle of a program if you did not leave enough room between your original line numbers.
RESAVE file-name—Replaces the named-file on disk with the file in memory. (ON many systems the same function can be accomplished with the SAVE command.)
RESET (position)—Turns off the pixel at the specified position on the video screen.
RESTORE [line-number]—Resets the counter for DATA values so the next READ command will copy in the first value on a DATA statement (even if it has already been READ once). If a line number is given, the next value will be the first one on the DATA statement in the specified line.
RESUME [line-number or NEXT]—Ends an error subroutine. (See ON ERROR GOTO.) If a line-number is given, that is where the program will go to continue processing. The word NEXT directs the computer to continue with the line that follows the statement where the error was detected.
RETURN—Ends a subroutine and directs the computer back to the statement following the GOSUB command.
RIGHT$ (string, length)—Picks off the last characters of a string. The resulting value is a string of the specified length composed of the RIGHT-most characters in the original string.
RND(expression)—Selects a random number. Different systems have different ways of controlling the random number. The standard range of random numbers is either a decimal value between zero and one, or between −1 and +1. In some versions of BASIC, the RND command will always produce a value in the standard range. Other versions produce a value in the standard range when the expression has a value of zero, and produce an integer between 1 and the value of the expression when the expression has a higher value. The other common version is to repeat the

last randomly produced value when the expression is zero, to produce a new value in the standard range when the expression is greater than zero, and to change the seed for the random number generator when the expression has a negative value.

ROT = integer—ROTates a stored shape for display by the DRAW command.

RSET field-variable = string—Copies the string into the specified field starting from the right. Any extra room at the front of the field is filled with blank characters.

RUN [file-name or line-number]— Causes the computer to start translating and following the program stored in memory. In some versions, it also clears the values of all variables to zero. If a line-number is specified, the program starts at that line number. If a file-name is specified that program is first LOADed into memory, then run starting with the first line.

SAVE file-name—Copies the program from memory onto a disk. On some systems, this command will not work if the disk already has a file with the specified name (in that case, use RESAVE instead).

SCALE = n—Sets the scale size for shapes to be displayed with the DRAW command.

SCR—Erases (or SCRatches) the memory. (Synonym: NEW.)

SCRATCH# file-number—Assigns a file to be used as a sequential file for output. (Synonym: OPEN "O", . . .)

SCRN (position)—Turns on a colored pixel at the specified screen position. (Synonyms: PLOT, SET.)

SET (position)—Turns on a pixel at the specified screen position. (Synonyms: PLOT, SCRN.)

SGN (expression)—Determines whether the value of the expression is positive, negative or zero.

SHLOAD—Loads a table of stored shapes for display with the DRAW command.

SIN(expression)—Finds the value of the trigonometric SINe function for the expression.

SOUND expression—Generates a sound based on the value of the expression.

SPACE$ (expression) or SPC (expression)—Generates a string of blank spaces for use in PRINT statements. The value of the expression gives the length of the string.

SPEED = value—Controls the rate of output of characters in PRINT commands.

SQR(expression)—Finds the positive square root of the value of the expression. The inverse of multiplying the expression by itself.

STEP expression—Used in FOR statements to determine the value added to the counter variable each time the loop is repeated. (See FOR and NEXT.)

STOP—Stops the program and prints a message. Produces the same effect as pressing the BREAK or INTERRUPT key. Can be used as a substitute for the END command.

STORE array—Copies all elements of the array in memory onto a disk. They can be brought back into memory by the RECALL command.

STRING$ (expression, character)—Produces a string with the specified character repeated the number of times indicated by the value of the expression.

STR$(expression)—Converts the value of the expression into a string of numeric characters. The inverse of the VAL function.

SWAP variable, variable—Swaps the values of the two named variables. In core BASIC, a temporary variable (T) and three LET statements are needed for a swap: LET T = V1: LET V1 = V2: LET V2 = T is the same as SWAP V1, V2.

SYSTEM—Signals the computer to stop running the BASIC translator and prepare for operating system commands. (Synonyms: DONE, CMD"S".)

TAB(expression)—In a PRINT statement, skips over to the column number specified by the value of the expression before continuing to print.

TAN (expression)—Finds the value of the trigonometric TANgent function. The inverse of the ATN function.

THEN line-number—In an IF statement, directs the computer to the next line to be executed if the condition is true.

**TIME$**—Variable whose value is a string representation of the current time. (Synonym: CLK$.)

TO—Used to indicate the range of values in a FOR statement.

TONE pitch, duration—Generates a musical tone.

TRACE—Causes the computer to display line numbers to trace the lines executed while a program is running. (Synonym: TRON.)

TROFF—Turns off the display of trace messages while a program is running. The inverse of TRON. (Synonym: NOTRACE.)

TRON—Turns on the display of trace messages while a program is running. The inverse of TROFF. (Synonym: TRACE.)

TYP (file-number)—Identifies the next value to be input from a sequential file to be a number, a string, or the end of file. Not available in most systems.

USING format or line-number—Controls the format for printing values. If a format string is specified, it is used as the image for printing the values. If a line-number is specified, that line must be an IMAGE statement.

USRn (expression)—Causes the computer to follow a user's machine language subroutine. (Used in conjunction with a DEF USRn statement.)

VAL (string)—Converts a string of numeric characters into a standard floating point value.
VARPTR (variable)—Finds the memory address assigned to the specified variable.
VLIN Y1, Y2 AT X—Draws a vertical line in column X on the video screen between the two specified Y coordinates.
VTAB integer—Moves the cursor up or down the screen to the specified row (Vertical TAB).

WAIT variable, value [,value]—Causes the computer to pause or wait for a value to arrive at a port.
WEND—Marks the end of a WHILE loop. Similar to NEXT.
WHILE condition—Marks the start of a test-before loop. The statements between the WHILE command and the WEND command will be repeated as long as the condition is true.
WIDTH integer—Specifies the maximum width (number of characters) for a print line. If a PRINT command produces a longer line, it will be split and continued on the following line.
WINDOW integer—Identifies the top lines of the screen as titles which will not be scrolled out of the display by additional PRINT statements.
WRITE list of expressions—A variation of the PRINT command.
WRITE# file-number, list of expressions—Copies the values of the listed expressions to the specified sequential file. String values are automatically enclosed in quotes and are separated by delimiters. (Synonym: PRINT#.)

XDRAW shape-code AT position—A reversed color version of the DRAW command.
XOR—Exclusive OR combination of conditions. Condition XOR condition is true only if one of the two conditions is true and the other is false. If both are true, or both are false, the result of the XOR will be false.

Index